1 PETER

JUDE AND 2 PETER

Sacra Pagina Series

Volume 15

1 Peter

Donald P. Senior, C.P.

Jude and 2 Peter

Daniel J. Harrington, S.J.

Daniel J. Harrington, S.J.
Editor

A Michael Glazier Book

THE LITURGICAL PRESS
Collegeville, Minnesota

www.litpress.org

A Michael Glazier Book published by The Liturgical Press.

1   2   3   4   5   6   7   8

Library of Congress Cataloging-in-Publication Data

Senior, Donald.
    1 Peter / Donald P. Senior. Jude and 2 Peter / Daniel J. Harrington ; Daniel J. Harrington, editor.
        p. cm. — (Sacra pagina series ; v. 15)
    "A Michael Glazier book."
    Includes bibliographical references and indexes.
    ISBN 0-8146-5817-2 (alk. paper)
    1. Bible. N.T. Peter—Commentaries.   2. Bible. N.T. Jude—Commentaries.
I. Harrington, Daniel J.   II. Title.   III. Sacra pagina series ; 15.

BS2795.53.S46   2003
227'.92077—dc21

                                                                2003044684

CONTENTS

JUDE AND 2 PETER

Introduction

JUDE

Introduction to Jude

Translation, Notes, Interpretation

2 PETER

Introduction to 2 Peter

Translation, Notes, Interpretation

Indexes

EDITOR'S PREFACE

Sacra Pagina is a multi-volume commentary on the books of the New Testament. The expression *Sacra Pagina* ("Sacred Page") originally referred to the text of Scripture. In the Middle Ages it also described the study of Scripture to which the interpreter brought the tools of grammar, rhetoric, dialectic, and philosophy. Thus *Sacra Pagina* encompasses both the text to be studied and the activity of interpretation.

This series presents fresh translations and modern expositions of all the books of the New Testament. Written by an international team of biblical scholars, it is intended for biblical professionals, graduate students, theologians, clergy, and religious educators. The volumes present basic introductory information and close exposition. They self-consciously adopt specific methodological perspectives, but maintain a focus on the issues raised by the New Testament compositions themselves. The goal of *Sacra Pagina* is to provide sound critical analysis without any loss of sensitivity to religious meaning. This series is therefore catholic in two senses of the word: inclusive in its methods and perspectives, and shaped by the context of the Catholic tradition.

The Second Vatican Council described the study of the "sacred page" as the "very soul of sacred theology" (*Dei Verbum* 24). The volumes in this series illustrate how biblical scholars contribute to the council's call to provide access to Sacred Scripture for all the Christian faithful. Rather than pretending to say the final word on any text, these volumes seek to open up the riches of the New Testament and to invite as many people as possible to study seriously the "sacred page."

DANIEL J. HARRINGTON, S.J.

AUTHORS' PREFACE

Crisis in the church is not a new phenomenon. In fact, the church has always been (and probably always will be) involved in some kind of crisis. Even in the apostolic period, which is regarded by many as the church's "golden age," there were serious crises coming both from the outside (as in 1 Peter) and from the inside (as in Jude and 2 Peter). The three short New Testament letters treated in this volume illustrate the kinds of problems early Christians faced as well as the rhetorical techniques and theological concepts with which they combated those problems.

In the first part of this volume Donald P. Senior, C.P. views 1 Peter as written from Rome in Peter's name to several churches in northern Asia Minor (present-day Turkey) in the latter part of the first century C.E. The new Christians addressed in 1 Peter found themselves "aliens and exiles" in the wider Greco-Roman society and so suffering a kind of social ostracism. The author presents them with a marvelous theological vision of who they have become through their baptism along with pastoral encouragement to stand firm, without leading them into a sectarian rejection of the world around them. He shows them how to take a "missionary" stance toward the outside world by giving the witness of a holy and blameless life to offset the slander and ignorance of the non-Christian majority, something that may possibly even lead them to glorify God on the day of judgment.

In the second part Daniel J. Harrington, S.J. interprets Jude and 2 Peter as confronting crises in the late first century that were perpetrated by Christian teachers, described polemically as "intruders" in Jude and as "false teachers" in 2 Peter. In confronting the crises within their churches the authors appeal frequently to the Old Testament and to early summaries of Christian faith. While Jude uses other Jewish traditions, 2 Peter includes most of the text of Jude as well as many distinctively Greek terms and concepts. It is clear that for both authors (despite their different social settings) what was at stake was the struggle for "the faith handed on to the saints once for all" (Jude 3), which is "a faith of equal standing" to that of the apostles (2 Pet 1:1).

The two commentators first met in the summer of 1965, in the early stages of their professional biblical formation, as students in an Arabic course at Harvard University. Although we have taken different routes in our graduate programs, academic concentrations, and teaching positions, our paths have crossed many times over the years, especially due to our common interest in Matthew's Gospel. We are grateful to have been given the opportunity to work together on this volume, which we believe is particularly timely in the midst of the crises in our church today.

Daniel J. Harrington, S.J.   Donald P. Senior, C.P.
Cambridge, Massachusetts   Chicago, Illinois

September 2002

ABBREVIATIONS

Biblical Books and Apocrypha

Gen	Nah	1–2–3–4 Kgdms	John
Exod	Hab	Add Esth	Acts
Lev	Zeph	Bar	Rom
Num	Hag	Bel	1–2 Cor
Deut	Zech	1–2 Esdr	Gal
Josh	Mal	4 Ezra	Eph
Judg	Ps (*pl.:* Pss)	Jdt	Phil
1–2 Sam	Job	Ep Jer	Col
1–2 Kgs	Prov	1–2–3–4 Macc	1–2 Thess
Isa	Ruth	Pr Azar	1–2 Tim
Jer	Cant	Pr Man	Titus
Ezek	Eccl (*or* Qoh)	Sir	Phlm
Hos	Lam	Sus	Heb
Joel	Esth	Tob	Jas
Amos	Dan	Wis	1–2 Pet
Obad	Ezra	Matt	1–2–3 John
Jonah	Neh	Mark	Jude
Mic	1–2 Chr	Luke	Rev

Other Ancient Texts

Ant.	Josephus, *Antiquities of the Jews*
CD	Cairo Geniza copy of the *Damascus Document*
m.	Mishnah
1QH	*Hodayot*
1QS	*Rule of the Community*
Sanh.	Sanhedrin
T. Benj.	*Testament of Benjamin*

Periodicals, Reference Works, and Serials

AB	Anchor Bible
ABD	*Anchor Bible Dictionary*, ed. David N. Freedman et al.

xiii

ANRW	*Aufstieg und Niedergang der römischen Welt*
AsSeign	*Assemblées du Seigneur*
AUSS	*Andrews University Seminary Studies*
BBET	Beiträge zur biblischen Exegese und Theologie
BDAG	F. W. Danker, reviser and editor, *A Greek-English Lexicon of the New Testament and Other Early Christian Literature* (3rd ed.)
Bib	*Biblica*
BL	*Bibel und Liturgie*
BS	*Bibliotheca Sacra*
BTB	*Biblical Theology Bulletin*
BZ	*Biblische Zeitschrift*
CBNT	Coniectanea Biblica, New Testament
CBQ	*Catholic Biblical Quarterly*
CNT	Commentaire du Nouveau Testament
EKKNT	Evangelisch-katholischer Kommentar zum Neuen Testament
EstBib	*Estudios Bíblicos*
ExpTim	*Expository Times*
FB	Forschung zur Bibel
FTS	Freiburger Theologische Studien
HTKNT	Herders theologischer Kommentar zum Neuen Testament
HTR	*Harvard Theological Review*
HUCA	*Hebrew Union College Annual*
ICC	International Critical Commentary
Int	*Interpretation*
JBL	*Journal of Biblical Literature*
JETS	*Journal of the Evangelical Theological Society*
JSJ	*Journal for the Study of Judaism*
JSNT	*Journal for the Study of the New Testament*
JSNTSup	JSNT, Supplement Series
JSOTSup	JSOT, Supplement Series
JSPSup	Journal for the Study of the Pseudepigrapha Supplement Series
JTS	*Journal of Theological Studies*
KEK	Kritisch-exegetischer Kommentar über das Neue Testament
NABPR	National Association of Baptist Professors of Religion
NAB Rev.	New American Bible Revised
Neot	*Neotestamentica*
NJB	New Jerusalem Bible
NovT	*Novum Testamentum*
NovTSup	Novum Testamentum Supplements
NRSV	New Revised Standard Version
NTD	Das Neue Testament Deutsch
NTM	New Testament Message
NTS	*New Testament Studies*
OTP	*The Old Testament Pseudepigrapha*, ed. James H. Charlesworth
ResQ	*Restoration Quarterly*
RevExp	*Review & Expositor*
RHR	*Revue de l'histoire des religions*

RB	*Revue Biblique*
RivB	*Rivista Biblica*
RSV	Revised Standard Version
RVV	Religionsgeschichtliche Versuche und Vorarbeiten
SBL	Society of Biblical Literature
SBLDS	SBL Dissertation Series
SBLMS	SBL Monograph Series
SNTSMS	Society of New Testament Studies Monograph Series
SNTSU	*Studien zum Neuen Testament und seiner Umwelt*
SUNT	Studien zur Umwelt des Neuen Testaments
TBT	*The Bible Today*
THKNT	Theologischer Handkommentar zum Neuen Testament
TynBull	*Tyndale Bulletin*
TZ	*Theologische Zeitschrift*
USQR	*Union Seminary Quarterly Review*
VT	*Vetus Testamentum*
WTJ	*Westminster Theological Journal*
WUNT	Wissenschaftliche Untersuchungen zum Neuen Testament
ZNW	*Zeitschrift für die neutestamentliche Wissenschaft*

1 Peter

Donald P. Senior, C.P.

1 PETER

INTRODUCTION

The First Letter of Peter is one of the New Testament's most eloquent and theologically rich books. This circular letter was written from Rome in the latter part of the first century C.E. to a series of Christian communities located north of the Taurus Mountains in several Roman provinces of Asia Minor. Its stated intent was to give witness to the sustaining beauty and power of the Christian faith and thereby to encourage the recipients who were suffering harassment and verbal abuse from the dominant non-Christian culture (5:12). Purportedly written by the apostle Peter (1:1; 5:1) and delivered through his trusted associate Silvanus (5:12), the letter may have originated from a "Petrine group" in Rome that took its inspiration from the venerable apostle and his missionary associates (including Mark; see 5:13) and now carried forward his teaching and his pastoral encouragement to the far-flung Christian communities that were growing in Asia Minor.

This is the basic view of the letter and the circumstances of its composition assumed in the commentary that follows. The Introduction will amplify some of the key points and help prepare the reader for the detailed commentary. On virtually every point there has been considerable discussion in the profusion of studies of 1 Peter that continues unabated in contemporary biblical scholarship. It should be noted at the outset that English-language readers are particularly well served; in recent years two major commentaries have appeared, that of Paul J. Achtemeier in the Hermeneia series (*1 Peter* [Minneapolis: Fortress, 1996]) and John H. Elliott in the Anchor Bible commentaries (*1 Peter* [New York: Doubleday, 2000]). Elliott in particular offers a nearly comprehensive review of the literature on this letter. Both provide thorough discussions of disputed issues in interpretation of the letter and have been most helpful resources for this commentary. Although both authors concur in their views about

3

the authorship, origin, dating, and general purpose of the letter, they take different paths in assessing the content of 1 Peter in some key passages.

1. *Authorship and Origin*

Because the question of authorship is so entwined with other introductory issues such as the date, origin, and purpose of the letter, it will be taken up first. The letter itself clearly identifies "Peter, an apostle of Jesus Christ" as the author of the letter (1:1). While the body of the letter contains no clear personal reference, the author returns to the first person in 5:1, referring to himself as a "co-elder and witness of the sufferings of Christ, and also as one who shares in the expected glory to be revealed" (5:1).

Traditional interpretation took these references at face value and assumed that Peter the follower of Jesus and the apparent leader of the disciples was in fact the author of the letter. That view still has its defenders (see, for example, Norman Hillyer, *1 and 2 Peter, Jude.* New International Biblical Commentary [Peabody, Mass.: Hendrickson, 1992] 1–3), although most recent scholarship has cast doubt on the Petrine authorship of the letter. Several reasons work against the probability of Peter being the actual author of this text: (1) The quality of the Greek used in the letter and the evidence of some classical rhetorical training on the part of the author seem improbable for a Palestinian fisherman. (2) The letter quotes consistently from the Greek Septuagint (LXX) version of the Bible rather than from the Hebrew as one might expect from the original Peter. (3) There is no mention of any circumstances of Jesus' life or Peter's experience with him, as one might expect to find. The self-designation as a "co-elder" is unique to 1 Peter and the claim to be a "witness of the sufferings of Christ" is generic and does not seem to be a reference to Peter's role in the events of Jesus' final days (see below, commentary on 5:1). (4) If the letter was written from Rome by Peter himself it is strange that there is no mention of Paul, who would have been there at that time, nor do we have any evidence that Peter was acquainted with the communities in Asia Minor to whom the letter is addressed. (5) The fact of established leadership in these communities (see "elders" in 5:1-4) may suggest a later level of church organization than would be likely during Peter's lifetime.

While not absolutely decisive, these are strong reasons for concluding that the letter was written by someone other than Peter. A mediating position is to suggest that the letter was written by a secretary in Peter's name or by Silvanus himself. While Paul and other ancient letter-writers certainly dictated letters through secretaries, there is no solid internal evidence in 1 Peter to support this. In contrast to 1 Cor 16:21 where Paul signals that he is dictating his letter ("I, Paul, write this greeting with my own hand"), the personal reinsertion of the author in 1 Pet 5:1 does not imply that he was taking over from a secretary. In any case, if Peter had dictated this letter to a secretary it is still strangely silent on the kind of personal references or experiences of the first follower of Jesus that one might expect. Likewise, the phrase "through Silvanus" (5:12) is not strong support that Peter is naming his missionary companion as the author of the letter. In virtually all examples of this phrase in other ancient literature it designates the *bearer* of the letter, not the author (see commentary at 5:12). Most interpreters assume that "Silvanus" is the name of the early missionary mentioned in the Pauline letters as a companion of Paul and Timothy (see 2 Cor 1:19; 1 Thess 1:1; 2 Thess 1:1), and identified also with "Silas"—the Aramaic form of Silvanus—who is mentioned in Acts as the missionary companion of Paul, Barnabas, and John Mark (Acts 15:22, 27, 32, 40; 16:19, 25, 29; 17:4, 10, 14, 15; 18:5). In the Acts of the Apostles Silvanus performs a similar role to that conjectured here, namely bringing (along with Paul, Barnabas, and Judas Barsabbas) the letter from the council at Jerusalem to the community at Antioch and providing verbal commentary on it (see Acts 15:27). First Peter presents Silvanus, "the faithful brother," as the one who brings the letter to the various communities and adds the prestige of his presence and knowledge to its presentation.

The most likely solution is that 1 Peter is a pseudonymous writing, that is, a text written by a later author who invokes Peter's name as the author of the letter. Such a rhetorical device was not unknown in the ancient world, especially when a later disciple or follower of a great leader or teacher wished to endow the writing with the authority of a revered teacher or to extend the tradition of his teaching to a new situation. The attachment of an earlier and revered author's name to a text composed after that author's lifetime serves as both homage to the author and an acceptable "therapeutic lie" for the common good of the community that receives it (see Achtemeier, *1 Peter* 40).

While the actual author of 1 Peter may have been such an individual disciple, more recent scholarship has hypothesized that a "Petrine group" at Rome may account for the origin of the letter (see the extended discussion in Elliott, *1 Peter* 127–30). The letter itself refers not only to the apostle Peter but also to Silvanus (5:12) and Mark (5:13), both of whom Acts describes as "leaders among the brethren" of the Jerusalem church (Acts 15:22). From Acts and Paul we know that Peter was charged in a particular way with the mission to the Jewish community but at the same time was something of a mediating figure between the Jewish Christian churches and the growing number of Gentile communities, especially those evangelized by Paul (see Acts 10:1-48 [i.e., the symbolic role of Peter's baptizing the first Gentile convert], 15:6-11 [Peter's leadership role at the Jerusalem council]; also Paul's testimony in this regard in Gal 2:7-9). Paul's frustration with Peter's withdrawal from table fellowship with Gentiles in Antioch is testimony to the importance of Peter's role in this regard (see Gal 2:11-14). As mentioned above, Silas or Silvanus was a prominent companion with Paul and John Mark (probably to be identified with "my son Mark," mentioned in 1 Pet 5:13). Mark himself first comes on the New Testament stage as known to Peter (Acts 12:12) and then as a coworker with Paul, Barnabas, and Silas (see Acts 12:25; 15:37, 39). He is also mentioned in Colossians as a cousin of Barnabas (Col 4:10) and a trusted coworker with Paul and Timothy (2 Tim 4:11; Phlm 23). Later tradition derived from Papias and reported by Eusebius places Mark at Rome as a companion and "secretary" to Peter, a tradition that has a great deal of probability (see C. Clifton Black, *Mark: Images of an Apostolic Interpreter* [Columbia: University of South Carolina Press, 1994] especially 77–94; Martin Hengel, *Studies in the Gospel of Mark* [Philadelphia: Fortress, 1985] especially 31–63).

The letter probably originated at Rome, which in both Jewish and Christian literature after 70 C.E. was sometimes called "Babylon" (see commentary on 5:13), particularly because of its repression of the Jewish revolt in 66–70 C.E. and the resulting destruction of Jerusalem and its Temple. While the author of 1 Peter is respectful of imperial authority and counsels the readers to "submit" to proper authority, there is also a careful circumscribing of any imperial claims to divine authority (see 2:17) and awareness of the suffering that the non-Christian majority brought upon the community. The recipients are addressed as "aliens and exiles," and their communities are designated as part of the "diaspora"—a description of their vulnerability and dislocation in the midst of the empire that the author also seems to experience in a similar way. Thus the term "Babylon"—the traditional symbol of exile and dispersion in Jewish tradition—is apt for early Christian wariness about Rome.

The effect of all this is to surmise that both the Pauline and Petrine missionary efforts and their respective pastoral and theological traditions and styles intersected in Rome in the sixties through the presence of these two great apostles and some of their coworkers. This concentration, plus the pivotal importance of the imperial city itself, would give Rome a crucial role in the development of Christianity in the early centuries (see Raymond E. Brown and John P. Meier, *Antioch and Rome: New Testament Cradles of Catholic Christianity* [New York: Paulist, 1983] 87–210). Writing from this evolving center, leaders belonging to this "Petrine" group would have had the moral authority to encourage outlying communities such as those in Asia Minor, beginning a tradition that would be taken up by Clement, writing from Rome to the Corinthian church in the late first century (c. 96 C.E.) and later by other bishops of Rome. The blend of traditions at Rome would also explain some of the distinctive features of 1 Peter's theology (see below): its affinity with Pauline tradition, its use of moral exhortation influenced by sayings of Jesus, and its effortless assimilation of Old Testament allusions and symbols. Evoking the name of the founding apostle and first witness of the resurrection of Jesus, later members of this Petrine group sent words of encouragement and solidarity to their fellow Christians by means of the letter we call 1 Peter.

2. *Date and Circumstance of the Letter*

If the above scenario regarding authorship is correct, then 1 Peter was probably written sometime in the last quarter of the first century. The establishment of churches throughout the regions of Asia Minor cited at the beginning of the letter (1:1), the presence of Peter in Rome, and the post-70 use of the term "Babylon" for Rome all suggest that a date sometime after 70 C.E. and the martyrdoms of Peter and Paul (65–66 C.E.) is likely. The letter may be alluded to in 1 Clement (written at the end of the first century) but this is disputed (in favor see Elliott, *1 Peter* 138–40; however Achtemeier, *1 Peter* 45, doubts it). A clearer case can be made for Polycarp, who appears to cite 1 Peter in his letter to the Philippians written about 140 C.E.

Another ingredient for determining the date of the letter is the series of references to suffering and persecution found throughout 1 Peter. Some have suggested that the author's mention of a "fiery ordeal" befalling the community (4:12) is an allusion to the persecution by Nero in the wake of the fire of 64 C.E., thus suggesting an early date for the letter. However, Nero's persecution of the Christians, while brutal, was largely confined to Rome and did not extend to the communities of Asia Minor addressed in the letter. There is a strong consensus among contemporary interpreters that the kind of suffering mentioned in the letter is not official state persecution but local and sporadic harassment visited on the Christians because their values and mores were a source of resentment and misunderstanding on the part of the dominant culture. The letter mentions verbal abuse (2:12), threats to slaves by arbitrary non-Christian owners (2:18), the pressures of religious conformity placed upon the wives of non-Christian husbands (3:1), and revilement and rejection because the Christians no longer participate in practices and associations they adhered to before their conversion (4:4). The author senses that these could lead to more deadly and systematic persecution (4:12), but for the moment the persecutions experienced by the community are on a local, sporadic, and informal basis. Writing from the same general area in Asia Minor in the first part of the second century, Pliny sought direction from the emperor Trajan (97–117 C.E.) concerning a policy for dealing with Christians, including the threat of capital punishment. His correspondence demonstrates that at that time there was still no set state policy of that kind. Although the emperor Domitian (81–96 C.E.) at the end of the first century was notorious for requiring emperor worship, was suspicious of foreign groups in the east, and had a reputation for arbitrary cruelty, there is no evidence that he engaged in wholesale persecution of Christians as such. Statewide persecution of this type would not befall Christianity until the reign of the emperor Decius in 249–51 C.E. (see the helpful discussion in Achtemeier, *1 Peter* 28–36). Thus the kind of persecution experienced by the communities addressed in 1 Peter fits with what we know of the circumstances in Asia Minor in the latter part of the first century.

The letter offers a few hints about the social circumstances of the communities it addresses and these, too, are compatible with the time period in the last quarter of the first century. Christianity made rapid advances in Asia Minor through the work of Paul and other early Christian missionaries. The regions mentioned in the address of the letter are five provinces north of the Taurus Mountains, which stretch east-west across central Asia Minor (i.e., Pontus, Galatia, Cappadocia, Asia, and Bithynia; see commentary on 1:1). This is a vast area of nearly 130,000 square miles whose inhabitants at the time the letter was written were mainly rural, living in small villages and hamlets, with some port cities on the Black Sea and the Aegean. Acts 2:9 includes pilgrims from Cappadocia, Pontus, and Asia in the list of Jewish pilgrims who came to Jerusalem for Pentecost and heard Peter preach. It is likely that through some of these Jewish communities scattered throughout the region Christian missionaries first penetrated the area. First Peter implies that many of the Christians were fairly new converts with memories of their former associations with their pagan counterparts still fresh in their minds (e.g., 4:3-4). The letter gives scant information about the organization of these communities, but the author's address to the "elders" *(presbyteroi)* in 5:1-4 suggests that there were at least some basic structures in place. The order in the listing of the regions probably reflects the circular route that the bearer of the letter (probably Silvanus) would take—moving east along the northern coast through Pontus and Galatia, then south and west through Cappadocia and Asia, and finally completing the circle at Bithynia. The fact that these communities circulated letters among themselves, as well as the link of the Roman community with them, implies a good deal of communication and development among the Christian communities of the region.

The author's address to the Christians in these communities as "aliens and exiles" (2:11) and his use of the designation "exiles of the diaspora" (1:1) have triggered debate about the social circumstances of these communities. Traditional interpretation tended to understand these terms in a purely metaphorical way, implying that the Christians were "exiles" on earth, dispersed strangers longing for their true heavenly home. More recent interpretation, however, has viewed these designations from a more horizontal rather than "vertical" perspective. The commentary of Leonhard Goppelt first published in 1978 led the way on this, suggesting that the values and practices espoused by the Christians put them at odds with the surrounding dominant majority and brought true estrangement. Because of their Christian commitment they became real "aliens and exiles" in their own land (see Leonhard Goppelt, *A Commentary on I Peter* [Grand Rapids: Eerdmans, 1993]). A more radical stance has been championed by John H. Elliott. In his monograph *A Home for the Homeless: A Sociological Exegesis of 1 Peter, Its Situation and Strategy* (Philadelphia: Fortress, 1983) and in his recent commentary (*1 Peter* 94–103) he argues that the term "alien" *(paroikoi)* should be taken literally in its social and legal sense, as it is consistently used this way in other biblical and ancient texts. As he notes, "*Paroikoi,* 'by-dwellers,' were distinguished legally from complete strangers *(xenoi)* and belonged to an institutionalized class ranked socially below the citizen population and above freedpersons, slaves, and complete strangers" (*1 Peter* 94). He concludes that many of the Christians in these communities were, in fact, resident aliens who had migrated to the region for work or other reasons. This social status set the stage for further alienation and estrangement caused by their religious allegiance: "Their different languages, clothing, customs, religious traditions, and foreign roots set these aliens apart and exposed them to suspicion and hostility on the part of the native population and to charges of wrongdoing and conduct injurious to the well-being of the commonwealth and the favor of the gods" (*1 Peter* 94).

It is impossible to determine whether Elliott's analysis of the social status of the Christians is correct, and some aspects of the letter seem to contradict his hypothesis. First of all, the letter implies that before becoming Christians the addressees were able to mingle freely with their non-Christian neighbors and were considered one with them; this is some of the reason for the current dismay and anger on part of the non-Christians now that the Christians refuse to join in with them (4:3-4). Likewise, in addressing the slaves and wives the author does not refer to their "alien" status as a further complication (see 2:18-21; 3:1-7). And the author's designation of the communities as "exiles of the dispersion" (1:1; also 2:11), as well as the use of the term "Babylon" for Rome, both indicate that he is thinking in metaphorical terms from the outset. The biblical memory of the Babylonian exile and the resulting Jewish diaspora were powerful metaphors expressive not only of Israel's eschatological longings for final peace and security but also for describing the religious distance Judaism had to maintain from the surrounding Gentile culture. In this instance as in so many others in the letter the author seamlessly absorbs biblical metaphors and symbols and applies them to Christian experience. The importance of seeing this set of metaphors—"alien," "exile," "diaspora" —from a social perspective is that the distinctive values and convictions of the Christian community were not purely spiritual realities but had significant social consequences—a major concern of the letter.

3. *Form, Style, and Structure*

Virtually all modern interpreters of 1 Peter defend its literary unity and its form as a circular letter. Some commentators had speculated that 1 Peter was a composite of two or more documents, based in part on the doxology that appears to conclude the text in 4:11, with the subsequent section 4:12–5:14 appearing to move from potential persecution in the first part to actual persecution in the second (see 4:12, "Beloved, do not be astounded at the fiery ordeal which is happening to you as a test for you . . ."; proposed by E. Richard Perdelwitz, *Die Mysterienreligion und das Problem des I. Petrusbriefes: Ein literarischer und religionsgeschichtlicher Versuch.* Religionsversuche und Vorarbeiten 11/3 [Giessen: Alfred Töpelman, 1911]). Others suggested that the body of the letter derived from a baptismal homily, a theory prompted especially by the reference to baptism in 3:21 ("and baptism, which is a representation of this, now saves you . . ."). F. L. Cross proposed that this in fact was a homily situated during the Easter triduum, similar to the *Apostolic Tradition of Hippolytus*, explaining the many references to Christ's Passion in the letter (see Frank Leslie Cross, *I Peter: A Paschal Liturgy* [London: Mowbray, 1954]).

However, the arguments for these theories about the composite nature and origin of the letter are not persuasive. Doxologies consistently appear in the midst of early Christian letters, and not as conclusions (see commentary on 4:11). The references to suffering in 4:12 and following are not substantially different from those in the preceding sections and can be explained by the eschatological emphasis of the author as he moves to the conclusion of his letter (see commentary on 4:12). While baptism as the entry point for Christian existence is important in 1 Peter, it is by no means the sole or major focus of the author's theology. There are in fact no compelling reasons to question the literary unity of 1 Peter. Its genre as a circular letter seems straightforward and it includes the essential elements of an early Christian letter in the Pauline model. (The extent to which Paul's letters actually influenced the form of other New Testament and early Christian texts is debated; on the form of the Pauline letters see Jerome Murphy-O'Connor, *Paul the Letter Writer: His World, His Options,*

His Skills. Good News Studies 41 [Collegeville: The Liturgical Press, 1995]). The author begins with a formal address to the communities (1:1-2) and concludes with personal greetings and a final commendation (5:12-14). The opening words of the body of the letter are a prayer of blessing that also signals some of the major theological motifs of the letter (1:3-12). The main body of the letter encompasses 1:13–5:11.

The author writes with an accomplished, if not elegant Greek style, with relatively few Semitisms and most of those attributable to the biblical quotations and allusions that dot the text. His vocabulary is rich, with sixty-one words found nowhere else in the New Testament (see the extensive discussion of 1 Peter's style in Elliott, *1 Peter* 41–80). As noted in the commentary, even when drawing on common New Testament tradition the author often gives a distinctive formulation all his own.

Based on structural elements and content discussed in the commentary, the letter may be outlined as follows:

A. The Address of the Letter 1:1-2

B. The Body of the Letter 1:3–5:11

1:3-12   The Foundation of Christian Life

1:13-16   The Call to Holiness

1:17-21   Fear Before a God of Hope

1:22–2:3 Earnestly Love One Another From the Heart

2:4-10   The Living Stones and the Household of God

2:11-12   Freedom and Responsibility

2:13-17   Commitment in the World

2:18-25   The Christian Witness of the Slaves

3:1-7   The Witness of Christian Wives and the Responsibilities of Christian Husbands

3:8-12   The Obligations of Community

3:13-17   Giving a Testimony of Hope

3:18-22   The Ascent and Exaltation of the Triumphant Christ

4:1-6   Living by the Will of God

4:7-11   Living in Awareness of the Endtime

4:12-19   Suffering as a Christian

5:1-5   Responsibility of the Elders

5:6-11   Confidence in the God of All Grace

C. Final Word 5:12-14

4. *The Sources, Pastoral Strategy,*
and Major Motifs of the Letter

The author's own statement of his purpose in writing the letter should be taken at face value: ". . . I have written to you briefly, encouraging and testifying that this is the true grace of God; stand fast in it" (5:12). The purpose of the letter, written in the name of a venerable apostle and historic follower of Jesus and from the center of the Roman world, is both to give a confident witness to Christian faith in the risen and exalted Christ and, through that witness, to encourage Christian communities under siege.

The letter is not intended to be a theological treatise, but employs traditional motifs for a pastoral purpose. The author makes abundant use of the Old Testament and some non-canonical Jewish literature (e.g., the allusion to the *Testament of Abraham* in 3:5-6; the traditions about Noah drawn from *1 Enoch* in 3:19-20). In addition to several explicit quotations (see, for example, Isa 40:6 in 1:24-25; Isa 28:16 in 2:6; Ps 118:22 in 2:7; Isa 8:14 in 2:8; Hos 1:6, 9 in 2:10; Ps 33:13-17 in 3:10-12; Prov 11:31 in 4:18; Prov 3:34 in 5:5), the letter is filled with Old Testament allusions and images (see the extended list in Elliott, *1 Peter* 12–17). One of the noted features of 1 Peter is, in fact, the ease with which it absorbs Old Testament traditions and applies them to the Christian community. There is no hint in the letter of any tension with Judaism or of any need to situate the Christian community in relationship to Israel. No mention is made of Israel's own fate or destiny in the wake of Christ's appearance. As noted below, the author seems to take it for granted that the church is Israel and that all of the promises God lavished on Israel come to fruition in the life of the Christian community.

The author is also steeped in Christian tradition. The content of the letter is not innovative in this regard, but draws on motifs common to a number of early Christian texts: Christ's redemptive sufferings, his resurrection, his exaltation; baptism as the initiation into Christian life; exhortations for mutual love within the community; non-retaliation for injury; the importance of good deeds; the parousia of Christ and the expectation of final judgment; and eschatological anticipation. Even though these motifs are part of the common fund of early Christianity, as indicated in the commentary, 1 Peter often casts them in a distinctive way and uses unique vocabulary with few parallels in other New Testament texts.

There has been considerable discussion about the relationship of 1 Peter to the Pauline writings. As noted above, the author follows the literary format of the Pauline letters. Likewise, many of the theological motifs in 1 Peter have affinity with Pauline theology. As discussed in the commentary, however, there is no strong evidence that the author of 1 Peter drew directly on any Pauline (or deutero-Pauline) letter. The affinity is best explained by contact with more general Christian tradition that itself may have been influenced by Paul's letters. If the conjecture is correct that 1 Peter is written from Rome and comes from a group that included Silvanus and others acquainted with Paul's theology, this would help to explain the influence of Pauline theology on 1 Peter.

The apparent influence of some sayings of Jesus on 1 Peter has also been a point of discussion (see Achtemeier, *1 Peter* 10–12, especially the list of possible sayings of Jesus with echoes in 1 Peter, p. 10 n. 97). Two of the most striking examples are 3:14 ("But even if you should suffer for the sake of righteousness, you are blessed"; see also 4:14), which is similar in form and content to Jesus' beatitude in Matt 5:10, and 2:12 (". . . from seeing your good deeds they will glorify God on the day of visitation"), which echoes the saying of Jesus in Matt 5:11-12. But here, too, there are some subtle differences in wording and context that suggest the author did not draw directly on Matthew's Gospel but was aware of ethical traditions in the early community that themselves were anchored in sayings of Jesus.

In short, 1 Peter stands in the stream of developing early Christian tradition and drew freely from it, along with abundant use of the Bible (mainly in its Greek form), to articulate his theological vision and its pastoral consequences for the communities addressed.

If the circumstances of the community were as described above, this meant that the Christians in these regions were under severe pressure, acute enough to cause suffering. Their Christian commitment was leading to slander, estrangement, and abuse from their neighbors because they no longer shared their non-Christian values and were no longer free to participate in many of the events, practices, and associations as they did formerly. The sanction for this was not only social alienation but could have included economic consequences as well—loss of jobs and opportunities that membership in the guilds and their celebrations helped facilitate. Apparently many of the Christians in these communities were relatively new converts who had only recently stepped away from their former way of life. The pressure for conformity may have been severe and could have caused some Christians to distance themselves from the community or even to renounce their faith.

This pastoral concern may well have prompted the letter. The author, representing a leadership group in Rome that felt some responsibility for the health of the communities in Asia Minor, writes to bolster the faith and perseverance of his fellow Christians. The author's strategy is clear. In the opening part of the letter he lays out an exuberant vision of the Christians' destiny (1:3-12). They are blessed because through God's mercy they have been given the gift of salvation, born anew into a salvation effected through the death and resurrection of Christ (1:3). This is the unfading inheritance that will finally be theirs at the end of time, a cause for great joy anticipated even now (1:4-6). Christ's own experience becomes the model for the Christians themselves: even though for a while he had to suffer trials and even death, he ultimately was raised from the dead and triumphantly exalted at God's right hand (3:17-22). Christ's victory over death and the powers of evil is not just a model or pattern for Christian destiny, but also the dynamic force that makes it possible (1:18-21; 2:24-25). His death was redemptive and his resurrection and exaltation spelled defeat and subjugation for the hostile spirits of the universe and for Satan himself (3:19-22).

The author perceives that this drama of salvation that the Christians now enjoy spans all of time. Through the power of Christ's Spirit already at work in the world, it was anticipated by the prophets of old who longed to see it (1:10)—and its full and glorious consummation will take place at the final coming of Jesus (1:5), an end that is not far into the future (4:7). Because they have been chosen by God, the followers of Jesus are the inheritors of all the promises that God has given to his people (2:9). As Achtemeier notes, the "controlling metaphor" the letter applies to the Christians is that of "Israel" itself (Achtemeier, *1 Peter* 69–72). The Christians are the elect community; they *are* Israel—and therefore the author can rhetorically lavish on the Christians all the biblical imagery and symbols that described Israel and its destiny (see, for example, the profusion of Old Testament symbols and allusions in the key passage, 2:4-10).

This bountiful theological vision is the foundation for the author's pastoral encouragement for the communities he addresses. Even though they are under threat from their uncomprehending neighbors and even if the devil seeks to consume them (5:8), they should not succumb to fear, because Christ has radically defeated the powers of evil and even death itself and will lead the Christians unharmed to God (3:18-22). The only one they are to "fear," that is, render complete reverence to, is God (2:17). The Christians live not in servile fear but with "living hope"—a key virtue in the letter, derived directly from its convictions about Christ's victory over death.

This theological vision serves the pastoral encouragement the author wants to give to the communities. He first of all underscores their great privilege as God's own people (2:9-10), the inheritors of all the promises made to their ancestors in faith. The author's ecclesiology is particularly rich. Here one of the key images for the community comes into play. Drawing out the varied symbolic meanings of "stone" in biblical literature, the author describes the community as a "living stone" built into a "spiritual house" (2:4). Most commentators agree that 1 Peter uses this image to portray the community as the "temple" where "spiritual sacrifices acceptable to God through Jesus Christ" can be offered (2:5), a metaphor for the church found in other New Testament traditions (note that Elliott is a strong dissenting voice in this interpretation, contending that the term *oikos* [house or household] does not mean "temple" in this context but literally means "household," a key theological metaphor for the church as the true "home" for the Christians; see the discussion in the commentary on 2:4-10). At the same time 1 Peter draws on Isa 8:14 and Ps 118:22 to speak of the "rejected cornerstone" and the "stumbling stone" to anticipate the experiences of opposition and suffering the community will experience. This elect and sacred community is to maintain a holy way of life expressed in good deeds (1:14-15), live actively "conscious" of God's presence (2:19; 3:16, 21), and have strong mutual love among its members (1:22; 3:8-12; 4:8-11).

The author resists falling into a purely sectarian stance in the face of outside threats. One of the remarkable features of the letter is its ability to thread its way between maintaining the integrity of Christian commitment within the life of the community and conformity with the social mores of the surrounding culture. The author in effect urges that the community take a "missionary" stance toward the outside world, giving a testimony of a holy and blameless life to offset the slander and ignorance of the non-Christian majority and possibly to lead them to glorify God on the day of judgment (2:11-12). Therefore all of the members of the community are to "submit" to or participate in the normal, created structures of society (2:13). Slaves, drawing inspiration from the sufferings of the innocent Christ (2:18-25), should not resist or resent unjust masters, and wives of non-Christian husbands should show proper respect for their spouses and perhaps win them over by their gracious behavior (3:1-6). In fact these two groups within the community—vulnerable because of their social standing—serve as models of Christian witness for all the rest (3:8). All are to be good citizens, respectful of authority (while aware of its limits, 2:13-17), not retaliating for the suffering they have to endure from others (2:9), and ready to give a witness for the Christian hope that sustains their life (3:15).

The author sets all of this exhortation within a perspective of unfolding history. Their ancestors in faith prepared for this moment and longed to see it (1:10-12). Christ brought the Christians God's gift of salvation and gave them an example of how to endure unjust suffering (1:20-21; 2:21). Now he has gone before them in triumph to God, subjugating the evil spirits and reigning at God's right hand (3:18-22) until he returns at the end of time—a consummation of history that is not long in coming (4:7). Because the time is short and because they have to endure suffering—and also because the devil prowls the world (5:8)—the Christians are to be vigilant and disciplined (4:7; 5:8), yet at the same time they should not be gripped by fear or anxiety (3:14; 4:12). While awaiting Christ's triumphant return they should persevere in doing good and entrust their lives to "a faithful Creator" (4:19).

5. *Text and Translation*

The Greek text used as the basis for this commentary is that found in the 27th edition of Nestle-Aland, *Novum Testamentum Graece,* edited by Barbara and Kurt Aland, Johannes Karavidopoulos, Carlo Maria Martini, and Bruce M. Metzger (Stuttgart: Deutsche Bibelgesellschaft, 1993). The earliest full text of 1 Peter is contained in $\mathfrak{P}^{72}$, a papyrus manuscript dating from the third or fourth century.

Where well-attested variant readings have some impact on the interpretation of a passage, the commentary notes the alternatives. For a more complete accounting of variant readings for 1 Peter the reader is referred to the massive commentaries of Achtemeier or Elliott.

A word needs to be said about the translation that accompanies the commentary. To the extent possible the translation closely follows the Greek text. Rather than attempt a graceful English version, the author intends here to enable the reader to follow the grammatical and exegetical explanations in the commentary. Thus good English idiom has often been sacrificed in the interests of literalness.

6. *The Abiding Significance of 1 Peter*

The goal of the Sacra Pagina series is "to provide sound, critical analysis without any loss of sensitivity to religious meaning." The contemporary Christian reader will surely benefit from sensitivity to the vigorous pastoral theology of 1 Peter. Although written at a time far different from our own, the letter continues to have exceptional appeal and relevance. The challenge for the Christian communities addressed in the letter was to maintain the integrity of their Christian lives in a world that had no sympathy for their faith and values and considered them moral strangers in their own land. Rather than draw the wagons in a circle and attempt to seal themselves off from that hostile environment, the author of 1 Peter counsels his Christians to continue to be good citizens, participating in the ordinary human structures of their society, while maintaining the integrity of their faith in Christ and their loyalty to one another.

Commentators on the letter have different opinions on how successfully 1 Peter maintained the precarious balance between Christian integrity and societal participation. Some, for example, feel that 1 Peter conceded too much in counseling Christian wives to be submissive to their nonbelieving husbands and to submerge their dignity under the traditional virtues of gentleness and modesty (3:1-6). For many the letter's counsel to slaves to endure unjust punishment (2:18-21) without, at the same time, saying anything about the responsibilities of slaveowners is also a flawed surrender to social conformity. These are serious questions that will continue to be debated whenever thoughtful Christians turn to this letter. In the author's mind the virtues of gentleness and modesty were not based primarily on social expectations but were Christian virtues—drawn from the example of Jesus himself—and required of all Christians, not just wives (3:8). And while for us the whole institution of slavery is morally repugnant, for a first-century Christian slave rebellion against harsh masters was not a very likely option, whereas finding meaning in the midst of unavoidable suffering was. A first-century slave may have stood on the lowest rungs of a free society in the Roman world, but for the Christian community slaves who suffered unjustly were an icon of the crucified Christ and an example for the entire community.

Even though contemporary circumstances in most parts of the world are vastly different from first-century Asia Minor or Rome, the challenge of maintaining one's Christian commitment while participating in a non-Christian (and sometimes hostile) world is an urgent one for many Christians today, including those in societies at one time considered "Christian." First Peter does not simply frame a perennial problem, but gracefully points the way to its solution: maintaining awareness of the gospel's profound vision of human destiny and the dignity and beauty of the church, consciousness of God's abiding presence, exercising the virtues of discipline and alertness, living in hope without fear, building communities based on mutual love and respect, seeking thoughtful means of giving witness without offense, and offering leadership that is rooted in faith and not overbearing. Reflection on this vigorous and thoughtful message of 1 Peter will benefit Christians of any age.

7. General Bibliography

Commentaries

Achtemeier, Paul J. *1 Peter*. Hermeneia. Minneapolis: Fortress, 1996.
Beare, Francis Wright. *The First Epistle of Peter: The Greek Text with Introduction and Notes*. 3rd ed. Oxford: Blackwell, 1970 [1st publication 1947; 2nd ed. 1958].
Best, Ernest. *I Peter*. NCB. London: Oliphants; Grand Rapids: Eerdmans, 1971.
Brox, Norbert. *Der erste Petrusbrief*. EKKNT 21. 2nd ed. Zurich: Benziger; Neukirchen-Vluyn: Neukirchner Verlag, 1986 [1st ed. 1976].
Craddock, Fred B. *First and Second Peter and Jude*. Westminster Bible Companion. Louisville: Westminster John Knox, 1995.

Dalton, William J. "The First Epistle of Peter," in Raymond E. Brown, Joseph A. Fitzmyer, and Roland E. Murphy, eds., *The New Jerome Biblical Commentary*. Englewood Cliffs, N.J.: Prentice Hall, 1990, 903–908.

Elliott, John H. *1 Peter*. AB New York: Doubleday, 2000.

Fitzmyer, Joseph A. "The First Epistle of Peter," in Raymond E. Brown, Joseph A. Fitzmyer, and Roland E. Murphy, eds., *The Jerome Biblical Commentary*. Englewood Cliffs, N.J.: Prentice-Hall, 1968, 2:362–68.

Garland, David E. "1 Peter," *The New Interpreter's Bible. Volume XII. Hebrews, James, 1 & 2 Peter, 1, 2, and 3 John, Jude, Revelation*. Nashville: Abingdon, 1998, 229–319.

Goppelt, Leonhard. *A Commentary on I Peter*. Edited by Ferdinand Hahn; translated and augmented by John E. Alsup. Grand Rapids: Eerdmans, 1993.

Hillyer, Norman. *1 and 2 Peter, Jude*. NIBC. Peabody, Mass.: Hendrickson, 1992.

Hort, Fenton John Anthony. *The First Epistle of St. Peter I. I–II, 17: The Greek Text, With Introductory Lecture, Commentary, and Additional Notes*. London: Macmillan, 1898.

Kelly, J.N.D. *The Epistles of Peter and of Jude*. HNTC. New York: Harper & Row, 1969.

Krodel, Gerhard. "1 Peter," in *The General Letters: Hebrews, James, 1–2 Peter, Jude, 1–3 John*. Proclamation Commentaries. Rev. ed. Minneapolis: Fortress, 1995, 42–83, 146–47.

Michaels, J. Ramsey. *1 Peter*. WBC 49. Waco, Texas: Word, 1988.

Perkins, Pheme. *First and Second Peter, James, and Jude*. Interpretation. Louisville: John Knox, 1995.

Selwyn, Edward Gordon. *The First Epistle of St. Peter: The Greek Text with Introduction, Notes, and Essays*. 2nd ed. London: Macmillan; New York: St. Martin's, 1947 [1st ed. 1946].

Senior, Donald P. *1 & 2 Peter*. New Testament Message 20. Wilmington: Michael Glazier, 1980.

Spicq, Ceslas. *Les Épîtres de Saint Pierre*. Sources Bibliques 4. Paris: Gabalda, 1966a.

Windisch, Hans. *Die katholischen Briefe*. HNT 4/2. Tübingen: J.C.B. Mohr (Paul Siebeck), 1911.

Other literature

Achtemeier, Paul J. "Suffering Servant and Suffering Christ in 1 Peter," in Abraham J. Malherbe and Wayne A. Meeks, eds., *The Future of Christology*. New York: Crossroad, 1993, 176–88.

Agnew, F. H. "1 Peter 1:2: An Alternative Translation," *CBQ* 45 (1968) 68–73.

Aland, Barbara, Kurt Aland, Johannes Karavidopoulos, Carlo Maria Martini, and Bruce M. Metzger. *Novum Testamentum Graece*. Stuttgart: Deutsche Bibelgesellschaft, 1993.

Applegate, J. K. "The Coelect Woman of 1 Peter," *NTS* 32 (1992) 587–604.

Balch, David L. *Let Wives Be Submissive: The Domestic Code in I Peter*. SBLMS 26. Chico: Scholars, 1981.

_____. "Early Christian Criticism of Patriarchal Authority: 1 Peter 2:11–3:12," *USQR* 39 (1984) 161–73.

Balch, David L., and Carolyn Osiek, *Families in the New Testament World: Households and House Churches.* Family, Religion, and Culture. Louisville: Westminster John Knox, 1997.

Bammel, Ernst. "The Commands in I Pet .ii. 17," *NTS* 11 (1964–65) 268–81.

Barth, Gerhard. "1 Petrus 1,3-9: Exegese, Meditation und Predigt," *Estudios teologicos* 6 (1966) 148–60.

Bauckham, Richard J. "Spirits in Prison," *ABD* 6:177–78.

Bechtler, Stephen R. *Following in His Steps: Suffering, Community, and Christology in 1 Peter.* SBLDS 162. Atlanta: Scholars, 1998.

Best, Ernest. "1 Peter II 4-10: A Reconsideration," *NovT* 11 (1969) 270–93.

Black, C. Clifton. *Mark. Images of an Apostolic Interpreter.* Columbia: University of South Carolina Press, 1994.

Blazen, I. T. "Suffering and Cessation from Sin According to 1 Peter 4:1," *AUSS* 21 (1983) 27–50.

Boismard, Marie-Émile. "La typologie baptismale dans la première épître de Saint Pierre," *La Vie Spirituelle* 94 (1956) 339–52.

_____. "Une liturgie baptismale dans la *Prima Petri,* II: Son influence sur l'épître de Jacques," *RB* 63 (1957) 161–83.

Borchert, Gerald L. "The Conduct of Christians in the Face of the 'Fiery Ordeal' (1 Pet 4:12–5:11)," *RevExp* 79 (1982) 451–62.

Brown, Raymond E. *The Churches the Apostles Left Behind.* New York: Paulist, 1984.

Brown, Raymond E., Karl P. Donfried, and John Reumann, *Peter in the New Testament: A Collaborative Assessment by Protestant and Roman Catholic Scholars.* New York: Paulist, 1973.

Brown, Raymond E., and John P. Meier, *Antioch and Rome: New Testament Cradles of Catholic Christianity.* New York: Paulist, 1983.

Brox, Norbert. "Tendenz und Pseudepigraphie im ersten Petrusbrief," *Kairos* 20 (1978) 110–20.

Cahill, Lisa Sowle. *Love Your Enemies: Discipleship, Pacifism, and Just War Theory.* Minneapolis: Fortress, 1997.

Carter, Warren. *Matthew and Empire: Initial Explorations.* Harrisburg, Pa.: Trinity Press International, 2001.

Cook, J. D. "I Peter iii.20: An Unnecessary Problem," *JTS* 31 (1980) 72–78.

Cothenet, Edouard. "Le réalisme de l'espérance chrétienne selon I Pierre," *NTS* 27 (1981) 564–72.

Cross, Frank Leslie. *I Peter: A Paschal Liturgy.* London: Mowbray, 1954.

Dalton, William J. "The Interpretation of 1 Peter 3,19 and 4,6: Light from 2 Peter," *Bib* 60 (1979) 547–55.

_____. *Christ's Proclamation to the Spirits: A Study of I Peter 3:18–4:6.* AnBib 23. 2nd rev. ed. Rome: Pontifical Biblical Institute, 1989.

_____. "So That Your Faith May Also Be Your Hope in God," in L. L. Morris, ed., *Reconciliation and Hope.* Grand Rapids: Eerdmans, 1974.

Danker, Frederick W. "1 Peter 1:14–2:17—A Consolatory Pericope," *ZNW* 58 (1967) 95–102.

Deterding, Paul. "Exodus Motifs in First Peter," *Concordia Journal* 7 (1981) 58–65.

Donahue, John R. *Are You the Christ? The Trial Narrative of Jesus in the Gospel of Mark.* SBLDS 10. Missoula: Scholars, 1973.

Dupont-Roc, Roselyne. "Le jeu des prépositions en 1 Pierre 1,1-12: De l'espérance finale à la joie dans les épreuves présentes," *EstBib* 53 (1995) 201–12.

Elliott, John H. "Disgraced yet Graced: The Gospel according to 1 Peter in the Key of Honor and Shame," *BTB* 25 (1995) 166–78.

_____. *The Elect and the Holy: An Exegetical Examination of 1 Peter 2:4-10 and the Phrase basileion hierateuma*. NovTSup 12. Leiden: Brill, 1966.

_____. "Ministry and Church Order in the New Testament: A Traditio-Historical Analysis (1 Pt 5,1-5 and parallels)," *CBQ* 32 (1970) 367–91.

_____. "Salutation and Exhortation to Christian Behavior on the Basis of God's Blessings (1 Pet 1:1–2:10)," *RevExp* 79 (1982) 415–25.

_____. "Silvanus and Mark in 1 Peter and Acts," in Karl H. Rengstorf, ed., *Wort in der Zeit*. Leiden: Brill, 1980.

_____. *A Home for the Homeless: A Sociological Exegesis of I Peter, Its Situation and Strategy*. Philadelphia: Fortress, 1981.

_____. *A Home for the Homeless: A Social-Scientific Exegesis of I Peter, Its Situation and Strategy, With a New Introduction*. Minneapolis: Fortress, 1990.

_____. "1 Peter, Its Situation and Strategy. A Discussion with David Balch," in Charles H. Talbert, ed., *Perspectives on First Peter*. NABPR Special Study Series 9. Macon: Mercer University Press, 1986.

Feinberg, John. "1 Peter 3:18-20, Ancient Mythology, and the Intermediate State," *WTJ* 48 (1986) 303–36.

Feldmeier, Reinhard. *Die Christen als Fremde: Die Metapher der Fremde in der antiken Welt, im Urchristentum und im 1. Petrusbrief*. WUNT 64. Tübingen: J.C.B. Mohr [Paul Siebeck], 1992.

Francis, James. "'Like Newborn Babes'—The Image of the Child in 1 Peter 2:2-3," *JSNT Suppl. Ser.* 3 (1980) 111–17.

Gärtner, Bertil. *The Temple and the Community in Qumran and the New Testament*. SNTSMS 1. Cambridge: Cambridge University Press, 1965.

Giesen, Heinz. "Gemeinde als Liebesgemeinschaft dank göttlicher Neuzeugung. Zu 1 Petr 1,22–2,3," *SNTSU* 24 (1998) 135–66.

_____. "Lebenszeugnis in der Fremde. Zum Verhalten der Christen in der paganen Gesellschaft (1 Petr 2,11-17)," *SNTSU* 23 (1998) 113–52.

Golebiewski, R. P. E. "Dieu nous console dans l'épreuve (1 P 5,6-11)," *AsSeign* 57 (1965) 17–23.

Gross, C. D. "Are the Wives of 1 Peter 3.7 Christians?" *JSNT* 35 (1989) 89–96.

Grudem, Wayne A. "Christ Preaching through Noah: 1 Peter 3:19-20 in the Light of Dominant Themes in Jewish Literature," *Trinity Journal* 7 (1986) 89–96.

Hall, R. "For to This You Have Been Called: The Cross and Suffering in 1 Peter," *ResQ* 19 (1976) 137–47.

Hanson, Anthony T. "Salvation Proclaimed, I: 1 Peter 3:18-22," *ExpTim* 93 (1981–82) 100–112.

Hellerman, Joseph H. *The Ancient Church as Family*. Minneapolis: Fortress, 2001.

Hemer, Colin J. "The Address of 1 Peter," *ExpTim* (1989) 239–43.

Hengel, Martin. *Studies in the Gospel of Mark*. Philadelphia: Fortress, 1985.

Hiebert, D. Edmond. "Designation of the Readers in 1 Peter 1:1-2," *BS* 137 (1964) 64–75.

_____. "Living in the Light of Christ's Return: An Exposition of 1 Peter 4:7-11," *BS* 139 (1982) 243–54.

_____. "Selected Studies from 1 Peter. Part I: Following Christ's Example—An Exposition of 1 Peter 2:21-25," *BS* 139 (1982) 32–45.

_____. "Selected Studies from 1 Peter. Part 4: Counsel for Christ's Under-Shepherds—An Exposition of 1 Peter 5:1-4," *BS* 139 (1982) 330–41.

Hill, David. "'To Offer Spiritual Sacrifices . . .' (1 Peter 2:5): Liturgical Formulations and Christian Paraenesis in 1 Peter," *JSNT* 16 (1982) 45–63.

_____. "On Suffering and Baptism in 1 Peter," *NovT* 18 (1976) 181–89.

Hillyer, Norman. "'Rock-Stone' Imagery in 1 Peter," *TynBul* 22 (1971) 58–81.

Horrell, David G. "The Product of a Petrine Circle? A Reassessment of the Origin and Character of 1 Peter," *JSNT* 86 (2002) 29–60.

Johnson, D. E. "Fire in God's House: Imagery from Malachi 3 in Peter's Theology of Suffering (1 Pet 4:12-19)," *JETS* 29 (1986) 285–94.

Jossa, Giorgio. "La sottomissione alle autorita politiche in 1 Pt,13-17," *RivB* 44 (1996) 205–11.

Juel, Donald. *Messiah and Temple: The Trial of Jesus in the Gospel of Mark.* SBLDS 31. Missoula: Scholars, 1977.

Kendall, Daniel. "On Christian Hope. 1 Peter 1:3-9," *Int* 41 (1987) 66–71.

_____. "The Literary and Theological Functions of 1 Peter 1:3-12," in Charles H. Talbert, ed., *Perspectives on First Peter.* Macon, Ga.: Mercer University Press, 1986, 103–20.

Kiley, Mark. "Like Sara: The Tale of Terror Behind 1 Peter 3:6," *JBL* 105 (1987) 689–92.

Kline, Leslie L. "Ethics for the Endtime: An Exegesis of 1 Pt. 4: 7-11," *ResQ* 7 (1963) 113–23.

Klumbies, Paul-Gerhard. "Die Verkündigung unter Geistern und Toten nach 1 Petr 3,19f und 4,6," *ZNW* 92 (2001) 207–28.

Koenig, John. "Hospitality," *ABD* 3:299–301.

Langkammer, H. "Jes 53 und 1 Petr 2,21-25: Zur christologischen Interpretation der Leidenstheologie von Jes 53," *BL* 60 (1987) 90–98.

Légasse, Simon. "La soumission aux authorités d'après 1 Pierre 2. 13-17: Version spécifique d'une parénese traditionelle," *NTS* 34 (1988) 378–96.

Manns, Frédéric. "La morale domestique de 1 P," *Didaskalia* 30 (2000) 3–27.

Martin, Troy W. "The Present Indicative in the Eschatological Statements of 1 Pet 1,6, 8," *JBL* 111 (1992) 307–12.

_____. "The TestAbr and the Background of 1 Pet 3,6," *ZNW* 90 (1999) 139–46.

_____. *Metaphor and Composition in 1 Peter.* SBLDS 131. Atlanta: Scholars, 1992.

McCartney, D. "Logikos in 1 Peter 2:2," *ZNW* 82 (1991) 352–59.

Michaels, J. Ramsey. "Eschatology in 1 Peter iii.17," *NTS* 13 (1966/67) 394–401.

Minear, Paul S. "The House of Living Stones: A Study of 1 Peter 2:4-12," *Ecumenical Review* 34 (1982) 238–48.

Murphy-O'Connor, Jerome. *Paul the Letter Writer: His World, His Options, His Skills.* Good News Studies 41. Collegeville: The Liturgical Press, 1995.

O'Connor, Daniel. "Holiness of Life as a Way of Christian Witness," *International Review of Missions* 80 (1991) 17–26.

Omanson, Roger. "Suffering For Righteousness' Sake (1 Pet 3:13–4:11)," _RevExp_ 79 (1982) 439–50.

Osborne, T. P. "Guide Lines for Christian Suffering: A Source-Critical and Theological Study of 1 Peter 2,21-25," _Bib_ 64 (1983) 381–408.

Ostmeyer, Karl-Heinrich. _Taufe und Typos. Elemente und Theologie der Taufetypologien in 1. Korinther 10 und 1. Petrus 3._ WUNT 2nd ser. 118. Tübingen: J.C.B. Mohr [Paul Siebeck], 2000.

Patterson, D. K. "Roles in Marriage: A Study in Submission—1 Peter 3:1-7," _Theological Educator_ 13 (1982) 70–79.

Perdelwitz, Emil Richard. _Die Mysterienreligion und das Problem des I. Petrusbriefes: Ein literarischer und religionsgeschichtlicher Versuch._ RVV 11/3. Giessen: Alfred Töpelman, 1911.

Perkins, Pheme. _Love Commands in the New Testament._ New York: Paulist, 1982.

_____. _Peter: Apostle for the Whole Church._ Columbia: University of South Carolina Press, 1994.

Pilch, John J. "'Visiting Strangers' and 'Resident Aliens,'" _TBT_ 29 (1991) 357–61.

Piper, John. "Hope as the Motivation for Love: I Peter 3:9-12," _NTS_ 26 (1980) 212–31.

_____. _"Love Your Enemies": Jesus' Love Command in the Synoptic Gospels and in the Early Christian Paraenesis. A History of the Tradition and Interpretation of Its Uses._ SNTSMS 38. Cambridge: Cambridge University Press, 1979.

Prasad, Jacob. _Foundations of The Christian Way of Life, According to 1 Peter 1,13-25: An Exegetico-Theological Study._ AB 146. Rome: Pontifical Biblical Institute, 2000.

Prostmeier, Ferdinand–Rupert. _Handlungsmodelle im ersten Petrusbrief._ FB 62. Würzburg: Echter, 1990, 449–71.

Reichert, Angelika. _Eine urchristliche praeparatio ad martyrium: Studien zur Komposition, Traditionsgeschichte und Theologie des 1. Petrusbriefes._ BBET 22. Frankfurt: Peter Lang, 1989.

Richards, E. Randolph. "Silvanus Was Not Peter's Secretary: Theological Bias in Interpreting _dia Silouanou . . . egrapsa_ in I Peter 5:12," _JETS_ 43 (2000) 417–32.

Richardson, R. L. Jr. "From 'Subjection to Authority' to 'Mutual Submission': The Ethic of Subordination in 1 Peter," _Faith and Mission_ 4 (1987) 70–80.

Rodgers, P. R. "The Longer Reading of 1 Peter 4:14," _CBQ_ 43 (1981) 93–95.

Scharlemann, Martin. "Exodus Ethics: Part One—I Peter 1:13-16," _Concordia Journal_ 2 (1976) 165–70.

Schertz, Mary H. "Nonretaliation and the Haustafeln in 1 Peter," in Willard H. Swartley, ed., _The Love of Enemy and Nonretaliation in the New Testament._ Louisville: Westminster, 1992, 258–86.

Scholer, David M. "Woman's Adornment: Some Historical and Hermeneutical Observations on The New Testament Passages 1 Tim 2:9-10 and 1 Pet 3:3-4," _Daughters of Sarah_ 6 (1980) 3–6.

Schutter, William L. "I Peter 4.17, Ezekiel 9.6, and Apocalyptic Hermeneutics," _SBL 1987: Seminar Papers._ SBLSP 26. Atlanta: Scholars, 1987, 276–84.

Schwank, Benedikt. _"Diabolus tamquam leo rugiens_ (I Petr. 5:8)," _Erbe und Auftrag_ 38 (1962) 15–20.

Schweizer, Eduard. "The Priesthood of All Believers: 1 Peter 2:1-10," in Michael J. Wilkins and Terence Paige, eds., *Worship, Theology, and Ministry in the Early Church: Essays in Honor of Ralph P. Martin.* JNTSSup 87. Sheffield: JSOT Press, 1992.

Senior, Donald P. "The Conduct of Christians in the World (1 Pet 2:11–3:12)," *RevExp* 79 (1982) 427–38.

_____. *The Passion of Jesus in the Gospel of Mark.* Passion Series 1. Collegeville: The Liturgical Press, 1984, 25–28.

Snodgrass, K. R. "I Peter ii.1-10: Its Formation and Literary Affinities," *NTS* 24 (1977/78) 97–106.

Soards, Marion L. "1 Peter, 2 Peter, and Jude as Evidence for a Petrine School," *ANRW* 2 (1988) 3827–49.

Spicq, Ceslas. "L'Épître de Pierre: Prière, charité, justice . . . et fin des Temps (1 Pierre 4:7-11)," *AsSeign* 50 (1966) 15–29.

_____. "La place ou le rôle des jeunes dans certaines communautés néotestamentaires," *RB* 76 (1969) 508–27.

Stevick, Daniel B. "A Matter of Taste: 1 Peter 2:3," *Review for Religious* 47 (1988) 707–17.

Strobel, August. "Macht Leiden von Sünden frei? Zur Problematick von 1 Petr. 4,1f.," *TZ* 19 (1963) 412–25.

Talbert, Charles H. "The Educational Value of Suffering in 1 Peter," in idem, *Learning Through Suffering: The Educational Value of Suffering in the New Testament and in Its Milieu.* Collegeville: The Liturgical Press, 1991.

Unnik, W. C. van. "Le role de Noé dans les épîtres de Pierre," *Noé, L'homme universel.* Colloque de Louvain 1978. Brussels: Institutum Judaicum Bruxelles 3 (1979) 207–39.

_____. "The Critique of Paganism in I Peter 1:18," in E. Earle Ellis and Max Wilcox, eds., *Neotestamentica et Semitica: Studies in Honour of Matthew Black.* Edinburgh: T & T Clark (1969) 129–42.

Vancil, Jack W. "Sheep, Shepherd," *ABD* 5:1187–90.

Villiers, J. L. de. "Joy in Suffering in 1 Peter," *Neot* 9 (1975) 64–86.

Vogels, Heinz–Jürgen. *Christi Abstieg ins Totenreich und das Läuterungsgericht an den Toten: eine bibeltheologisch-dogmatische Untersuchung zum Glaubensartikel "descendit ad inferos."* FTS 102. Freiburg: Herder, 1976.

Warden, D. "The Prophets of 1 Peter 1:10-12," *ResQ* 31 (1989) 1–12.

Winter, Bruce W. "The Public Honouring of Christian Benefactors: Romans 13.3-4 and 1 Peter 2.14-15," *JSNT* 34 (1988), 87–103.

Zerbe, Gordon M. "Non-retaliation in 1 Peter: A Pragmatic or a Christological Ethic?" in idem, *Non-retaliation in Early Jewish and New Testament Texts: Ethical Themes in Social Contexts.* JSPSup 13. Sheffield: JSOT Press, 1993.

TRANSLATION, NOTES, INTERPRETATION

1. *The Address of the Letter* (1:1-2)

1. Peter, apostle of Jesus Christ, to the elect sojourners who belong to the diaspora in Pontus, Galatia, Cappadocia, Asia, and Bithynia, 2. [To you, chosen] through the foreknowledge of God the Father, in the sanctification of the Spirit, for obedience and for the sprinkling of the blood of Jesus Christ: May grace and peace be yours in abundance.

NOTES

1. *Peter, apostle of Jesus Christ:* The name "Peter" derives from the Greek word *petros* ("rock"), used for the disciple of Jesus in the Gospels and Acts. It translates the Aramaic word *Kêpāʾ*, the name apparently given to Simon bar Jona by Jesus himself (see Mark 3:16; Matt 16:18; Luke 6:14; John 1:42). Paul tends to use *Kēphas*, the transliteration of the Aramaic name, using *Petros* only twice (Gal 2:7, 8). The identifying phrase "apostle of Jesus Christ" has no article, which in this context may suggest a recognized title for Peter. It identifies him as an "apostle," that is, as "one sent," and, more importantly, an apostle "of Jesus Christ," thereby indicating the basis for Peter's authority. Paul, too, consistently identifies himself as an "apostle" in the address of his letters, although he frequently underscores his claim to that title by some explanatory phrase (e.g., as in Gal 1:1 ". . . not from human beings nor through a human being but through Jesus Christ and God the Father who raised him from the dead . . ."); in contrast, no explanatory phrase is added to Peter's apostolic title. The apostle will explicitly reassert himself as author of the letter only in 5:1.

to the elect sojourners who belong to the diaspora in Pontus, Galatia, Cappadocia, Asia, and Bithynia: The words used to describe the recipients are highly significant and signal major themes that will be amplified later in the letter. They are "chosen" or "elect" (the Greek term is *eklektois*), evoking Old Testament descriptions of Israel as the chosen people (e.g., Deut 30:4; Neh 1:9; Ps 147:2). Peter will take this motif up later in the letter (2:9-10). They are also "sojourners" or "aliens"; the Greek term *parepidēmois*, rarely used in the Bible, suggests someone who is living temporarily in a strange land (see also 2:11). And they belong to the "diaspora"—the term used frequently in Jewish and early Christian literature to refer to the Jewish people scattered from their homeland through persecution. Here the term is applied in a metaphorical sense to Christians who, though sojourners and scattered, belong to a chosen people.

Pontus, Galatia, Cappadocia, Asia, and Bithynia are areas in Asia Minor, present-day Turkey, north of the Taurus Mountains. Most of these are regions Paul did not evangelize, although Acts places him in parts of the district of Asia during his visits to Ephesus (Acts 19:10). Acts 2:9 includes Cappadocia, Pontus, and Asia in the list of areas from which come the crowds who visit Jerusalem and hear Peter on Pentecost, a further indication that Christian communities developed in these areas prior to Paul's mission. It is difficult to decipher the order in which the areas are listed, although it may be the sequence in which the carrier of the letter traveled as he contacted Christian communities scattered throughout these regions, beginning with a port on the Black Sea in the region of Pontus such as Sinope and then proceeding in a circular route, first south through Galatia and Cappadocia, then west to Asia, and then turning east and north back to the Black Sea region through Bithynia to Pontus. (At the time of the letter these last two regions formed one province.)

2. *[To you, chosen] through the foreknowledge of God the Father:* Each phrase of this verse defines the source, dynamism, and consequences of the Christians' elect status. The triadic references to Father, Son, and Spirit make this greeting unique in the New Testament (although see Matt 28:19; 2 Cor 13:13; Eph 4:6; Jude 20-21). The Greek preposition *kata* ("through" or "according to") references the noun "elect"; they are elected or chosen through the "foreknowledge" of God the Father. The word *prognōsin* implies not only "foreknowledge" but intent; the source and cause of the Christians' elect status is God's will. The designation of God as "father" reflects the graciousness and benevolence that suffuse the divine choice.

in the sanctification of the Spirit: The noun *hagiasmos* derives from the verb "to make holy," or "sanctify" and attributes to the Spirit the means or dynamism by which the Father's choice is effected.

for obedience: The preposition used here is *eis* and its precise meaning in this context is not easily determined. Technically speaking the preposition could be used in a causative sense and, coupled with the next phrase "sprinkling of blood," mean that sanctification is also effected through the obedience and shed blood "of Jesus Christ." More likely, however, it signifies the end or goal of the sanctification effected through the Spirit. In this case the word "obedience" stands on its own and means "obedience" or responsiveness to God's will revealed in Jesus. In 1:22 the letter uses the phrase "obedience to the truth," which has a similar connotation.

and [for] the sprinkling of the blood of Jesus Christ: This unusual phrase evokes the covenant ritual described in Exod 24:3-8 in which Moses pours the blood of sacrificed oxen on the altar and then sprinkles it on the congregation as a sign of the covenant bond between God and the people. It is noteworthy that here, too, Moses first calls for obedience to the "words of the Lord and all the ordinances" and then proceeds to the ritual of the blood. Thus the end point of election includes both obedience to the gospel and membership in the new covenant people. This notion is amplified in 1 Pet 1:18-20.

May grace and peace be yours in abundance (literally "be multiplied for you"): A greeting typical in later Christian letters (e.g., 2 Pet 1:2; Jude 2; *1 Clement* 1:1), which draws on Jewish traditional salutations, especially the reference to "peace." The word "grace" *(charein)* is also used as a salutation in Greco-Roman letters, but here it takes on a more religious significance, as it already had in Jewish texts (see Jas 1:1).

INTERPRETATION

The format of these opening verses follows, with some adaptation, the standard format of a Greco-Roman or Jewish letter of this period. All of Paul's letters begin in similar fashion. However, the long string of stately phrases and the absence of definite pronouns give this greeting a particular solemnity, perhaps suitable for a circular letter intended to be read in a number of communities. Although brief and formal, the salutation already signals some of the major concerns of the letter as a whole.

The author of the letter is identified as "Peter, apostle of Jesus Christ." While it is unlikely that the apostle Peter is the actual author of the letter (see Introduction), his authority and status underwrite the letter. The body of the letter contains only brief personal references, such as 5:1 where the author speaks of himself as "an elder" and "a witness of the sufferings of Christ." In 5:12 the author refers to "Silvanus, whom I consider a faithful brother." In contrast, 2 Pet 1:14, 16-18 is more autobiographical in content.

If the origin of the letter is Rome (see 5:13, "your sister church in Babylon") and the letter is directed to the communities of northern Asia Minor cited in 1:1, this provides an intriguing glimpse of the developing image of Peter at the end of the first century. There is no question that Peter was an important figure in the early church's mission. Paul notes Peter's importance several times in his letters (Gal 1:18; 2:9, 11; 1 Cor 1:12; 9:5) and his name is attached to the credal formula Paul cites in 1 Cor 15:5. He plays a leading role in the community of the disciples in all four Gospels, and however one interprets the significance of Matt 16:16-19, it surely portrays Peter as bearing authority within the community of the disciples. Acts gives Peter a crucial role in the evolving mission of the Jerusalem church, where he is the first to baptize a Gentile centurion (Acts 10) and is the mediating figure in the council of Acts 15. Paul, too, pays homage to Peter's important role in the Jewish Christian mission (Gal 2:7-10) and implicitly understands him as a key mediating figure when he expresses disappointment at Peter's behavior in Antioch (Gal 2:11-14).

There is no evidence that Peter had visited the churches of Asia Minor cited in the greeting, yet the letter invokes Peter's prestige as an apostle and an "elder" and "witness to the sufferings of Christ." Perhaps emissaries from the church at Rome had evangelized these churches or a relationship had been established in some other way. In any case the greeting implies that there is a relationship between the church at Rome and these scattered communities in Asia Minor that permits the church at Rome to send exhortations and encouragement to these fellow Christians.

The description of the addressees as "elect sojourners" and members of the "diaspora" compresses into succinct phrases theological viewpoints that suffuse the letter as a whole. The Christians in these communities are "sojourners" or "strangers" not primarily because of any legal status but because their Christian faith and the values that flow from it set them apart from the surrounding culture. The letter will emphasize this at several points, noting that the Christians have abandoned the "futile ways of their ancestors" (1:18) and must live a life of virtue and integrity not appreciated by their fellow non-Christians (e.g., 2:11-13). The hint of impending persecution that hangs over this letter seems to stem from the alienation caused by the contrasting lifestyles of the Christian communities. In the perspective of 1 Peter, therefore, the Christians' status as strangers or "aliens" (see 2:11) is not so much a "vertical" estrangement of those who long for heaven but are confined temporarily to earthly existence, but a "horizontal" estrangement caused by leading a life different from the expectations of the dominant culture.

At the same time the letter quickly sketches the extraordinary dignity and destiny of these exiled communities. They are a "diaspora"; that is, even though scattered in an alien land they belong to God's people. The Jewish notion of the diaspora contained this same paradoxical meaning. Even though scattered through persecution and exile, the peoples of the diaspora remain one people destined for return and reunion. 1 Peter uses this same concept; although the communities addressed in the letter lead a fragile existence in alien territory and may even face the threat of persecution and suffering, they are nevertheless God's own people and as such will endure.

That compelling dignity is sketched in bold strokes. They are an "elect" or chosen people, like Israel of old. That choice is rooted in God's own foreknowledge and intent. This is the foundation for their identity as a holy nation and a new temple or house of God. This strong ecclesiology will be spelled out particularly in 2:4-10. God's own spirit provides the dynamic power to sanctify them as God's people and leads them to a life of obedience. The body of the letter refers several times to the virtues and attitudes that characterize a holy people, and this life of holiness is the point of the letter's exhortations.

They are also chosen to be "sprinkled with the blood of Jesus Christ" (1:2), a phrase that evokes the Mosaic covenant. In Exod 24:3-8 Moses sprinkled the blood of oxen on the altar and then on the people to signify the ratification of the covenant and the people's pledge to obey God's ordinances. First Peter adapts this ritual description to assert the covenant bonds of this new people of God. They, too, are called to obedience and to the sprinkling of blood. Now, however, the blood is no longer that of oxen but the blood of Jesus Christ. This metaphorical adaptation of the temple ritual to describe the redemptive work of Jesus and its consequences is much more elaborately developed in Heb 9:18-21. In 1 Peter the phrase evokes the passion of Jesus and its redemptive meaning for the Christian, as will be taken up later in the letter (see, for example, 1:18-21; 2:21, 24; 3:18-19; 4:1, 11). Underlying this phrase may also be the baptismal theology of 1 Peter. Sprinkling with the blood of Christ implies contact with his redemptive death, and this is experienced in baptism (see 3:21), a concept with strong roots in Pauline theology.

It is interesting that while 1 Peter draws freely on traditional Jewish symbols that define Israel's status as God's people—election, exile, diaspora, covenant—it does not engage in any polemic versus Judaism. For some interpreters this suggests that, in fact, the letter and the communities it addressed were Jewish Christian and therefore still considered themselves as thoroughly within the orbit of Israel. (For interpreters holding this more traditional view see the listing in Brox, *Der erste Petrusbrief* 25.) However, being Jewish Christian did not exempt other early Christian communities from sharp polemic with other Jewish groups, as is the case, for example, with Matthew's gospel and John's gospel. If, as is likely, 1 Peter belongs to a mainly Gentile form of Christianity, it is noteworthy that the tension points are not with Jewish groups but with the surrounding Greco-Roman culture. We know from the letters of Pliny the Younger that such tension did, in fact, exist in regions of Asia Minor in the first part of the second century, and the book of Revelation also witnesses to sharp alienation between some Christian groups and the dominant culture in western Asia Minor in the latter part of the first century.

The use of rich Jewish symbolism in this letter, along with the absence of polemic versus Judaism, suggests that the traditions utilized in 1 Peter may have originated in a strong Jewish Christian tradition (a likely case for a community connected with the teaching and authority of Peter), but now at a later moment were being used for the evangelization of Gentile communities for whom tension with Jewish groups was not a prime concern.

Thus the formal greeting of the letter, which concludes with a lovely call for an abundance of grace and peace for the recipients, describes in quick strokes both the plight of Christians who must live in a world that does not share the values of the gospel and the extraordinary dignity and strength that enable these exiles of the diaspora to give hope-filled witness to that world.

FOR REFERENCE AND FURTHER STUDY

Agnew, F. H. "1 Peter 1:2: An Alternative Translation," *CBQ* 45 (1968) 68–73.
Brown, Raymond E. *The Churches the Apostles Left Behind.* New York: Paulist, 1984, 75–83.
Brown, Raymond E., Karl P. Donfried, and John Reumann, eds., *Peter in the New Testament: A Collaborative Assessment by Protestant and Roman Catholic Scholars.* New York: Paulist, 1973.
Feldmeier, Reinhard. *Die Christen als Fremde: Die Metaphor der Fremde in der antiken Welt, im Urchristentum und im 1. Petrusbrief.* WUNT 64. Tübingen: J.C.B. Mohr [Paul Siebeck], 1992.
Hemer, Colin J. "The Address of 1 Peter," *ExpTim* (1989) 239–43.
Hiebert, D. Edmond. "Designation of the Readers in 1 Peter 1:1-2," *BS* 137 (1964) 64–75.
Perkins, Pheme. *Peter: Apostle for the Whole Church.* Columbia: University of South Carolina Press, 1994.
Pilch, John J. "'Visiting Strangers' and 'Resident Aliens.'" *TBT* 29 (1991) 357–61.

2. *The Foundation of Christian Life* (1:3-12)

3. Blessed be the God and father of our lord Jesus Christ, who in accord with his abundant mercy has begotten us anew to a living hope through the resurrection of Jesus Christ from the dead, 4. to an inheritance that is immortal, undefiled, and unfading, one reserved in heaven for you, 5. who in God's power are guarded through faith for a salvation that is ready to be revealed in the end time. 6. In this you rejoice, even if now for a little while you may have to be grieved by all kinds of trials 7. so that the genuineness of your faith, more precious than gold that is perishable yet tested by fire, may prove to be for praise and glory and honor at the revelation of Jesus Christ, 8. whom, without having seen, you love, and, although not seeing him yet believing in him, you rejoice with inexpressible and glorious joy, 9. attaining the goal of your faith, the salvation of your souls. 10. Concerning this salvation the prophets, who prophesied about the grace that was to be yours, searched and investigated diligently. 11. They inquired about the circumstances or timing, which the spirit of Christ that was within them indicated, the very spirit that gave witness in advance about the sufferings that were to be Christ's and the

glory that would follow. 12. To [them] these prophets it was revealed that they were not serving themselves but you in these matters, which have now been announced to you through the good news proclaimed by the Holy Spirit sent from heaven, matters into which angels longed to look.

NOTES

3. *Blessed be the God and father of our lord Jesus Christ:* The notion of "blessing" *(eulogētos)* as a way of praising God is, as noted above (see comments on 1:1-2), one of many appropriations 1 Peter makes of biblical and Jewish concepts. The letter does not appear to suggest a contrast between Christian and Jewish notions, but instinctively absorbs ideas and literary forms common in the biblical heritage. Despite its strong christology the letter begins with a theocentric focus. God is identified as "the father of our lord Jesus Christ"; this, too, can be seen as a thoroughly Christian identification of the God of Israel and the God of Abraham.

who in accord with his abundant mercy has begotten us anew to a living hope through the resurrection of Jesus Christ from the dead: The nuance of this active aorist participle "begotten anew" *(anagennēsas)* is to emphasize the action of God in begetting the Christian anew—thus the translation "(God) has begotten us anew" rather than "being born again." While the notion of being begotten or regenerated by God is found in both Jewish and Greco-Roman traditions, the verb *anagennaō* appears in the New Testament only here and in 1:23 (the notion of "rebirth" is found in John 3:5, 7; Titus 3:5; Jas 1:18; 1 John 2:29).

Hope is a fundamental and characteristic virtue in 1 Peter, one that defines the experience of the Christian because of God's merciful act of salvation manifested in the resurrection of Jesus from the dead. The author may intend a contrast with pagan experience that is characterized by fatalism and despair (see a similar idea in Eph 2:12 and 1 Peter's characterization in 4:1-4 of the life the Christians lived prior to their rebirth). Some Greco-Roman authors devalued hope and considered it an illusionary vice (see Achtemeier, *1 Peter* 95 n. 25, referring to Sophocles [*Oed. Col.* 1225-26] and to the Stoics; see further Edouard Cothenet, "Le réalisme de l'espérance chrétienne selon I Pierre," *NTS* 27 [1981] 564–72). First Peter, by contrast, describes hope as "living," that is, as the symptom of the regeneration or salvation given the Christian by God's mercy.

4. *to an inheritance that is immortal, undefiled, and unfading:* The notion of "inheritance" *(klēronomia)* also draws deeply on Old Testament theology. The promises to Abraham and succeeding generations include the land of Israel and the experience of "peace" and blessing or prosperity. Introducing this metaphor here follows through on the notion of new birth; the birthright of the Christian is a "living hope," which the author now further defines by three negative adjectives used in the Wisdom literature to describe divine characteristics. It is "immortal" *(aphthartos),* that is, not subject to death or corruption (see Wis 12:1; also Rom 1:23; 1 Tim 1:17; in 1 Cor 15:52 it describes the state of those

resurrected); it is "undefiled" *(amiantos)* or "pure," like those in the state of cultic or sexual purity (see Wis 3:12; Heb 13:4; 2 Macc 14:36; 15:34); it is "unfading" *(amarantos)*, that is, not subject to erosion or the wear of time (as Wisdom itself in Wis 6:12; see also 1 Pet 5:4).

one reserved in heaven for you, 5. who in God's power are guarded through faith for a salvation that is ready to be revealed in the end time: This segment (vv. 3–5) closes with a forward glance. The Christian lives now in hope but looks forward in time to experiencing an eternal inheritance that is "reserved in heaven." God's power stands guard *(phrouroumenous,* from *phroureō)* as a protective sentry over the Christian (guarding not just the inheritance, but those who will receive it). That power is experienced not as an impersonal force but personally "through faith," and will lead to a salvation that will be revealed "in the end time" *(en kairǭ eschatǭ;* see also 5:6).

6. *In this you rejoice, even if now for a little while you may have to be grieved by all kinds of trials:* The verse begins with a preposition and pronoun, "in which" *(en hǭ).* The pronoun could be understood as masculine and refer to the immediately preceding "end time," *(en kairǭ eschatǭ),* with the sense that the Christian rejoices in the prospect of the approaching end time when salvation would be experienced. More likely, however, the pronoun is neuter and embraces the whole set of salvific realities that has been cited in the previous verses (see Gerhard Barth, "1 Petrus 1,3-9," 151; Ernest Best, *1 Peter* 77; Achtemeier, *1 Peter* 100). "You rejoice" *(agalliasthe)* can either be the second person plural present indicative or the imperative. Most interpreters prefer the former since at this stage the author has not turned to direct exhortation (Achtemeier, *1 Peter* 100). The rejoicing of the Christian is in contrast with the reality of present sufferings, which are "necessary" *(ei deon)* not simply because suffering is inevitable but also as a necessary means of purification. The sufferings are for a little while now (the most likely sense of the phrase *oligon arti;* see below at 4:7). The term *peirasmois,* "trials," comes from the root *peirazō,* which means to "test" as in the end time ordeals (see 1 Pet 4:12 and frequently in the synoptics: e.g., Matt 6:13; 26:41; Mark 14:38; Luke 4:13; 8:13; 22:40, 46).

7. *so that the genuineness of your faith, more precious than gold that is perishable yet tested by fire:* The purpose of these various trials or tests is to purify and strengthen the faith of the Christian in preparation for the final day of salvation. The reference to the purging of gold is a stock comparison in biblical and Greco-Roman literature (see particularly Wis 3:5-6; see below at 1 Pet 4:12). The implied contrast is that if gold, which is "perishable" *(apollymenou),* must be purified by fire, how much more the "genuineness of one's faith." The author plays off the words "genuineness" *(dokimion)* of faith and the proving or purging *(dokimazomenou)* of gold.

may prove to be for praise and glory and honor at the revelation of Jesus Christ: Through the test of suffering, the faith of the Christian ("faith" in this context is a comprehensive term, equivalent to one's entire relationship of trust with God) "attains" or is found ready for the experience of full redemption, namely "praise and glory and honor"—attributes that belong to God or the risen Christ in other parts of the New Testament and are bestowed on humans by the divine power (Goppelt, *1 Peter* 92; see Rom 2:29; 8:17; 1 Cor 4:5; Col 3:4). The verb "prove to be" translates the aorist passive subjunctive of *heuriskō* and has the literal sense of "to be found" (NRSV). Following through on the metaphor of gold purged by fire, the implication may be that suffering purifies the Christians and readies them for the attributes of salvation.

8. *whom, without having seen, you love, and, although not seeing him yet believing in him, you rejoice with inexpressible and glorious joy:* Although in general the New Testament speaks somewhat sparingly of "loving Jesus," here the author of 1 Peter speaks movingly of the Christian's love for Jesus Christ. The series of phrases defies easy translation. Beginning with a pronoun referring to the antecedent "Jesus Christ" at the end of v. 7, the author uses an aorist participle "not having seen" him—presumably referring to the fact that the audience of the letter did not know Jesus in the flesh. Likewise, they now believe in him (*pisteuontes,* the present participle) even though they do not now "see" (*horōntes,* the present participle of *horaō*)—probably meaning that they believe in the risen Christ even though they have not directly witnessed him (a thought repeated elsewhere in the New Testament as in Mark 15:32; John 4:48; 6:30; 20:29; 1 Cor 2:9; 2 Cor 4:18; 5:7; Heb 11:1, 3). In spite of not "seeing" Jesus in the historical modes of the past and present, the Christians still "love" *(agapate)* and believe *(pisteuontes)* in Jesus. In this complex phraseology the parallel intended by the author seems to be between "loving" and "rejoicing"; i.e., even though the Christians had not seen Jesus, they love him, and even though not seeing and yet believing in him, they rejoice with inexpressible and glorious joy. The gift of joy, an experience typically identified with salvation in the end time (e.g., Matt 25:21, 23; John 16:22; Rom 14:17), is anticipated now for the Christian through faith.

9. *attaining the goal of your faith, the salvation of your souls:* This verse firmly fixes the eye of the Christian on the future. The Christians who love Christ and believe in him rejoice because they are "attaining" *(komizomenoi)* the "goal" or "end point" *(telos)* of faith, which is "salvation of your souls." This latter phrase does not refer to immortality or the saving of the soul as distinct from the body. Since 1 Peter uses the term "soul" *(psychē)* as equivalent to the whole person as a living being (see 1:22; 2:11, 25; 3:20; 4:19), salvation here is comprehensive, referring to the salvation of the human person entirely (see Elliott, *1 Peter* 344).

10. *Concerning this salvation the prophets, who prophesied about the grace that was to be yours, searched and investigated diligently:* This segment (vv. 10-12) concludes the opening thanksgiving that began in v. 3. The word "salvation" *(sōteria)* provides the link to the preceding (v. 9), and whereas the previous segments considered the future (vv. 3-5) and present (vv. 6-9) meaning of salvation, this segment will focus on its past anticipation. The mention of the "prophets" here is probably a generic reference to Old Testament prophetic figures, although some commentators have suggested that New Testament prophetic figures may be intended (this is argued strongly by Selwyn, *First Epistle* 134, 259–68; Warden, "The Prophets," 12). The reference to the ministry of the Old Testament prophets sets up the contrast between past anticipation and present

and future fulfillment, which is fundamental to 1 Peter's theology and a staple of other New Testament writings (see, for example, Matt 13:16-17; Luke 10:23-24; 24:25-27; John 5:39, 45-47; 8:56; Acts 7:52; 8:30-32; 17:2-4). These Old Testament forebearers prophesied about the "grace that was to be yours." First Peter describes the prophets as having "searched" *(exezētēsan)* and "investigated diligently" *(exēraunēsan)*, two verbs nearly identical in meaning but coupled to emphasize the intensity and diligence of the prophets' work.

11. *They inquired about the circumstances or timing, which the spirit of Christ that was within them indicated:* Some of the grammar in this verse is ambiguous. "Circumstances or timing" translates the Greek phrase *tina ē poion kairon*. *Tina* can either be a substantive pronoun ("who") or, as suggested here, used adjectivally to modify "time," literally "which time." *Poion* is an interrogative pronoun meaning "what kind of" and clearly modifies "time." Thus the most literal translation would be "which or what kind of time," the gist of which is captured in the English phrase, "circumstances and timing" (see a similar type of question about the circumstances and timing of the end time in Mark 13:4; 13:32; 1 Thess 5:1). "The spirit of Christ that was within them" *(to en autois pneuma christou)*. This key phrase suggests a notion of Christ's preexistence, as already indicated in reference to 1:20, and reinforces the letter's conviction that through divine providence the experiences of Israel were being directed to their fulfillment in Christ.

the very spirit that gave witness in advance about the sufferings that were to be Christ's and the glory that would follow: The illumination that the prophets diligently sought *(eraunōntes,* repeating the verb of v. 10) and the "witness in advance" *(promartyromenon)* provided by the spirit of Christ both "indicated" *(edēlou)* the same fundamental gospel message, namely, the sufferings that belong to Christ *(ta eis christon pathēmata)* and the consequent glory *(tas meta tauta doxas)*. Some commentators have suggested that the sufferings and glory of the "Christ" refer in a generic manner to the anticipated apocalyptic sufferings and triumph of the messianic age, without a specific reference to Jesus Christ (Selwyn, *First Epistle* 112; Hort, *First Epistle* 54; Windisch, *Die katholischen Briefe* 54). However, 1 Peter gives particular emphasis to the sufferings of Jesus and to his resurrection and glorification throughout the body of the letter (1:21; 2:21-25; 3:18-22; 4:1, 13; 5:1) and this is clearly in view in this verse.

12. *To [them] these prophets it was revealed that they were not serving themselves but you in these matters which have now been announced to you through the good news proclaimed by the Holy Spirit sent from heaven, matters into which angels longed to look:* The author claims that it was "revealed" *(hois apekalyphthē)* to the prophets that they were serving not themselves but the recipients of the letter who are among those blessed to receive the gospel, a gospel announced to them *(euangelisamenōn)* by the "Holy Spirit from heaven." The reference to the Holy Spirit does not necessarily speak of Pentecost or any specific event, but again reinforces the divine origin and warrant of the message the Christians have received and toward which the entire prophetic mission of the Old Testament was ordained. The segment concludes with a reference to the angels who "longed" *(epithymousin)* to "look (into)" *(parakypsai,* literally to "look into" or

"peer into," suggesting an intensity of concentration and longing). The longing of the angelic beings to see what the Christians already experience further emphasizes the extraordinary grace of the gospel.

INTERPRETATION

Most of Paul's letters follow up the initial greeting with an encouraging passage that gives thanks to God for the faith and goodness of the Christian community he is addressing (e.g., 2 Cor 1:3). These verses in 1 Peter are similar, but are less a personal prayer for the recipients than a triumphant acclamation of praise to God for the Christian life the author and his fellow Christians share. There is a majestic, sweeping tone to the section that has led some interpreters to suggest that these verses may have been adapted from a liturgical hymn or poetry (e.g., Ralph P. Martin, "The Composition of 1 Peter in Recent Study," *Vox Evangelica* 1 [1962] 29–42). It is more likely that the author's elevated style is inspired by his attempt to portray in dramatic terms the very foundation of Christian existence in the world (see Achtemeier, *1 Peter* 90–91; Gerhard Barth, "1 Petrus 1,3-9," 148–60).

The body of the letter opens with a long and majestic periodic sentence, encompassing vv. 3-12, that lays the theological foundation for 1 Peter's vision of Christian existence and fuels the exhortations that will come later in the letter. Commentators divide the section in various ways, depending on which formal cues or aspects of the content one selects. The prepositions followed by relative pronouns at v. 6 and v. 10 are evident markers that divide the sentence into three basic sections: 1:3-5, 6-9, and 10-12 (see Achtemeier, *1 Peter* 90).

The buoyant theology of 1 Peter is immediately apparent in the opening segment (vv. 3-5) that follows the formal greeting of the letter to the churches of Asia Minor. The author praises God for the gift of salvation and new life effected through the resurrection of Jesus Christ from the dead. This burst of praise lays the groundwork for the entire letter. First of all it roots the experience of salvation in a definitive act of God's gracious mercy. In raising Jesus Christ from the dead, God made known his intent to save or "rebeget" the Christian. God is the center of focus and the object of praise for this act of mercy. The author does not pinpoint the setting or moment in which the Christian first experiences this salvation. The image of rebirth has suggested to some commentators that there is here an implicit baptismal theology or even that these verses derive from a baptismal liturgy in some manner (see, for example, Boismard, "La typologie baptismale," 339–52; "Une liturgie baptismale," 161–83; Kelly, *Epistles* 21–23). But the letter's use of this metaphor seems a step removed from such a specific liturgical or baptismal reference, even though its theology certainly lends itself to a theology of baptism (Elliott, *1 Peter* 333; Goppelt, *Commentary* 91). Rather, 1 Peter uses the image of "rebirth" to describe both God's sovereign power (God alone can give life) and the radical change salvation brings (from non-existence to existence).

This act of salvation gives meaning to the present existence of the Christian. The Christian is born to a "living hope," no longer condemned to living a life of despair or wanton aimlessness (see the author's description of such a life in 4:3-4), but alive with the hope that death in all its manifestations can be overcome just as Jesus was triumphant over death. The concept of "rebirth" or being "newly begotten" is a traditional and widespread metaphor in biblical tradition and even in Greco-Roman religion. In John's Gospel Jesus tells Nicodemus that one has to be "reborn from above" or recreated by God's living spirit in order to enter the kingdom of heaven (John 3:1-8). Similarly, Paul speaks of Christian existence as a "new creation" (2 Cor 5:17). Underlying this metaphorical language is the conviction that the human person could not escape death or a life doomed to frustration and despair except through the power of God. God's mercy gives the believer the power to live in an authentic and enduring way that would be utterly impossible apart from God's grace. God's salvation gives new life to the human being who otherwise would be condemned to a futile existence. Thus the "living hope" of the Christian is an existential stance or way of perceiving the world that is based on God's mercy. It gives the Christian hope but also makes the Christian a member of a scattered or "diaspora" people who live in "exile" in the midst of the uncomprehending and despairing world around them.

At the same time God's merciful salvation through the resurrection of Jesus also colors the Christian's expectations of the future. Christians live in the world confident that God has reserved for them a glorious and eternal inheritance. The Christians and their sure inheritance are "guarded" by God's protective power, a providential power felt with assurance now through faith. While the fullness of salvation will only be experienced in the end time, the Christians turn their faces toward that future with confidence, able to endure suffering as they await the fulfillment of God's promises.

As the word "exiles" has already hinted (1:1), the Christians addressed in this letter are experiencing some form of suffering. In fact, no other New Testament writing reflects on the meaning of suffering with the intensity of 1 Peter. In vv. 6-9 the mood is still upbeat, carried over from the burst of praise in v. 3. The Christians "rejoice" (vv. 6, 9) but that joy must coexist with the reality of suffering. Suffering can be experienced as a purification during the brief time before the end of the world (v. 7). Such a conviction is not deducible from abstract principles, but comes from faith experience. The sufferings that come to a believer because of his or her Christian faith (the kind of suffering the letter seems to have in mind) can "test" the strength of one's faith and deepen it; this has been the experience of persecuted Christians from the first century to the present day. Even the seemingly arbitrary sufferings brought on by illness or accident —although they remain tragic and unglamorous—can purify the humanity and the faith of the one who endures them.

But 1 Peter goes beyond speaking of suffering as mere clenched-teeth endurance. The author affirms that even in the midst of suffering the Christian has a right to joy, one of the gifts the Bible frequently associates with the experience of salvation. Such suffering endured in faith contributes to the glory, praise, and honor that will burst into view at the final revelation of Jesus Christ and can contribute to one's own salvation (vv. 7-8). The belief that suffering borne in faith has the power to bring about the transformation of the world is a major theme developed in subsequent sections of the letter.

The reference to the consummation of the world at "the revelation of Jesus Christ" (v. 7) prompts the author to dwell in a unique way on the figure of Jesus Christ. In beautifully poetic words the text speaks of loving Jesus and believing in him even though this be an experience of faith and love without actually "seeing" him. More typically, in the remainder of the letter the author will exhort the reader to consider the example of Jesus, especially in his sufferings (e.g., 2:21-25; 3:18-19; 4:1) and to have reverence for the teaching of Jesus (3:9; 4:14; 5:6-7).

The stress on joy is repeated at the end of this segment. Love and trust in Jesus, as well as the experience of God's saving power (v. 5), lead to "inexpressible and glorious joy" (v. 8). Christian joy is based on trust in God's faithfulness even in the midst of trial. The ultimate goal is to attain salvation "of [your] souls" (v. 9) that is a transformation of one's entire being.

The thanksgiving section begun in v. 3 now concludes (vv. 10-12). To this point the author has been directing the readers' attention to the future salvation God has in store for the believers (vv. 3-5) and to present anticipation of that joy through a life of faith and love (vv. 6-9). Now he expands that horizon by tilting their gaze backward to the past, a past that had anticipated both the present now experienced by the Christians and the future for which they longed, and thereby underscores the coherence and harmony of God's work in history.

The prophetic voices of the Old Testament proclaimed the very gift of "grace" that the Christians now experience and whose full realization they look forward to at the end of time. As indicated in the Notes, some commentators have interpreted "prophets" to mean not the Old Testament prophets but spirit-filled prophets of the early church who instructed the community on the meaning of Jesus (see, for example, 1 Cor 14:3-4). That would help explain the unusual reference to the "spirit of Christ" in v. 11, but in view of the temporal contrast intended between the earnest search of the prophets into the meaning of salvation (vv. 10-11) and the actual experience of this gift on the part of those who have had the gospel announced to them (v. 12), it is preferable to interpret the "prophets" as the prophetic utterances of the Old Testament. The inspired prophets and other great teachers in Israel directed their message to their contemporaries. As such, the Old Testament Scriptures have a message in their own right and not just as a prologue to or prediction of the future. But the purpose of 1 Peter in this passage is to help the Christians see how their gift of faith fits into the entire sweep of salvation history. The author does not draw any negative contrast with the Old Testament or Jewish experience, but simply appropriates its entire meaning into a Christian perspective. The Hebrew Scriptures themselves provide an opening for such a reading in that much of the prophetic perspective is future-oriented, calling the people of Israel to fidelity and hope as they look beyond present failure or travail to future deliverance and peace. Sensing this future orientation and convinced that the hopes of Israel come true in Jesus, many of the New Testament writings look upon the Old Testament as a prophecy of what was now coming to pass in the experience of the Christian community.

This perspective suffuses the passage under consideration. The author portrays the prophets (by which he probably means not only the classical prophets but all of the biblical authors) as searching for and inquiring about the salvation Christians now experience. They were driven to this by "the spirit of Christ that was within them." The precise meaning of this phrase is difficult to discern. Does the author mean the Spirit in a general sense, that is, the Spirit of God that gave the prophets insight into God's plan of salvation in which Christ would play the key role? Or, as the words literally say, were they driven by Christ's own Spirit, that is, by the mysterious presence of Christ at work even before his incarnation? The latter seems to be the meaning of the text. Not unlike the prologue to John's Gospel (John 1:1-18), the author affirms the pre-existence of Jesus at work in the world, guiding it to the climax of salvation history. This uniform divine action is the theological basis for the author's absorption of Old Testament images and metaphors into his portrayal of the Christian message (Elliott, *1 Peter* 352–53).

The Spirit of Christ led the prophets to prophesy the very heart of the gospel: Jesus' death and resurrection. The pattern of suffering leading to glory is constantly alluded to in 1 Peter, describing the essence of the Christian vocation (see 2:19-25; 3:18; 4:1-2, 13; 5:10).

The author considers the prophecy of salvation as a "service" for the Christians. How 1 Peter conceives of this service being "revealed" to the prophets (v. 12) is not clear. But now these "matters" (the predicted salvation) have been communicated to the Christians by those who preached the gospel (literally "the good news"). The power to proclaim the gospel is itself the work of the "Holy Spirit from heaven," a conviction that 1 Peter shares with many other New Testament traditions (see Acts 1:8; 5:32; 1 Cor 2:4; 1 Thess 1:5; Heb 2:4; see further Kelly, *Epistles* 63).

The cosmic scope of salvation history is evoked in the final words of v. 12. The angelic beings "longed to look at" the beautiful grace of salvation that God, through the agency of the Spirit, has given to the Christians. The author of the letter cannot conceal his sheer joy and pride in being a Christian.

FOR REFERENCE AND FURTHER READING

Barth, Gerhard. "1 Petrus 1,3-9: Exegese, Meditation und Predigt," *Estudios teologicos* 6 (1966) 148–60.
Boismard, Marie-Émile. "La typologie baptismale dans la première épître de Saint Pierre," *La Vie Spirituelle* 94 (1956) 339–52.
_____. "Une liturgie baptismale dans la *Prima Petri*, II: Son influence sur l'épître de Jacques," *RB* 63 (1957) 161–83.
Cothenet, Edouard. "Le réalisme de l'espérance chrétienne selon I Pierre," *NTS* 27 (1981) 564–72.
Dupont-Roc, Roselyne. "Le jeu des prépositions en 1 Pierre 1,1-12: De l'espérance finale à la joie dans les épreuves présentes," *EstBib* 53 (1995) 201–12.
Kendall, Daniel. "The Literary and Theological Functions of 1 Peter 1:3-12," in Charles H. Talbert, ed., *Perspectives on First Peter* (Macon, Ga.: Mercer University Press, 1986) 103–20.
_____. "On Christian Hope. 1 Peter 1:3-9," *Int* 41 (1987) 66–71.
Martin, Troy W. *Metaphor and Composition in 1 Peter.* SBLDS 131. Atlanta: Scholars, 1992.
_____. "The Present Indicative in the Eschatological Statements of 1 Pet 1,6, 8," *JBL* 111 (1992) 307–12.
Warden, D. "The Prophets of 1 Peter 1:10-12," *ResQ* 31 (1989) 1–12.

3. *The Call to Holiness* (1:13-16)

13. Therefore gird up the loins of your minds, being self-controlled; place your hopes completely on the grace that is being brought to you at the revelation of Jesus Christ. 14. As children of obedience, do not be conformed to the desires you previously experienced in your ignorance.

15. Rather, in accord with the holy one who called you, be yourselves holy
in your entire way of life. 16. For it is written, "Be holy, because I am holy."

NOTES

13. *Therefore gird up the loins of your minds, being self-controlled:* The conjunction *dio,*
    "therefore," signals a change of tone from the description of the graced state of
    the Christian in the opening segment (1:3-12) to the consequences of this grace
    for Christian life in the world. "Gird up the loins of your minds"—this mixed
    metaphor evokes images of the need for readiness and action from the Exodus
    journey of Israel (see Exod 12:11 with echoes in Luke 12:35). The word "gird
    up" *(anazōsamenoi)* is a first-person plural aorist middle participle. The trans-
    lation preferred here understands it as having imperative force in the context,
    especially following "therefore." Some commentators, however, translate it as
    a participle (see Achtemeier, *1 Peter* 117: ". . . people whose minds are girded
    for action"; similarly Elliott, *1 Peter* 335; both authors concede, however, that
    the participles pick up an imperative force from the context). The notion of
    being "self-controlled" or "sober-minded" *(nēphontes* derives from sobriety,
    but is used in a metaphorical sense) is important to 1 Peter and is found also in
    4:7 and 5:8. It signals the Christian stance of alert virtue in contrast to the
    "ignorance" and unbridled passions of the non-Christians (see v. 14).

    *place your hopes completely on the grace that is being brought to you at the revelation
    of Jesus Christ:* The adverb "completely" *(teleiōs)* could modify "being self-
    controlled," but the adverb does not usually precede the verb it modifies;
    therefore it is preferable to link it to "placing your hopes" *(elpisate)*. The Chris-
    tians are to base their hopes on the grace that will be fully revealed at the end-
    time with the triumphant return of Jesus. "Being brought to you" *(pheromenēn)*
    is a present participle even though "revelation of Jesus Christ" refers to the
    future parousia. This anticipated revelation provides active hope for the
    Christians now and recalls the fact that they have already been reborn to new
    life and hope through the death and resurrection of Christ, a point made in the
    opening lines of the letter (1:3-9).

14. *As children of obedience, do not be conformed to the desires you previously experi-
    enced in your ignorance:* The phrase "children of obedience" is the literal
    translation of the phrase *(tekna hypakoēs)* that the NAB and others prefer to
    understand in an adjectival sense ("obedient children"). "Obedience" carries
    the Old Testament notion of conforming one's life to the will of God; 1 Peter
    urges the Christians to live in precisely this manner—hence as "children of
    obedience." Addressing the Christians as "children" recalls the birth imagery
    of the opening section of the letter (1:3; see also 1:23; 2:2). Through faith the
    Christians have become new beings; through obedience they manifest the
    transformation that new existence requires. The author drives home the point
    that the Christians as "new beings" can no longer live in the pattern of their
    former existence. The verb "do not be conformed" *(syschēmatizomenoi)*, found
    in the New Testament only here and in Rom 12:2, is a middle participle

once again used with imperative meaning, contrasting with the subsequent command "be . . . holy" in v. 15. Unbridled "desires" or "passions" (Greek *epithymia*) and "ignorance" are negative traits frequently used to describe non-Christians in biblical literature (see Rom 1:24; Eph 5:16; 4:22; 1 Thess 4:5; Mark 4:19). Later in the letter the author will also label non-Christians as "ignorant" (2:15). The kind of "passions" or "desires" 1 Peter has in mind is illustrated in 4:1-5.

15. *in accord with the holy one who called you:* This translation takes "the holy one" *(ton kalesanta hymas hagion)* as a noun and the object of the preposition *kata* ("in accord with"). An alternate translation could be: "as the one who called you is holy," taking "the one who called you" as the substantive (see the NAB). The overall meaning is clear: the Christians are to be "holy in all your conduct" because the God who calls the Christian into being is holy. "Holiness" in this context fits well with its fundamental meaning in the Hebrew Scriptures as signifying the unique character of God as distinct from all impurity and death. Separated from the desires and ignorance of their former way of life, the Christians are to lead a life that testifies to their transformed state of being as children of God.

16. *For it is written, "Be holy, because I am holy":* The exhortation to imitate God is sealed with a quotation from Lev 19:2 (see also Lev 11:44-45; 20:7, 26). The letter will frequently quote from the Old Testament to ratify its exhortations (see 1:18, 24; 2:3, 4-10, 22-25; 3:10-12, 14, 15; 4:8, 18; 5:5, 7, 8). As in other instances, the author introduces the Old Testament quotation with the conjunction *dioti* (see 1:24; 2:6). First Peter keeps close to the LXX version of this key Old Testament text. In this context it reinforces the author's emphasis on the "holiness" of the Christian, understood in terms of God's holiness, which was not tainted by corruption or death. While living in the world, the Christians were, nevertheless, to lead lives distinctive because of their faith and virtue (see Goppelt, *Commentary* 109–11).

INTERPRETATION

Having scanned the foundations of Christian existence in the exuberant opening section of the letter (1:1-12), the author now turns to his immediate purpose: an exhortation to live a life of holiness. The sequence is not without significance. The letter does not begin with moral demands necessary for the Christians to be worthy of their vocation. Rather, in a pattern often used in Paul's letters, the reverse is the case. Only after strongly affirming the beauty and power of the Christians' vocation and the new mode of existence into which they have been drawn does the author proceed to the demands of living out this new mode of existence. The imperative follows upon the indicative: first the good news, then a search for the appropriate response to this grace (note the emphatic "therefore" that opens v. 13). The exhortations begun here will continue to the end of the first major division of the letter in 2:10. These first few verses (13-16) stress the call to "holiness."

The opening verse (13) begins with a "journey" image, evocative of the exodus experience of Israel as well as the "exile" status of the readers (see 1:1; 2:11). Literally they are to "gird the loins of (their) minds"—a call for readiness as they set out toward the full experience of salvation that will be theirs at the completion of human history when Jesus Christ is fully revealed (see also 1:7; 4:13). As in the previous segments, the author puts into play past, present, and future to present a coherent sequence of God's saving work in the world, a "grace" anticipated in the experience of Israel, to be fully realized at the end-time, and having a transforming impact on life now.

The demand to be "self-controlled" or "sober" (see also 5:8) and the reference to active "hope" are a typical blend of thought found throughout this epistle. The difficulty of living a gospel life in a world filled with alien values is never discounted; however, the cost of discipleship results not in grim endurance but in active hope. Later in the letter the author will spell out the implications of such witness for certain members of the community (see 2:11–3:7). The image of "girding" one's loins or belt and the call to a life of alert discipleship echo a number of gospel sayings (see Luke 12:35; 17:8; John 21:18; Acts 12:8; Eph 6:14).

The call to live a life of virtue grounded in hope is then repeated in other images. The Christians, as children of God through the rebirth of baptism, should also be "children of obedience" (v. 14), totally responsive not to the "passions" of their former "ignorance" but to the "holy" God who called them into a life of hope. Both Jewish and early Christian literature indicted the pagans for their "ignorance" of God (see Rom 1:18-32). This ignorance was deepened by the non-Christians' indulgence of their "passions" or unsound "desires." The author will cite a stock list of such desires in 4:3: licentiousness, drunkenness, lawless idolatry, etc. These are the symptoms of despair, signs of a life without hope or meaning. First Peter writes to Christians who had once been part of that world (v. 14, "previously experienced in your ignorance") and were still vulnerable to its pressures (see 4:4). But now the Christians have been born into a new life and their behavior must reflect that new mode of existence. The goal of this new life is "holiness" because the One who calls them into this life is holy. Note that the author does not describe "holiness" as requiring that the Christians withdraw from the world but rather as the transformation of their "entire way of life" (v. 15). As later passages will make clear (e.g., 2:11-12), 1 Peter wants holiness to be a manifest witness for the sake of a world without God.

A citation from Lev 19:2, "you shall be holy, for I am holy" (v. 16) punctuates this call to holiness and gives the exhortation the authority of the

Scriptures, a device used by the author in a number of exhortation passages (see 2:3; 3:10; 4:18; 5:5).

FOR REFERENCE AND FURTHER STUDY

Dalton, William J. "So That Your Faith May Also Be Your Hope in God," in Robert Banks, ed., *Reconciliation and Hope. New Testament Essays on Atonement and Eschatology Presented to L. L. Morris on his 60th birthday.* Grand Rapids: Eerdmans, 1974, 262–74.
Deterding, Paul. "Exodus Motifs in First Peter," *Concordia Journal* 7 (1981) 58–65.
Scharlemann, Martin. "Exodus Ethics: Part One—I Peter 1:13-16," *Concordia Journal* 2 (1976) 165–70.

4. *Fear Before a God of Hope* (1:17-21)

17. And if you invoke as Father the one who impartially judges a person's every work, conduct yourself in fear during the time of your exile. 18. You know that it was not with perishable things such as silver or gold that you were ransomed from the futile way of life that you inherited from your ancestors, 19. but with Christ's precious blood, like that of a lamb without blemish and spotless. 20. Having been already known before the beginning of the world, he has been made manifest at the end of time for you, 21. who through him believe in God, the one who raised him from the dead and gave him glory, so that your faith and hope are in God.

NOTES

17. *And if you invoke as Father the one who impartially judges a person's every work, conduct yourself in fear during the time of your exile:* The foundational perspectives of the opening section of the letter continue in this section, which in condensed form cites fundamental convictions of the Christian gospel. Here the author introduces the notion of judgment, a motif consistently linked to exhortation in the New Testament but found sparingly in other parts of 1 Peter (see 3:17; 4:17-18; in Paul see 2 Cor 5:10-11; Rom 14:10-11; 1 Cor 3:12-15; 4:4). The letter asserts that the notion of invoking God as "father," already cited in the opening of the letter (1:2, 3) and used as a favored address for God in both the gospels and Pauline tradition, is not incompatible with the sentiment of "fear." The word *phobos* ("fear") in this context does not imply servile fear or terror, but reverence and awe before the sovereignty of God (see, for

example, 3:2, 16; cf. Elliott, *1 Peter* 365–66). God is portrayed as holding a person accountable literally for "each deed" or each one's conduct, a traditional biblical conviction and one affirmed in Jesus' own teaching (see Matt 12:36-37; 25:31-46). God is an "impartial" judge whose integrity and equity cannot be questioned. The notion of living in "a time of exile" (*paroikias;* see also 2:11) coincides with the notion introduced in the opening salutation (1:1, "sojourners" of the "diaspora"), which suggests that the Christians' code of conduct makes them spiritual aliens alongside the dominant culture (see the extensive discussion in Elliott, *1 Peter* 367–68).

18. *You know that it was not with perishable things such as silver or gold that you were ransomed from the futile way of life that you inherited from your ancestors:* Some suggest that this and the following verses may be citing an early Christian hymn or credal formula, but that is hard to determine (see Boismard, "Une liturgie baptismale"; Kelly, *Epistles* 72, who suggests that vv. 18-21 have "been filled out with catechetical, credal or liturgical material"). In any case the author recalls for the reader of the letter fundamental convictions they already "know" (*eidotes;* see below at 5:9). The first is that they have been "redeemed" or "ransomed" by the blood of Christ, liberating them from the futile way of life to which they were formerly enslaved (see 1:14; 4:1-4). The verb *lytraomai* ("free by ransom" or "redeem") is used in Greco-Roman literature to refer primarily to the manumission of slaves or liberation of prisoners (BDAG, 606). It is applied elsewhere in the New Testament as a metaphor for the redemptive power of Christ's death (see Mark 10:45; Titus 2:14; Heb 9:12; also Luke 24:21). This in turn surely draws on Old Testament and Jewish tradition that used the word to signify the liberating power of God toward Israel in the Exodus or in the return from exile (see, for example, Exod 6:6; Deut 7:8; Isa 42:23; 51:11; 52:3).

19. *but with Christ's precious blood, like that of a lamb without blemish and spotless:* This emphasis on the pristine condition of the lamb and its connection with liberation may suggest that the author has in mind Passover imagery rather than that of the sacrificial lamb applied to the Servant in a key text such as Isa 53:7 (Elliott, *1 Peter* 374–75). Portraying Jesus as the Passover lamb in connection with redemption from sin is a strong motif in Johannine literature (John 1:29, 35; 19:36; see also a similar passage in Heb 9:12-14). The connection of Jesus' death with Passover is also asserted in the Last Supper narratives of the synoptics (see Matt 26:17-19 and parallels) and in Paul (1 Cor 5:7).

20. *Having been already known before the beginning of the world, he has been made manifest at the end of time for you:* The perfect past participle *proegnōsmenou* ("having been known before") suggests the preexistence of Christ in the mind of God (see above at 1:11). This reality that existed "before the beginning of the world" (*pro katabolēs kosmou;* see also John 17:24; Eph 1:4) is now revealed for the Christians (literally "for you") in "the end of time" (literally "the last of the ages," *ep' eschatou tōn chronōn;* some variants use "the last days," but this is the preferred reading), a line that sweeps through all of created existence. First Peter foresees the appearance of Christ as leading to the consummation of history in the not too distant future (4:5, 7, 17; 5:10).

21. *who through him believe in God, the one who raised him from the dead and gave him glory, so that your faith and hope are in God:* The author returns to words of encouragement and hope, with the phrase "in God" *(eis theon)* anchoring the beginning and end of the verse. Christians make God the foundation for their trust and hope because God has been faithful to Jesus in raising him from the dead and glorifying him (see the same fundamental affirmation in 1:3). Although the affirmation of God's raising Jesus from the dead and glorifying him are both common New Testament motifs, the formula that combines them here is unique to 1 Peter (see a similar description in Peter's sermon in Acts 3:13, "God . . . has glorified his servant, Jesus" and 3:15, ". . . whom God raised from the dead"). The conjunction "so that" *(hōste)* usually states an accomplished result, and that is most likely the case here: because of God's resurrection and glorification of Jesus, the Christians can place all their trust in God. Because there is no article before the word "hope" *(elpida),* it is possible that this final phrase could be translated "so that your faith is also hope in God" (thus Elliott, *1 Peter* 379–80). The preference here is to see the article before "faith" *(tēn pistin hymōn)* as applying to both "faith" and "hope" as fundamental perspectives of the Christian that are linked in the author's mind (see Achtemeier, *1 Peter* 133).

INTERPRETATION

The invitation to a transformed life of holiness continues in this section, but now with new imagery. The gift of Christian life brings with it the ability to invoke God as "Father" (see 1:2, 3 and a similar perspective in Rom 8:15-17), but God remains the awesome God who is the author of life and the one to whom all human life is responsible. This line of reflection moves the author from the theme of "holiness" (1:13-16) to that of "fear" or "awe" before God as judge. Since the newborn life of the Christian is destined for God and bound up with God, each one's conduct will be impartially evaluated by God. Therefore the Christians cannot take their call to holiness casually. The Christian sojourn in "exile" must be shot through with "fear" of God. The whole tenor of 1 Peter suggests that the notion of "fear" implied here is not that of anxious or servile fear before an avenging God, but a sense of reverence or awe before the mystery of God and the sovereignty of God over all life. Such an attitude of reverence has marked biblical piety from Moses to Jesus and is not incompatible with confident trust in God's love (as 1 Peter will conclude in 1:21).

The author recalls some fundamental Christian convictions already known to his readers (v. 18, "you know . . .") but reaffirmed in condensed fashion here at the outset of the letter. The first of these is that the "precious blood of Christ" has "ransomed" Christians from a life of futility. Drawing on biblical tradition that portrayed God as one who ransomed and liberated Israel from slavery and sin, and on New Testament tradition that applied this motif to the redemptive power of Christ's death, the author reaffirms that humanity has been redeemed through the suffering and death of Jesus.

What the Christians are redeemed from is described as "the futile way of life that you inherited from your ancestors" (v. 18; see also 1:14). The metaphor of displacement already cited in 1:1 ("elect sojourners who belong to the diaspora") is repeated here: during their "exile" (v. 17) the Christians have been empowered to leave behind their former life of futility and despair and are able to live now a life of hope in God expressed in good conduct.

In connection with the ransom image the author speaks of Jesus as "a lamb without blemish and spotless." Isaiah 53:7 refers to the redemptive figure of the Servant as a "lamb" who silently submits to shearing or slaughter. Although this Isaiah text may be intended by 1 Peter, his description of the lamb as without blemish or spot suggests that he is describing Jesus as the Passover lamb. According to the ritual laid down in Exodus 12 the slaughter of the lamb "without blemish" (Exod 12:5) celebrated the liberation of Israel from slavery. Paul explicitly calls Jesus "our Paschal lamb" in 1 Cor 5:7 and the Gospel of John clearly portrays Jesus as the Passover lamb in the manner of his death (see the citation of Exod 12:5 in John 19:36). Similarly, in the synoptic gospels Jesus interprets his death in sacrificial terms as "for the many" (Mark 14:24) or "given for you" (Luke 22:19) or "for the forgiveness of sins" (Matt 26:28) in the context of the Passover meal. First Peter, therefore, stands in an already well established New Testament tradition that interpreted the redemptive power of Jesus' death by using Passover imagery.

The same cosmic sweep of history expressed in 1:10-12 returns in v. 20. Christ was already known by God (the implied subject of the passive participle in this verse) before the beginning of the world, but was revealed or made manifest at the climax of history for the sake of the Christians ("for you"). As in the reference to the "spirit of Christ" that instructed the prophets in v. 11, so here the author affirms the pre-existence of Christ in the mind of God. Jewish thought roughly contemporary with 1 Peter had similar notions of pre-existence, as seen for example in *1 Enoch,* which portrays the "Son of Man" being given a name by God in the "before" time and then later revealed to the "holy ones" (see *1 Enoch* 48:3, 6-7; 62:7). Romans 16:25-26 and Eph 3:5, 9-10 speak of the mystery of salvation in similar terms, i.e., hidden with God from the beginning of time and now revealed in the last days (see J. R. Michaels, "Eschatology in 1 Peter," 67).

Although this segment begins by calling on the reader to fear God and with a reminder of judgment (v. 17), it ends with a reaffirmation of confidence and hope (v. 21). Because of Jesus' death and resurrection the Christians can have confidence in God (literally "faith" or trust). First Peter's perspective is ultimately God-centered: Because God raised Jesus from death and gave him glory the Christians have a sure basis for hope.

FOR REFERENCE AND FURTHER STUDY

Boismard, Marie–Émile. "Une liturgie baptismale dans la *Prima Petri*, II: Son influence sur le épître de Jacques," *RB* 64 (1957) 161–83.
Unnik, W. C. van. "The Critique of Paganism in I Peter 1:18," in E. Earle Ellis and Max Wilcox, eds., *Neotestamentica et Semitica; Studies in Honour of Matthew Black*. Edinburgh: T & T Clark, 1969, 129–42.

5. *Earnestly Love One Another from the Heart* (1:22–2:3)

22. Having purified your lives through obedience to the truth in order to attain genuine mutual love, now earnestly love each other from the heart. 23. You have been born anew, not from perishable seed but from imperishable, through the living and abiding word of God. 24. "For all flesh is as grass and all its glory is as a blossom of grass; the grass withers and the blossom fades away, 25. but the word of the Lord abides forever." This is the word that has been preached to you. 2:1 Therefore rid yourselves of all evil and all deceit and hypocrisy and envy and all slander. 2. Like newborn infants, long for pure spiritual milk so that with it you may grow into salvation, 3. for you have tasted that the Lord is good.

NOTES

22. *Having purified your lives through obedience to the truth in order to attain genuine mutual love, now earnestly love each other from the heart:* This verse recapitulates the fundamental message of salvation evoked in the opening sections of the letter and now moves in a new direction, namely the exhortation to communal love. The verb *hagnizō* ("purify") is used in the Old Testament to refer to ritual purification (see, for example, Exod 19:10; 2 Chr 31:18), but 1 Peter uses the term in reference to moral purification. The perfect participle of the verb suggests the act of conversion or initiation into the community that drew the readers into the path of salvation. Some find here an allusion to baptism. Although this cannot be excluded, the author may have a more generic reference in mind to the starting point of Christian life through God's grace, which includes baptism (Elliott, *1 Peter* 382; Goppelt, *Commentary* 126; Kelly, *Epistles* 78–79). The term "your lives" translates "your souls" *(psychē)*, which in the context is to be taken as a reference not just to the "souls" but to the entire lives of the Christians. The phrase "obedience to the truth" *(en tę̄ hypakoę̄ tēs*

alētheias) also recalls key elements of the opening lines of the letter: the Christians have been chosen by God for "obedience" to Jesus Christ (1:2), an "obedience" that turns them away from their previous lives of futility (1:14). "Truth" in this context does not mean "truth" in a general abstract sense, but refers to the gospel or the entire Christian message (see v. 25, the "word that has been preached to you"). Authentic conversion is expressed in love for the community. The term "mutual love" *(philadelphia,* literally "brotherly love") and the imperative "earnestly love each other from the heart" in this instance focus Christian love on the other members of the community, a major concern of 1 Peter (see 2:17; 3:8-9; 4:8-11; 5:14).

23. *You have been born anew, not from perishable seed but from imperishable, through the living and abiding word of God:* In the pattern of the previous verse the author begins with another key past participle that evokes the state of the Christian who has now experienced salvation. "Having been born anew" (the perfect passive participle of *anagennaō)* recalls the resounding claim of 1:3. While this, too, could be taken as a reference to baptism, it is likely that the author refers to the entire inaugural experience of the Christian, one rooted in God's own act of salvation, signified in the baptismal ritual of initiation and expressed in a transformed moral life. The "imperishable seed" that gives life to the Christian contrasts with the fragile and transitory nature of the created world that will be portrayed in the quotation from Isa 40:6-8 that follows in the next verse. The "living and abiding word of God" is yet another way of describing the entirety of the Christian message experienced by the readers of the letter. While the "word of God" *(logos . . . theou)* could be taken as a reference to Christ, the reference to the "word" in the following Isaiah quotation and the author's identification of the word as the "word that has been preached to you" make it clear that the author means the gospel in a generic sense when he refers to the word of God.

24. *"For all flesh is as grass and all its glory is as a blossom of grass; the grass withers and the blossom fades away, 25. but the word of the Lord abides forever":* The author quotes Isa 40:6-8 to emphasize the abiding power of God's word in contrast to the transitory created world, no matter how beautiful or alluring it may seem for a time ("all its glory"). The term "all flesh" *(pasa sarx)* refers to the entirety of the human condition with emphasis on its mortality, much as it is used in Pauline tradition (see similar uses in 3:18 and 4:1 in reference to Christ's death, and in 4:2, 6 referring to the human condition). The Greek quotation used here is close to the Septuagint version, although one notable change from both the LXX and the Masoretic text is in the phrase "word of the Lord" where 1 Peter substitutes the term "Lord" *(kyrios)* for "God" *(theos),* which is found in both the Hebrew and Septuagint versions. Since the term "lord" is often applied to Jesus it is possible that the author may want to suggest, in accord with a similar perspective in 1:10-12, that the words of Isaiah had anticipated the gospel embodied in Jesus and proclaimed by the community. Here the author twice uses the term *rēma* for "word" in accord with the LXX quotation, but there does not seem to be any different nuance of meaning from the formulation in 1:23 where he uses his preferred term *logos* for "word" (see also 2:8; 3:1).

2:1 *Therefore rid yourselves of all evil and all deceit and hypocrisy and envy and all slander:* It is difficult to determine if the author aims the list of vices named here (i.e., "evil," "deceit," "hypocrisy," "envy," "slander") at specific problems in the communities he addresses or whether it is a stock list of the kinds of behaviors that would poison any community that aspired to "mutual love." In fact, 1 Peter, in contrast to several of Paul's letters and other New Testament epistles, is remarkable for the absence of any specific complaints about internal divisions or strife in the communities. The real threat seems to be how the community can withstand hostility directed at Christians from outside.

2. *Like newborn infants, long for pure spiritual milk so that with it you may grow into salvation:* Developing the metaphor that the experience of salvation is "rebirth" (1:3, 23), the author addresses the Christians as "newborn infants" and encourages them to long for "pure spiritual milk." Presumably this refers to the gospel preached to them (1:25) and even more fundamentally to their experience of the Risen Christ, for they have "tasted that the Lord *(kyrios)* is good." This milk is "spiritual" or "metaphorical" (the term *logikon* has the connotation not just of "spiritual" as in the usual term *pneumatikos*, but also of something metaphorical [BDAG 598]) in contrast to mere human food (i.e., in the realm of the "flesh," following the contrast made earlier in this segment) and "pure" *(adolon)*, that is, "unadulterated" or "authentic" and in accord with the message proclaimed to them.

3. *for you have tasted that the Lord is good:* As he does several times in the letter, the author confirms an exhortation with a quotation from Scripture (e.g., 1:16, 24-25; 2:6; 3:10-12; 5:5). This is from Ps 33:8 ("O taste and see that the Lord is good"). The author will quote the psalm again in 3:10-12 and seems to have a particular affinity for its theme of God's help in distress (Kelly, *Epistles* 86–87). The quotation generally follows the Septuagint version, but 1 Peter has adapted it to the context, adding the opening conjunction "for" or "since" *(ei)*, reaffirming the strong foundation on which their Christian experience rests (see 1:22), and in the same vein changing the original imperative ("taste" *geusate*) to an aorist indicative *(egeusasthe,* "you have tasted"). Likewise the author omits the reference to "seeing" ("taste and see"), focusing on the experience of tasting. While in the original "Lord" referred to God, here it refers to Christ (as in 1:25). Some commentators have suggested that the metaphors of nourishment and tasting may refer to the Eucharist, especially since the psalm was often connected with the Eucharist in early Christianity (see Kelly, *Epistles* 87). However, these metaphors of spiritual milk and good taste may more immediately capture the joyous and life-giving experience of the Christians whose lives are rooted in Christ.

INTERPRETATION

This section recapitulates some of the fundamental themes already cited in the opening lines of the letter but now, for the first time, it turns to an exhortation for mutual love within the community. This will be a pattern

repeated later in the letter (see 3:8-12; 4:8-11; 5:5). This is not simply a rhetorical pattern, but reflects the deepest convictions of the author about the
nature of Christian life. Through the gift of salvation the Christian takes
on a new existence, leaving behind a life of futility and made part of a new
people graced by God (a theme that will be emphatically developed in the
following section beginning in 2:4). Christian life is not solitary, but gives
the believer a new identity as part of the people of God bound together in
mutual love (see 2:9-10). Because this "mutual love" is the consequence of
God's salvation, the vibrant communal life of the Christians is a witness to
the world about the reality of God's grace (2:9, 11; 4:11).

The call to "earnestly love each other from the heart" is based, therefore, on the very nature of Christian existence. Their "souls," their very
beings (see 1:9) have been purified by "obedience to the truth." By "obedience to the truth" the author means living a life of faith, a life totally
responsive to the ultimate truth of God's love proclaimed in the gospel.
In 1:2 and 1:14 the author uses "obedience" in the same sense. This total
response to God's love has the effect of purifying one's life from the self-
indulgent and dead-end desires that make human life shallow (see 1:14).
Being open to God's love means leading a life that is now capable of
"genuine mutual love" for the other members of God's people.

First Peter puts the term "purified" in the past tense (v. 22). The primary
referent here is to the gift of salvation that the Christians have experienced, an experience that transforms their lives. Does the author also have
in mind the specific moment of baptism as the ritual act of initiation signifying this transformation and marking their entrance into the Christian
community? Commentators debate this point. Those who favor a baptismal reference point to the image of "rebirth" in 1:3 and 1:23, as well as
to the explicit reference to baptism in 3:21. It is impossible to be decisive
about the author's intention here. In any case, the emphasis is not on the
ritual act of baptism as such but on the entire effect of God's grace on the
human person, an effect that is also signified in baptism whether the author intends an explicit allusion or not. (The same could be said for the
entire letter, which offers a profound theology of baptism or reflection on
the gift of salvation, whether an explicit baptismal context is in view or
not. See the Introduction.) The author points to the power of the "living
and abiding word of God" (v. 23) as the impulse for this new life of the
Christian. "The word of God" is a way of speaking of the gospel in its
most dynamic and comprehensive sense, ultimately as a metaphor for the
saving force of God's own presence in human life, a presence embodied in
Jesus and the gospel. This abiding and enduring nature of the word is
emphasized in the quotation from Isa 40:6-8 (see v. 24). While "all flesh" is
mortal and transitory, the sustaining power of God's word endures
forever. That word of God is identified with the "good news" or "gospel,"

which the Christians had preached to them and that ultimately led them to conversion and baptism.

In effect, the author identifies sincere mutual love "from the heart" as the sign of authentic conversion, a basic tenet of the entire New Testament. This is repeated with another set of metaphors in the first three verses of ch. 2. The Christians should "take off" or "rid themselves" of the old ways of sin as if they were filthy garments (an image found also in Rom 13:12; Col 3:8; Eph 4:22, 25; Jas 1:21). Here again there is a possible but hardly conclusive baptismal allusion to the shedding of garments and the taking on of the baptismal robe (Kelly, *Epistles* 83–84). The list of vices to be shed does not seem to describe actual specific problems in the communities addressed by the letter, but is a warning about the kind of generic behaviors that destroy communal relationships. The list here (and in 4:3) finds echoes in other stock New Testament texts (see, for example, Rom 1:29; 2 Cor 12:20; Eph 4:31; Col 3:8).

The stripping away of sin is only one side of the conversion process; the plunge into new life is the other. Verse 2 develops the metaphor of "rebirth" used earlier to describe the transforming effect of salvation (1:3, 23) by inviting the Christians as "newborn infants" to "long for pure spiritual milk so that with it you may grow into salvation." The author views the gospel as an invitation to a new life, a life that begins a process of growth leading to the full experience of salvation. This harmonizes with the journey imagery used in 1:13-21 and with the call to perseverance through trial in 1:3-9. In each instance 1 Peter conceives of Christian life not as an instantaneous and easily attainable experience but as a lifelong process of growth toward the full beauty of one's humanity before God. In 1 Cor 3:1-3 and Heb 5:12-14 the metaphor of milk for the newborn is used with a pejorative tone; weak and immature Christians get mere milk in contrast to the hearty diet of the mature believer. But here in 1 Peter "milk" is not a grudging concession to weakness but a hope-filled sign of God's nourishment intended for those who are growing toward maturity.

An allusion to Ps 34(33):8 ("O taste and see that the Lord is good") rounds out the passage. The Christians have in fact tasted the goodness of the Lord. The "if" (*ei*) found at the beginning of this phrase in 2:3 is not intended as a condition, but in the emphatic sense of "since. . . ." The entire first section of the letter affirms that the Christians have already experienced the goodness of God through the redemptive work of Jesus' death and resurrection (1:8-21) and in the resulting call to live a life of hope and mutual love (1:22-25). It is this sure experience that gives Christians the motivation to continue in the process of salvation. Psalm 34 is also quoted in Heb 6:4-5 in reference to religious experience. Here, as in many other places in the letter, the author draws on a wide range of traditional imagery. The title "Lord" probably refers to Jesus, the one through whom God's life has been made available to the Christian (1:21), and one whose definitive presence was already anticipated in the prophetic writings. The opening verse of the next section builds on this, inviting the Christian to further embrace Jesus Christ (2:4-10).

FOR REFERENCE AND FURTHER READING

Danker, Frederick W. "1 Peter 1:14–2:17—A Consolatory Pericope," *ZNW* 58 (1967) 95–102.

Elliott, John H. "Salutation and Exhortation to Christian Behavior on the Basis of God's Blessings (1 Pet 1:1–2:10)," *RevExp* 79 (1982) 415–25.

Francis, James. "'Like Newborn Babes'—The Image of the Child in 1 Peter 2:2-3," *JSNT Suppl. Ser.* 3 (1980) 111–17.

Giesen, Heinz. "Gemeinde als Liebesgemeinschaft dank göttlicher Neuzeugung. Zu 1 Petr 1,22–2,3," *SNTSU* 24 (1998) 135–66.

Jobes, Karen H. "Got Milk? Septuagint Psalm 33 and the Interpretation of 1 Peter 2:1-3," *WTJ* 64 (2002) 1–14.

McCartney, D. "Logikos in 1 Peter 2:2," *ZNW* 82 (1991) 352–59.

Snodgrass, K. R. "I Peter ii.1-10: Its Formation and Literary Affinities," *NTS* 24 (1977/78) 97–106.

Stevick, Daniel B. "A Matter of Taste: 1 Peter 2:3," *Review for Religious* 47 (1988) 707–17.

6. *The Living Stones and the Household of God* (2:4-10)

4. Come to him, a living stone, rejected by human beings but chosen and honored by God. 5. And as living stones let yourselves be built up as a spiritual house so as to become a holy priesthood offering spiritual sacrifices acceptable to God through Jesus Christ. 6. For it is contained in the Scriptures, "Behold I am placing in Zion a precious and chosen cornerstone, and the one who believes in him will not be disgraced." 7. Therefore [this is] honor to you who believe, but for those who do not believe, this very stone rejected by the builders has become the cornerstone, 8. and a stone that causes stumbling and a rock that is an obstacle. The ones who stumble against [this stone] are those who do not believe in the word, for which they were destined. 9. But you are a chosen nation, a royal priesthood, a holy people, a people treasured, in order that you may proclaim the great deeds of the one who called you out of darkness into his marvelous light. 10. Once you were not a people, but now you are people of God; [once] you had not experienced mercy, but now you experience mercy.

NOTES

4. *Come to him a living stone, rejected by human beings but chosen and honored by God:*
The verb "come" *(proserchomenoi)* is a present participle in the Greek but can
be translated as an imperative as part of the ensemble of verbs begun in 1:13
(Goppelt, *Commentary* 140 n. 28; Achtemeier, *1 Peter* 153; Elliott, *1 Peter* 409
prefer an indicative in parallel with the indicative verb "built up" in v. 5). The
pronoun "him" refers to Christ, who was explicitly mentioned in the previous
verse, although in the Old Testament "rock" or "stone" is used as a metaphor
for God (Deut 32:4; 2 Sam 23:3; Isa 26:4; 30:29; Pss 1:3; 19:15; 62:3, 7). As discussed below, this section of the letter introduces another set of rich Old Testament symbols: the notion of a primal foundation stone as in Isa 28:16 and the
stone as paradoxically both rejected and designated as cornerstone as in
Ps 118:22. The switch from the notion of nourishment (2:1-3) to the metaphor
of rock may have been inspired by Psalm 133's portrayal of God as a place of
"refuge" (see Achtemeier, *1 Peter* 153). The Greek word *lithos* ("stone") can be
used in a generic sense but often implies a dressed or specially cut stone suitable for building. In personifying Christ as the "stone" the author creates the
somewhat dissonant metaphor of "living stone," no doubt affirming Christ as
risen, a strong motif of the letter as a whole (see 1:3). This living stone is "rejected" by human beings; the perfect tense of the participle *apodedokimasmenon*
carries the connotation that the rejection of Christ is not simply the past event
of his Passion and death, but continues in the rejection of Christ and the
gospel experienced by the communities to which the letter is addressed. The
author sharply contrasts such rejection with the chosen status and honor
Christ receives from God through his resurrection and exaltation.

5. *And as living stones let yourselves be built up as a spiritual house so as to become a
holy priesthood offering spiritual sacrifices acceptable to God through Jesus Christ:*
This section binds together the destiny of the Christians with their crucified
and risen Master. The Christians, too, are "living stones." The translation of
this verse is challenging. The one preferred here takes the verb *oikodomeisthe*
("let yourselves be built up") as the middle voice, which gives it an imperative
cast in line with the other exhortatory verbs in this section (see above, v. 4, and
the comment of Goppelt, *Commentary* 140). Others read this as a passive voice,
presumably with God as the ultimate implied agent (". . . are being built";
see Achtemeier, *1 Peter* 155; Elliott, *1 Peter* 413). This translation also interprets
"a spiritual house" as in apposition to the Christians as "living stones" rather
than as the object of "build up." The preposition "into" *(eis)* in fact comes after
the phrase "a spiritual house" and is attached directly to "a holy priesthood."

The term *oikos* can mean either the "house" as a building or the "household" as the family community itself. Both nuances seem to be present here in
the wake of the author's use of the metaphor "living stones." The Christians
form a "spiritual *house*," fitting the author's view of the community as the new
temple, a notion reinforced in the subsequent references to priesthood and
offering of sacrifices. But they also form a spiritual "household" whose members have strong mutual responsibilities, as the author's exhortations to

charity make clear. The adjective "spiritual" (*pneumatikos*) underscores the fact that this "house" is not an ordinary material dwelling of stone and wood, but it may also convey the sense that this household is animated by God's Spirit (see, for example, 1:2).

Although a few have questioned whether in using the term *oikos* 1 Peter views the community as the new temple, it is hard to escape that conclusion. (The most ardent opponent of this view is Elliott, who finds no connection to the temple in 1 Peter; see his extensive discussion in his *1 Peter* 415–18 and earlier, *A Home For the Homeless*, 165–266.) The word *oikos* is used to refer to the Temple in the Septuagint (e.g., 2 Chr 36:23; Ps 69:9; Isa 56:7) as is the verb *oikodomeō* ("build"), used to describe the construction of the Temple (e.g., 2 Sam 7:5-6; 1 Kgs 8:27; Isa 66:1). Likewise the motif of the community as a new temple is found elsewhere in the New Testament and in Qumran literature (see the Interpretation below). The references to "priesthood" (see also v. 9) and "sacrifice" that follow clearly suggest the author is exploiting the temple motif.

The notion of "spiritual" sacrifices (*pneumatikas thysias*) harmonizes with the fundamental quality of this community and its temple (i.e, "spiritual house"), but may also imply a contrast to "non-spiritual" sacrifices. This is not necessarily a critique of the ancient Jewish sacrificial system of animals, birds, or grains, but more likely is the type of implied criticism already found in Judaism itself that frowned on sacrifice that was not an expression of an inner spiritual disposition (see, for example, Isa 1:12-17). In other words, the sacrifices of this "holy priesthood" and "spiritual temple" are to be authentic and therefore "acceptable to God." The efficacy of such "spiritual sacrifice" rests ultimately on the redemptive power of "Jesus Christ"—a conviction already strongly affirmed in the opening paragraphs of the letter (see, for example, 1:3, 13, 18-21).

6. *For it is contained in the Scriptures, "Behold I am placing in Zion a precious and chosen cornerstone, and the one who believes in him will not be disgraced":* The conjunction "for" (*dioti*) implies that the Scripture quotation cited here provides both the authority and the source for the author's collection of metaphors in this section (see above at 1:24). The phrase *periechei en graphē* literally means "it is contained in (the) Scriptures" but may have been a stock phrase equivalent to "the Scriptures say." The quotation is from Isa 28:16 but deviates to some extent from both the Masoretic and Septuagint texts (see Achtemeier, *1 Peter* 159 n. 126). Most of the changes are minor, although the addition of the phrase "in him" after "believes"—a change from the Hebrew, but one found in some LXX versions—reinforces the christological interpretation of the quotation. The quotation is apt for this context because it recapitulates the christological motifs that 1 Peter stresses in this opening section of the letter. Through his death and resurrection Christ has become the "cornerstone" (*lithon akrogōniaion*) of God's people, a stone that is "precious" and "chosen." At the same time the rejection of the cornerstone cited above is also implied here: those who believe in this "cornerstone" will "not be disgraced."

7. *Therefore [this is] honor to you who believe, but for those who do not believe, this very stone rejected by the builders has become the cornerstone:* This intertwined motif of

acceptance and rejection continues in the next two verses. "Honor" *(timē)*, a major social and religious value in the first-century Mediterranean world, redounds to those who believe, but for those who fail "to believe in the word for which they were destined" and thereby reject the cornerstone placed by God as the foundation of the saved community, there is only "stumbling" and "obstacles." In v. 7 the author quotes from the Septuagint version of Ps 118:22, "the very stone rejected by the builders has become the cornerstone," a text cited in similar contexts elsewhere in the New Testament (see Mark 12:10-11; Matt 21:42; Luke 20:17; Acts 4:11).

8. *and a stone that causes stumbling and a rock that is an obstacle:* The author freely cites Isa 8:14, "a stone that causes stumbling" *(lithos proskommatos)* and "a rock that is an obstacle" *(petra skandalou); lithos* ("stone") usually implies a dressed stone used in building such as the cornerstone; *petra* ("rock") is more generic and may refer to a loose rock found in the pathway. Paul, too, quotes both of these Isaian passages in Rom 9:33, but merges them into one. The appearance of these two quotations and the "stone" motif in various New Testament texts suggests that they each drew on a fairly widespread early Christian tradition rather than being a result of the literary dependence of one text directly on another.

   The ones who stumble against [this stone] are those who do not believe in the word, for which they were destined: Those who trip over the stumbling rock are those who "disobey the word" *(tō logō apeithountes)*—presumably these are the outsiders who harass the Christians because of their beliefs and thereby "disobey" or reject the Christian message (see similarly 3:1 in referring to the non-Christian husbands of women in the community). Such a fateful choice on the part of nonbelievers is, in the view of the author, their "destiny."

9. *But you are a chosen nation, a royal priesthood, a holy people, a people treasured, in order that you may proclaim the great deeds of the one who called you out of darkness into his marvelous light:* Here again the author weaves together several Old Testament quotations to describe the dignity and status of the Christian community as chosen by God, redeemed through Jesus Christ, and formed into a living temple. Principal texts are Isa 43:20-21, "a chosen nation" *(genos eklekton;* see also the notion of election introduced in 1:2), and Exod 19:6 "a royal priesthood" *(basileion hierateuma)* and "a holy people" *(ethnos hagion).* The term *basileion* should be taken as an adjective ("royal") rather than as a noun ("kingdom"), although the latter is possible and would follow the Masoretic text (literally "a kingdom of priests"). But interpreting *basileion* as an adjective brings it into parallel with the other two phrases describing the Christian community, each of which consists of a noun and modifying adjective. In this instance ("royal priesthood") the adjective precedes the noun, as in the Septuagint word order for Exod 19:6 *(basileion hierateuma).*

   The phrase "a people treasured" *(laos eis peripoiēsin)* is not a direct quotation, but is close to Isa 43:21 ("my people that I formed for myself" LXX: *laos mou hon periepoiēsamen*). Similarly, the purpose of God's election "in order that you may proclaim the great deeds" [of the one who called you out of darkness into his marvelous light] also echoes the intent of God's election of Israel as stated in Isa 43:21b, "so that they might declare my great deeds" *(hopōs tas aretas exaggeilete;* LXX *tas aretas mou diegeisthai* ["to declare my great deeds"]). The Greek word *aretē* can be translated "praise" as in the NAB, but in Greco-Roman literature usually means the actions or performance that elicit praise, hence "great deeds" or "mighty acts" [NRSV] or "glorious deeds" [NEB]. To experience God's saving acts on their behalf also means a responsibility to proclaim them to the world; the compound verb *exaggellō* (literally "to proclaim out") as distinct from the more common *aggellō* ("announce") or *euaggellō* ("announce good news") is found only here in the New Testament.

The most evident and fundamental of God's "great deeds" is his calling the people from "darkness into his marvelous light." This metaphor for conversion and new life reaffirms a recurring motif of the letter as a whole (see, for example, 1:2; 1:3, 14-15, 18, 23; 3:18). The notion of "call" or "election" is also a characteristic Old Testament motif favored by 1 Peter (see a similar use of the verb *kaleō*, "call," in 1:15; 2:21; 3:9; 5:10).

10. *Once you were not a people, but now you are people of God; [once] you had not experienced mercy, but now you experience mercy:* At the conclusion of the segment the author once again uses Old Testament allusions to define the new life that belongs to the Christian community redeemed by Christ, and to contrast that life with the plight of their own past and that of the people who continue to reject the gospel. While not a direct quote, the phrases in v. 10 are evidently inspired by Hos 1:6, 9 (LXX 2:25): compare 1 Pet 2:10a, "once you were not a people, but now you are people of God" *(ou laos nun de laos theou)* with Hos 1:9 "you are not my people" *(hymeis ou laos mou)* and Hos 2:25b "I will say to Lo-ammi [i.e., "not my people"] 'You are my people'" *[laos mou ei su]*. Similarly, the phrase "once you had not experienced mercy, but now you experience mercy" *(ouk eleēmenoi nun de eleēthentes)* draws on Hos 1:6-7 "Name her 'No-mercy' *(ouk eleēmenē)*, for I will no longer have pity *(ou me prosthesō eti eleēsai)* on the house of Israel or forgive them. But I will have pity *(eleēsō)* on the house of Judah, and I will save them by the Lord their God." Paul also quotes these same verses from Hosea in Rom 9:25 in a similar vein, emphasizing the elect status of the Christians.

INTERPRETATION

This is an exceedingly rich segment of the letter, bringing to a close the entire opening section that lays out the theological foundation of Christian life. The profusion of Old Testament allusions in this passage rivals or exceeds any other text in the New Testament. The previous segment (2:1-3) used the image of new birth; now the author draws other images from his quiver, that of "living stones" built into a "spiritual house" or temple, and the recurring image of God's "call" and "election" of the Christians as a new people.

"Stone" or "rock" is used as a metaphor or symbol with a variety of meanings in both the Old and New Testaments. One basic meaning develops the idea of "foundation stone." According to a mythology current in several ancient Near Eastern cultures the creation of the world began with the laying of a foundation stone or "capstone" that marked the center of the universe. This stone capped the chaotic waters of the subterranean seas and became the starting point for the construction of the rest of the world. Usually the sacred capital city and its temple are said to have been built on this hub. Isaiah 28:16, which 1 Peter cites in 2:6, reflects this kind of mythology. Mount Zion, on which Jerusalem and its Temple are built, is the site of this cosmic cornerstone; it is thus a sure and unshakable foundation for God's people.

Another dimension of the stone symbol is that of "obstacle" or stumbling rock. The stone stands immovably in the way, an image of strength and a challenge to those who would circumvent it. This image is applied to God in Isa 8:14, a text cited in 1 Pet 2:8.

A third facet of the stone symbol seems to combine both foundation stone and stumbling stone. Psalm 118:22 uses the metaphor of a stone or rock rejected by the builders yet becoming the cornerstone of the building. In the psalm this image is applied to the plight of the psalmist, who seems to express his thanksgiving for victory in battle. The king (or whoever the psalmist may represent) was rejected by enemies among his people, but with God's help has prevailed.

Each of these metaphorical or symbolic uses of "stone" or "rock" is found in the New Testament. The symbol of "foundation stone" seems to influence Matt 16:18, where Jesus declares Peter to be the "rock" or foundation stone on which he will build his new community. The fact that the name "Peter" in both Aramaic *(kēpha)* and Greek *(petra)* means "rock" is the basis for the wordplay in the saying. At the same time Jesus also declares Peter to be a *skandalon* or "obstacle" for his attempt to dissuade Jesus from his pilgrimage to the cross (Matt 16:23), an echo of Isa 8:14. Somewhat closer to the sense of 1 Peter, however, is Eph 2:20-22. Here Jesus himself is the cornerstone *(akrogōniaion,* as in 1 Pet 2:6) while the apostles are the "foundation" *(themelios)* upon which the community is built as a "holy temple in the Lord; in whom you also are built into it for a dwelling place of God in the Spirit." Although the language is not identical with 1 Peter, this passage links together Jesus as the "cornerstone," the apostles as "foundation," and the motif of the community as the temple filled with the Spirit. Qumran also drew on Isa 28:16 to describe the community itself as the "precious cornerstone" (1QS 8.5-10) and a place where authentic sacrifice will be offered (1QS 9.4-5; on the motif of the community as a temple in the Qumran literature see further Bertil Gärtner, *The Temple and the Community* 22–44). John 2:19-22 ("destroy this temple and in three days I will raise it up") explicitly portrays the risen Jesus as the personification of a new temple. The saying of Jesus in Mark 14:58 about a new temple "not made by hands" (see also Matt 26:61, where the accusation is simply "I am able to destroy the temple of God and to build it in three days") implies a similar motif, that is, through the death and resurrection of Jesus a new temple will be built, present either in the risen Christ himself as the locus of the divine presence or in the community (see John Donahue, *Are You the Christ?*; Donald Juel, *Messiah and Temple*; Donald Senior, *Passion* 25–28).

The motif of the "rejected cornerstone" is also found in the New Testament. Mark cites Ps 118:22 as a commentary on the meaning of the parable of the vineyard (Mark 12:10-11). Both the lightly concealed allegory of the parable and the psalm quotation refer to the death and resurrection of Jesus. Matthew (21:42) follows Mark faithfully in this, but Luke 20:17-18 expands the quotation from the psalm by adding the image of the stumbling block from Isa 8:14. For those who reject Jesus he is both an obstacle and a sign of judgment, but for those who accept him he is a precious cornerstone. Thus Luke combines themes and Old Testament quotations in a manner similar to 1 Peter. This is a sure sign that these images for Jesus and the community were already in circulation before either Luke or 1 Peter put them in writing.

Having reviewed this diverse and complex use of the stone motif, we can now return to the text of 1 Pet 2:4-10. The segment begins with an exhortation to "come to him [Christ]." 1 Peter portrays Jesus Christ as both the inauguration and the culmination of the process of salvation. The death and resurrection of Jesus formed the saving act of God that gave birth to living hope (1:3). Even before the foundation of the world Jesus was present in the mind of God (1:20); his Spirit moved the prophets to prepare the way of salvation (1:11), and the endpoint of that journey is the full revelation of Jesus at the completion of history (1:13). While on this journey through history the Christians are to love their Lord without seeing him and to trust and rejoice in him (1:8). All of this experience of salvation is summed up in 2:3: "you have tasted that the Lord is good." This testimony to the central role of Jesus in the Christian experience of salvation gives urgency and meaning to the plea: "come to him." The Christians are invited to plunge fully into the way of salvation, to leave behind their previous lives of futility, and to live out their baptismal call. The warm, inviting tone of the opening phrase is reminiscent of the saying of Jesus in Matt 11:28, "Come to me, all you who labor and are heavy laden, and I will give you rest."

The introduction of the stone imagery causes a slight mixing of metaphors: the invitation to "come" to a "living stone, rejected by human beings but chosen and honored by God" (2:4). This description of Jesus as a "living stone" draws on two of the symbolic meanings of stone we have discussed above. Jesus is both the "foundation stone," as affirmed by the quotation from Isa 28:16 in v. 6, and a "rejected cornerstone," as illustrated in the quotation from Ps 118:22 in v. 7. The Christians are invited to base their life of discipleship on Jesus himself and thereby to share completely in his destiny. They are to find in him the confidence needed for their Christian witness (as in 1:21). He is a "living" stone, one who in spite of rejection and death has been raised up by God. One of the most insistent themes of 1 Peter is the pattern of death-resurrection for Jesus himself and for the Christians who believe in him. Suffering for the sake of the gospel is a redemptive act (see the discussion below at 2:21-25).

The bond between Jesus "the living stone" and the Christians brings life to them; in v. 5, therefore, they, too, are called "living stones." By building their lives and their community on the foundation of Jesus the Christians are being constructed into a "spiritual house." Although some scholars have questioned this, it seems most probable that by "house" 1 Peter means the *temple*. The following phrases speak of "priesthood" and "sacrifices." Thus, as in Eph 2:20-22, the Christian community is now designated as a living temple. The historical Jerusalem Temple was a central institution of Jewish life and the taproot of its identity as a people, serving as the unique locus of the divine presence, the center of worship, and the seat of authoritative teaching. First Peter, drawing on a theological tradition already developed in the early Christian community (with a parallel development in the Qumran literature), applies this powerful symbol to the Christian community itself (in addition to Eph 2:20-22 see 1 Cor 3:16-17; 2 Cor 6:16; 1 Tim 3:15; Heb 3:6). The temple is no longer a building or an institution, but a living community or "household" (the alternate connotation of the Greek word *oikos*). Here is where God is present and where true worship is to be offered to God. Therefore the Christians form a "holy priesthood" (a name for Israel in Exod 19:6 and Isa 61:6), that is, they are the custodians and leaders in this living temple. To be part of a sacred place or household requires "holiness" (see also 1:13-16). It also demands a life of dedication, which 1 Peter expresses in cultic language, "offering spiritual sacrifices acceptable to God through Jesus Christ" (v. 5). The language used here requires careful analysis. By "spiritual sacrifices" the author does not mean simply "spiritual" as opposed to the "material" (i.e., animal, fowl, and grain) sacrifices of the Jewish temple cult. Rather, the sense of "spiritual" here is that the sacrifices offered to God express the inner disposition of the one who offers them. They are not merely external acts, but spring from a committed and virtuous heart. This motif of sacrifices "acceptable to God" is neither a Christian invention nor necessarily an implied critique of material sacrifice, but was a recurrent motif in Judaism. Psalm 51:7 proclaims that the "sacrifice acceptable to God is a broken spirit; a broken and contrite heart, O God, thou wilt not despise" (see also Pss 69:30-33; 141:2). The prophets challenged the leaders of Israel on the hypocrisy of liturgical sacrifice that coexisted with injustice (see, for example, the classic text of Isa 1:10-20). And during the turbulent period of the first century C.E. both the Pharisees and the Essenes (the reform group most likely represented at Qumran) reminded the people that sincere obedience to the Law was an acceptable and authentic form of sacrifice. Thus to be a holy priesthood offering sacrifices in a spiritual temple does not mean withdrawal into some sacred zone, but is a plea for a life fully convinced of its sacredness and fully committed to acts of integrity.

First Peter describes the "temple" not as a static reality but as under construction, "being built up." This implies that the process of conversion is ongoing for the Christian community (as in 2:2). Paul speaks similarly of the "building up" of the church in 1 Cor 14:12. Ephesians 4:11-12 cites the various ministries in the community and says that the purpose of these "gifts" is "to equip the saints . . . for the building up of the body of Christ." These exhortations share a common perspective, namely that the building up of the church as a living temple is an ongoing process, a "way" of discipleship rather than an achieved status.

Verses 7 and 8 add a final comment on the stone symbolism. For the believers Christ is indeed the precious foundation stone on which they base their new life. But for those who reject Jesus and the gospel, who choose to remain in their lives of futility, this "stone" becomes the "stumbling stone." Although both Ps 118:22 and Isa 8:14 are cited, it is the mood of the latter that dominates. Those who experience God's judgment are not unbelievers in general, but those who "do not believe in the word, for which they were destined." The "word" of God, the gospel, is the way to life for the believer (1:24-25). Their belief in this word helped them shed a life of meaningless indulgence (1:22; 2:1) and set them on the way to salvation. But those to whom the gospel is offered, yet who reject it, have invited death into their lives. First Peter does not consider encounter with the gospel a casual affair without consequences, but a matter of life and death. In this sense the person of Jesus (as proclaimed by the word and witness of the community) stands as an immovable rock in the flow of human history. Those whose God-given destiny brings them into knowing contact with it must either cling to it and build their lives upon it or attempt to skirt the rock and ignore it. To choose the latter course, in the perspective of 1 Peter, is fatal; those who do so will find the "rock" an obstacle, and they will trip and fall.

In the final verses of this rich section (2:9-10) 1 Peter turns to another Old Testament set of images connected with the covenant and Israel's election. In applying covenant terms to the Christian community 1 Peter draws on a theme that was already part of early Christian self-understanding (see, for example, the reference to the death of Jesus as a "new covenant" in Mark 14:24; Luke 22:20; 1 Cor 11:25). This tradition generally assumes that the Christian community was the new covenant community, heirs to the promises made to Israel. But here, too, 1 Peter in using covenant imagery does not comment on the fate of Israel or draw a negative inference about Israel on the basis of the Christian community's status as an elect people.

First Peter seems to draw on two key Old Testament texts, each with a different mood: the triumphant sense of election as God's people as described in Exodus 19 and Isaiah 43, and the more muted description of a renewed covenant in Hosea 1–2.

Verse 9 opens with a contrast: "But *you*. . . ." The previous verses (2:4-8) recalled both God's choice or election of the Christians and the tragedy of those who refuse the invitation of the gospel. A string of powerful names is given to the Christians as God's people: these come from Exod 19:6, part of the Sinai covenant text, and Isa 43:20-21, a passage that refers to a future renewal of the covenant. The first phrase, "a chosen nation," comes from Isa 43:20 and captures the basic mood that 1 Peter wants to convey. The Christians are chosen by God and thereby become God's elect people. This consciousness is the basis for hope and the ultimate source for Christian witness in the world.

A second phrase, "a royal priesthood," builds on the first and recapitulates the temple motif found earlier in the passage. Here 1 Peter draws on Exod 19:6, quoting literally from the Septuagint. This description of the Christian community fits into 1 Peter's collage of images. In 2:5 it already spoke of the community as a "spiritual house," a temple. In 4:17 the church will be named "the household of God" (*tou oikou tou theou*). All of these are justified in 1 Peter's theological perspective because of the author's conviction that God and God's Spirit are present and at work in the Christian community. The image of the Christians as "priests" was also introduced in 2:5. Because the church is God's temple, the members of the community are chosen to be in God's presence, to reflect God's holiness, and to be active in worship and service on God's behalf. Both of these "priestly" labels for the church (2:5 and 2:9) have been the focus of a sometimes tense debate in post-reformation Christianity (see the extended discussion in Elliott, *1 Peter* 449–55). Some consider these texts the basis for a "priesthood of believers" that, in effect, would deny the possibility of a specific priestly ministry in the church. But in referring to a "priesthood" exercised by all Christians 1 Peter is neither affirming nor denying the possibility of a specific liturgical role in the church, just as the author of Exodus 19 could speak of the entire Israelite community as "priestly" without thereby passing judgment on the Levitical priesthood. Instead, the letter uses these biblical images metaphorically to affirm the dignity of the Christian community, which through the salvation effected by Jesus Christ is now called to authentic worship of God and dedicated service in the world.

Two more descriptive phrases from Exodus 19 and Isaiah 43 drive home the community's sense of being chosen by God. In the words of Exod 19:6, they are a "holy people." The term "people" or "nation" accurately picks up the connotation of the Greek term *ethnos* used here. The Christians in Rome, Pontus, Galatia, Cappadocia, and Bithynia (1:1) had differing ethnic roots, but their common calling as Christians cut through the frontiers of culture and history and gave them a sense of common identity, setting them apart from the surrounding peoples who did not believe. (The author is conscious of this bond among the Christian communities throughout the world; see 5:9.)

A final title directly underscores their chosen status. In the words of Isa 43:21, the Christians are "a people treasured." The Greek word *laos* ("people") is the term most frequently used in the Bible to describe Israel as a community chosen by God. In applying such a title to the church, the author appropriates for the Christian community the elect status ascribed to Israel. As noted throughout the letter, the author does this without any explicit contrast to Israel, reflecting none of the Jewish-Gentile polarity that is a dominant concern in other New Testament literature.

The author stresses that such election or chosen status is for the purpose of mission. The Christians are chosen "in order that you may proclaim the great deeds of the one who called you out of darkness into his marvelous light" (v. 9). The first half of this statement seems to be a paraphrase of Isa 43:21 ("the people whom I formed for myself that they might declare my praise"). First Peter uses the quasi-technical New Testament root verb "proclaim" *(exaggeilēte)* in place of Isaiah's more generic "declare" *(diegeisthai)*, although the compound verb with the prefix *ex-* ("out," therefore literally "to proclaim out") is found only here in the New Testament. The Christian mission is to proclaim publicly to the world the "great deeds" of God, that is, the acts of salvation that have given life to the Christians and are offered to all who would accept the gospel. As the opening section of the letter repeatedly notes, the Christians themselves have experienced these "great deeds"—summed up in the metaphorical phrase "called . . . out of darkness into [God's] marvelous light." The movement from "darkness" to "light" as a description of conversion is stock biblical imagery (in the New Testament see Matt 4:16; 6:22-23; Luke 1:79; Acts 26:18; 2 Cor 4:6; 6:14; 1 Thess 5:4-5; Eph 5:8; Col 1:12-13; 1 John 1:6-7), and at several points in the letter the author portrays the pre-converted life of the Christians as a time of ignorance and futility (see, for example, 1:14; 4:3-4) while the experience of conversion is described as a new birth (1:3, 23) and as rescue from a life of futility (1:14, 18). The phrase "marvelous light" has a special beauty and may suggest the author is speaking of God's own glorious presence, to which the Christians are called and which will be manifest at the end of time (see similarly the rich descriptions of the end point of salvation in 1:4; 5:10). For the Christians, therefore, preaching the gospel is living testimony of a people whose lives have been profoundly transformed by God. This testimony will be the primary concern of 1 Peter in the next major section of the letter (see 2:11).

In the final verse of the segment the author turns to the rich theology of Hosea. Hosea recasts the mood of covenant theology by reflecting on the bond between Israel and God in the light of his own experience of a broken marriage. Hosea reflects on his own experience as a metaphor for Israel's troubled covenantal relationship with God. His wife Gomer, apparently a former prostitute at a Canaanite shrine, repeatedly leaves Hosea to return to her former way of life. However, neither her repeated infidelities nor even the illegitimate children she bears (wryly named "No-mercy" and "Not-my-people"; see Hos 1:6-9) discourage Hosea from renewing his bond with her, an experience that serves as an illustration of God's relentless love for Israel.

First Peter draws on this remarkable theological metaphor to complete its word-portrait of the church. Prior to their encounter with the gospel the Christians were "not a people," caught in the same meaningless lives as their contemporaries (see 1:14, 18; 2:1; 4:2-4). But now through their belief in the gospel and the power of God's salvation in Jesus Christ they have become the "people of God." Once they had experienced "no mercy," but now they have experienced mercy. Even as 1 Peter describes the church in lavish biblical metaphors as a living temple and the covenant people, the author does not forget the futile situation from which they were rescued and in which the surrounding peoples are still mired.

FOR REFERENCE AND FURTHER STUDY

Best, Ernest. "1 Peter II 4-10: A Reconsideration," *NovT* 11 (1969) 270–93.

Donahue, John R. *Are You the Christ? The Trial Narrative of Jesus in the Gospel of Mark.* SBLDS 10. Missoula: Scholars, 1973.

Elliott, John H. *A Home for the Homeless: A Sociological Exegesis of I Peter, Its Situation and Strategy.* Philadelphia: Fortress, 1981.

_____. *The Elect and the Holy: An Exegetical Examination of 1 Peter 2:4-10 and the Phrase basileion hierateuma.* NovTSup 12. Leiden: Brill, 1966.

Gärtner, Bertil. *The Temple and the Community in Qumran and the New Testament.* SNTSMS 1. Cambridge: Cambridge University Press (1965) 22–44.

Hill, David. "'To Offer Spiritual Sacrifices . . .' (1 Peter 2:5): Liturgical Formulations and Christian Paraenesis in 1 Peter," *JSNT* 16 (1982) 45–63.

Hillyer, Norman. "'Rock-Stone' Imagery in 1 Peter," *TynBul* 22 (1971) 58–81.

Juel, Donald. *Messiah and Temple: The Trial of Jesus in the Gospel of Mark.* SBLDS 31. Missoula: Scholars, 1977.

Minear, Paul S. "The House of Living Stones: A Study of 1 Peter 2:4-12," *Ecumenical Review* 34 (1982) 238–48.

Schweizer, Eduard. "The Priesthood of All Believers: 1 Peter 2:1-10," in Michael J. Wilkins and Terence Paige, eds., *Worship, Theology, and Ministry in the Early Church: Essays in Honor of Ralph P. Martin.* JNTSSup 87. Sheffield: JSOT Press, 1992.

Senior, Donald P. *The Passion of Jesus in the Gospel of Mark.* Passion Series 1. Collegeville: The Liturgical Press, 1984, 25–28.

7. *Freedom and Responsibility* (2:11-12)

11. Beloved, I urge [you] as strangers and sojourners to avoid those desires of the flesh that wage war against [your] very lives, 12. keeping your conduct blameless before the gentiles so that when they speak against you as evildoers, from seeing your good deeds they will glorify God on the day of visitation.

NOTES

11. *Beloved, I urge [you] as strangers and sojourners to avoid those desires of the flesh that wage war against [your] very lives:* These verses introduce a major new section of the letter (2:11–4:11) and establish a fundamental theological principle for 1 Peter's view of Christian conduct in the world. The recipients are affectionately addressed as "beloved" *(agapētoi),* a typical Christian greeting found in other New Testament literature (e.g., Rom 12:19; 1 Cor 10:14; 2 Cor 7:1; Jas 1:16, 19; 2:5) but also expressive of 1 Peter's concern for mutual love and respect within the community (see 1:22; 3:8; 4:8). The verb to "urge" or "entreat" *(parakalō)* is used here without an express object, but "you" seems implied. As he begins this new section the author returns to a designation of the Christian's place in the world similar to that with which the letter began. They are "strangers" or "aliens" *(paroikous,* literally someone who is away or apart from home; see similarly Eph 2:19). This term was also applied to Israel during its displacement in Egypt (e.g., Wis 19:10; see Acts 13:17). And they are "sojourners" or "aliens" as those living only temporarily in a strange land *(parepidēmous;* cf. 1:1). Both terms evoke the sense of displacement and distance from the surrounding peoples and culture brought on by the Christians' conversion to a new way of life. While the term "desire" *(epithymia)* can be used in a neutral or positive sense, it obviously has a negative connotation here. These are desires "of the flesh" *(tōn sarkikōn epithymiōn)* that "wage war

against [your] very lives." The term "of the flesh," or literally "fleshly," does not necessarily mean only sexual promiscuity, but all those misguided and unrestrained desires that reflect a life of the flesh as opposed to a life of the Spirit (similar to Pauline theology: see, for example, Rom 7:14; 2 Cor 1:12). Such desires have the capacity to "wage war against" *(strateuontai)* the Christians' "lives," literally *psychē*, which can mean "soul" or "life" in the sense of the very being of the person.

12. *keeping your conduct blameless before the gentiles so that when they speak against you as evildoers, from seeing your good deeds they will glorify God on the day of visitation:* The participle *exontes* ("keeping" or "holding") can be translated as an imperative or, as here, as the means by which the Christians avoid the destructive desires of the flesh. The Christians are to maintain good conduct before the "gentiles" *(ethnesin)*, a biblical term that stressed the difference between the chosen people Israel and the "nations" or "gentiles." In the context of 1 Peter the term does not mean "non-Jew" but anyone outside the community or a "nonbeliever." The purpose of this witness is that (literally *en hō*, on that occasion or circumstance) when nonbelievers "speak against" or "slander" *(katalalousin)* the Christians as "evildoers" *(kakopoiōn)*, their exemplary lives (literally their "good works," *kalōn ergōn*) will persuade the gentiles to glorify God "on the day of visitation." The slander against the Christians was probably not formal charges in a court of law but the kind of well-documented contempt that the dominant society of the Greco-Roman empire had for Christians because of their customs and beliefs and their refusal to join some of the religious and social practices of the day. The reference to the "day of visitation" may be an echo of Isa 10:3 (LXX "What will you do on the day of visitation?" *[en tē hēmera tēs episkopēs]*; similarly Luke 19:44, ". . . you did not recognize the time of your visitation from God," *[ton kairon tēs episkopēs sou]*) and refers to the time of final judgment. The whole spirit and some of the language of the verse recall the saying of Jesus in Matt 5:16 instructing the disciples to "let your light shine before others so that they may see your good works *(ta kala erga)* and give glory *(doxasōsin)* to your father in heaven."

INTERPRETATION

With these verses the author moves to a new major section of the letter that will ultimately extend to 4:11. In the opening section 1:1–2:10 the author described the foundation of Christian existence in God's act of salvation through the death and resurrection of Jesus and the resulting status of the community as a living temple, a spiritual household, and a chosen people. Throughout the opening section the author had contrasted the new existence of the Christians with their previous lives of futility in which the surrounding cultures and people were still embedded. With this foundation in place, the author now turns more decisively to describe what Christian life in the world is to be.

The author signals a turning point in the letter by renewing his address to the recipients. They are "beloved," a term that is not a mere stock phrase but expressive of the author's vision of the church. In 1:22 the author had urged the believers "to earnestly love each other from the heart." The Christian has been born anew; each one is a sacred creation of God, a living stone in God's new temple. This is the "truth" that leads to a "genuine mutual love" (1:22). The author also invokes the opening address of the letter when he again calls his fellow Christians "strangers" and "sojourners" (see 1:1). Some interpreters think that these terms may describe the actual legal status of the Christian communities addressed in the letter, who represented displaced peoples or migrant workers in the region of Asia Minor encompassed by the letter (see Elliott, *1 Peter* 476–83; he suggests that the literal status of the recipients as aliens made way for a possible metaphorical use of the term). Their identity as Christians would have compounded the social alienation they already experienced as resident aliens.

But there is no compelling reason to see 1 Peter's use of these terms as describing anything other than the situation glimpsed in the letter itself, i.e., the Christians are aliens or strangers because their Christian values and community identity put them at a distance from the pagan society around them. They are "exiles" not simply in the sense that they are living an earthly existence while awaiting the full revelation of God at the end of the world (1:6-7), but because their non-Christian neighbors are perplexed by their manner of life and "speak evil" of them, thereby giving the Christians a sense of alienation and displacement from the surrounding society.

The author recalls this "exile" status now because he intends to discuss how one should live in a world that appears alien to the gospel. These first two verses of the section lay down basic principles of Christian existence in the world. A life based on the gospel demands inner freedom from destructive desires or values, but it also means giving a public witness so that the example of a good life can have an impact on non-Christians. This is a key insight of the letter and gives it perennial significance. The author is convinced that many of the values and suppositions of the surrounding culture are opposed to and destructive of human life as envisioned by the gospel. But instead of demanding full separation from the world as a protection from its corrosive influence the author encourages the Christians to make their good lives transparent for the world to see. In this sense 1 Peter chooses a course that is different from the fully sectarian or separatist stances of a community such as Qumran or even from a New Testament perspective such as found in Revelation, which strongly counsels complete condemnation of and separation from the surrounding society that is deemed "demonic" in spirit.

Verse 11 lays down one of the basic principles for the kind of "witness" spirituality suggested in 1 Peter: the Christian must abstain from "desires of the flesh that wage war against [your] very lives." In 1:14 the author had used the term "desires" or "passions that you previously experienced in your former ignorance" *(en tę̄ agnoią hymōn epithymiais)*, that is, desires or passions symptomatic of a meaningless life unaware of the truth of the gospel. The expression "desires of the flesh" is similar. In speaking of the "flesh" the author is not limiting desires to sensuality or sexual excess. "Flesh" as used in the New Testament connotes a whole dimension of human existence—not the body as opposed to the soul, but the limited and egotistical tendencies of the human being as opposed to the spiritual and self-transcendent potential of human life that is animated by grace. Paul uses the contrast of "flesh" and "spirit" in a similar fashion, as for example in Rom 8:1-12.

Some Greek philosophical traditions had also counseled control of or abstinence from unbridled "desires" to achieve a moral life. In the context of 1 Peter this language does not imply detachment from emotion or human feeling, but portrays a life of discipline in which desires are channeled to virtue and a life of "good deeds" in contrast to a life of "ignorance" (1:14) and excess (see the list of vices in 4:3-4).

But the call for inner freedom and self-control is only one side of the coin. Verse 12 lays down the corresponding principle of giving public witness. The Christians are to maintain good conduct so that nonbelievers (the "gentiles") may eventually be moved to glorify God. Much of the spirit of 1 Peter is compressed into this verse. The demands of Christian life are not something to be pursued only within the safe confines of the Christian community. Rather, Christians are to witness to the dominant society even as that society maligns them. The Christian way of life is to be sustained in the hope that it will ultimately convince the nonbelievers to glorify God "on the day of visitation." As indicated in the notes, this call to the witness of good deeds even in the face of slander is similar to the saying of Jesus in Matt 5:16, where the disciples are urged to "let your light shine before all, so that they see your good works and give glory to your Father who is in heaven." First Peter foresees that this transformation of the "gentiles" from being slanderers to those who glorify God may take place only on the final day of judgment (i.e, "the day of visitation"), implying perhaps both a foreshortened view of history (see 4:7) and a certain resignation that such a transformation is a slow process. Placing the moment when the gentiles will glorify God at the end-time also gives a cosmic and triumphant scope to the Christian community's mission in the world. Ultimately the new life that animates the Christians will bring the gentiles themselves to acknowledge the truth of the gospel.

FOR FURTHER STUDY AND REFERENCE

Elliott, John H. "1 Peter, Its Situation and Strategy. A Discussion with David
    Balch," in Charles H. Talbert, ed., *Perspectives on First Peter.* NABPR Special
    Study Series 9. Macon: Mercer University Press, 1986, 61–78.
Feldmeier, Reinhard. *Die Christen als Fremde: Die Metapher der Fremde in der antiken
    Welt, im Urchristentum und im 1. Petrusbrief.* WUNT 64. Tübingen: J.C.B.
    Mohr [Paul Siebeck], 1992.
Giesen, Heinz. "Lebenszeugnis in der Fremde. Zum Verhalten der Christen in der
    paganen Gesellschaft (1 Petr 2,11-17)," *SNTSU* 23 (1998) 113–52.
Pilch, John J. "'Visiting Strangers' and 'Resident Aliens,'" *TBT* 29 (1991) 357–61.
Senior, Donald P. "The Conduct of Christians in the World (1 Pet 2:11–3:12),"
    RevExp 79 (1982) 427–38.

8. *Commitment in the World* (2:13-17)

13. Be subject to all created structures for the sake of the Lord, whether to
the king as superior, 14. or to governors as sent by him to render justice
to evildoers but praise for those who do good 15. because such is the will
of God, that in your doing good [you] silence the ignorance of foolish
people. 16. [Live as] free people but not having freedom as a cover for
evil; [live] rather as servants of God. 17. Honor all people, love the
brethren, fear God, honor the king.

NOTES

13. *Be subject to all created structures for the sake of the Lord, whether to the king as
    superior:* The verb "be subject to" or "be subordinate to" is the aorist passive
    imperative of the Greek *hypotassō,* and is frequently used in exhortations to
    civil obedience (e.g., Rom 13:1, 5) or with household codes (Col 3:18; Eph 5:21;
    Titus 2:5, 9; 3:1). In this context it does not connote servile conformity or sub-
    missiveness, but rather proper subordination to legitimate authority. The
    Christians are to be subject to "all created structures" *(pasę anthrōpinę ktisei)*—
    this unique phrase is challenging to translate properly. The noun *ktisis* derives
    from the verb *ktizō,* "create," and literally means "something created." In this
    context the author is referring to authority structures, as indicated in the in-
    junctions that will follow, i.e., kings, governors, etc. Hence the translation here
    prefers "created structures." The nuance of the word "created" may also help
    the author to deflect any notion of imperial authority as divine. The phrase
    "for the sake of the Lord" *(dia ton kyrion)* gives the Christian motivation for
    such obedience, which is based ultimately on God's authority, not that of the

king or emperor. The final phrase in the verse begins a series of examples, starting with "the king" *(basilei)*, a term that refers to the Roman emperor who stands in the "superior" *(hos hyperechonti)* or supreme position within the political hierarchy.

14. *or to governors as sent by him to render justice to evildoers but praise for those who do good:* The "governors" *(hēgemosin,* a term frequently used for provincial governors) are authorized by the emperor to render justice or punish evildoers (see a similar role assigned to political authorities in Rom 13:1-5). It should be noted that 1 Peter explicitly has the governors' authority deriving from that of the emperor who sends them, and does not make any claim for divine authority underwriting either the governors or the emperor. This differs substantially from Rom 13:1-2, which bases the authority of the ruling governors in God's authority, so that in disobeying the ruler one disobeys God (see the discussion in Achtemeier, *1 Peter* 180–82).

15. *because such is the will of God, that in your doing good [you] silence the ignorance of foolish people:* The will of God is that the Christians "do good" *(agathopoiountas).* This notion is very important in the theology of 1 Peter; various forms of the word occur six times in the letter (2:15, 20; 3:6, 17; similarly 2:14; 4:19). The good conduct of the Christians will silence the "ignorance" *(agnōsian)* of foolish people. "Ignorance" here does not mean a shortage of education, but a lack of spiritual insight or understanding; that is, these are people who have not accepted the gospel (see 1:14). As seems to be the case throughout the letter, the problems the Christians are encountering are probably not formal legal denunciations, but ridicule and criticism because the Christian code of conduct does not conform to usual customs and practices.

16. *[Live as] free people but not having freedom as a cover for evil; [live] rather as servants of God:* The verse begins without an explicit subject, and this translation supplies the "you" that is still operative from the second-person imperative that began v. 13 ("Be subject to . . ."). Christians are to live as "free" men and women *(hos eleutheroi),* but not as those who use freedom as a "cover" *(epikalymma)* or "pretext" for doing evil *(tēs kakias).* The final phrase of the verse is also elliptical, literally: ". . . but as servants of God" *(hōs theou douloi).* The ellipsis to be supplied also derives from the opening words of v. 13—i.e., Christians are to subject themselves to legitimate authority, but they are truly free, not using freedom as a pretext for evil but living as servants of God. As the final verse makes clear, the only one to whom the Christian owes total allegiance is God, and this is the source of Christian freedom.

17. *Honor all people, love the brethren, fear God, honor the king:* This verse is carefully worded. Its staccato cadence and calculated sequencing of verbs vividly illustrate 1 Peter's perspective on the varying relationships that make a claim on Christian conduct and help define what "doing good" means. (The remaining part of the section up to 4:11 will also spell this out.) They are to "honor all people" *(pantas timēsate).* "Honor" was a prime societal value in traditional Mediterranean culture and implies respect and deference proper to a person's standing in the community. The Christian as a member of society was also to

conform to this good conduct. The Christians owe other members of the community more than honor. The Christians are to "love" (*agapate,* a term used repeatedly in 1 Peter for love of Christ [1:8] or for the love of the community members among themselves [1:22; 3:10; 4:8; 5:14]) the "brethren" (*adelphotēta,* literally a community of brothers and sisters or fellowship; see 5:9). The sequence of relationships moves to its summit with the next phrase: the Christians are to "fear God" (*ton theon phobeisthe*). Reverential fear—often used in the Bible to describe one's homage to God—is reserved solely for God. This natural climax of the sequence of verbs serves as a sharp contrast with the concluding phrase: "honor the king" (*ton basilea timate*). The king or emperor is to receive the same respect owed to all men and women. There is clearly no deference here to the divine authorization of the ruler, much less to any claim to divine status or power on the part of the emperor.

Interpretation

This segment of the letter builds on the fundamental theological principle expressed in 2:11-12, giving particular attention to how Christians are to maintain "blameless conduct before the gentiles." These verses, 2:13-17, review the basic obligations Christians have to political authorities, setting them in the guiding context of their allegiance to God. The concern for how Christians are to live in the world will preoccupy the entire midsection of the letter. After a general statement on political involvement (2:13-17) the author singles out two difficult conflict situations, that of Christian slaves in non-Christian households (2:18-25) and that of Christian wives married to non-Christian husbands (3:1-6). A final section cuts across all the roles of the community (3:7–4:11).

The section considered here (2:13-17) stays on the level of principle: "Be subject to all created structures for the sake of the Lord. . . ." This injunction needs careful analysis to catch the subtlety of 1 Peter's theological perspective. The verb "be subject to" does not connote blind conformity or submission to political authority, as the overall letter makes clear. The word can be properly decoded if one keeps in mind the alternative that is being rejected. "Be subject to" is not used in contrast to "rebel against" (advice not found in any of the New Testament writings) but to "withdraw from." In other words, the choice before the Christians who are "exiles" and "sojourners" in the surrounding society is either to retreat into a fully sectarian stance, attempting to avoid any contact with the surrounding society, or to interact publicly with that society while attempting to maintain the integrity of their faith. The latter choice is implied in the exhortation "be subject to." This stance puts 1 Peter's theological perspective in contrast with the exhortations of the book of Revelation, which demanded of the Christian communities in Western Asia Minor that they not participate in any fashion in the surrounding society, whose political authorities and cultural values the author considers fundamentally demonic in spirit. Similarly, in Judaism at a period contemporary with 1 Peter a sectarian community such as Qumran (probably to be identified as Essenes) also chose a radical sectarian stance that required its members to physically and spiritually withdraw from participation in the priestly society of Jerusalem because it was deemed thoroughly corrupt and doomed to destruction. First Peter, on the other hand, while sharply criticizing the false values and futile ways of the dominant "gentile" culture, nevertheless exhorts the community to respect political authorities and to "do good" in a public manner calculated to defuse the slanders and suspicions directed at the Christian minority.

One of the reasons for this stance of 1 Peter may be the author's conviction about the course of history. He seems to believe that the consummation of the world is not long in coming (see 1:6; 4:7; 5:10). In view of the short span of history that must be endured, the author's advice to the Christians is that they remain within the social and political situations they were in when they first heard the gospel. Even though the Christian vision foresees a world order that can and will be very different, the community should patiently stay involved in the present world until the time of God's visitation. This is similar to Paul's stance in 1 Corinthians: ". . . everyone should live as the Lord has assigned, just as God called each one" (1 Cor 7:17; see also 1 Cor 7:20, 24), and may in part be the motivation for his own exhortations to obey political authorities (although Paul also considers legitimate political authority as divinely warranted, a stance not affirmed by 1 Peter; see Rom 13:1-2).

This eschatological perspective does not reduce the message of 1 Peter to that of merely feigning participation while waiting out the arrival of the end-time. The author sees a "missionary" purpose in the "good conduct" of Christians, in that such conduct will help protect the community from slander (2:15) and ultimately may bring the non-Christians also to glorify God at the end-time (2:12). This purposeful stance is implicit in the careful wording of v. 13. Christians are to be subject to created structures "for the sake of the Lord." The term for "created structures," as indicated in the Notes, is *ktisis,* derived from the Greek verb "to create" *(ktizō).* The noun form *ktisis* has the sense of "that which is created," that is, a fundamental structure or institution or the established authority that results from a created system or structure (BDAG 572–73). By referring to political structures as "created" or "human" structures the author subtly subordinates all political structures and authorities to the sovereignty of God, the one who is the source of all creation and will ultimately guide it to its purpose. This is implied in the phrase "for the sake of the Lord" and will be affirmed again in the hierarchy of obligations stated in v. 17.

The author now states in generic terms what such subjection to political structures implies. The Christians should "be subject to" the "king" or emperor because he is the "supreme" political authority and to "governors" or provincial authorities because they hold legitimate authority derived from that of the king who "sends" them. As noted above, 1 Peter does not base the authority of the emperor or governors directly on divine warrant (in contrast to Rom 13:1-2). The "governors"—the kind of provincial authorities with whom the communities in the province of Asia were most directly familiar—have a worthy societal purpose of punishing evil and rewarding good, stock terms used to describe the ideal function of political authorities. The letter implies that this proper function, rooted in their authorization by the supreme political authority of the emperor, is the basis for the respect owed these officials.

"Praise for those who do good . . ." slants the message of the next verse (v. 15) toward the call for active witness. It is God's will that the Christians do good, a point already stressed in 2:12. "Doing good" did not necessarily mean that the Christians would always conform to the expectations of the surrounding society. "Doing good" based on the virtues expressive of the gospel in a society alien to that vision could (and apparently did) lead to ridicule, slander, isolation, and even active persecution. But there is a strong optimism in this letter that the Christians' virtuous lives will ultimately silence the "ignorance of foolish people" (2:15).

The capacity to "do good" depended on the inner freedom of the Christians and their allegiance to God. Thus the recipients are exhorted to "live as free people." The nature of this "freedom" is clear: it is not a pretext for license, but is paradoxically expressed in living as "servants of God" (see a similar thought on "freedom" as a pretence for license in Gal 5:13; also 1 Cor 6:12). As the letter has already stated, true freedom is experienced in leaving behind the destructive "desires" of the Christians' former lives and rooting their lives in God's grace (see above at 1:21; 2:4, 11). Paul, too, uses this kind of imagery: "But now that you have been freed from sin and have become slaves of God, the benefit that you have leads to sanctification, and its end is eternal life" (Rom 6:22; cf. also 1 Cor 7:22-23).

The dual bases of 1 Peter's perspective on life in the world—inner freedom and active public witness—are subtly joined in the remaining verse of this passage (v. 17). The words chosen for each relationship in the spectrum of society and the order in which they are presented demonstrate incisive care on the part of the author. The Christians are to "honor" all human beings, reflecting not only a common cultural value in Greco-Roman society, which prized honor, but also, as a fundamental value of the gospel itself, giving respect to every person as a creature of God called to a destiny of glory. Even though 1 Peter speaks unhesitatingly of conflict and judgment, a sense of respect for all human beings, not just community members, pervades the letter (see, for example, 2:12, 18; 3:1, 7, 9, 15-16). More, however, is owed fellow members of the community: *"love* the brethren." The members of the community share in a common new life through the gift of salvation (1:3), have a new identity as the living temple and God's chosen people (2:4-10), and share a destiny with Christ in the end-time (1:4). Therefore the mutual love that binds the community together must be transparent (1:22; 3:8; 4:8; 5:5). The Christian's relationship with God is singular: God alone, as the source and end-point of all life, is owed reverential "fear" or "awe." The relationship to the emperor comes last, not as the climax to what has been a mounting sense of obligation (honor, love, awe), but as a deliberate anticlimax. The emperor deserves "honor," the same obligation owed to all human beings. As the "supreme" civil ruler the king is to be obeyed (2:13), but in no way can the emperor command the allegiance reserved to God alone. Because of the difficulty of precisely dating the letter (see Introduction), it is impossible to know if 1 Peter intends this pointed exhortation as a counterweight to claims of divine status and authority for the emperor. Emperor worship would be a problem for Christian communities toward the end of the first century and beyond, but it is difficult to know if it was already a problem for the communities 1 Peter addresses. In any case this verse makes clear that "being subject to" the emperor or "doing good" as a citizen did not mean unqualified submission to political authority. The "freedom" of the Christians as "servants of God" enabled them to be conscious of both the obligations and limits of civil participation. No doubt such a stance aggravated non-Christian observers of the community and became the source of their criticism and slander. Consciousness of one's obligation to God and to legitimate political authority was also expressed in the famous saying of Jesus, "Render to Caesar the things that are Caesar's and to God the things that are God's" (Mark 12:17 and parallels), as well as in Matthew's account of Jesus' advising Peter to pay the half-shekel tax in order to avoid scandal while remaining conscious that the "children [of the king] are free" from such taxation (Matt 17:24-27; on this see Carter, *Matthew and Empire* 130–44).

FOR REFERENCE AND FURTHER STUDY

Balch, David L. "Early Christian Criticism of Patriarchal Authority: 1 Peter 2:11–3:12," *USQR* 39 (1984) 161–73.
Bammel, Ernst. "The Commands in I Pet. ii. 17," *NTS* 11 (1964–65) 268–81.
Carter, Warren. *Matthew and Empire: Initial Explorations.* Harrisburg, Pa.: Trinity Press International, 2001, 130–44.

Jossa, Giorgio. "La sottomissione alle autorita politiche in 1 Pt,13-17," *RivB* 44
    (1996) 205–11.
Légasse, Simon. "La soumission aux authorités d'après 1 Pierre 2. 13-17: Version
    spécifique d'une parénese traditionelle," *NTS* 34 (1988) 378–96.
Richardson, R. L. Jr. "From 'Subjection to Authority' to 'Mutual Submission': The
    Ethic of Subordination in 1 Peter," *Faith and Mission* 4 (1987) 73–90.
Winter, Bruce W. "The Public Honouring of Christian Benefactors: Romans 13.3-4
    and 1 Peter 2.14-15," *JSNT* 34 (1988) 87–103.

9. *The Christian Witness of the Slaves* (2:18-25)

18. Household slaves, be subordinate to your masters with all reverential
fear, not only to those who are good and considerate but also to those
who are crooked. 19. For this is a grace if, through consciousness of God,
one endures pain while suffering unjustly. 20. For what glory is there if
you sin and are beaten for it and endure it? But if you do good and suffer,
yet endure, this is a grace before God. 21. For to this you have been
called, because Christ also suffered for you, leaving you an example in
order that you may follow closely in his footsteps: 22. [Christ] who committed no sin, nor was deceit found in his mouth, 23. who when he was
reviled, he did not revile in return; when he suffered, he did not threaten,
but handed himself over to the one who judges justly; 24. [Christ] who
himself bore our sins in his body on the tree in order that having died to
sins we might live to righteousness; by his wounds you have been
healed. 25. For you were as sheep going astray, but now you have been
turned back to the shepherd and overseer of your souls.

NOTES

18. *Household slaves, be subordinate to your masters with all reverential fear, not only to
    those who are good and considerate but also to those who are crooked:* The term *oiketai*
    ("household slaves") refers specifically to those slaves who worked within the
    household. Whether the author also intended to evoke the notion of the spirit-
    ual "household" (see 2:5) to which the servants or slaves also belonged as
    Christians is impossible to determine. In any case, their way of living out their
    Christian life is "to be subordinate *(hypotassomenoi)* to [their] masters." The
    verb *hypotassō* was used in v. 13 and applied to all Christians who were en-
    couraged to "be subordinate to" or stay involved in the created order of which
    they were a part, yet to do so from a Christian motivation and with a Christian
    manner. This spirit may be indicated by the phrase "with all reverential fear,"

literally "with all fear" (*en panti phobō*). The word "fear" (*phobos*) in this context cannot mean servile fear on the part of the slaves, but "respect" or "reverence" shown to God, as indicated in v. 17 (see also v. 19, "consciousness of God"). The Christian slaves' respectful demeanor must be extended both to masters who are "crooked" (the literal translation of *skoliois*) as well as to good and "considerate" or "tolerant" (*epieikesin*) ones.

19. *For this is a grace if, through consciousness of God, one endures pain while suffering unjustly:* The term "grace" (*charis*), which has a rich array of meanings in the New Testament, in this context has the sense of something that is favorable or admirable in the sight of God (see 2:20, *charis para theō*). What makes unjust suffering worthwhile is one's "consciousness of God." The term *syneidēsis* is used by Paul to refer to one's moral "conscience" (e.g., Rom 2:15); in this context it has the sense of "consciousness" and implies "awareness" of God's presence in the midst of this experience.

20. *For what glory is there if you sin and are beaten for it and endure it? But if you do good and suffer, yet endure, this is a grace before God:* The term *kleos* means "glory" in the sense of "fame" or "honor." There is no cause for glory or honor in suffering endured because one in fact has done something worthy of a beating, but if one endures unjust suffering for having done good then this is a "grace before God" (*charis para theō*), a phrase that links with the notions of "consciousness of God" and "reverential fear" in the previous verses. The participle *hamartanontes* ("sin") anticipates the allusions to Isaiah 53 in the verses that follow (see vv. 22, 24).

21. *For to this you have been called, because Christ suffered for you, leaving you an example in order that you might follow closely in his footsteps:* At this point the letter addresses all Christians through the example of the household slaves. The notion of Christian life as a "call" to follow the pattern of Christ will be repeated in 3:9. The verb "to suffer" (*paschein*) becomes a quasi-technical term in 1 Peter referring both to Christ's paradigmatic suffering (2:21, 23; 3:18; 4:1) and to the sufferings of the Christians (2:19, 20; 3:14, 17; 4:16, 19; 5:10). The word for "example" (*hypogrammos*) is used only here in the New Testament; it carries the notion of a writing sample whose pattern is to be followed. The phrase "follow closely in his footsteps" (*epakolouthēsēte tois ichnesin autou*) turns from the notion of imitating Christ's example or pattern to the more dynamic metaphor of following in his "footsteps" (*ichnesis*). The prefix on the verb "follow" (*epakolouthein*), instead of the more common New Testament term *akolouthein*, adds the sense of exactness or intensity, hence the translation "follow closely." The manner or pattern of Jesus' suffering will be spelled out in vv. 22-24.

22. *[Christ] who committed no sin, nor was deceit found in his mouth:* The author cites Isa 53:9b. The only change from the Septuagint version is the use of the term *harmartia* ("sin") instead of *anomia* ("lawlessness"), thereby adapting the quotation more readily to the discussion of wrongdoing (see above, 2:20).

23. *who when he was reviled, he did not revile in return; when he suffered, he did not threaten, but handed himself over to the one who judges justly:* This verse is not a

direct quotation from Isaiah 53, but takes its inspiration from the plight of the Suffering Servant and from the Passion story of Jesus, which the author probably knew in some form. The verb *loidorein* ("revile" or use abusive speech toward) no doubt reflects the experiences of slaves, who could be treated with contempt by their masters; it also evokes the experience of Jesus during his interrogation and the revilement of the bystanders at the cross. Likewise the experience of "suffering" (*paschōn;* see above, v. 21) does not lead to retaliation against the slaves' masters, something that was greatly feared by Roman society and severely sanctioned. The verb "to hand over" or "deliver" (*paredidou*) is used repeatedly in the synoptic tradition to refer to Jesus' Passion (see, for example, Matt 17:22; 20:18-19; 26:2; Mark 9:31; 10:33; 14:41; Luke 9:44), often in the passive voice, implying that God is the ultimate agent of delivering Jesus to his enemies. Here the term is used to describe Jesus' entrusting himself to God who judges justly.

24. *[Christ] who himself bore our sins in his body on the tree:* The opening phrase ("bore our sins") is not a direct quotation, but seems to merge phrases from Isa 53:4 and 53:11-12 (e.g., Isa 53:4, *houtos tas hamartias hēmōn pherei*—"this one bears our sins"; 53:11, *kai tas hamartias autōn autos anoisei*—"and he himself will bear their sins"; 53:12, *kai autos hamartias pollōn anenenken kai dia tas hamartias autōn paredōthē*—"and he himself has borne the sins of many and on account of their sins he was handed over"). The phrase "on the tree" refers to the crucifixion of Jesus; the word *zylon* means something made from wood or can refer to a tree. With the latter meaning it is used in reference to the cross (see, for example, Gal 3:13; Acts 5:30; 10:39).

in order that having died to sins we might live to righteousness: The notion of "dying to sins" is similar to Pauline thought (see Rom 6:11); the reference here is to the fundamental decision of the Christians to turn from their former way of life, a theme emphasized earlier in the letter (see 1:14, 22, 23). The term "righteousness" (*dikaiosynē*) also has strong resonance with Pauline theology, although for Paul this term refers primarily to the "righteousness" that is a gift of God (e.g., Rom 6:1-12) whereas in 1 Peter it refers primarily to good deeds (see 2:15, 20; 3:6, 11, 17; 4:19; cf. Elliott, *1 Peter* 535–36). In the context of 1 Peter "living in righteousness" refers to the kind of behavior and exemplary witness that is enjoined on the household slaves and, beyond them, on all Christians.

By his wounds you have been healed: This is a direct quotation from the Septuagint version of Isa 53:5, with the exception of changing "we" (have been healed) to "you," adapting the quotation to the context of exhortation in 2:24.

25. *For you were as sheep going astray, but now you have been turned back to the shepherd and overseer of your souls:* The imagery now shifts to that of shepherd and sheep, probably taking its lead from Isa 53:5-6, which does the same (". . . All we like sheep have gone astray *[hōs probata eplanēthēmen];* we have all turned to our own way . . ."). Jesus is the "shepherd" (*poimēn*) and "overseer" (*episkopos*) of the Christians who have "turned back" (*epestraphēte*) to him. "Turning back" as used here does not imply that the Christians have lapsed, but refers to the fundamental conversion spoken of throughout the first part

of the letter (1:14, 22, 23). The use of "shepherd" imagery as applied to Christ and the Christian community is found elsewhere in the New Testament (Mark 6:34; 14:27; Matt 9:36; 10:6; 15:24; 26:31; John 10:11-18) and is applied to the leadership of the community in 1 Pet 5:2-3, where Christ in 5:4 is designated as the "chief shepherd" *(archipoimenos)* who comes at the end of time. The term *episkopos* ("overseer") is used elsewhere in the New Testament to refer to leaders within the community (Acts 20:28; Phil 1:2; 1 Tim 3:2; Titus 1:7). The word "soul" *(psychē)* has a comprehensive meaning here, not simply "soul" as opposed to body (as implied in 2:11) but equivalent to "your lives" (see also 1:9, 22; 3:20; 4:19).

INTERPRETATION

The fundamental principles for Christian life in the world presented in 2:11-17 are now applied to specific roles within society: slaves (2:18-25), wives (3:1-6), and husbands (3:7). The literary device of directing moral exhortations to various members of the household was common in Greco-Roman literature, although slaves were not usually singled out. Such "household" codes are also found in the New Testament (see Col 3:18–4:1; Eph 5:22–6:9). In 1 Timothy and Titus a list format is used to describe qualities needed for various offices or ministries in the community. In 1 Peter the list concerns Christians' conduct not within the community but within the context of their societal roles. The author singles out two groups for special attention: slaves or household servants and wives, especially those married to non-Christian husbands. Of all the Christians living in society these were the two groups that were the most vulnerable and had to endure the most painful conflict between their fidelity to their Christian faith and their efforts to conform to societal expectations. The Christian slaves and wives become the prime exemplars of a commitment and struggle that ultimately all Christians had to face in their own settings.

The first segment (2:18-20) directly addresses the Christian slaves, but in 2:21-25 the letter begins to move beyond the slaves to an exhortation to all Christians. In using the term *oiketai* the author seems to have in mind domestic slaves or servants under the control of their "masters," the patriarchal heads of households. While many household slaves lived in better circumstances than some free persons did, nevertheless they were not free and faced severe sanctions if they were to disobey or rebel, whether their masters were benign or cruel. There is little doubt that the sense of freedom and dignity intrinsic to the gospel message must have created a deep tension in the lives of Christians trapped in slavery. It is no accident that several New Testament letters attempt to encourage and comfort these Christians (see, for example, 1 Cor 7:21-24; Col 3:22-25; Eph 6:5-8). Paul emphasizes the essential equality of all—whether slave or free—within the community itself (see 1 Cor 7:22). Although in 1 Corinthians Paul tells slaves to take advantage of any opportunity to gain their freedom (an exception to his rule that all should continue in the same condition in which they received the gospel; see above, 2:13-17), neither Paul nor any other New Testament writer offers a wholesale condemnation of slavery, nor do they encourage rebellion on the part of slaves. The pervasiveness of the system in the Greco-Roman world and the high risk to the community's existence that such a subversive stance would entail argued against such a radical step for the early Christian community. Only much later in Christian history would the essential incompatibility between the system of slavery and the Christian message become clear and opportunity to address it possible. But the roots of that liberation were already present in the Christian message itself and can be found in the directives of 1 Peter. The slaves are spoken to directly in the letter, without apology or condescension, as full members of the community. In fact, the slaves—along with the wives of non-Christian husbands—are singled out because they become exemplars of how suffering can be endured in the pattern of Christ himself.

Thus the slaves are to "be subordinate to" their masters. This advice fits neatly into the theology of 1 Peter. The slaves, like all Christians (see 2:13), are to be fully active and responsible in the societal institutions and structures to which they belong. This entails working with "good and considerate" masters, but also with ones who are "crooked." But the author does not call for a dehumanizing servility. The slaves' obedience to their masters is to be in a spirit of "reverential fear" of God, who alone can require total submission. This "reverential fear" or "awe" of God describes the religious consciousness of Christian slaves as they go about their duties. This is exactly what 2:19 and 2:20 state: to act out of reverence for God is a "grace," or something that wins favor with God, as the principles of 2:11-17 had stated earlier. The Christian lives and acts in the world with "consciousness of God" (2:19). This is particularly true when one has to suffer unjustly. The slave who has to suffer the conflict of working for a cruel or unjust master keeps his or her integrity and continues to do good while maintaining that inner freedom that is grounded in one's relationship with God in Christ. As is typical of 1 Peter's perspective, the tenacious pursuit of good is at stake here (2:20), not merely as an expression of good citizenship or coerced social conformity but as expression of one's Christian commitment to do good.

Therefore punishment that comes from doing evil is of no value. But when suffering comes as the result of doing good, because of one's loyalty to God, then this is suffering in the pattern of the suffering Christ and is a "grace" before God. The plight of the slaves illustrates for the whole community what is the vocation of the Christian in the world. Because Christians have been reborn to a new way of life they are to see the world through God's eyes ("conscious of God"). The Christian task is to build up a universe that will ultimately give glory to God.

This broader lesson for all the Christians comes to the fore in vv. 21-25. "For to this you have been called. . . ." "This" is precisely the commitment to pursue good even in the midst of suffering. The vocation of the Christian is to follow the way of redemptive suffering that was laid out by Jesus himself. This "pattern" or example of Jesus in his suffering now commands the attention of the author and is a major motif of the letter (see also 1:18-21; 3:18-22). The sufferings of Christ have two levels of meaning. His way of suffering was "an example" for the Christian, showing how one can suffer conflict, even death, and still be "conscious of God." But the sufferings of Jesus have an additional dimension in that they have the redemptive power to bring about good. In the pattern of the Suffering Servant of Isaiah 53, Christ suffered "for us."

Both dimensions of suffering are reflected in the poetic words of 2:22-25. As in 1:18-21, much of the imagery is drawn from the suffering servant oracles of Isaiah 53. The smooth cadence of these four verses suggests to some interpreters that the author may have borrowed them from an already existing Christian hymn, but it is also quite possible that they are the careful formulation of the author himself (see the extensive discussion in Elliott, *1 Peter* 543–50, who concludes that appeal to a source other than the inspiration of Isaiah 53 is not necessary). Verses 22-23 dwell on the exemplary manner of Jesus' suffering; vv. 24-25 underscore the transformative power of that suffering.

The words of 2:22 paraphrase Isa 53:9, emphasizing the innocence of Jesus ("who committed no sin, nor was deceit found in his mouth"). Verse 23 reshapes Isa 53:7, affirming that Jesus did not allow abuse or suffering to compromise his goodness. Although suffering unjustly, Jesus does not render evil for evil. The silence of Jesus before his captors is something that caught the attention of the evangelists (see Mark 14:61; 15:5; Matt 26:63; 27:14; Luke 23:9; John 19:9-10). Matthew has Jesus explicitly reject the option of a violent response to his arrest (Matt 26:52-54), echoing the instruction of Jesus in the Sermon on the Mount (Matt 5:39). As the slaves were encouraged to suffer "conscious of God" and with "reverent fear," so Jesus, while suffering, hands "himself over to the one who judges justly" (2:23).

Verses 24-25 turn from the exemplary nature of Christ's sufferings to their transforming power. Like the suffering servant of Israel who "bears our iniquities" (Isa 53:12), Jesus takes on the burden of sin in his Passion (2:24). The crucifixion of Jesus is graphically stated: "bore our sins in his body on the tree." The consequence of that death is salvific, enabling the

Christian to be dead to sin and alive to "righteousness" (2:24). The language echoes that of Paul in Rom 6:11. It also resonates with 1 Peter's repeated use of a variety of images to assert the transformation that grace effects in the Christian's life (see 1:3, 14-15, 18-19, 22-23; 2:1-3, 9-10; 3:18, 21; 4:1-2). Another image in 2:24 taken from Isa 53:5—"by his wounds you have been healed"—reasserts the same conviction.

The final verse also draws on Isaiah 53, but uses pastoral imagery to describe the pre-conversion plight of the Christians: "for you were as sheep going astray." But now, having put aside their former way of life, the Christians have "turned back" to the "shepherd and overseer" of their lives. The image of the "shepherd" is applied to God in the Old Testament as in Psalm 23, or in Ezekiel 34, where a contrast is drawn between God as the compassionate and faithful shepherd and the leaders who are unfaithful and treacherous shepherds. In the New Testament the image of shepherd is also common. The parable of the "good shepherd" is used as a justification of Jesus' own mission in Luke 15:1-7 or as an example of responsible pastoral care for the "little ones" in Matt 18:10-14. John's gospel, drawing on the tradition of Ezekiel 34, applies the image directly to Jesus as the "good shepherd" who cares for his sheep in contrast to the example of the religious leaders who neglect the sheep. As a title for Jesus, shepherd is also found in Heb 13:10 ("Jesus, the great shepherd of the sheep") and in Rev 7:17. The term "overseer" reinforces the shepherd's role as one of care and protection. The Greek word *episkopos* is also a title used for leaders in the community in 1 Pet 5:1-4; they are to exercise their leadership after the example of the "chief shepherd" (5:4), which in this section of the letter is described as giving one's life for the sheep. Thus 1 Peter sees the example of Jesus' sufferings as the pattern for all Christians, from the slaves to the community's overseers.

For Reference and Further Study

Achtemeier, Paul J. "Suffering Servant and Suffering Christ in 1 Peter," in Abraham J. Malherbe and Wayne Meeks, eds., *The Future of Christology*. New York: Crossroad, 1993, 176–88.

Hall, R. "For to This You Have Been Called: The Cross and Suffering in 1 Peter," *ResQ* 19 (1976) 137–47.

Hiebert, D. Edmond. "Selected Studies from 1 Peter. Part I: Following Christ's Example—An Exposition of 1 Peter 2:21-25," *BS* 139 (1982) 32–45.

Langkammer, H. "Jes 53 und 1 Petr 2,21-25: Zur christologischen Interpretation der Leidenstheologie von Jes 53," *BL* 60 (1987) 90–98.

Manns, Frédéric. "La morale domestique de 1 P," *Didaskalia* 30 (2000) 3–27.

Osborne, T. P. "Guide Lines for Christian Suffering: A Source-Critical and Theological Study of 1 Peter 2,21-25," *Bib* 64 (1983) 381–408.

Zerbe, Gordon M. "Non-retaliation in 1 Peter: A Pragmatic or a Christological Ethic?" in idem, *Non-retaliation in Early Jewish and New Testament Texts: Ethical Themes in Social Contexts*. JSPSup 13. Sheffield: JSOT Press, 1993, 270–91.

10. *The Witness of Christian Wives and the Responsibilities of Christian Husbands* (3:1-7)

1. Similarly, wives, be subordinate to your own husbands, so that, even if some of them disobey the word, through the conduct of [their] wives they may be won over without a word, 2. when they have observed your pure manner of life [that you maintain] in reverential fear. 3. Let not yours be the external braiding of your hair and the wearing of gold or the wearing of worldly garments, 4. but [that of] the hidden person of the heart, [expressed] in the immortal [quality] of a gentle and peaceful spirit—this is what is precious before God. 5. For thus formerly also the holy women who put their hopes in God adorned themselves by being subordinate to their own husbands 6. as Sarah obeyed Abraham, calling him lord, whose children you have become in order to do good and not fear any intimidation. 7. Similarly, husbands, live together [with your wives] with awareness, according honor to the woman as the weaker vessel, but also as those who are co-heirs [with you] of the gift of life in order that your prayers may not be thwarted.

NOTES

1. *Similarly, wives, be subordinate to your own husbands:* The adverb *homoiōs* ("similarly," "in like fashion") links advice to wives of non-Christian husbands to the previous exhortation to the domestic slaves; the author will introduce his exhortation to husbands in the same manner (v. 7). All three groups within the community—slaves, wives, husbands—are to be guided by the fundamental principles stated in 2:11-17. The participle form "be subordinate" (*hypotassomenai;* see v. 18) functions as a mild imperative but also suggests the instrumentality by which wives exercise their Christian responsibility. The modifier "your own" *(idiois)* implies that the text is not a generic comment on the subordination of women but focuses on the specific relationship that Christian women have to their [non-Christian] husbands.

so that, even if some of them disobey the word, through the conduct of [their] wives they may be won over without a word: The purpose of the Christian wives' deference is "missionary" in character. The description of their husbands as those who "do not obey the word" *(apeithousin tǭ logǭ)* implies not only indifference

but perhaps active opposition or hostility to the Christian community (identified by its commitment to the Christian message or "the word")—a circumstance that would put the Christian wife in a very difficult situation. The
mission strategy suggested by the letter for "winning over" *(kerdēthēsontai)* the
non-Christian husband is not direct confrontation (hence "be subordinate,"
"be subject to") but the persuasiveness of "good conduct"; the noun *anastrophē*
connotes a principled way of life (see 2:12; similarly in Gal 1:13 where Paul
refers to his former way of life in Judaism). The author plays on the concept of
"word" *(logos)*; the husbands who do not obey the "word" *(tǭ logǭ;* i.e., the
Christian message) will be won over "without a word" *(aneu logou;* i.e., without direct proselytizing or confrontation).

2. *when they have observed your pure manner of life [that you maintain] in reverential
   fear:* There are variant readings for the tense of the verb "observe"; the aorist—
   implying that *after* observing the wives' conduct they will be won over—is
   probably to be preferred. The wives' conduct is described literally as a "pure
   life of principle" *(hagnēn anastrophēn);* the word *hagnos* does not simply mean
   "purity" in the sense of "chaste" but has a cultic sense of "holy." This manner
   of life is conducted "in [reverential] fear" *(en phobǭ);* the meaning is not that
   the wife lives in fear of her husband, but that she lives conscious of the reverence or awe owed to God (see above, 2:17, 19).

3. *Let not yours be the external braiding of your hair and the wearing of gold or the
   wearing of worldly garments:* Following similar exhortations in both Jewish and
   Greco-Roman literature against extravagant dress or ornamentation for
   women, the author contrasts superficial outward ornamentation with the
   inner beauty of the Christian woman (v. 4). *Emplokēs trichōn* refers to an elaborate and fashionable braiding of the hair. *Krysiōn* literally means pure gold,
   but by extension refers to jewelry or ornaments made of gold. Similarly the
   notion of "worldly" *(kosmos)* garments means fine women's apparel; this is the
   only example in the New Testament, but it is used in this sense in classical
   literature as well as in Philo and Josephus (BDAG 561).

4. *but [that of] the hidden person of the heart, [expressed] in the immortal [quality] of a
   gentle and peaceful spirit—this is what is precious before God:* The sentence is awkward grammatically, although the author's point is clear: external ornamentation is contrasted with the hidden interior beauty of an authentic Christian
   spirit, which expresses itself in treasured virtues. The graphic phrase "hidden
   person of the heart" *(ho kryptos tēs kardias anthrōpos),* or the "inner self," is
   what is contrasted with the outward appearance and ornamentation in the
   previous sentence. The adjective "immortal" *(aphthartos)* is used here as a
   noun (i.e., literally "the immortal"), hence "immortal quality." The quality of
   the Christian's inner or hidden self "of the heart," which was thought of as the
   locus of choice and determination, is expressed in a "gentle and peaceful
   spirit" *(tou praeōs kai hēsychiou pneumatos).* The virtue of "gentleness" or
   "meekness" is praised in Jesus' beatitude (see Matt 5:5) and is used to describe
   his own spirit (Matt 11:29). A "quiet" or "serene" *(hēsychios)* spirit is also
   prized in Pauline literature (see 1 Thess 4:11; 2 Thess 3:12). The final phrase is
   key: the inner spirit and virtuous life of the Christian wife, not external orna-

mentation, are what is pleasing to God—another way of expressing what it means to live in "reverential fear" or with "consciousness of God."

5. *For thus formerly also the holy women who put their hopes in God adorned themselves by being subordinate to their own husbands:* As the reference to Sarah in the next verse suggests, by "holy women" the author has in mind the great women who appear in the story of Israel ("formerly"). Their fundamental stance is similar to that which the author exhorts the slaves and wives of non-Christian husbands to adopt, namely "putting their hopes in God." Because they too had reverence for God they "adorned" (*ekosmoun;* see v. 3) themselves not with fine apparel but with proper obedience to their own husbands.

6. *as Sarah obeyed Abraham, calling him lord:* The author uses the matriarch Sarah as a specific example of one of these "holy women" of former times. She "obeyed" (*hypēkousen*) Abraham, calling him "lord" (*kyrios*), a term of deep respect. Here the author defines the notion of "being subordinate" (*hypotassein*) as respectful obedience to one's husband. Many authors appeal to the Septuagint version of the story of Abraham and Sarah in Gen 18:1-15 (Achtemeier, *1 Peter* 215; Elliott, *1 Peter* 571) or to other passages where Sarah is prominent, such as Genesis 12 and 20 (see Mark Kiley, "Like Sara"). However, a more convincing parallel is Sarah's portrayal in the Testament of Abraham, where she is a model of obedience to Abraham (e.g., TestAbr A 5, 12-13; A 6, 2, 4, 5, 8; A 15, 4; etc.) and an example of fearlessness and good deeds—precisely the points 1 Peter wants to make. In this text, which either predated or was contemporary with 1 Peter, she is also called mother of the "elect," which is another important connection to 1 Peter (see T. W. Martin, "The TestAbr").

whose children you have become in order to do good and not fear any intimidation: As Martin suggests (p. 144), the participles "doing good" and "not fearing" are best understood as "circumstantial participles expressing purpose." The wives have become children of Sarah, the mother of the elect, so that they may act similarly to her, that is, by "doing good" (*agathopoiousai;* to "do good" is another way the author summarizes proper Christian action as a whole; see 2:15) and, despite their highly vulnerable situation, by not fearing any "intimidation" (*ptoēsis,* literally something terrifying or intimidating). The author is consistent in his expectations of the Christian stance in the world; only God is to be "feared" or given ultimate reverence (2:17)—no husband, however threatening, can require that of the Christian wife.

7. *Similarly, husbands, live together [with your wives] with awareness:* Christian husbands are not in the vulnerable situations of slaves and wives, but the letter includes them briefly in this series of household exhortations. "Similarly" (*homoiōs,* as in 3:1), that is, they too must live in accord with the principles outlined in 2:11-17. This is done in "living together" with their wives "with awareness" (*kata gnōsin*), that is, with the kind of "consciousness of God" (2:19) or "reverential fear of God" (3:2) that was also enjoined on the slaves and wives.

according honor to the woman as the weaker vessel: The husband is to show honor (*timēn*) or respect to his wife, in part because as a woman (*gynaikeios*) she is a "weaker vessel" *(asthenesterǭ skeuei)*. Here the author is speaking not of the husband-wife relationship as such, but of the deference a man owes to women as the physically weaker "vessels." The word *skeuos* ("vessel") was used in Greco-Roman and early Christian literature to refer to the body (e.g., 2 Cor 4:7; 1 Thess 4:4). "Weaker vessel" implies that both man and woman share the frailty of mortal bodies, but the woman's body is weaker and thus she deserves consideration from the physically stronger male.

but also as those who are co-heirs with you of the gift of life: Although the woman is thought to be weaker physically, on the level of their Christian life the man and woman are equal. Therefore husbands are to show honor to their wives because they are "co-heirs" *(sygklēronomois)* of the "gift of life" *(charitos zōēs)*—probably referring to the eternal inheritance promised in the opening lines of the letter (1:3-4).

in order that your prayers may not be thwarted: Failing to treat their wives with respect would result in the husbands' prayers being "thwarted" or "blocked" *(egkoptesthai)*. The passive form of the infinitive implies that God is the one who would not hear the prayers of a husband who treats his wife without respect.

INTERPRETATION

The plight of Christian slaves, especially those in a vulnerable situation with unjust masters, had triggered a long reflection on the meaning of suffering (2:18-25) and how one is to live as a Christian while remaining immersed in a difficult social role. Now another challenging Christian role—that of women married to non-Christian husbands—will also serve as a paradigm for the entire community to consider. As is well documented, traditional patriarchal Greco-Roman society presumed that a woman would adopt the social circle and religious persuasions of her husband as head of the household (see Joseph H. Hellerman, *The Ancient Church as Family;* David Balch and Carolyn Osiek, *Families*). While Roman law gave women some degree of autonomy, the basic social mores required a subordinate role for women within the household. The Christian wife married to a non-Christian husband who not only did not share but may even have been hostile to the Christian way of life was in a difficult position.

The basic principles of 1 Peter's "witness spirituality" (see 2:11-17) are applied to the women as they were to the domestic slaves. While obviously a part of its first-century social context, the letter does not simply accept the presumed social roles designated for women. Although women were assigned a subordinate role in society, 1 Peter addresses them as equal in standing within the Christian community and, indeed, as exemplars of authentic life for the entire community. As the author had enjoined on slaves, wives of non-Christian husbands are to be "subordinate" to their husbands. In the context of the letter, to be "subordinate" has a connotation beyond that of the deference normally expected of wives within Greco-Roman society. In 2:13 the author had urged all members of the community to "be *subordinate to (hypotagēte)* all created structures for the sake of the Lord"—that is, not to withdraw from their roles within society nor to violate the normal social canons. This stance has a "missionary" purpose: namely, to give the surrounding culture the witness of "doing good," which could both protect the community from hostility (2:15) and, above all, persuade outsiders about the beauty of the Christian message and ultimately lead them to give glory to God (2:12).

In the case of the wives this mission need not be accomplished by direct religious persuasion, which was unlikely to be successful. Instead, the letter consistently calls for the eloquent witness of a "good way of life" (2:12, 15, 20). This is how the Christian citizen (2:13-17) or the Christian slave (2:18-25) first preaches the gospel. The same advice is now offered to wives whose husbands "disobey the word" (3:1). Their response, too, is in the pattern of the suffering Christ that was encouraged for the slaves, namely done "without a word." The wives' silence coupled with the transparent goodness of their lives can "win over" their husbands. This non-aggressive demeanor on the part of the woman, while a societal value within the Greco-Roman world, is not motivated simply by cultural mores, but is also a missionary strategy. The Christian woman acts out of "reverential fear" of God (2:2); it is this "consciousness of God" (2:19) that enables the woman to maintain her principled way of life and her Christian identity even in the face of hostility on the part of her husband.

The author goes on to contrast external, superficial beauty with the beauty that springs from an interior life of authentic virtue in the eyes of God (3:3-4). While the lines of the comparison are somewhat convoluted, the author's point is clear. External and transitory marks of beauty and wealth—fashionably braided hair, gold jewelry, and fine garments—are contrasted with the "hidden person of the heart" whose signs are the immortal qualities of "a gentle and quiet spirit." Here, too, the author suffuses traditional moral axioms with a Christian consciousness. Non-Christian authors also decried ostentatious ornamentation for women and praised modesty and gentleness as apt feminine virtues. For 1 Peter, however, these societal virtues have a particular Christian resonance and are not confined to women; in 3:16 *all* Christians are exhorted to give witness through "gentleness" or "meekness" *(meta prautētos)*, a virtue that Jesus' beatitude honors (Matt 5:5, "Blessed are the meek," *hoi praeis*), and that describes Jesus himself (Matt 11:29, ". . . for I am meek," *hoti praus eimi*). Similarly, the quality of a "serene" *(hēsychios)* or "quiet" spirit is also enjoined on the whole community in Pauline literature in contexts where

Christians are urged to lead good but quiet lives in witness to those outside the community (see 1 Thess 4:11; 2 Thess 3:12; 1 Tim 2:2).

These virtues have their source in the "hidden person of the heart"
(3:4), a quaint phrase that points to the inner transformation and grace
that are the heritage of the Christian and the source of a transformed life.
The notion of the interior and hidden person transformed to goodness
echoes some of the teaching of Jesus in the gospel literature. Both Mark
7:1-23 and Matt 15:1-20 emphasize that what determines human goodness
is not external, but what emerges from the interior, from the human heart.
Likewise, Jesus' teaching on authentic piety emphasizes that almsgiving,
prayer, and fasting should be done "in secret" or "hidden" *(en kryptō)*,
where God alone can see it (Matt 6:4, 6, 18).

This notion of a transformed interior life as the source of Christian
virtue runs throughout the letter. The opening lines describe the "new
birth" experienced by the Christian that leads to an immortal inheritance
(1:3-5). This Christian faith is more precious than "gold," which is perishable (1:7, 18; see also 1:23), and it results in a profound interior transformation whose external manifestation is a good and virtuous life. This
interior transformation and its external manifestation are sources of
wonder to the wider society, which expects the Christians to be as they
were before (4:1-4).

An Old Testament example closes out 1 Peter's exhortation to wives.
The "holy women" of the Scriptures who, like their Christian descendants, "put their hopes in God" (3:5; see 1:21), adorned themselves in the
same manner, not with fine jewelry but through their subordination to
their husbands. As is the case throughout the letter, the author effortlessly
adopts Old Testament imagery and examples into his message (see Introduction). The example of these holy women is precisely what the author
enjoins on the Christians, right behavior rooted in their faith in God.

The example of Sarah is singled out (3:6), probably under the inspiration of her portrayal as an obedient wife, examplar of fearlessly doing good,
and mother of the elect (see Notes). Abraham and Sarah were important
Old Testament figures for the early Christians as well as for Judaism. Paul
cites the examples of Abraham's trust in God in spite of Sarah's barren-
ness (Rom 4:19) and the surety of God's promises exemplified in Sarah's
giving birth to a son (Rom 9:9; see also Gal 4:22-31). Similarly, Heb 11:11
cites Abraham as an example of faith in having a son even though Sarah
was barren. Luke's infancy narrative seems to portray Zachary and Eliza-
beth as models of Abraham and Sarah. First Peter finds Sarah exemplary
in that she "obeyed" *(hypēkousen)* her husband and called him "lord" or
"master" *(kyrios)*, a term of deep respect and deference. In this instance
the author defines being "subordinate" as "obedience" and showing marks
of respect toward her husband. This returns the exhortation to the specific

situation of the wives of non-Christian husbands. The Christian wives prove to be daughters of Sarah and other such holy women by "doing good" and "not fearing any intimidation." The insistence on doing good reaffirms the author's insistence on a virtuous life as the sign of authentic faith; the verb "to do good" *(agathopoiein)* and its cognates appear six times in the letter to describe Christian life (see 2:14, 15, 20; 3:6, 17; 4:19), in addition to the noun or adjective forms "good" *(agathos)* or "goodness" used with similar meaning (see 3:11, 13, 16 "to do good"). The encouragement "not to fear any intimidation" relates specifically to the vulnerable position of the wives. Consistent with the principle laid out in 2:17, "fear" *(phobos)* is owed only to God. The non-Christian husband can expect not only "honor"—which is owed to everyone—but the kind of obedience appropriate to the social role of husband and wife. However, the Christian should not fear or be awed by anything "intimidating" or "frightening." In the case of the wife married to a non-Christian husband it would be the threat of punishment or hostility because of her Christian allegiance, just as the Christian slave might have to face a harsh master (2:18). Christians in other circumstances might anticipate ridicule or harassment because of their faith (3:16; 4:4), or even the prospect of more dire persecution (4:12-19). In each instance ultimate allegiance is owed to God alone. The difficult circumstances of slaves and the wives of non-Christian husbands exemplify this Christian stance in a clear way for the whole community.

The author turns to the final segment of his "household code" with an exhortation to Christian husbands (v. 7). The husbands, too (i.e., "similarly"), fall under the same principles for Christian life in the world as the slaves and wives, but obviously under different social circumstances. There is no reference to any duress or suffering that the husbands might have to endure within the specific circumstances of their social role. The husband is to pay honor to the woman because she is the "weaker vessel," that is, because the woman is physically weaker (3:7). The author here steps outside the marital role to speak of the situation of "women" *(gynaikeios)* in general, voicing a commonplace observation in Greco-Roman literature. Yet this inequality on a physical level is not to determine the relationship of husband and wife on the level of their Christian life. Women are "co-heirs" of the "gift of life"—not just life in a physical sense but the gift of a transformed and eternal life that is the birthright of the Christian (1:3-5). Therefore on the deepest and most determinative level of reality from the letter's point of view women are equal to men. The fact that the Christian woman is endowed by God with the gift of this divine life becomes a more compelling reason *(hōs kai . . .)* for the husband to owe honor and respect to his wife. For the husband to act otherwise toward his wife might cause his prayers to be "blocked" or "hindered," an unusual phrase suggesting that God would be offended by such dishonor and not hear the prayers of the husband—an indication of the seriousness with which the author takes this matter. Such a stance on God's part will be illustrated in the subsequent quotation from Psalm 34, "For the eyes of the Lord [are] on the just and his ears [are open] to their petitions, but the face of the Lord [is] against those who do evil" (see below, 1 Pet 3:12).

First Peter's teaching concerning the role of women is both conformative and subversive: conformative in that the letter's exhortations reflect widespread first-century Jewish and Greco-Roman social mores about women as being physically "weaker" and therefore requiring protection on the part of the male (3:7), about the required deference of the wife to the husband in the marital relationship (3:1), and about the expectation that women would exemplify the more passive virtues of modesty and gentleness (3:3-4). (On the status of women in the Greco-Roman world see the extensive bibliography in Elliott, *1 Peter* 599.) Yet the letter is subversive in that it affirms the woman's right to freely make a choice to belong to the Christian community despite her husband's views, regards the woman as a full and exemplary member of the community and "co-heir" with men in the Christian vision of life, considers the "feminine" virtues of gentleness and serenity to be required of all Christians and, in the case of the Christian wives, a missionary tactic to "win over" their husbands to the Christian way, and subordinates any social obligation—including that of wife to husband—to the woman's interior freedom based on consciousness of God.

FOR REFERENCE AND FURTHER STUDY

Balch, David L. *Let Wives Be Submissive: The Domestic Code in I Peter.* SBLMS 26. Chico: Scholars, 1981.

Balch, David L,. and Carolyn Osiek, *Families in the New Testament World: Households and House Churches.* Family, Religion, and Culture. Louisville: Westminster John Knox, 1997.

Gross, C. D. "Are the Wives of 1 Peter 3.7 Christians?" *JSNT* 35 (1989) 89–96.

Hellerman, Joseph H. *The Ancient Church as Family.* Minneapolis: Fortress, 2001.

Kiley, Mark. "Like Sara: The Tale of Terror Behind 1 Peter 3:6," *JBL* 105 (1987) 689–92.

Martin, Troy W. "The TestAbr and the Background of 1 Pet 3,6," *ZNW* 90 (1999) 139–46.

O'Connor, Daniel. "Holiness of Life as a Way of Christian Witness," *International Review of Missions* 80 (1991) 17–26.

Patterson, D. K. "Roles in Marriage: A Study in Submission—1 Peter 3:1-7," *Theological Educator* 13 (1982) 70–79.

Scholer, David M. "Woman's Adornment: Some Historical and Hermeneutical Observations on The New Testament Passages 1 Tim 2:9-10 and 1 Pet 3:3-4," *Daughters of Sarah* 6 (1980) 3–6.

11. *The Obligations of Community* (3:8-12)

8. Finally, all of you, [be] of one mind, sympathetic, loving one another, compassionate [for each other], humble minded, 9. not rendering evil for evil or abuse for abuse, but on the contrary, bestowing a blessing, for to this you were called in order that you might inherit a blessing. 10. For the one desiring to love life and to see good days should keep his tongue from evil and his lips from speaking deceit. 11. Let him turn aside from evil and do good, seek peace and strive for it. 12. For the eyes of the Lord [are] on the just and his ears [are open] to their petitions, but the face of the Lord [is] against those who do evil.

NOTES

8. *Finally, all of you, [be] of one mind, sympathetic, loving one another, compassionate, humble minded*: This section concludes ("finally," *to de telos*) the string of instructions that began in 2:18, but now extends its scope from "slaves" (2:18), "wives" (3:1), and "husbands" (3:7) to all of the community members. The verb governing the series of adjectives in this verse is an ellipsis, probably to be understood as an exhortative imperative ("be") in the manner of the participles that appeared in the previous segments. As with the instructions in the household code, this exhortation to all the community members spells out the principles for Christian life in the world stated in 2:11-17. Some of the words used in this verse are unique to the New Testament, but the general content harmonizes with similar exhortations found elsewhere, particularly in Rom 12:9-18 (but see also 1 Thess 5:13-15; Col 3:12-15; Eph 4:1-3, 31-32). "Of one mind" *(homophrones)* is found in Hellenistic literature but not in the New Testament; it has the connotation of being harmonious toward others. "Sympathetic" literally translates *sympatheis,* is unique to the New Testament, and has the connotation of "being understanding." "Loving the brethren" *(philadelphoi)* refers to love toward other community members rather than love in general (see above, 1:22; also Rom 12:10; 1 Thess 4:9). *Eusplanchnoi* ("compassionate") is found only here and in Eph 4:32. It derives from the word for "intestines" *(splanchna),* which were considered the seat of emotions; thus *eusplanchna* (i.e., good or healthy intestines) implies tender or compassionate feelings toward another. The adjectival form "humble minded" *(tapeino-phrones)* is found only here in the New Testament (see the noun form in 1 Pet 5:5).

9. *not rendering evil for evil or abuse for abuse*: The exhortation not to retaliate, which has strong resonance in the New Testament, turns the direction toward relationships with outsiders, reminiscent of the previous instructions to the slaves and wives. The term for "abuse" *(loidorian)* implies abusive or highly insulting speech (see 1 Tim 5:14, where it also refers to abuse from outsiders).

but on the contrary, bestowing a blessing, for to this you were called in order that you might inherit a blessing: *Tounantion* couples the pronoun *tou* with the adverb *enantion,* with the meaning "on the contrary" or "on the other hand." The participle *eulogouontes* ("bestowing a blessing") provides a link to the previous phrase: the Christian responds to evil or abusive speech not in kind, but by bestowing a blessing on the one who attacks. The "this" *(eis touto)* to which the Christian is called is probably this exacting manner of life being described throughout this section, although the following phrase about "inheriting a blessing" is also part of the Christian calling. The notion of God's ultimate blessing as an "inheritance" for the Christian appears in 1:4 and in the reminder to husbands that their wives are "co-heirs" with them of the gift of life (3:7).

10. *For the one desiring to love life and to see good days should keep his tongue from evil and his lips from speaking deceit. 11. Let him turn aside from evil and do good, seek peace and strive for it. 12. For the eyes of the Lord [are] on the just and his ears [are open] to their petitions, but the face of the Lord [is] against those who do evil:* With only a few adaptations these verses are a quotation from Ps 33(34):13-17a. The form generally follows the LXX version, with the notable exception of changing the address from the second person to the third person and adapting the beginning of the Psalm quotation to the context of the letter (LXX Ps 33:13, "Who is the one desiring . . . ?"; 1 Pet 3:10, "For the one desiring . . ."). First Peter also adds the conjunction "for" or "because" *(hoti)* to v. 12; it is absent in the LXX version. These changes may have happened because the author quoted this snatch of psalm from memory and fitted it into the exhortation of the letter. The quotation is apt because it ratifies the main points of the preceding exhortations: namely, not rendering evil for evil, striving to "do good," and the warning not to hinder one's prayer (3:7). Similarly, the psalm's words about "desiring to love life" *(ho gar thelōn zōēn agapan)* echoes 1 Peter's phrase in 3:7 about husbands and wives being "co-heirs of the gift of life" *(charitas zōēs).* "Life" in the context of 1 Peter refers to the eternal life the Christian inherits through baptism and conversion (see above, 3:7; 1:3-5).

INTERPRETATION

The author closes his words to slaves, wives, and husbands with an exhortation extended to the whole community, calling for compassion and mutual love among the community members themselves and the witness of forbearance and non-retaliation toward those hostile to the community. Similar messages anchored his exhortations in ch. 1 (1:22) and will do so again in ch. 4 (4:8-11) and ch. 5 (5:5). Although this plea is cast in somewhat different terms from the exhortations to the previous specific members of the community, in fact the virtues enjoined on the whole community are quite similar in spirit. The author characteristically emphasizes mutual respect and compassion as well as, in a spirit of witness, refraining from violence or hostility even when provoked. This demonstrates that the kinds of virtues prized by the author cannot be reduced simply to cultural assumptions for behavior proper to slaves and women but, in the author's mind, are virtues exemplified by Christ himself and therefore characteristic of any follower of Jesus who has been transformed by grace. Similar lists of virtues are found in Paul and in other New Testament writings, suggesting that 1 Peter is drawing on a common pool of tradition (see particularly Rom 12:9-18, which has particular affinity with 1 Pet 3:8-9).

The author cites five qualities that should characterize Christian conduct, particularly among the members of the community themselves (3:8). One does not have a sense that the author is responding to specific problems or tensions within the community, as is the case in some of the Pauline materials, but rather that he is continuing his general instruction on what "doing good" means for Christian life. All are to be "of one mind" *(homophrones)*, which does not mean simply having similar ideas, but refers to a harmonious kinship of spirit and mutual respect (see also Phil 2:2-5, where Paul pleads in similar fashion that the community members be of the "same mind" *[to hen phronountes]*). A second quality is that the members be "sympathetic" *(sympatheis)*, literally feeling or experiencing with the other and therefore being "understanding" toward the other, reminiscent of Paul's words in Rom 12:15 ("Rejoice with those who rejoice, weep with those who weep"; see also 1 Cor 12:26, where Paul uses a similar word to describe the sympathy the members of the body of Christ should have for each other: "if one member suffers, all suffer together with it" *[sympaschei panta ta melē]*). "Loving the brethren" *(philadelphoi)* confirms that at this point the author is concentrating on relationships within the community. In the opening part of the letter the author had urged that the community members strive "to attain genuine mutual love" *(eis philadelphian anypokriton)* and to "earnestly love each other from the heart" (1:22). The word is used in similar fashion in Pauline and other New Testament literature to refer to the mutual love and respect that should characterize relationships among the community members as a "family" under God (see Rom 12:10; 1 Thess 4:9; Heb 13:1; 2 Pet 1:7).

The word "compassionate" *(eusplanchnoi)*, derived from the notion of the intestines *(splanchna)* as the seat of emotion, adds a sense of strong feeling to the relationships of love and sympathy. The root word appears in the gospel literature to describe deep and positive feelings toward another stirred by love and concern, such as the response of the father to his lost son in the parable of the prodigal son in Luke 15:20, or the Samaritan toward the victim of robbery in the parable of the Good Samaritan (Luke 10:33), or the king toward the errant servant in the parable of the unjust steward in Matt 18:27. The gospels also attribute this strong emotion to Jesus himself, as in his reaction to the plight of the leper in Mark 1:41 or toward the hapless crowds in Matt 14:14 and 15:32. Paul expresses his love for the Philippian Christians with the very "feeling" that Christ had for them (Phil 1:8, *en splanchnois christou Iesou*).

Moreover, the Christians are to be "humble minded" *(tapeinophrones)*. Humility is a standard Christian virtue; the emphasis in this word is on one's perspective or frame of mind. Being "humble minded" fits here into the spirit of the author's exhortations, which deal with the way the Christians perceive and treat each other. Such humility also reflects 1 Peter's emphasis on the need for "consciousness of God" (2:19) or "reverential fear" (2:17) that leads the Christian to view human relationships with a transformed spirit and profound understanding.

With v. 9 the exhortations turn to relationships with those outside the community, since in other parts of the letter the author refers to abuse directed at the community from non-Christians, not only toward slaves with abusive masters (2:18-25) or wives with husbands who are hostile to Christianity (3:1), but also to the community as a whole (2:12; 3:16; 4:4, 12-16; 5:6-11). Rather than "rendering evil for evil or abuse for abuse," the very nature of the Christians' vocation urges them to react with a "blessing" (3:9). This is characteristic of 1 Peter's entire view of Christian existence rooted in the example of Christ himself and ultimately in God's own manner of relating to the world. Christ had left an example of non-retaliation and of suffering unjustly for the sake of the world (2:21-25). And God, out of mercy, had fashioned a people from those who once were "no people" (2:9-10). These fundamental theological convictions undergird the author's exhortations to the Christians about their own conduct, particularly when dealing with hostility and abuse. By their own God-like and Christ-like witness of rendering a "blessing" instead of a curse they, too, might effect a transformation in those who inflict suffering upon them and lead them not only to confound their opponents (3:16) but also to "glorify God" (2:12). This is the same spirit in which the author had counseled the slaves and the wives—the most vulnerable members of the community, who serve as moral beacons for the rest of the members.

The quotation from Ps 33(34):13-17 concludes the section and ratifies the author's teaching (3:10-12). As is typical of the letter, the author does not alert the reader that he is quoting Scripture but simply incorporates it without comment into his argumentation, perhaps able to assume that his readers will recognize the Psalm. The quotation fits quite well into the author's purpose here. The "blessing" the Christians are to inherit (v. 9) is the gift of new and eternal life, which God graciously bestows on those redeemed by Christ (1:3-9). That "life" will be experienced fully at the end-time but is already anticipated by the Christian now and is expressed in a life of "good conduct," whose qualities the author has been describing in this section of the letter. This is the pattern of thought that leads into the opening line of the quotation and suffuses it with new meaning: "the one desiring to love life and to see good days" is the Christian blessed by God, whose commitment to "doing good" is expressed in "seeking peace" and refraining from evil speech. God's favor is assured for those who live as followers of Christ, but God's "face is against" those who do evil, just as husbands had been warned not to treat their wives with disrespect for fear that their prayers would not be heeded by God (3:7).

FOR REFERENCE AND FURTHER STUDY

Cahill, Lisa Sowle. *Love Your Enemies: Discipleship, Pacifism, and Just War Theory.* Minneapolis: Fortress, 1997.

Perkins, Pheme. *Love Commands in the New Testament.* New York: Paulist, 1982, 89–96.

Piper, John. *"Love Your Enemies": Jesus' Love Command in the Synoptic Gospels and in the Early Christian Paraenesis. A History of the Tradition and Interpretation of Its Uses.* SNTSMS 38. Cambridge: Cambridge University Press, 1979.

_____. "Hope as the Motivation for Love: I Peter 3:9-12," *NTS* 26 (1980) 212–31.

Schertz, Mary H. "Nonretaliation and the Haustafeln in 1 Peter," in Willard H. Swartley, ed., *The Love of Enemy and Nonretaliation in the New Testament.* Louisville: Westminster, 1992, 258–86.

12. *Giving a Testimony of Hope* (3:13-17)

13. And who is the one who will harm you if you become zealous for the good? 14. But even if you should suffer for the sake of righteousness, you are blessed. Do not fear their fear or be disturbed 15. but in your hearts sanctify Christ as lord, always ready for a testimony to anyone who asks you the reason for the hope that is in you 16. but [do so] with gentleness and reverence, having a good conscience, so that in the event you are slandered, those who mistreat you will be put to shame on account of your good way of life in Christ. 17. For it is better to suffer, if that should be God's will, for doing good rather than for doing evil.

NOTES

13. *And who is the one who will harm you if you become zealous for the good?:* This segment is part of the extensive exhortation that began in 2:11, but takes its immediate lead from the previous section, which concluded with the words of Psalm 34 about "doing good" and "avoiding evil" (see 3:10-12). No one can truly "harm" (*kakōsōn*, literally "to do evil against" or "harm") the Christian

because, as the quoted words of the psalm proclaim, "the eyes of the Lord are on the just" (3:12). The Christian is not only to avoid evil but to become "zealous" *(zēlotai)* for doing good. The word "zealous" was often used in the Bible to refer to God's ardor or jealousy versus Israel (e.g., Exod 20:5; 34:14; Deut 4:24; 6:15; Nah 1:2) but was also used in Greco-Roman and Jewish literature for the commitment to virtue (BDAG 427).

14. *But even if you should suffer for the sake of righteousness, you are blessed:* Being protected by God from ultimate evil does not preclude having to "suffer" *(paschoite),* a verb used more frequently in 1 Peter than in any other New Testament book (see 2:29, 20, 21, 23; 3:17, 18; 4:1, 15, 19; 5:10). The form of the verb is the optative, which may imply that the experience of suffering is hypothetical, yet, as other parts of the letter make clear, suffering in the form of harassment has already taken place and more severe persecution is very possible (see 5:12). So the sense here is not purely hypothetical (i.e., "if" suffering should come), but conditional (i.e., in those instances when suffering does come). As the author already made clear in describing the situation of the wives of non-Christian husbands and that of Christian slaves, suffering that leads to blessing is not because of wrongdoing but "for the sake of righteousness." The term "righteousness" *(dikaiosynē)* is a key New Testament concept and, as in 1 Pet 2:24, refers to the full life of Christian virtue made possible by the redemptive power of Christ. The formulation of this verse and its coupling with the notion of "blessing" *(makarioi)* evokes the beatitude found in Matt 5:10 ("Blessed *[makarioi]* are those who are persecuted for righteousness' *[dikaiosynēs]* sake, for they will be filled"); its fundamental meaning of suffering because of commitment to a life of virtue fits exactly into 1 Peter's perspective. It is likely that this saying of Jesus had quickly become part of the ethical tradition of early Christianity, particularly in finding meaning in suffering. The notion of being "blessed" for such suffering will be repeated in 4:14 where the eschatological perspective of ultimately being vindicated in the end time for such suffering is clearer, although that same perspective is at work in this verse as well.

Do not fear their fear or be disturbed: The author quotes from Isa 8:12, but in his usual fashion gives no indication that he is citing Scripture, apparently presuming his readers will recognize the citation. The literal translation—"do not fear their fear"—is awkward in English but implies that the Christians are not to be agitated by the fear that those hostile to the community generate. The author stays close to the Septuagint, but adapts the quotation to the context. Isaiah refers to the fear generated by "conspiracy," and the people are exhorted not to fear "it"; 1 Peter uses a plural pronoun ("their"), referring to all those who cause the Christians to suffer.

15. *but in your hearts sanctify Christ as lord:* This, too, is prompted by the Isaiah quotation. Isaiah 8:12b exhorts the people "to sanctify your Lord and this will be your fear" *(kyrion autōn hagiasate kai autos estai sou phobos).* First Peter adopts the first part of the phrase, retaining the verb "sanctify" *(hagiasate)* and the title "Lord" *(kyrion).* But now the quotation is applied to Jesus as "Lord," and the characteristic notion of sanctifying or reverencing "in your hearts" is

added (a later reading has "God" instead of "Christ," but the reference to "Christ" is the preferred reading). The wives of non-Christian husbands were encouraged to find their beauty in the "hidden person of the heart" (3:4). Likewise, all Christians are able to love one another "from the heart" once they have purified their lives through obedience to the truth (1:22). There is a parallel in the letter between the idea of interior purification and integrity on the part of the individual leading to a life of virtuous testimony and that of the community as a whole retaining its internal integrity and commitment while giving a corporate witness of hope to the world.

always ready for a testimony to anyone who asks you the reason for the hope that is in you: This is one of the most often quoted verses of the letter, and it eloquently states the fundamental mission of witness that the author encourages the community to accept. Even though faced with suffering from those who want to harm the community, the Christians are nevertheless to be always ready to give a "testimony" or defense of their hope to anyone who questions them. The word "testimony" translates the Greek term *apologia*, which can be used in a strictly legal sense as an "apologia" or "defense" of one's position (see, for example, Luke 12:11-12, where the disciples have to defend themselves before "rulers" or "authorities," or Acts 22:1 and 25:16 where Paul gives a more formal defense of his position). It is possible that 1 Peter is referring to instances in which Christians would be brought before magistrates to defend their beliefs and practices, as the Letters of Pliny described for this same general area of Asia Minor some years later. However, the word seems to be used here in a more general context (i.e., "to anyone who asks you") and therefore the translation "testimony" or giving an account of one's Christian faith seems more appropriate (see Achtemeier, *1 Peter* 234–35). The author beautifully characterizes Christian faith and practice as "the hope that is in you"; this is similar to the keynote statement of 1:3, which describes Christian existence as "a new birth into a living hope" (see also 1:21). The use of the term "hope" expresses the fundamental eschatological perspective of 1 Peter; while committed to living within the structures of the created world (2:13) and being prepared to give witness to those outside the community, the Christians are still "aliens" and "exiles" who look forward in hope to the fullness of life with God in the endtime. Achtemeier raises the question whether in referring to the hope that is "within you" the author is thinking primarily of the individual Christian's interior life or of the hope that characterizes the community as a whole. The latter is more probable, given the overall communitarian focus of the letter.

16. *but [do so] with gentleness and reverence, having a good conscience:* Here, too, the author's characteristic perspective is in evidence. The testimony to those who ask is to be given with "gentleness" *(meta prautētos)*, as was the case with the wives of non-Christian husbands who were urged to eschew the superficial beauty of rich clothing and jewelry for the "immortal quality of a gentle and peaceful spirit." As its use in this general exhortation makes clear, the author does not view gentleness simply as a customary social virtue for women, but as a characteristic Christian virtue that imitates Jesus himself in his comportment under duress. Similarly, the attitude of "reverence" (literally "fear" *[phobos]*) is

not a reaction of servile deference or fear of the one who challenges the Christian, but springs from the profound sense of awe and reverence one owes to God alone (2:17). This is the point of the next phrase: "having a good conscience" *(syneidēsin echontes agathēn)*. Although the word *syneidēsis* can mean "conscience" or moral awareness (as in Rom 2:15; 9:1; 1 Cor 10:29a; 2 Cor 1:12; 4:2; 5:11), 1 Peter uses the word in its more fundamental meaning of "awareness" or "consciousness." This was the case in 2:19, where he encourages the slaves to endure suffering while having "consciousness of God," and that same sense of the term seems to be at work here (see also 3:21). The Christians have a "good conscience" because they live with an interior awareness of God and God's protection of them that allows them to endure suffering and threat with serenity.

so that in the event you are slandered, those who mistreat you will be put to shame on account of your good way of life in Christ: As is the case throughout this section and the letter as a whole, the sufferings the Christians are likely to experience are those of "slander" or verbal abuse rather than physical harm (literally *katalalein,* to "speak against"). Those who assault the Christians in this way will ultimately be put to shame because of the Christians' "good way of life in Christ" (literally "your good *[hymōn tēn agathēn]* in Christ"). The phrase "in Christ" is more characteristic of Pauline theology, referring to the fundamental redeemed status of the Christian (see a similar use in 1 Pet 5:10, 14); here it has more of an adjectival quality, describing the life of virtue and good deeds expected of the Christian. The emphasis on "good conduct" is typical of 1 Peter and has been the leitmotif of this entire section of the letter. It is not clear how or when the nonbeliever will be shamed by the good way of life of the Christian. Does the author hope that such good example may have an immediate impact, as in the case of the husbands who will be "won over" by the virtuous conduct of their wives (3:1-2)? Or, as in 2:12, will such a conversion take place only on the Day of Judgment?

17. *For it is better to suffer, if that should be God's will, for doing good rather than for doing evil:* The concluding verse of this segment restates the thesis with which it began. Suffering because one has done something evil has no merit (see 2:20). But "if" or "when" one suffers (although the verb is in the optative form the letter presumes in fact that suffering is taking place) because of one's Christian way of life, that is a blessing (3:14). This also recapitulates the message of the quotation from Psalm 34 that concluded the previous section: God will protect those who do good, but will punish evildoers.

INTERPRETATION

Throughout this exhortation section of the letter (2:11–4:11) the author has presumed that discipleship exacts a cost. For particularly vulnerable members of the community such as the wives of non-Christian husbands (3:1-6) or slaves (2:18-25) it may bring open abuse. For all in the community it means the disciplined love needed for community living and the constant effort to witness to a life of integrity. This cost of discipleship now becomes the dominant concern in the latter half of the exhortation section (3:13–4:11).

The quotation from Psalm 34 that concluded the previous section (3:10-12) had summed up 1 Peter's exhortations in the basic contrast between "doing good" and "doing evil." The pursuit of good in the face of evil is where this new segment picks up the thread of the letter. Even though they live as if "in exile" and have to endure slander and may face even greater suffering in the near future, no ultimate harm or threat can penetrate the love and hope that are God's gift to the Christians. This confident assessment of ultimate protection in the face of suffering is reminiscent of Paul's confidence in Rom 8:35-39.

In pursuing good, Christians are not only confident that God will protect them from ultimate harm but they are, in fact, "blessed" to suffer in the cause of righteousness. The words paraphrase Jesus' beatitude in Matt 5:10: "Blessed are those who are persecuted for righteousness' sake, for theirs is the kingdom of heaven." The sufferings envisioned by the letter are those that are a direct consequence of the Christians' perseverance in doing good, maintaining their virtuous way of life even in the face of ridicule and challenge. As the author pointed out in the case of the wives and slaves, such suffering aligns them with the example of Jesus himself who, though innocent, suffered unjustly and in so doing redeemed humanity (2:21-23). The author will return to the example of the suffering Christ as the letter continues (see 3:18; 4:1).

In the midst of such suffering the Christians are not to live in fear of those who assault them (3:14); awe or reverential fear is owed to God alone (see also 2:17). Instead they are to live in a profound spirit of faith, "in their hearts" sanctifying Christ as Lord (3:15). Here and throughout the letter the author sees the interior life (i.e., "in their hearts"; also, in 3:4, the "hidden person of the heart") both of the individual Christian and by extension of the community as a whole as a place of peace and serenity that stands as a bulwark against fear and becomes the source for a radiant life of hope. That interior center is illumined by a "consciousness" of God and God's loving providence (3:16; see also 3:19) that quenches fear and restrains the impulse to render evil for evil.

Similarly, this interior centerpoint in the life of the Christian also leads to a responsibility for witness. In what may be the most frequently quoted verse of the letter the Christians are urged to be prepared to give a defense of the hope that is in them to anyone who asks (3:16). Practically every word in the verse is a distillation of 1 Peter's central message. "Hope" stands in 1 Peter for the entire attitude a Christian should have toward life. It is equivalent to what Paul calls "faith"; a radical trust in God that shapes one's entire consciousness. God's mercy is the basis for hope (1:3) and God's promise of salvation shapes the Christian expectation about the future (1:4). This sense of hope and the life of virtue to which it leads are what ultimately separate the Christians and their communal life from the worldview of their non-Christian neighbors and lead to their consternation.

To those who demand to know the reasons for such hope the Christians should be ready to make a "defense" or explanation. In fact, the entire letter is itself an explanation of the reasons for hope, rooting hope in God's act of salvation in Christ, relating it to the history of Israel, describing the way of life to which it leads, and assuring the Christians of an ultimate blessed future despite their experience of alienation and suffering (the author will describe the purpose of the letter as "encouragement" and "witness"; see 5:12). The exercise of this witness must be imbued with the same values that are intrinsic to a life of hope: namely with "gentleness," the compassionate concern and respect that typify the way a Christian relates to every human being as a creation of God (see 2:13-17; also the exhortation to wives in 3:4), and with "reverence," the attitude of reverential fear that 1 Peter has consistently used to describe one's relationship to God (1:17; 2:17, 3:2). Thus "reverence" or "fear" is not the attitude to be taken toward the non-Christian questioner—which would contradict the advice in the previous verse ("Do not fear their fear or be disturbed")—but toward God. In other words, in dealing gently with the questioner the Christian is bolstered by a sense of reverence and awe for God. Looking at the whole situation with the eyes of faith is what enables the Christians to have hope in the first place and that same vantage point impels them to give such witness to others.

The atmosphere of this passage and of the letter as a whole suggests that the encounter between the nonbeliever and the Christian envisioned here is not a dispassionate discussion but a more aggressive challenge to the Christian way of life mounted by the dominant majority that has little sympathy for these spiritual "aliens." This is clearly the implication of vv. 16 and 17, which continue the discussion of the disposition needed to mount such a witness of hope. The Christians are to have a "good conscience" (3:16), meaning here not simply freedom from awareness of moral guilt but, as the author uses this term elsewhere, having an "awareness" of God (see, for example 2:19; 3:21). Such awareness of God will maintain Christians in their good conduct and thereby not only help them to endure slander and mistreatment but, they may hope, will put the perpetrators of such slander to shame. Only a life thoroughly rooted "in Christ" is likely to withstand the pressure to conform.

The segment concludes as it began. Suffering abuse that is caused by wrong behavior on the Christian's part has nothing to recommend it. But suffering that results from the integrity and witness of an authentic Christian life is under the will of God and puts one in the footsteps of the Christ whose suffering brought life to the world.

FOR REFERENCE AND FURTHER STUDY

Hanson, Anthony T. "Salvation Proclaimed, I: 1 Peter 3:18-22," *ExpTim* 93 (1981–82) 100–112.

Michaels, J. Ramsey. "Eschatology in 1 Peter iii.17," *NTS* 13 (1966/67) 394–401.

Omanson, Roger. "Suffering for Righteousness' Sake (1 Pet 3:13–4:11)," *RevExp* 79 (1982) 439–50.

Reichert, Angelika. *Eine urchristliche praeparatio ad martyrium: Studien zur Komposition, Traditionsgeschichte und Theologie des 1. Petrusbriefes.* BBET 22. Frankfurt: Peter Lang, 1989.

Talbert, Charles H. "The Educational Value of Suffering in 1 Peter," in idem, *Learning Through Suffering: The Educational Value of Suffering in the New Testament and in Its Milieu.* Collegeville: The Liturgical Press, 1991.

13. *The Ascent and Exaltation of the Triumphant Christ* (3:18-22)

18. For Christ also suffered for sins once for all, the righteous for the sake of the unrighteous, in order that he might bring you to God, having been put to death in flesh but being made alive in spirit, 19. in which also having gone to those spirits in prison he announced 20. to those who had disobeyed formerly when the patience of God waited expectantly in the days of Noah, while the ark was being built, in which a few, that is, eight persons, were rescued through water, 21. and baptism, which is a representation of this, now saves you, not as a removal of dirt from the flesh, but as an appeal of a good consciousness to God, through the resurrection of Jesus Christ, 22. who has gone into heaven at the right hand of God, with angels and authorities and powers made subject to him.

NOTES

18. *For Christ also suffered for sins once for all, the righteous for the sake of the unrighteous:* The segment 3:18-21 is one of the most challenging passages in the letter, both from a linguistic and theological point of view. It begins with an affirmation of a fundamental New Testament doctrine about the redemptive and atoning power of the death of Christ, who, although "righteous" *(dikaios),* willingly suffered for the sins *(hamartiōn)* of the "unrighteous" *(adikōn).* The language appears to draw on the Old Testament image of the Suffering Servant

(see especially Isa 53:11, "The righteous one [LXX *dikaios,* as in 1 Pet 3:18a], my servant, shall make many righteous *(dikaiosai),* and he shall bear their iniquities [LXX *hamartia,* as in 1 Pet 3:18a]"). Earlier the author had anchored his exhortations to the slaves about enduring unjust suffering by an appeal to the example of Christ, whose unjust sufferings were not only exemplary but had redemptive power (2:21-23), and he will do the same here. Similar appeals will come in 4:1 and 4:13 (see also the references to Christ's redemptive blood in 1:2 and 1:19). Here in this passage the author will extend his reflection beyond Christ's sufferings to his resurrection, heavenly ascent, and exaltation at the right hand of God. While most New Testament formulations refer to Christ's "death" (e.g., Rom 5:6-8; 1 Cor 15:14-15; Gal 1:4; 2:21; 1 Thess 5:10; Heb 10:12; 1 John 2:2), 1 Peter uses its characteristic word "suffer" *(epathen);* as noted above (see 2:21), this word appears more often in 1 Peter than in any other New Testament book. Although a number of alternate readings revert to "died" *(apethanen),* "suffer" is to be preferred. The reason for the choice of word may be that by referring to Christ's "suffering" the author can more readily use the example of Christ to give meaning to the sufferings of his community. In any case, the formula "Christ suffered for sins . . ." surely includes the notion of his redemptive death (which is explicitly mentioned in the latter half of the verse).

The conjunction "for" *(hoti)* links this section to the previous exhortation about doing good and avoiding evil (see 3:13-17); Christ's sufferings are not only the model for how to bear unjust suffering but the dynamic power that enables the Christian to remain hopeful and serene in the midst of such suffering. The adverb "once for all" *(hapax)* underscores the traditional affirmation of the unique and decisive quality of Jesus' redemptive suffering (see, similarly, Heb 9:26, 28; Rom 6:9-10). This unique character of Jesus' redemptive suffering was affirmed at the beginning of the letter, where the author stated that the Christians were able to experience the sufferings and glory of Christ—something the prophets had anticipated and angels longed to contemplate (see 1:10-12).

in order that he might bring you to God: With this phrase the author states the ultimate redemptive purpose of Christ's sufferings and death and also begins to move his reflection in a cosmic direction, namely to the heavenly ascent of the Risen Christ. The purpose *(hina)* of Christ's death was to "bring you to God." The verb *prosagein* (used here in the aorist subjunctive) has the basic meaning of "leading someone" or, as here, bringing someone into another's presence. The verb is also used in the Septuagint in conjunction with bringing sacrifice to the sanctuary (see Exod 29:10; Lev 1:2; 8:24; Num 8:9-10) which suggests to some interpreters that 1 Peter intended such a cultic nuance here (see Dalton, *Christ's Proclamation to the Spirits* 135, who also refers to Hebrews). The reading "you" *(hymas)* is contested, with a number of other manuscripts preferring "us" *(hēmas),* but the author has used the second-person address throughout this section and that would seem to be the case here.

having been put to death in flesh but being made alive in spirit: This reference to the death and resurrection of Christ affirms a traditional conviction, but does so in a distinctive way (see 1 Cor 15:3-4; 1 Tim 3:16; in reference to the Christian see also Rom 8:10; 1 Cor 15:42-44). The structure is balanced and formulaic, suggesting to some commentators that it may be a quotation from an early hymn or credal statement (e.g., Beare, *First Epistle* 169; Kelly, *Epistles* 150–51; Selwyn, *First Epistle* 197). The phrase parallels two contrasting aorist passive participles ("having been put to death" *[thanatōtheis]* and "being made alive" *[zōopoiētheis]*), as well as two contrasting dative nouns ("in flesh" *[sarki]* and "in spirit" *[pneumati]*). The verb "put to death" clearly refers to the crucifixion of Jesus, and the passive form harmonizes with the idea of unjust suffering endured by Christ that has been emphasized in the letter. The verb *zōopoiein* is used to refer to the resurrection of Jesus or God's life-giving power in other New Testament texts (1 Cor 15:45; Rom 4:17; 8:11; 1 Tim 6:13), and its passive voice here refers to God's act in raising Jesus from the dead (already affirmed by the author in 1:3, 21). The contrast between "flesh" and "spirit" is not that between "body" and "soul" (i.e., Christ's body died but his spirit did not), nor simply that between moral dimensions of the human person (i.e., the flesh as corrupt and the spirit as divine or pristine). "Flesh" here refers to the inherent dimension of the human person that encompasses not only the physical reality of flesh and bone but also its limited and mortal nature (see 1 Pet 1:24; 4:1). "Spirit," by contrast, is that equally inherent dimension that touches upon the intelligent and transcendent aspects of the human person that can be responsive to grace. Paul uses these terms in a similar fashion in referring to Jesus himself (see Rom 1:4; 8:3-4) as well as to the dynamics of Christian life (e.g., Gal 3:3-5; 5:16-19; 6:8) and in his explanation of the resurrected body in 1 Cor 15:44. In other words, 1 Peter affirms that "in flesh," that is, in accord with his status as a mortal human being, Jesus experienced death (i.e, being put to death undeservedly). But "in spirit" he was raised from the dead by God, that is, in accord with the power of God that is uniquely related to Jesus and, by extension, with the capacity of the human being to be transformed by God's redemptive power. Paul Achtemeier argues that the dative case of these two nouns should be understood not as a dative of reference as suggested here, but in an instrumental sense; i.e., Jesus was put to death "by flesh" (i.e., unjustly by sinful human beings) but was raised to life "by the spirit" (i.e., by the power of God). This seems forced, however, since the term "flesh" is rarely used to refer to hostile human beings as such (he refers to 1:24 but in this instance, too, the point is the mortal nature of the human person).

19. *in which also having gone to those spirits in prison he announced:* This may be the most enigmatic sentence in the passage, but its interpretation is key to the meaning of the passage as a whole. The syntax is problematic, beginning with the question of how to determine the antecedent of the opening words, "in which" *(en hō)*. While it could refer in a narrow sense to the immediately preceding word "in spirit" *(pneumati)*, the more likely antecedent is the entire phrase, "being made alive in spirit." The sense of the phrase "in which" would be equivalent to "in the state of" or "in the condition of" having been raised from the dead; thus the activity about to be ascribed to Christ in this verse takes place *after* his resurrection.

What Christ did in this state is *"also"* to "have gone to those spirits in prison." The word *kai* ("also") is used here adverbially, implying that there are other activities the Risen Christ will do, namely his ascent to the right hand of God and the subjection of the cosmic powers (see 3:22). The enigmatic reference to the "spirits in prison" ushers in one of the most controverted passages in the letter. Several lines of intepretation have developed, depending on the identification of these "spirits," the nature and location of their "prison," and the decision about when this activity of Christ took place (i.e, before or after his resurrection).

It is useful to examine each of the elements of the verse before reviewing possible interpretations (see the Interpretation). The author asserts that while in his resurrected state (see discussion of v. 19a above) Christ began a journey: "having gone to the spirits in prison." The verb used is *poreutheis,* the aorist participle of the verb *poreuein,* meaning "go" or "travel"; the verb itself does not reveal the direction of the journey (i.e., neither "ascent" nor "descent"), although it is used in Acts 1:10-11 to describe the ascension of Jesus and in the Gospel of John to refer to the ascent of Jesus to God (John 14:2, 3, 28; 16:28). The end point of the journey is "those spirits in prison"; the word "spirits" is the dative plural of *pneuma* and has a broad range of meanings: i.e., "air," "wind," "life-breath" of the human body, or the spiritual dimension of the human person (see above, 3:18), noncorporeal beings such as good or evil spirits, or, finally, the divine Spirit (see BDAG 832–36). While some traditional interpretations have assumed that the "spirits" referred to in 3:19 are the spirits or "souls" of dead human beings, "spirit" *(pneuma)* is rarely used to refer to human beings (see Heb 12:23, "the spirits of the righteous made perfect," the only New Testament example; 1 Enoch also uses "spirit" in this sense but couples it with a qualifying phrase, e.g., 1 Enoch 22:3, "spirits of the souls of the dead"). Therefore the most likely reference is to some sort of noncorporeal beings such as angels or demons. In line with the Enoch traditions (see especially 1 Enoch 6–16; 18), 1 Peter may be thinking of the "sons of God" in Gen 6:1-4 who took human wives, or possibly the children of what the Bible considers this perverse union (Gen 6:4; see J. Ramsey Michaels, *1 Peter* 207). In any case these are likely to be evil spirits or quasi-spirits engendered by the fallen angels who are hostile to human beings, and whose ultimate defeat is part of the drama of the end-time.

These spirits are confined to some sort of "prison" *(phylakē),* but no hint is given of its location. The word "prison" is not used to refer to the Hades or the abode of the dead in any of the New Testament literature—a further argument against supposing these are human souls. The term is used elsewhere to refer to the abode of demons or a place of restraint for them (see Rev 18:2; 20:7; 1 Enoch 10:4; 14:5; 15:8, 10; 18:12-14; while not explicitly mentioning a "prison" 2 Pet 2:4 refers to God casting the demons into Hades and binding them with chains).

The finite verb in the sentence comes last: Christ "announced" *(ekēryxsen,* the aorist of the verb *kēryssein).* The basic meaning of the word is "proclaim" or make an official announcement or public declaration, often of victory. In the New Testament it is frequently used in a quasi-technical sense to describe the missionary preaching of the community, often coupled with the word "gospel" (e.g., Matt 24:14; Mark 1:14; 13:10; 14:9; Luke 8:1; Col 1:23; 1 Thess 2:9). Although normally followed by an object, it is sometimes used intransitively, as here (e.g., Mark 1:38, 45; 3:14; Luke 4:44; Rom 2:21; 10:15; 1 Cor 9:27; 15:11; see Achtemeier, *1 Peter* 262). Thus the translation "announced" or "proclaimed"; the content or tone of the announcement is not revealed in the word itself.

If we take the elements of this verse as a whole there is little explicit support for the traditional association of this passage with the "descent into hell" motif whereby Christ after his death, but prior to his resurrection, descended into the realm of the dead, thereby affirming the reality of his own death and also bringing redemption to the souls of the just who had been languishing in the nether world awaiting redemption. This concept is similar to 1 Pet 4:6, which refers to preaching even to the dead. The traditional motif of the descent into hell is first found in Justin's *Dialogue With Trypho* (72). Beginning with Irenaeus it would become a common motif in patristic writings and would find expression in the apostolic creed. However, 1 Pet 3:19 was not associated with this view until the end of the second century with Clement of Alexandria. There were various explanations for the precise identity of the "spirits" in prison, either referring generically to all the just dead, or to the generation of Noah, or to all the just prior to the time of Noah and the flood. A variant on this motif was proposed by Augustine (*Epistula ad Euodium* 164.14-18), who asserted that it was the pre-existent Christ who preached to the generation of Noah.

However, the text of 3:19 appears to place this activity of Christ *after* his resurrection yet *before* his exaltation at God's right hand (3:22), perhaps during his heavenly ascent. The "spirits" in prison are more likely to be evil spirits than the souls of dead human beings. And the nature of Christ's "announcement," while possibly salvific in intent, is not necessarily so.

The combination of these factors suggests that the most likely backdrop for understanding 3:19 is not the traditional descent into hell motif, but Jewish traditions about Enoch (see Gen 5:24; these are found especially in 1 Enoch) referring to the punishment of the fallen angels described in Gen 6:1-4 whose promiscuous union with daughters of humans earns them God's punishment. Their wickedness seems to lead directly to God's despair about the human race and the threat of the flood, thus connecting the story with Noah (see Gen 6:5-7). This connection is made directly in Enoch (see 1 Enoch 106:13; 2 Enoch 7:3). The fallen angels are confined to imprisonment in the heavenly realm, and they and their offspring will be finally condemned on the day of judgment. In 1 Peter, Christ's heavenly ascent begins with a visit to the realm in which these evil angelic spirits are imprisoned. The author does not locate this "prison" although a number of Jewish apocalyptic texts envisioned stages of ascent and located places where evil spirits abided even in the heavenly realm.

Christ's "announcement" to the evil spirits is most likely an announcement of his own victory over death and is meant as a further condemnation of or act of triumph over the forces of evil, fitting into the general context of the letter, in which the suffering Christians are assured of ultimate victory. The

author now extends the exemplary force and redemptive power of Christ beyond that of his suffering, death, and resurrection to his victorious ascent to
God and his ultimate triumph over all evil spirits and powers (3:22).

20. *to those who had disobeyed formerly when the patience of God waited expectantly in
the days of Noah, while the ark was being built:* The author now explicitly identifies the spirits in prison with "those who had disobeyed *(apeithesasin)* formerly" during "the days of Noah." As noted above (3:19), the most likely
suspects are the fallen angels of Gen 6:1-4 as described in the Enoch traditions,
or possibly their quasi-human offspring. Their wickedness ignited God's
anger and led to the flood. The verse quaintly describes the "patience of God
waiting expectantly" *(apexedecheto)*. While this word can have a positive connotation of waiting eagerly for a good outcome (e.g., all of creation awaiting
redemption in Rom 8:19); or with patience for God's salvation (1 Cor 1:7;
Rom 8:25), here God's forbearance seems to extend only to Noah and his clan
while the ark is being built; after that, God's punishment would be unleashed
(the exasperation of God is noted in Gen 6:3; see a similar thought in 2 Pet 2:5).

in which a few, that is, eight persons, were rescued through water: The author makes
the point that only a "few" were rescued—perhaps a subtle warning to the
readers that the way of salvation is narrow (the flood and Noah's rescue are
used for this type of moral example in Luke 17:27). The number is specified at
"eight," surely referring to the Bible's enumeration of Noah's family to include Noah and his wife, his three sons, Shem, Ham, Japheth, and their three
wives. These are explicitly mentioned as entering the ark to escape the flood
waters (see Gen 7:7; 1 Peter's phrase "into it," namely the ark, seems to allude
to this verse as well). These were "rescued," with the passive voice of the verb
signifying that God is the author of this rescue, "through water" *(di' hydatos)*.
The meaning of the preposition *dia* is somewhat ambiguous here; it can be
used in an instrumental sense ("by means of the water") or in a locative sense
("through the waters"). Obviously the author is setting up the parallel with the
waters of baptism that will follow in the next verse. In Noah's case the flood-
waters are an instrument of destruction yet, because of God's forbearance in
directing him to build the ark, Noah and his family are saved in the midst of the
waters. The author may intend to embrace both meanings of the preposition.

21. *and baptism, which is a representation of this, now saves you:* The author now
draws a parallel between the rescue of Noah and his family and the effect of
baptism for the Christians. This is the first and only time that "baptism" *(bap-
tisma)* is explicitly mentioned in the letter, although some interpreters have
suggested that the entire letter originated as a baptismal homily or reflection
(Introduction). However, the author's more fundamental concern in the letter
as a whole is with the sure hope of salvation that Christ's death and resurrection have given the Christian, and the consequent need for a life of virtue and
the responsibility of witness. The waters of baptism are an effective sign of
Christ's saving action and the purification and strength that result.

The syntax of the verse is hard to decipher. The opening neuter pronoun
"which" *(ho)* could refer either to the immediately preceding word "water" at

the end of v. 20 or, what is more likely, to the entire event previously described, namely the salvation of Noah and his family "through the flood." The Greek word *antitypon* ("representation," "type"), used somewhat awkwardly as a compound subject with baptism, is rare in the New Testament, found only here and in Heb 9:24, where the Temple is described as a "representation" *(antitypa)* of the heavenly sanctuary. In 1 Peter, however, the word could not imply that baptism is somehow inferior to the waters of the flood. Hence the word suggests that the ancient flood waters, which because of God's power became a means of salvation for Noah and his ark, are a prefigurement of the waters of baptism which *now (nyn)* actually "save" *(sōzei)* the Christians.

not as a removal of dirt from the flesh, but as an appeal of a good consciousness to God: Unlike Paul, who in Rom 6:3-4 reflects on the experience of baptism as immersion into the death, burial, and resurrection of Christ, the author of 1 Peter focuses on the renewal of "consciousness" transmitted through baptism that results from the effects of Christ's resurrection, ascension, and triumphant enthronement at the right hand of God (3:22). The author underscores that the experience of baptism is not an external cleansing, i.e., a "removal" or "putting off" *(apothesis)* of dirt from the "flesh." Here "flesh" *(sarx)* is used in its most physical sense (see above 3:18). The author's point seems to be to contrast external purification with an interior transformation, similar to earlier concerns in the letter (see the exhortation to wives in 3:1-4; also 1:22; William J. Dalton's suggestion that "removal of filth from the flesh" may refer to circumcision, based on the declaration in Lev 19:23 and Jer 4:1-4 that the foreskin is unclean, is not persuasive; see Dalton, *Christ's Proclamation* 199–206; also Kelly, *Epistles* 161–62; Achtemeier, *1 Peter* 269). The effect of baptism is an "appeal of a good consciousness to God," a phrase with some ambiguity. The noun "appeal" *(eperōtēma)* is used only here in the New Testament. The verb form *eperōtaō* ("ask," "appeal") is much more frequent and may guide the meaning of the noun in this instance. In non-Christian literature the verb is also used in legal, contractual contexts meaning "to pledge" (see Achtemeier, who argues for this meaning, *1 Peter* 270–72; also Elliott, *1 Peter* 679–80). Also difficult to determine is the connection to "good consciousness to God" *(syneidēseōs agathēs . . . eis theon)*. As discussed above, 1 Peter uses the term *syneidēsis* in its literal sense of "consciousness" or "awareness" (see above, 3:16). The "good consciousness" is directed "to God"; this is consistent with the overall theology of the letter that Christians should maintain the discipline of good conduct and interior purity in order to be mindful of God, who alone is worthy of reverence. Less clear is the connection between the word "appeal" and "good consciousness"; if the genitive case of *syneidēseōs* is understood as a subjective genitive, then the meaning would be that baptism results in effective prayer, that is, the appeal or persuasiveness to God of a good consciousness. If, what is more likely, the genitive is an objective genitive, then the effect of baptism is the Christian's appeal (in this instance the connotation of "pledge" would also make sense) for a good consciousness directed to God. In other words, the effect of baptism (equivalent to salvation) is not simply an external cleansing but the powerful and effective appeal to God to transform the Christian's consciousness, similar to the notion of rebirth found in the opening lines of the letter (1:3-5).

through the resurrection of Jesus Christ, 22. who has gone into heaven at the right hand of God, with angels and authorities and powers made subject to him: With this concluding verse the author opens up the full vista of Christ's triumph over death as the ultimate source of the Christian's transformation into a new consciousness. The saving power of baptism is effected "through the resurrection of Jesus Christ," who has also "gone into heaven at the right hand of God." The passive participle *poreutheis* ("having gone") repeats the reference to Christ's heavenly journey initiated in v. 19, which began with the risen Christ's visit to the evil spirits in their prison. Now that journey carries Christ "to the right hand of God," a traditional affirmation of the triumphant exaltation of Christ derived from Ps 110:1, "The Lord says to my lord, 'Sit at my right hand until I make your enemies your footstool'" (Matt 22:44 [par.]; 26:64; Acts 2:33-34; 5:31; 7:55-56 [standing at the right hand of God"]; Rom 8:34; Col 3:1; Heb 1:13; 8:1; 10:12; 12:2). Christ's triumphant ascent to God and his exaltation at the right hand of God also result in the subjection of "angels and authorities and powers to him." The verb *hypotassō* (here as a perfect passive participle: "been made subject to") was used earlier in the letter to describe the required subjection of all the community to proper human authority (2:13), and specifically of slaves to their masters (2:18) and wives to their husbands (3:1). In the triumphant context of 3:22 the note of subjugation is more apparent; the Risen and Exalted Christ had already "announced" his victory to the imprisoned evil spirits (3:19), and now the entire spirit world is made subject to him. The description of these spirits as "angels *(angelōn),*" "authorities" *(exousiōn),* and "powers" *(dynameōn)* is traditional and has echoes in the Pauline literature (see a similar listing in Rom 8:38: "neither angels *[angeloi]* nor rulers *[archai]* . . . nor powers *[dynameis]*"; also 1 Cor 15:24, "every ruler *[archēn],* authority *[exousian]* and power *[dynamin]*"). Since Christ subjugates them, one should assume that these are hostile spirits who are also threatening to human beings (similar to Paul's thought in 1 Cor 15:24-25, where the spirits are called "enemies"). Thus Christ's victory over the powers of death is now complete, and the sure foundation for Christian hope and fearlessness is definitely established.

INTERPRETATION

As was the case twice before in the letter, an exhortation to Christian good conduct and witness is followed by a reflection on the redemptive sufferings of Christ (see 1:18-21; 2:22-25). Virtually all commentators note that this is one of the most difficult passages in the letter, both grammatically and theologically. Yet the overall thrust of the passage is clear. Christ's suffering, death, and resurrection are not only exemplary for Christian conduct in the world, but provide the effective power to be able to lead this way of life with confidence. In this segment, which is part of the major exhortation section that began in 2:11 and will conclude in 4:11, the author extends his reflections on the drama of Christ's redemption beyond his resurrection to his heavenly ascent to God, his triumphant enthronement at God's right hand, and the final subjugation of the hostile spirits of the cosmos. This definitive victory of Christ is the ultimate basis for Christian hope.

More immediately, this segment is linked to 3:13-17, which began and concluded with the letter's characteristic emphasis on good conduct and urged that Christians be ready, when challenged, to give an account of the hope that is in them (3:15). Even if they are slandered and so suffer unjustly for their faith, they should remain steadfast in doing good (3:17) and be assured that no radical harm can befall them (3:13). Awareness that maintaining Christian integrity may still be costly leads the author to turn to the example of Christ's death and resurrection (see the causal link, "for," at the beginning of 3:18).

The passage begins by citing the example of Christ's innocent redemptive suffering, "the righteous for the sake of the unrighteous" (3:18; see also 3:14; note the similarity to the saying of Jesus in Matt 5:10, which blesses those who suffer "for the sake of righteousness" [*dikaiosynē*]). The author evokes the image of the Suffering Servant of Isaiah 53, a tradition exploited elsewhere in the New Testament (on this motif in 1 Peter and the New Testament see the discussion in Elliott, *1 Peter* 543–50). Throughout this passage 1 Peter affirms fundamental New Testament traditions about the death, resurrection, ascension, and exaltation of Christ but does so in terms that are not identical with Pauline or other formulations. This suggests that the author draws on a common fund of early Christian tradition but does not hesitate to adapt language that fits the rhetorical purpose of the letter. Here, for example, the expression "Christ also *suffered* for sins" instead of the more common "*died* for sins" fits the letter's exhortative purpose. The Christians who may suffer unjustly because of their virtuous lives can look to the example of the suffering Christ, whose own innocent sufferings were hardly in vain.

Yet in citing Christ's sufferings the author intends more than simply lifting up the example of Christ; he is also intent on affirming the basis on which all Christian hope and even the ability to lead a life of integrity stand. Christ's sufferings are not simply one example of virtuous suffering among many; his suffering was "for sins" (*peri hamartiōn*) and was definitive—that is, "once" (*hapax*; similar to Rom 6:10, "The death [Christ] died, he died to sin [*tē hamartia*] once [*ephapax*]"). As the author says directly to the readers of the letter: the ultimate intent of Christ's suffering (which includes the reality of his death) was "to bring you to God" (3:18). The journey to God that Christ undertakes reveals the triumph of God over the cosmic powers of death and is the reason why no one can truly "harm" the Christian (3:13). The notion of Christ leading Christians on a heavenly journey to God has echoes in other New Testament traditions (see, for example, Heb 12:1-2, although the author portrays Jesus as entering the heavenly sanctuary as the eternal high priest, a conception absent from 1 Peter; the Gospel of John, which frequently refers to Jesus' death and resurrection as an ascent to God, also speaks of Jesus as returning to God in order to prepare a place for the disciples; see John 14:1-7).

Christ experiences the full brunt of mortality, being "put to death in flesh"; thus his sufferings, like those facing the Christians, were genuine and threatening. Yet, through the power of God, Christ was "made alive in spirit." The resurrection of Christ is, therefore, also exemplary, demonstrating that Christians are no longer trapped within the bounds of mortality imposed by the "flesh" but also, through the power of God, can live fully in the "spirit" (3:18). Here the author's description of the death and resurrection of Christ are similar but not identical to Paul's reflections on the transformation that will be experienced by the Christian at the resurrection of the dead (see 1 Cor 15:35-57). In 1 Cor 15:44 Paul contrasts the "physical body" *(sōma psychikon)* with the "spiritual body" *(sōma pneumatikon)*; in 15:54 "this perishable [body] *(to phtharton touto)*" will put on "imperishability" *(aphtharsian)*, and "this mortal [body]" *(to thnēton touto)* will put on "immortality" *(athanasian)*. The realms of "flesh" and "spirit" cannot be reduced to the distinction between "body" and "spirit" or "soul." "In the flesh" refers to the physical, mortal, and inherently limited dimensions of Christ's humanity signified in his experience of death. "In the spirit," by contrast, refers to "that state of Christ's existence most demonstrably controlled and animated by God's life-giving Spirit" (Elliott, *1 Peter* 647).

Tracking how the author conceives of Christ's journey to God is the major challenge of this passage. The translation of v. 19 explained in the notes favors the interpretation that the journey takes place *after* Christ's resurrection. The opening phrase of the verse, "in which," refers not simply to the immediately preceding word (v. 18, "in spirit") but to the entire preceding phrase that describes the newly resurrected state of Jesus ("being made alive in spirit"). In the course of this ascent or journey Christ went to "the spirits in prison." This enigmatic reference has often been understood as part of the traditional motif of Christ's descent into hell or Hades during the time between his death and his resurrection, whereby the full reality of Christ's death is affirmed and, at the same time, the salvific victory over death that comes with the resurrection is anticipated. However, the text of 1 Peter offers scant ground for this interpretation. The verb "having gone" describes neither a descent nor an ascent, although the verb *poreuein* is used elsewhere in the New Testament to refer to the ascent of Jesus to God (see Acts 1:10-11; John 14:2, 3, 28; 16:28). As J. Ramsey Michaels notes, the "location of [the spirits'] strongholds, and hence the geography of Christ's mission to them, is not Peter's main concern" (p. 210). Similarly, the word "spirit" *(pneuma)* is rarely used of dead human beings (in the New Testament only in Heb 12:23), but often refers to noncorporeal beings, whether good or evil. The term "prison" is not used in the New Testament as a metaphor for Hades or the abode of the dead but in some instances does refer to a place of restraint or confinement for evil spirits. Finally, the main verb of the verse, "[Christ] announced" (the aorist of the verb *kēryssein*, "announce" or "proclaim") is often used to refer to early Christian missionary proclamation and has a connotation of an announcement of victory. If the "spirits" are in fact evil spirits, then the tenor of Christ's announcement is not a benign message offering liberation from death to just souls languishing in Hades, but a triumphant announcement of victory over the forces of death and evil hurled at hostile spirits.

As noted above, many recent commentators suggest that 1 Peter may have been drawing on Jewish traditions about Enoch and his revelations about the fate of the fallen angels inspired by the story in Gen 6:1-4. The "spirits" 1 Peter refers to are, therefore, not the souls of dead humans from the generation of Noah (v. 20), but most likely either the fallen angels whose promiscuity with daughters of the earth was condemned by God, or the children of these supernatural beings who themselves partake of the nature of evil spirits. Therefore, these are evil spirits connected with the history of Noah and the flood yet still lurking in the universe and needing to be restrained. As Michaels and others have pointed out, the connotation of evil spirits for a first-century audience would be a threatening one, that is, beings who were capable of tormenting humans with suffering and illness and, in some mysterious way, having the power to influence human fate (Michaels, "Eschatology," 206–209).

The sense of this passage in 1 Peter begins to emerge. The redemptive death of Jesus and his triumphant resurrection find their full expression in his ascent to God and his enthronement at God's right hand (3:22). This triumph of Christ has profound consequences for the destiny of the Christians. Christ's example as he endures unjust suffering shows the way for the Christians, who also must endure unjust suffering. More fundamentally, Christ's triumph over death through the power of God redeems the Christians from the power of evil and death and gives them a new birth and a fundamental reason for hope. Because Christ's triumph is complete, culminating in the defeat and subjugation of all threatening forces of the cosmos, the Christians can live with the assurance that no ultimate harm can befall them. As 3:19 asserts, this triumph of Christ over the powers of evil begins immediately following his resurrection; while yet on his way to God—a path the Christians will also follow—Christ announces his victory to the evil spirits who are restrained in their prison.

Baptism is the means through which the Christian experiences this overwhelming redemptive power of Christ. The author leads into his reflection on baptism by a series of links with his description of the Risen Christ's visit to the spirits in prison. Whatever their precise identity—whether the fallen angels of Gen 6:1-4 or their offspring—these spirits are connected to the time of Noah (3:20). As the text of Genesis 6 implies and the Enoch traditions would amplify, immediately after the story of the heavenly beings mingling with the daughters of the earth and impregnating them God regrets having created humans because of their wickedness and decides to destroy them with the flood (Gen 6:5-7). Only a "few," that is, eight members—Noah and his family—are to be spared because Noah "found favor in the sight of the Lord" (Gen 6:8; the members of Noah's family are enumerated in Gen 7:13). Thus God's punishment falls on those "who formerly had disobeyed" (1 Pet 3:20; see also the same link in 2 Pet 2:4-5; 3:5-6). "The patience of God," which the Genesis story portrays as exasperated by the prevalence of evil, "waits expectantly" only to allow time for the ark to be built (3:20). Safe in the ark, Noah and his family "were rescued *through water*." First Peter's use of the instrumental dative (the more probable reading; see the Notes)—"through" the water —is somewhat awkward in that the flood waters are the instrument of God's wrath. But, as the Genesis story also notes, the waters bear up Noah and his family (safe in the ark) and lift them high above the earth (Gen 7:17-18). For the obedient Noah the waters become a means of rescue— providing the basis for the author's comparison with baptism, which is a "representation" of this ancient story of rescue through water (*antitypon*; 3:21).

Baptism "saves" the Christian not by cleansing dirt from the flesh but as "an appeal of a good consciousness to God" (3:21). While the literally translated words may be somewhat awkward in English, the thought is consistent with the theology of 1 Peter. The experience of baptism is salvific because through the waters of baptism the Christian experiences the redemptive power of Christ's death, resurrection, and triumphant exaltation. As a consequence of baptism the Christian is endowed with the effective "appeal" of a sound or good "consciousness" (*syneidēsis*) directed to God. Transformed by the redemptive power of Christ in baptism, the interior life of the Christian is purified and illumined, becoming conscious of God and directing the full attention of one's life and thought to the divine presence. This emphasis on a profound interior disposition that enables the Christian to endure external threat and suffering is characteristic of 1 Peter. The author had urged his readers to "gird up the loins of your minds" and to be "self-controlled," with their hopes set entirely on God's grace (1:13); they were to "purify" their lives through "obedience to the truth" (1:22); the slaves were urged to maintain "consciousness" (*syneidēsis*) of God, even when enduring unjust suffering (2:19); wives married to non-Christian husbands were to adorn themselves with "the hidden person of the heart" (3:4); husbands should live together with their wives "with awareness" of God (3:7); and the entire community was urged not to give way to fear but to sanctify Christ "in your hearts" and to have a "good consciousness" (3:15).

The saving effect of baptism enables the Christian to experience this interior purification and alert spiritual consciousness of God. This is the kind of rebirth that effectively "appeals" to God, giving reason for hope and assurance of God's protection from ultimate harm. The noun *eperōtēma* is used in some non-Christian literature in a legal sense of "pledge." If the word carries that meaning here, it would imply that in the inaugural experience of baptism the Christian makes the "pledge" to live with a good consciousness directed to God. Because 1 Peter speaks of baptism as "saving" the Christian, it seems preferable to see baptism as not simply the occasion for a formal "pledge" on the part of the new Christian but an interior transformation that enables the Christian to now be equipped with a "good consciousness [directed] to God."

The final verse of the passage reaffirms the basis for the salvation lavished on the Christian (3:22). All of this takes place "through the resurrection of Jesus Christ," who in his triumph over death goes into heaven to be "at the right hand of God," with the supernatural spirits made subject to him. As discussed in the Notes, the author uses traditional formulations to lay out the full span of Christ's triumph over death—from resurrection through exaltation at the right hand of God. The author's purpose is not simply theological but soteriological: through his triumph Christ is able to finally defeat the cosmic spirits who threaten the created world. This is the reason the Christians have nothing to fear (3:13) and why they can summon up the moral courage to endure slander and suffering, while also giving a testimony of vigorous hope.

The final verse of the passage (3:22) forms an inclusion with 3:18; the purpose of Christ's sufferings for sin (and by implication the resurrection and triumph to which his sufferings lead) was to bring the Christians to God. Christ himself leads the way on that heavenly journey, boldly proclaiming victory to the evil spirits restrained in their prison and finally subjugating all the cosmic powers that threaten the universe.

FOR REFERENCE AND FURTHER STUDY

Bauckham, Richard J. "Spirits in Prison," *ABD* 6:177–78.

Cook, J. D. "I Peter iii.20: An Unnecessary Problem," *JTS* 31 (1980) 72–78.

Dalton, William J. "The Interpretation of 1 Peter 3,19 and 4,6: Light from 2 Peter," *Bib* 60 (1979) 547–55.

_____. *Christ's Proclamation to the Spirits: A Study of I Peter 3:18-4:6.* AnBib 23. 2nd rev. ed. Rome: Pontifical Biblical Institute, 1989.

Feinberg, John. "1 Peter 3:18-20, Ancient Mythology, and the Intermediate State," *WTJ* 48 (1986) 303–36.

Grudem, Wayne A. "Christ Preaching through Noah: 1 Peter 3:19-20 in the Light of Dominant Themes in Jewish Literature," *Trinity Journal* 7 (1986) 89–96.

Hanson, Anthony T. "Salvation Proclaimed: I. 1 Peter 3:18-22," *ExpTim* 93 (1982) 100–115.

Hill, David. "On Suffering and Baptism in 1 Peter," *NovT* 18 (1976) 181–89.

Klumbies, Paul-Gerhard. "Die Verkündigung unter Geistern und Toten nach 1 Petr 3,19f und 4,6," *ZNW* 92 (2001) 207–28.

Ostmeyer, Karl-Heinrich. *Taufe und Typos. Elemente und Theologie der Tauftypologien in 1. Korinther 10 und 1. Petrus 3.* WUNT 2. Tübingen: J.C.B. Mohr (Paul Siebeck), 2000.

Unnik, W. C. van "Le role de Noé dans les épîtres de Pierre," *Noé, L'homme universel.* Colloque de Louvain 1978. Brussels: Institutum Judaicum Bruxelles 3 (1979) 207–39.

14. *Living by the Will of God* (4:1-6)

1. Christ, therefore, having suffered in the flesh, you also arm yourselves with the same way of thinking, for the one who suffers in the flesh has ceased from sin, 2. so as to live in the flesh in the time remaining no longer according to human cravings but by the will of God. 3. For enough of the time past [has been given over to] accomplishing the will of the gentiles, living in a lack of self-control, cravings, drunkenness, revelry, drunken orgies and disgusting idolatry. 4. In this they are astonished that you do not run with them in this flood of dissipation, [and so] they blaspheme. 5. They will have to give an account to the one who is ready to judge the living and the dead. 6. For to this purpose the good news was proclaimed even to the dead, in order that having been judged in the flesh according to humans, they might live in the spirit according to God.

NOTES

1. *Christ, therefore, having suffered in the flesh:* This segment resumes the motif of Christ's exemplary and efficacious sufferings found in the previous section (3:17-22, especially 3:18). Having affirmed the ultimate triumph of Christ over the threatening spirits, the author now exhorts the recipients of the letter to conform their manner of life and their perspective to those of Christ. The conjunction "therefore" provides the transition. The author refers to Christ

"having suffered," using his favored term *pathontos* to describe Christ's Passion and death (see 2:21, 23; 3:18; 5:1 [*pathēmatōn*]), a word also used for the innocent sufferings endured by the Christians (2:19, 20; 3:14, 17; 4:15, 19; 5:10). Some variants substitute the verb *apothanontos* ("died"), which may be an attempt to align the phrase with more traditional language referring to Christ's redemptive death, but "suffering" is the preferred reading (as in 3:18), enabling the author to link the sufferings of the community to those of Christ, a major concern of 1 Peter. (Note that some manuscripts also add the phrase "for us" [*hyper hēmōn*], also an attempt to conform the description of Christ's death to traditional formulae.) The author states that Christ suffered "in the flesh" (*en sarki*), underscoring the human context of his sufferings and reprising the affirmation of 3:18 ("having been put to death in the flesh").

you also arm yourselves with the same way of thinking: The Christians are to live in the pattern of the suffering Christ ("you also . . ."). The author uses a stock military metaphor ("arm yourselves"), found in other exhortatory passages in the New Testament and in Greco-Roman and Jewish literature (see, for example, 1 Thess 5:8; 2 Cor 6:7; Rom 13:12-14; Eph 6:11-17). The Christians are to equip themselves with "the same way of thinking"; the word used here is *ennoia*, which derives from the root word for mind or thought (*nous*) and has the connotation that the Christians are to take on the same pattern of thought or perspective as that of Christ.

for the one who suffers in the flesh has ceased from sin: The precise meaning of this passage is difficult to determine. First of all, the phrase introduced by the conjunction *hoti* could be understood in a causal sense, "because," i.e., supplying the reason why the Christians should take on Christ's way of thinking. Or as this translation implies, the conjunction could have an "explanatory" meaning ("for"); i.e., the phrase that follows explains or teases out in a quasi-parenthetical manner the rationale implicit in the exhortation to take on Christ's way of thinking.

Equally challenging is determining the subject and precise meaning of the statement, "the one who suffers in the flesh has ceased from sin." Does "one" refer to Christ? Or to the Christians? Or is this a kind of proverbial statement referring generically to those who suffer? Although Judaism and Stoic philosophy spoke aphoristically of the purifying effects of suffering of the innocent or righteous person, it seems unlikely that 1 Peter would turn to such generic wisdom in a letter that makes constant reference to the efficacious suffering of Christ and of Christians (Elliott, *1 Peter* 715, maintains that it is a generic observation but that the author already has in mind the specific application to Christian suffering stated in vv. 2-3).

If the subject is Christ, a problem arises in understanding how he could have "ceased from" sin since 1 Peter, along with the entire New Testament, understands Christ as sinless (see 1:19; 3:18). Some interpreters who identify the subject as the Christian point to the similarity of this verse with Rom 6:7 ("whoever has died is freed from sin"), where Paul speaks of baptism as immersion in the death of Christ (see Rom 6:1-11). However, the link between these two passages is tenuous. Paul's phrase speaks of "dying" whereas

1 Peter refers to "suffering," and there is no hint that 1 Peter is referring to baptism here. The concern evident in 1 Peter is how the Christians are to endure innocent suffering caused by harassment on the part of the dominant culture (see 4:3-4; see also 2:12; 2:20-24; 3:16-18).

Perhaps the most persuasive interpretation sees the subject of the phrase as the Christian. The sense is not the same as Rom 6:7, where Paul refers to the salvific effect of Christ's death experienced in baptism. For 1 Peter the sufferings involved are the harassment and persecution the Christians are experiencing from the surrounding culture. The letter parenthetically states why it is efficacious for the Christian to take on the mindset of Christ, who endured suffering and thereby overcame the hostile spirits and now reigns triumphantly at God's right hand (3:18-22). By taking on Christ's "way of thinking" the Christian who "suffers in the flesh" is also empowered by Christ to be free from the tyranny of sin. This thought will be further illustrated in the verses that follow; namely, in putting aside the futile ways of their contemporaries the Christians are prepared for God's judgment and the life in the spirit it promises (4:6).

2. *so as to live in the flesh in the time remaining no longer according to human desires but by the will of God:* The author now begins to spell out what "ceasing from sin" and taking on Christ's "way of thinking" mean on an ethical level. The time remaining between now and the final judgment is relatively short (see also 1:6; 4:7, 17; 5:10), adding urgency to the need to lead their human lives (i.e., "living in the flesh") according to "God's will" (see also, 3:17; 4:19) rather than by "human cravings" *(anthrōpōn epithymiais).* The English translation "cravings" catches the connotation of the word *epithymia* ("desire") in this context. Although the word can be used in a neutral or positive sense of desiring something legitimate or good, it was often used in ethical contexts in both Greco-Roman and other New Testament literature to refer to crude, inordinate cravings or to unbridled sexual desire (see BDAG 372). First Peter used the term earlier to refer to "desires of the flesh that wage war against your very lives" (2:11).

3. *For enough of the time past [has been given over to] accomplishing the will of the gentiles, living in a lack of self-control, cravings, drunkenness, revelry, drunken orgies and disgusting idolatry:* The author refers again to the conversion of life that has been experienced by the Christians. With a trace of irony the author notes that since time is short (v. 2), "enough" of it has been given to achieving the "will of the gentiles" *(to boulēma tōn ethnōn),* i.e., doing what gentiles choose to do. While the author uses the term "nations" or "gentiles," the letter does not seem to refer to the distinction between Jews and gentiles here. More likely he is once again appropriating traditional biblical terms that viewed the mores of gentiles or nonbelievers as corrupt (see also 2:12).

The list of vices that follows enumerates some of these typical corruptions that characterize the gentile way of life *(peporeumenous,* literally the way they "conduct themselves" or "live"). The specific categories of vice echo similar citations in other New Testament texts: "lack of self-control" *(aselgeia)* implies conduct that goes against all morality and acceptable social behavior (see also

Eph 4:19; 2 Pet 2:2; Rom 13:13; 2 Cor 12:21; Gal 5:19; Mark 7:22); "cravings" *(epithymia)*, here as in v. 2 referring to base desires or cravings and probably to sexual lust (see, for example, Rom 7:7; Gal 5:24; 1 Thess 4:5; Col 3:5; 1 Tim 6:9; 2 Tim 2:22; Jas 1:14-15); "drunkenness" *(oinophlygia)*, literally one who is sotted with wine; "revelry" *(kōmos):* originally derived from a festival of Dionysus, the word generally refers to excessive feasting or carousing (see also Rom 13:13; Gal 5:21); "drunken orgies" *(potoi)*, literally drinking parties; "and disgusting idolatry" *(kai athemitois eidōlolatriais):* different from the other categories that imply physical excesses of lust and drinking, this is a more sweeping indictment. Judaism generally condemned pagan religious practices as "idolatry"; here 1 Peter adds the term "disgusting" or "unseemly" *(athemitos)*, implying that in their ritual practices the Gentiles performed immoral or even illegal acts.

4. *In this they are astonished that you do not run with them in this flood of dissipation, [and so] they blaspheme:* The "this" referred to is the fact that the Christians no longer indulge in the kind of life described here (i.e., they have "ceased from sin," vv. 1-2), namely "run(ning) with them in this flood of dissipation" *(tēs asōtias anachysin,* literally this flood or stream of that which is the opposite of salvation or preservation *[sōtia];* see also Eph 5:18; Titus 1:6). The non-Christians are "astonished" *(xenizontai)* at this turn of events; the verb used here derives from the root *xenos*, which means "strange" or "foreign" and thus implies that their "astonishment" is in the form of estrangement or incipient hostility. The author emphasizes again that the cause of such alienation is the fact that the Christians no longer indulge in the immoral lifestyle they had previously shared with their non-Christian contemporaries. This leads the non-Christians to "blaspheme." Because the non-Christians are hostile precisely because of the Christlike way of life that the community now adheres to (see also 2:12), their hostility is a form of "blasphemy" and will lead to God's judgment against them, as the following verse states.

5. *They will have to give an account to the one who is ready to judge the living and the dead:* The verb *apodōsousin* ("yield," "fulfill") coupled with the object *logon* (here "account") implies an obligation that will have to be fulfilled. The "one" who will judge the "living and the dead" could be Christ, but more frequently in 1 Peter the role of judge is assigned to God (see 1:17; 2:23; 4:17-19; 5:10).

6. *For to this purpose the good news was proclaimed even to the dead:* This verse, too, offers some challenging ambiguities. The referent of the opening phrase, "for to this purpose" *(eis touto gar)* is most likely the transformation the Christians have experienced in leaving behind their former way of life (i.e., "ceasing from sin," v. 1; living "by the will of God," v. 2). The sense is that the proclamation of the good news is for the purpose of such transformation, a transformation that will also stand them in good stead on the day of judgment. The aorist passive verb *euēggelisthē* ("the gospel was proclaimed") has no express subject and could be understood in an impersonal sense, i.e., "the gospel was proclaimed to the dead" although there are few if any instances of an impersonal subject with a passive verb in the New Testament (see Kelly, *Epistles* 172–76, who has an excellent discussion of this passage). Or one could assume

that the implicit subject is Christ, i.e., "Christ was proclaimed to the dead." The most likely referent is Christian preaching: i.e., Christ was proclaimed by Christians.

But a further complication is that this aorist verb refers to a specific past activity whose object was "the dead." Here, too, there has been a great deal of speculation about what "dead" are being referred to. One classical view related this verse to 3:19, assuming that in both instances 1 Peter is citing the tradition of Christ's descent into hell to save the souls of the just imprisoned there. However, there are substantial differences between 3:19 and 4:6. In 3:19 Christ "announces" *(ekēryxen)* to the "spirits" (not the "dead") who are "in prison." As noted above (see 3:19), this is not the descent into Hades motif but refers to Christ's triumphant confrontation with the hostile spirits and is part of 1 Peter's description of the ultimate victory of Christ over the hostile powers of the universe (see 3:22). In 4:6, by contrast, the text refers to Christian preaching of the gospel to the dead *(nekrois)*.

Some have suggested that "the dead" refers to those who are "spiritually" dead, thus smoothing the way to understanding how the "dead" can be preached to. However, giving a metaphorical sense to the term "dead" is not persuasive in view of the fact that in both 4:5 ("the living and the dead") and in 4:6b ("judged in the flesh") actual human death is assumed.

The most coherent explanation is that "the dead" in this context refers to those Christians who heard and accepted the gospel yet subsequently died. Concern about the fate of those who died prior to the triumphant return of Christ was a pastoral problem for early Christianity (Paul addresses this issue in 1 Thess 4:13-18; see the discussion in Achtemeier, *1 Peter* 288–91; Elliott, *1 Peter* 733–34).

in order that having been judged in the flesh according to humans, they might live in the spirit according to God: The final segment of the passage helps clarify its overall meaning. The Christians' concern about the fate of community members who had died is exacerbated by the fact that their experience of death is an implicit "judgment" or condemnation of them, despite their acceptance of the gospel. They are thus "judged in the flesh according to humans"; more than likely this reflects some of the hostile derision nonbelievers had directed at the community. If Christ saved them, why did such believers experience death like everyone else? (This might also be the point of 3:15, where the author exhorted the Christians to be prepared to give a testimony to those who ask about the reason "for the hope that is in [them]").

This final segment has a clear parallel structure that contrasts judgment in the flesh with life in the spirit and human standards with divine standards. Convinced of the ultimate triumph of Christ over death and the future inheritance of eternal life by the Christians who believe in the gospel, the author affirms that although in the human realm *(kata anthrōpous)* the dead have been "judged in the flesh," according to the divine realm *(kata theon)* they "live in the spirit." Thus the Christians—including those already dead—participate in the triumph of Christ over death that the author had described in the preceding passage (3:18-22).

INTERPRETATION

This section of the letter builds on the immediately preceding reflection on the redemptive work of Christ (see 3:18-22), but now turns to its implications for the life of virtue the Christians must lead. The following segment (4:7-11) will extend the author's moral exhortations to the quality of life that should characterize the Christian community as a whole, bringing to a close the main body of the letter that began in 2:11.

As was the case earlier in the letter, the author grounds his exhortations on the example of the suffering Christ (4:1; see 2:21-25; 3:17-18). Christ's "suffering in the flesh," that is, the innocent suffering he had to endure for the sake of others (3:18), entailed a self-transcendence that is the very opposite of sin. That suffering was redemptive; though put to death in the flesh, Christ was made alive in the spirit (3:18). The Christians are to arm themselves with the same "way of thinking" (4:1). Transformed by grace, they, too, although "suffer(ing) in the flesh," have "ceased from sin" (4:1).

This section emphasizes the transformed life Christians must now lead, a life that distinguishes them from their non-Christian contemporaries. Leading such a manner of life different from the dominant culture will itself be a cause of alienation and suffering for the community. Conscious that the end of time may be near, the author emphasizes that the time remaining must be dedicated to living in accord with God's will (4:2). Somewhat wryly the author notes that enough time has already been given over to leading the kind of squandered life that the "Gentiles"—i.e., the non-Christians—lead, a way of life in which those who are now Christians once participated (4:3). That life is described in its worst light as characterized by cravings that are not in accord with God's will and unbridled sensuality and indulgence (4:3). Even the religious practices of the non-Christians are branded as "disgusting idolatry," implying that their rituals involve illicit and immoral behavior.

As the author graphically states, refusing to go along with this "flood of dissipation" is shocking to the dominant culture and provokes hostility toward the Christians (4:4). This section demonstrates that the suffering endured by the community is not yet the result of formal persecution, but is the kind of resentment, derision, and hostility that the nonconforming behavior of the Christians provokes in their neighbors. This moral stance of the Christians had a potentially severe social cost. By refusing to participate in some of the public festivals and guild celebrations where no doubt much of the revelry criticized in the letter took place the Christians effectively removed themselves from much of the social and commercial interaction of their contemporaries. The experience of such isolation and hostility stands behind the author's addressing the Christians as "exiles" and "aliens" in their own society (1:1; 2:11).

The author labels such hostility on the part of the non-Christians "blasphemy" (4:4). Because the Christian manner of life is rooted in God's will and manifests the fruits of Christ's own redemptive power and exemplary way of life, to attack it is, in effect, to blaspheme and to make one liable to judgment (4:5). Thus they will have to give an account to God ("who is ready to judge the living and the dead") on the day of judgment (4:5).

At the same time that the unbridled desires and wanton behavior of the "Gentiles" put them on the road to condemnation, the Christians are on a journey to God. In the previous section the author affirmed that the purpose of Christ's Passion, resurrection, and exaltation was to "bring (the Christians) to God" (3:18). This was the very reason the gospel was proclaimed to the community, that "they might live in the spirit according to God" (4:6). This holds true even for those members of the community who had accepted the gospel yet had now died. There was no need for anxiety about the fate of such Christians, even if in the view of skeptics they seemed to have ended up no better than the nonbelievers who feasted and died (i.e., "judged in the flesh according to humans"). They, too, would live in the spirit through the power of God. Thus the victory of the Risen and Exalted Christ over the hostile powers of the universe proclaimed in 3:18-22 would envelop all those who believed in Christ and led lives worthy of the gospel.

FOR REFERENCE AND FURTHER READING

Blazen, I. T. "Suffering and Cessation from Sin According to 1 Peter 4:1," *AUSS* 21 (1983) 27–50.

Dalton, William J. "The Interpretation of 1 Peter 3,19 and 4,6: Light from 2 Peter," *Bib* 60 (1979) 547–55.

Omanson, Roger. "Suffering For Righteousness' Sake (1 Pet 3:13–4:11)," *RevExp* 79 (1982) 439–50.

Strobel, August. "Macht Leiden von Sünden frei? Zur Problematick von 1 Petr. 4,1f." *TZ* 19 (1963) 412–25.

Vogels, Heinz-Jürgen. *Christi Abstieg ins Totenreich und das Läuterungsgericht an den Toten: eine bibeltheologisch-dogmatische Untersuchung zum Glaubensartikel "descendit ad inferos."* FTS 102. Freiburg: Herder, 1976.

15. *Living in Awareness of the End-time* (4:7-11)

7. The end of all things is at hand; therefore be serious-minded and sober for prayer, 8. above all having constant love for one another, because love covers a multitude of sins, 9. (being) hospitable toward one another without muttering, 10. as each has received a gift, using it in service for one another, as good stewards of the diverse gifts of God. 11. If someone speaks, (speak) as (with) the oracle of God; if someone serves, (let them serve) as from the strength that God supplies, in order that in all things God may be glorified through Jesus Christ, to whom is the glory and the power forever and ever. Amen.

NOTES

7. *The end of all things is at hand:* The author begins this segment by citing the eschatological perspective that was evoked in the previous section, where he spoke about the passing of time (4:2-3), and is found in other parts of the letter (see 4:17 and the references to a "little while" in 1:6 and 5:10). Here the "end of all things" *(pantōn . . . to telos)*—clearly referring to the end of the present age or world—is "at hand." The verb *ēggizein* ("approach" or "come near") is often used in New Testament texts referring to the parousia and the end of the world (e.g., Matt 4:17; 10:7; Mark 1:15; Luke 10:9, 11; Rom 13:12; Phil 4:5; Heb 10:25; Jas 5:8; Rev 1:3); the perfect tense implies that the end has already drawn near and is therefore "at hand."

    therefore be serious-minded and sober for prayer: The first set of injunctions deals with the discipline of mind and spirit needed first of all for prayer and, by extension, for the virtues required for authentic Christian community. The imperative *sōphronēsate* ("be serious-minded") implies thinking in a sound and serious way with discipline and focus. The accompanying verb *nēpsate* ("be sober"), which derives from the word for sobriety or temperance (in drink, but by extension to other passions as well), has a similar connotation in this context. The connection between clear thinking and prayer probably reflects the notion of "consciousness" of God cited earlier in the letter's advice to slaves (see 2:19) and the warning to husbands to respect their wives so that their prayers would not be thwarted (3:7).

8. *above all, having constant love for one another:* The phrase "above all" *(prō pantōn)* seems to be a word play on the opening phrase of v. 7 *(pantōn de to telos)*. Even as the end of "all things" is at hand, the first requirement of Christian life ("above all") remains charity (see, of course, Paul's famous hymn to charity as the primary Christian virtue in 1 Cor 13:1-13). The participle *exontes* ("having") no doubt has imperative force here, but retaining its participial form brings out the underlying structure of this overall section. The Christians are directed to be "serious-minded and sober" for prayer (v. 7), and this is expressed in the qualities that follow both as illustration and exhortation in the participle form ("having constant love . . . ." "being hospitable . . . ." ". . .

serving one another"). It is clear that the author is talking about the love and respect that is directed to other members of the community, i.e., "to one another" (*eis heautous;* see also 1:22; 2:17; 3:8; 5:14). That love *(agapē)* is to be "constant"; the adjective used here, *ektenē,* implies perseverance and therefore deep devotion (some translations favor the word "fervent," which focuses on the devotion that undergirds perseverance).

because love covers a multitude of sins: This often-quoted proverbial expression derives from Prov 10:12 ("Hatred stirs up strife, but love covers all offenses") and is also cited in Jas 5:20 (". . . whoever brings back a sinner from wandering will save the sinner's soul and will cover a multitude of sins"). The quotation in 1 Peter is closer to the Hebrew text of Proverbs; since the author usually quotes from the Septuagint it is likely that he is not directly quoting from Proverbs here but citing a proverbial expression that had passed into general Christian tradition. The precise meaning of the passage is open to debate. To have one's sins "covered" or "hidden" (the literal meaning of the verb *kalyptō*) probably means to have them forgiven or "overlooked" by God on the impending day of judgment (see Ps 32:1, "Happy are those whose transgression is forgiven, whose sin is covered [LXX *epekalyphthēsan]*"). But whose sins are being hidden? The one who loves? Or the one who is loved? The author may not have parsed the saying in such detail; the general sense may simply be that when Christians exercise the primary value of love God is pleased and reconciliation takes place—for all concerned.

9. *(being) hospitable toward one another without muttering:* The author refers to another important early Christian virtue that is a practical expression of love, namely hospitality *(philoxenoi,* literally "love for strangers"); in line with the sense of the previous verse, the participle imperative is implied ("being"). Care and hospitality for the sojourner and stranger were hallmarks of the Jewish Bible and also respected in Greco-Roman writings (see John Koenig, "Hospitality," 299–301). Given the minority status of early Christianity and the extraordinary mobility of its members, hospitality for traveling preachers and other community members was a practical necessity (as implied in the mission texts such as Matt 10:11-15; 25:35; see also Rom 15:7; 1 Cor 11:17-34; 1 Tim 3:2; Titus 1:7; Jas 2:1-7). One can also understand that abuses could easily take place, as the Didache warns *(Did.* 4:7), with some wandering Christians overextending their stay or exploiting the good-natured hospitality of others. Paul Achtemeier suggests that the specific context in 1 Peter may refer to worship within house churches (Achtemeier, *1 Peter* 297). Some community members who had homes large enough for community gatherings may have felt put upon and therefore "muttered" about it (the colorful word *gongysmos* used here literally means saying something in a low voice, hence "muttering" or "grumbling").

10. *as each has received a gift, using it in service for one another, as good stewards of the diverse gifts of God:* The grammatical construction of this verse is somewhat convoluted, although its meaning is clear. As in the previous phrases, the participle *diakonountes* ("using [it] in service for") has imperative force but also retains some of its role as a participle illustrating the qualities that should

characterize a vibrant Christian community. The author affirms that each member of the community has received a gift from God. The notion of the Christian being endowed with "gifts" or "charisms" *(charisma)* is found also in the Pauline and deutero-Pauline literature. Especially important is Paul's citing of the varied gifts *(charismata)* of the Spirit in 1 Cor 12:4-11 and in Rom 12:6-8. For Paul the manifold gifts come from the one Spirit and are given to the varied members of the community so that they can work together in complementarity and harmony to form the one body of Christ, just as the members of a human body must work in harmony. In 1 Peter the focus is on the individual Christian who has received a gift "of God" and is to use it in service for the members of the community *(eis heautous auto diakonountes)*; there is no mention of the Spirit. The dominant image for 1 Peter is not that of the "body of Christ," but of "stewardship." Each member of the community, having been endowed by God with a "charism," should, like "good stewards of the diverse gifts of God," put these at the service of the community as a whole. John H. Elliott suggests that the term "steward" *(oikonomos,* literally one who manages a household) reflects one of the dominant images of the letter, namely the church as the "household" of God (see 2:5, "spiritual household" *[oikos pneumatikos],* and 4:17, "household of God" *[oikos tou theou];* see Elliott, *1 Peter* 756). These differences from the Pauline materials suggest once again that 1 Peter does not depend directly on Paul but draws from a common fund of early Christian tradition to which the author gives his own distinctive expression.

11. *If someone speaks, (speak) as (with) the oracle of God:* The author now describes in eloquent fashion the spirit in which two basic gifts or charisms are to be expressed, one of speech and the other of action or service. While the gift of speech could be understood as any instance in which someone speaks, the reference to the "oracle of God" suggests that the author particularly has in mind preaching or teaching in the public assembly or worship. The translation "oracle of God" *(logia theou,* literally "words of God") derives from the common occurrence of this phrase in cultic or oracular contexts in the Old Testament (see, for example, LXX Num 24:4, 16; Ps 106:11; cf. Achtemeier, *1 Peter* 298) and similarly in other New Testament texts (e.g., Acts 7:38 referring to Moses; Rom 3:2, the oracles entrusted to the Jewish people; Heb 5:12, Christian teachers). The sense is that whenever such teachers or preachers use their gift they are to do so in a manner worthy of God's own utterance.

if someone serves, (let them serve) as from the strength that God supplies: The notion of *diakonia,* or humble service, is central in 1 Peter as a summary of Christian action. As with the charism of speech, "service" could refer to any act on behalf of another but the author may particularly have in mind public roles of service within the community. Whoever serves in such a capacity is to do it not as if they were the source of strength but as dependent solely on God. Here again is an instance of the "God consciousness" the author has referred to previously (2:19; 3:16).

in order that in all things God may be glorified through Jesus Christ, to whom is the glory and the power forever and ever. Amen: The segment concludes with a doxology. While a few commentators consider this as evidence of a literary seam that brings into question the original unity of the letter as a whole, the fact is that New Testament doxologies often appear in the midst of a text and not at the conclusion (e.g., Rom 11:36; Gal 1:5; Eph 3:20-21; 1 Tim 1:17; 6:16; 2 Tim 4:18; Heb 13:20-21). The doxology is triggered by the preceding reference to the strength of God (v. 11a) and it rings down the main body of the letter and prepares for the final exhortations that bring the letter to a close. The author emphatically states a fundamental perspective of the letter: the ultimate purpose of all Christian existence and every Christian act *(hina en pasin)* is to glorify God (see 1:7; 2:12 [even the nonbelievers on the day of judgment]; 4:16). The glorification is made possible "through Jesus Christ"; as the author had stated at the very outset of the letter, the hope of rebirth and the promise of eternal life was given by God through the death and resurrection of Jesus Christ (1:3). The precise referent of the conclusion of the doxology is debated; i.e., does the dative pronoun "to whom" *(hǭ)* refer to the immediately preceding "Jesus Christ" or to "God?" While the most grammatical conclusion would be that the immediate antecedent is "Jesus Christ," it seems more in character with 1 Peter's overall theology that the doxology is addressed to God. Throughout the letter Jesus is presented as the agent of God's salvation and the one who is exalted by God in triumph. The opening greeting of the letter refers to God the Father (1:1) and the body of the letter begins with a doxology addressed to God (1:3) that could be seen as forming something of an inclusion with the doxology that concludes this section. The letter as a whole will conclude with another doxology that clearly refers to God (5:10-11). The language of the doxology is traditional, attributing to God "glory" *(doxa)* and "power" *(kratos)* "forever and ever" (literally "unto the ages of ages," *eis tous aiōnas tōn aiōnōn*). The doxology concludes with the word "Amen," a Hebraism found frequently in New Testament liturgical texts and used here as a concluding acclamation.

INTERPRETATION

This segment brings to a conclusion the main body of the letter that began in 2:11 and prepares for the conclusion that will stretch from 4:12 to 5:14. It begins with an eschatological perspective that prompts the exhortation that follows, a motivation found in many New Testament texts (e.g., Matt 24:45–25:13; Mark 13:33-37; Rom 13:11-14; Phil 4:4-6; 1 Thess 5:1-15; Heb 10:23-25; Jas 5:7-11). Whereas 4:1-6 concentrated on the conversion of life and consistent virtue required of the community in its dealings with those outside the community, this set of exhortations concentrates on relationships within the community. This repeats a pattern found in 3:8-10, where the author counsels mutual love and respect within the community at the conclusion of a series of exhortations to slaves and wives in dealing with non-Christian masters and spouses. As will be the case throughout this section, the author draws on traditional Christian concepts and language to make his points.

This is one of the most lyrical passages in the letter. In the previous segment the author had spelled out what was required for Christians who lived surrounded by an uncomprehending and hostile dominant culture (4:1-6). They could no longer indulge their human cravings as they may have in their non-Christian past but had to live lives of beauty and discipline, even if it cost them suffering in being hounded and ostracized by their non-Christian neighbors. The author now turns to the inner life of the community and describes the spirit that should characterize the relationships among those called to salvation in Christ. This type of sequence —dealing with the community's relationship to outsiders and then turning to the dynamics within the community—repeats that found in 3:8-10 after a series of instructions to slaves dealing with their masters and wives of non-Christian husbands in dealing with their spouses. This segment in 4:7-11, which concludes with a doxology, will bring to a close the entire main body of the letter, which began in 2:11, and serves as a transition to the final section, 4:12–5:14.

The passage begins with a reminder that the end of the present age or world is near. The author's eschatological perspective breaks out in a number of passages in the letter, and a concern about judgment was apparent in the previous section where the author warned that the non-Christians who attack the community are "blaspheming" and are therefore liable to God who is "ready to judge the living and the dead" (4:5). While 1 Peter does not speculate on the precise cosmic timetable for the parousia, it implies that it will be "soon" (see 1:6; 4:2-3; 5:10). More important is the way of life one should lead when conscious that this world is transitory and that all will have to give an account to God (see similarly 1 Thess 5:1-10; Mark 13:33-37).

The author spells out some key virtues or attitudes that should characterize Christian life in this meantime before the advent of Christ. First and foremost, the Christians should be fully aware of the new reality brought about by their rebirth in Christ. They are to be "serious-minded and sober," a stance that probably reflects the God-consciousness the author has enjoined on the slaves in 2:19 and on the entire community in 3:16. Surrounded by a hostile culture and under pressure to conform, the Christians needed to have inner discipline that kept them focused on God. This would result first of all in readiness for prayer (4:7), as the author had counseled the husbands in 3:7, but by extension it would also enable them to speak and act in accord with the gospel and the new reality of their life in Christ.

In describing the manner of life within the community the author draws on common early Christian tradition. There are echoes of Paul's theology, but not in the sense the author directly quotes Paul; instead, 1 Peter draws on a common fund of tradition, one that may also have been earlier influenced by Pauline teaching. "Above all," the Christians are to have "constant love" for the other members of the community (4:8). Here 1 Peter reflects a fundamental Christian tradition, found most eloquently in Paul (see 1 Cor 13:1-13) and in the Johannine tradition (John 15:12-17). The author does not address the issue of love toward those outside the community, as for example in the "love of enemy" teaching in Matt 5:43-48. First Peter speaks with more restraint regarding the Christians' relationship to outsiders: they are to "honor" all people (2:17), give witness to them (2:12; 3:1-2; 3:15-16), and not render violence for violence (3:9). But, as in 2:17, "love" *(agapē)* is reserved for the members of the community (see also 1:22; 3:8; 5:14). Such love "covers a multitude of sins." This axiom is found in both the Old Testament (Prov 10:12; Ps 32:1) and in James (5:20), as well as in early Christian literature (see *1 Clement* 50:5; *2 Clement* 16:4). Although the precise meaning is elusive, the general sense is that in loving others one carries out the primary command of the gospel, with the result that forgiveness and reconciliation abound (both among members of the community and in the eye of God), and therefore God's judgment about other lesser failings is abated.

A similar virtue is hospitality (4:9), one prized in both Jewish and Greco-Roman literature (see the Notes above). In a sense hospitality is a practical expression of communal love and that is probably the logic that leads to it being placed here after the injunction to love one another. Mobility was common in the first-century Mediterranean world and travelers often depended for lodging on the kindness of friends or family acquaintances. This virtue was even more urgent for the early Christian communities, particularly those that felt threatened by the dominant culture, as was the case for the Christians addressed in 1 Peter. As the opening line of the letter itself indicates (see the list of areas addressed in 1:1), there was a far-flung network of communities in Asia Minor and they apparently had contact with each other and even with communities in other parts of the Mediterranean world such as Rome (cf. 5:13). While the circulation of Christian travelers and itinerant missionaries was cherished, there is no doubt that abuses also occurred. Some interpreters suggest that more particularly the author has in mind the hospitality required of Christians within the community to offer their homes (and provisions) for communal meetings and worship (this may be the context for some of the dissension Paul is concerned about in 1 Cor 11:17-34). In any case, despite the burden such hospitality might entail, Christians should not "grumble," but see this as an expression of their mutual love for each other.

The author's vision of the community is expressed in eloquent terms (4:10-11). Each member has been "gifted" by God and is to use those gifts in service to the community as a whole. The Christians are to be "good stewards of the diverse gifts of God" (4:10). This notion of the Christians as endowed with varied "gifts" or "charisms" and using them harmoniously for the good of the community as a whole echoes Paul's famous portrayal of the community as the "body of Christ," with each member endowed with gifts *(charismata)* by the Spirit and using these diverse gifts for the sake of the unity and harmony of the body as a whole (see 1 Cor 12:4-11; Rom 12:6-8). Here again, 1 Peter seems to tap into a common fund of early Christian exhortation that has similarities to Paul but enough differences to suggest the author is not directly dependent on the Pauline correspondence. In this instance 1 Peter does not use the dominant Pauline image of the "body," and attributes the gifts not to the Spirit but to God. For 1 Peter the dominant image is that of "stewardship"; each member has been entrusted with a gift of God and, like a good manager of the household (the literal meaning of *oikonomos*), is to use them in "service" for the other members of the community. The notion of good stewardship particularly while awaiting the end-time is also found in the gospel literature (see Matt 24:45-51; 25:14-30; Luke 12:42-48).

The notion of "service" is a rich Christian concept important for this letter (see 4:10, 11; also 1:12 in reference to "prophets of old"). The verb itself has a range of meanings in Greek, referring to public service performed on behalf of others by an intermediary or official functionary or to more humble domestic tasks such as serving at meals. In the gospel literature it is applied to Jesus' own mission of humble service (see Mark 10:45; Matt 20:28; Luke 22:27) and by extension as the essence of discipleship (Mark 9:35; 10:43; Matt 20:26; 23:11; Luke 22:26; John 12:26). This broader sense of humble, unassuming, and Christlike service seems to be the meaning intended by the term in 1 Peter. Each gift or "charism" entrusted to the Christian by God is to be used not for self-aggrandizement but in loving service for the community.

Two fundamental categories of gifts are used to illustrate such a spirit of service and good stewardship (4:11). Those who speak should do so as if speaking an "oracle of God." Literally the text refers to the "words of God" *(logia theou)*, which might imply that the author is referring to any context in which the Christian speaks, giving this exhortation the broadest possible application (i.e., "whenever one speaks, speak as if uttering the word of God"). However, the term *logia theou* is used in the biblical literature in oracular or cultic contexts (see the Notes). It is likely that the author is singling out as examples public instances such as speaking in the assembly. In a setting such as worship in a house church the teacher or preacher is to use his or her gift in such a way that it is manifestly an "oracle of God." Likewise, if one is "serving"—again probably in some visible, public role—one is to do that in a way that communicates that the strength and authority of one's actions come from God, and not from oneself.

Even if the author has in mind limited public roles as examples of proper use of God's gifts, the fundamental intent is that all of the varied gifts God gives to individual Christians are to be used in this same spirit. In all instances Christians are to use their gifts, conscious that God is working through them for the good of the community as a whole, whether in speech or in action. Here again "God-consciousness" is at stake. That is why the Christians need the discipline of mind and spirit to be aware of the ultimate truth that surrounds them, namely the fact that they have been reborn to a new life of hope in Christ (1:3-9), that they must put aside the destructive way of life in which they may previously have indulged (4:1-6), and that the time is short before the end of all things and the day of judgment will come.

This notion of "God-consciousness" or awareness of truth through the eyes of faith is a key underlying motif of the letter and it emerges again in the final doxology (4:11b). This new consciousness is the effect of baptism (3:21) and it should mark every aspect of Christian existence. The goal of living in community in this way is "in order that in all things God may be glorified through Jesus Christ." First Peter's vision of a world ready to break out in worship of God is summoned up again (see 2:12). Throughout the long list of exhortations and instructions begun in 2:11 the author has had his eye fixed on this vision of glory. All of Jesus' life, all of his exemplary suffering on behalf of others, was directed to God and had as its purpose to bring the Christians to God (3:18). Through his redemptive suffering Christ triumphed over the hostile powers and was exalted at God's right hand (4:22). So, too, every act of the Christian—bearing the suffering imposed on slaves and wives, the struggle for freedom from disordered human cravings, giving witness through lives of virtue and integrity, the effort to build a community of love and service—all of this must be directed to God's glory.

The author concludes with a doxology that gives homage to God's "glory" and "power." While the object of the doxology could be Jesus, it is more likely directed to God in the same manner as the final words of praise will be dedicated to the "God of all grace" (5:10). First Peter clearly portrays Christ as God's agent of salvation and as a divine figure at the right hand of God, yet the fundamental orientation of the letter is theocentric—seeing the mission of Jesus and the goal of Christian life finding their ultimate origin and end in God.

For Reference and Further Reading

Elliott, John H. *A Home for the Homeless: A Social-Scientific Exegesis of 1 Peter, Its Situation and Strategy, With a New Introduction.* Minneapolis: Fortress, 1990, 145–48, 162–64.

Hiebert, D. Edmond. "Living in the Light of Christ's Return: An Exposition of 1 Peter 4:7-11," *BS* 139 (1982) 243–54.

Kline, Leslie L. "Ethics for the Endtime: An Exegesis of 1 Pt. 4: 7-11," *ResQ* 7 (1963) 113–23.

Koenig, John. "Hospitality," *ABD* 3:299–301.

Spicq, Ceslas. "L'Épître de Pierre: Prière, charité, justice . . . et fin des Temps (1 Pierre 4:7-11)," *AsSeign* 50 (1966) 15–29.

16. *Suffering as a Christian* (4:12-19)

12. Beloved, do not be astounded at the fiery ordeal that is happening to you as a test for you, as if something strange was coming upon you. 13. Rather, inasmuch as you share in the sufferings of Christ, rejoice, in order that you may also rejoice with exultation at the revelation of his glory. 14. If you are insulted in the name of Christ, blessed are you, because the spirit of glory and of God is resting on you. 15. However, let none of you suffer as a murderer or a thief or an evildoer or as a troublemaker; 16. but if (one suffers) as a Christian, do not be ashamed, but glorify God in that name. 17. For the time has come for judgment to begin with the house of God; but if first with us, what [will be] the end of those who have not obeyed the gospel of God? 18. And if the just can hardly be saved, where will the godless and sinner appear? 19. So then, those who suffer in accord with God's will should entrust their lives to a faithful creator in doing good.

NOTES

12. *Beloved, do not be astounded at the fiery ordeal that is happening to you as a test for you, as if something strange was coming upon you:* The affectionate address "beloved" *(agapētoi)* recalls the opening of the main body of the letter, where the author also began a series of urgent exhortations with *agapētoi* (2:11). The use of this term as an address is common in the New Testament letters (e.g., Rom 12:19; 1 Cor 10:14; 2 Cor 6:7; Phil 2:12; Heb 6:9; Jas 1:16; 2 Pet 3:14; 1 John 3:2; Jude 20), and here it echoes the author's frequent reference to the mutual love that should characterize the inner life of the community (see 1:22; 2:17; 3:8; 4:8; 5:14).

The Christians should not be "astounded" or taken by surprise *(xenizesthe)* at the ordeal they have to face. This same verb was used to describe the reaction of the non-Christians who were "astonished" that the Christians no longer shared their immoral way of life (4:4); in that instance the astonishment was negative and would lead to hostility. The Christians, by contrast, should not be surprised that fidelity to the gospel would bear the cost of suffering. Throughout the letter the author has warned that suffering is an inevitable part of Christian experience (1:6; 2:21; 3:13-14, 17; 4:1) and in so doing the letter joins many other New Testament texts that alerted the Christians to the prospect of suffering, particularly in anticipation of the final age (e.g., Matt 10:24-25; Luke 6:40; John 13:16; 15:18-21; 16:1-4, 33; 1 Thess 3:3; 2 Tim 3:12; 1 John 3:13). Here 1 Peter describes those sufferings as a "fiery ordeal" *(pyrōsei)* that is coming upon the Christians as a "test" *(peirasmos)* for them. The notion of suffering as "fire" that "tests" or purifies the one who suffers was already cited by the author in 1:7 and reflects a traditional biblical motif (see Prov 27:21, "The crucible is for silver, and the furnace *[pyrōsis]* is for gold; so a person is tested by being praised"; Ps 65:10 "For you, O God, have tested us, you have tried us *[epyrōsas]* as silver is tried *[pyrōutai]*; Wis 3:5-6, "Having been disciplined a little, they will receive great good, because God tested *[epeirasen]* them and found them worthy of himself; like gold in the furnace he tried them, and like a sacrificial burnt offering he accepted them"; 1 Cor 3:13, ". . . the fire *[pyr]* will test what sort of work each has done"; F. W. Beare, *First Epistle* 190, suggests that the reference to fire may be an allusion to the burning of Rome under Nero in 64 C.E., but this is not persuasive). The author reaffirms his point at the conclusion of the verse. Given their circumstances in society and the common wisdom of the biblical peoples before them, suffering should not be seen as something "strange" *(xenos)* or unexpected for those who follow the way of Christ.

13. *Rather, inasmuch as you share in the sufferings of Christ, rejoice:* The disjunctive "rather" *(alla)* underscores the author's point that far from seeing suffering as something alien or strange, Christians should even rejoice *(chairete)* in it because in this way they share in the sufferings of Christ. "Inasmuch as" translates the adverb *katho*, which literally means "to the extent that" or "to the degree that"; in this context, however, the author sees sharing in Christ's sufferings not as a hypothetical possibility but as an actual reality for the Christians. The Christians share in common *(koinōneite)* with the sufferings of Christ, as the author had already emphasized earlier in the letter, because they follow his example, suffering unjustly but not rendering evil for evil, the just for the sake of the unjust (2:21; 3:9; 3:17-18; 4:1). Because of this bond with the suffering (and triumphant) Christ, paradoxically the Christian can actually "rejoice" in the midst of suffering (see also 1:6).

in order that you may also rejoice with exultation at the revelation of his glory: The author now adds another dimension to the Christian perspective on suffering. By sharing in the sufferings of Christ they will also rejoice on that day when Christ's glory is revealed *(en tę apokalypsei tēs doxēs autou)*. This affirms that the Christian stance is not some sort of warped enjoyment of suffering as such but, while finding strength in enduring suffering in solidarity with Christ, the Christian anticipates that day of liberation and great joy (the participle *agalliōmenoi* suggests exultation or exuberant joy associated with the triumph of the end-time) when all suffering will be overcome in Christ's triumphant return (see 3:22). The author describes this final moment as "the revelation of his glory," presumably the parousia of Christ (see 5:4). Anticipation of this moment of ecstasy for the Christians, when all trials would cease and the glory of Christ would be fully revealed, was cited at the very beginning of the letter (1:3-9). "Glory" *(doxa)* is a key term in this letter and refers to the manifestation of God's transcendent power that is also attributed to the triumphant Christ (1:7, 11, 21; 4:11; 5:1, 10).

14. *If you are insulted in the name of Christ, blessed are you:* Although the conditional "if" *(ei)* is used here, it is clear from the overall context of the letter that the Christians will not escape denunciation and abuse because of their allegiance to Christ and in fact have already experienced this (2:12; 3:16; 4:4). The "fiery ordeal" that comes upon the Christians as a "test" is not formal state persecution or even threat of death at this point, but the steady drumbeat of hostile criticism from the dominant non-Christian majority and the social alienation that results. The verb *oneidizein* ("denounce," "demean," "insult") refers to this kind of verbal abuse (see also the mockery of Jesus on the cross: Matt 27:44; Mark 15:32; also Heb 11:26).

Such abuse is done "in the name of Christ" *(en onomati christou),* a unique formulation. In other similar New Testament examples the phrase "in the name of Jesus Christ" or its equivalent usually refers to something done in solidarity with Christ or under the authority of Christ (e.g., Mark 9:41; Acts 16:18; Eph 5:20; 2 Thess 3:6). But this is the sole example where it refers to a hostile act. The most likely sense here is that the Christians are abused precisely because of their allegiance to Christ or because of the fact that they are identified as "Christians" (see 4:16; Elliott, *1 Peter* 779–80, suggests the translation "because of Christ"). Those who are insulted and suffer because they belong to Christ are indeed "blessed" *(makarioi).* The wording and the sentiment are strongly reminiscent of Jesus' beatitude in Matt 5:11 (see also Luke 6:11)— "Blessed are you when they insult you *(makarioi este hotan oneidisōsin hymas)* . . . on account of me *(heneken emou)."* The author had pronounced a similar "beatitude" in 3:14 ("But if you should suffer for the sake of righteousness, you are blessed") that was reminiscent of Matt 5:10 ("Blessed are those who are persecuted for the sake of righteousness . . ."). In both cases it is likely that 1 Peter draws on a common fund of Christian tradition that included these proverbial sayings of Jesus.

because the spirit of glory and of God is resting on you: The fundamental reason why *(hoti,* "because") the Christians are "blessed" even in the midst of such suffering is that the "spirit of glory which is also the spirit of God" rests upon them. The notion of God's Spirit abiding with the Christian in the midst of suffering and persecution is found in other New Testament texts (see, for example, Matt 10:19-20; Luke 12:11-12; John 14:26; 16:7-15). The phrasing here is somewhat awkward; literally the text says "the spirit of the glory and of God" *(to tēs doxēs kai tou theou pneuma).* The phrase should probably be understood as a hendiadys as this translation tries to suggest, i.e., where two modifying phrases ("of the glory," "of God") attach to the one noun ("spirit"). The formulation of the phrase may be influenced by Isa 11:2, "The spirit of the Lord shall rest on him" (LXX: *kai anapausetai ep' auton pneuma tou theou).* First

Peter adapted the quotation by putting the verb "rest" in the present tense *(anapauetai)* and changing the phrase "upon him" *(ep' auton)* to "upon you" *(eph' hymas)*. Paul Achtemeier suggests that the addition of the phrase "of the glory" *(to tēs doxēs)* to the original "spirit of God" may have been influenced by the string of genitive phrases that follows in the Isaiah quotation (i.e., "the spirit of wisdom and of understanding, the spirit of counsel and might, the spirit of knowledge and the fear of the Lord"); the author of the letter wanted to make clear "that the prophecy described by Isaiah has now been fulfilled within the Christian community" (Achtemeier, *1 Peter* 308). As noted above, the concept of "glory" is especially important for 1 Peter (see 4:13); now the transcendent glory that belongs to God and to Christ rests upon the Christians themselves, who have been joined to Christ in an intense way through the bond of innocent suffering. Some manuscripts and later versions add to the end of this verse the phrase "for them it is blaspheming, but for you glorification" *(kata men autous blasphēmeitai, kata de hymas doxazetai).* While most commentators consider it a later gloss, some do defend it as authentic; see P. R. Rodgers, "The Longer Reading," 93–95.

15. *However, let none of you suffer as a murderer or a thief or an evildoer or as a trouble-maker:* By way of contrast (the sense of the emphatic *mē gar* that begins the sentence) the author cites other reasons for "suffering" that do not constitute a share in the suffering of Christ. The first two items in the list refer to classic crimes that are clearly wrong and illegal: a "murderer" *(phoneus,* also roundly condemned in the Decalogue [see also Matt 19:18] and other New Testament texts, e.g., Rev 21:8; 22:15; the invitees to the wedding feast who mistreat the king's messengers are described as "murderers" in Matt 22:7, as are the religious leaders in Acts 7:52; in Acts 28:4 Paul is thought to be a cursed "murderer" when he escapes shipwreck only to be bitten by a poisonous snake); and a "thief" *(kleptēs,* a crime likewise forbidden in the Ten Commandments [Matt 19:18] and listed as an example of evil in 1 Cor 6:10; Rom 2:21; Eph 4:28).

The other two examples seem more generic; the notion of "evildoer" (the literal meaning of *kakopoios)* or "criminal" (see John 18:30) was mentioned earlier in the letter (2:12; 2:14). This is the kind of broad accusation hurled at the Christians by nonbelievers (2:12). The word "troublemaker" *(allotriepiskopos)* is more difficult to pin down since this is the only occurrence of the word in the New Testament. The etymology of the word, combining "what belongs to another" *(allotrios)* and "overseer" *(episkopos),* suggests the notion of someone who causes trouble by meddling in the affairs of another. Another possibility is that of "spy" or "informer" (see BDAG 47). This final word in the list of four is introduced by the phrase "or as" *(ē hōs),* which may indicate the author viewed this category of offense as distinct from the rest or was simply using this grammatical device to bring the list to a close.

16. *but if (one suffers) as a Christian, do not be ashamed, but glorify God in that name:* Although the sentence begins with a conditional "but if" *(ei de),* the actual meaning is "when," since the experience of suffering for the community is not hypothetical (as in v. 14). The verb to be supplied here might either be "suffer" as in the preceding verse, or "insulted" as in v. 14. Since "suffer" occurs in the

immediately preceding verse, it is the more likely candidate. The term "Christian" was probably not a self-designation for the community at this period. The only other occurrences of the word are in Acts 11:26 (". . . and it was in Antioch that the disciples were first called 'Christians'") and Acts 26:28 (Agrippa's challenge to Paul: "Are you so quickly persuading me to become a Christian?")—both instances in which an outsider names the community. Given the context in 1 Peter, the term "Christian" may have been used contemptuously by those hostile to the community. The author's point is that to be ridiculed or to suffer "as a Christian" is not a cause for shame but paradoxically an opportunity to glorify God in being given that name.

Both the verbs "be ashamed" *(aischynesthō)* and "glorify" *(doxazetō)* are in the third person singular imperative (i.e., "let one not be ashamed," "let one glorify") but are best rendered in English in the direct imperative form. The author's point is to set up a paradoxical contrast between the two verbs. While the non-Christians heap ridicule on the Christians because they are linked to Christ and his community of followers, in fact such suffering becomes an opportunity to glorify God because of the name the community bears. The root verb "to be ashamed" *(aischynomai)* is found in other New Testament texts referring to shame on account of one's allegiance to Christ or the gospel (used with the prefix *epi* or *kata:* see Mark 8:38; Luke 9:26; Rom 1:16; 2 Tim 1:8, 12). The phrase "in that name" *(en tǭ onomati toutǭ)* undoubtedly refers to the name "Christian" although it is also equivalent to the similar phrase "in the name of Christ" (4:14). The name "Christian" carries forward the paradox; it is a name of opprobrium for those outside the community but for community members themselves it is a badge of honor and in bearing it at a terrible cost they give glory to God. A majority of later manuscripts substitute the reading "in this way" *(en tǭ merei)* for "in this name"; see J. Ramsey Michaels, *1 Peter* 257, who defends the authenticity of this reading on the grounds that it is the more difficult reading.

17. *For the time has come for judgment to begin with the house of God:* The eschatological perspective of the author is always close to the surface, and so he returns now to the expected moment of judgment cited at the beginning of this segment (vv. 12-13). The experience of suffering in the name of Christ is also linked to the final day of judgment (i.e., the causative sense of the "for" *[hoti]* that begins the verse). The verb "come" or "be at hand" is implied. The word used for "time" *(kairos)* has the meaning of "opportune" or "critical" time and is repeatedly linked to the end-time or the day of judgment in the New Testament (e.g., Matt 8:29; 13:30; 16:3; 26:18; Mark 1:15; 13:33; Luke 18:30; 19:44; 21:8; John 7:6, 8; Rom 13:11; 1 Cor 4:5; 7:29; 2 Cor 6:2; Gal 6:9; Eph 1:10; 1 Thess 5:1; 2 Thess 2:6). Both the nearness of the final day (4:17; see also 1:6; 5:10) and the notion of the impending "judgment" *(krima;* see 1:17; 2:23; 4:5) are recurring ideas in the letter. Now the author asserts that God's act of judging will begin with "the house of God" *(apo tou oikou tou theou).* The author portrayed the community as a "spiritual house" or household in 2:4 where a cluster of temple images (see especially 2:4-9) also suggests that the author views them as both a community (i.e., a "household") and the locus of a new spiritual

"temple" (i.e., a "house" of God). Some commentators suggest that the idea that judgment will begin with the community itself may be influenced by this temple motif since there are Old Testament texts such as Ezek 9:6, Jer 25:29, and Mal 3:1-6 that describe judgment and destruction beginning with the Temple and its precincts (see Achtemeier, *1 Peter* 315–16). However, the link with these texts seems tenuous. In Ezekiel, for example, the Temple and the city and its elders are viewed as corrupt and worthy of judgment; in 1 Peter the community has not been portrayed in such negative terms. More likely the author evokes a more generalized conviction that because they are God's chosen people and the object of God's redemptive work, i.e., the "household of God," it is only logical that the day of judgment should begin with the community itself. Such a general conviction that judgment begins with Israel is found in Jewish literature (see, for example, *2 Bar.* 13:9-10; 13:1-12; *T.Benj.* 100:8-9; 1QS 4:18-21; 1QH 8:30-31; 9:10; 11:8-10).

but if first with us, what [will be] the end of those who have not obeyed the gospel of God?: The author's point here is in fact to reassure the community. Although judgment may begin with the community (literally "but if first from us," *ei de prōton aph' hēmōn*), that does not mean it is in disfavor with God. Quite the contrary: the community that bears suffering in Christ's name will be infinitely better off on the day of judgment than those who "are disobeying the gospel of God" *(tōn apeithountōn to tou theou euangelion)*. Earlier the author had described the nonbelieving spouses of Christian wives as those "who disobey the word" (3:1). The phrase "gospel of God" is equivalent to the entirety of the Christian message (i.e., similar to "the word") and is traditional language found elsewhere in the New Testament (see Mark 1:14; Acts 20:24; Rom 1:1; 15:16; 2 Cor 11:7; 1 Thess 2:2, 8, 9; 1 Tim 1:11). The author implies that the "end" or "goal" *(telos)* toward which those who have rejected the gospel are moving is calamitous.

18. *And if the just can hardly be saved, where will the godless and sinner appear?:* The author repeats his point about the contrasting fates of those who accept the gospel and those who reject it by quoting from Prov 11:31. The quotation is remarkably close to the Septuagint version, with the only change being the addition of "and" *(kai)* at the beginning of the verse and the omission of the contrasting particle *(men)* that is found before the word "just" in Proverbs. The adverb "hardly" *(molis)* implies something accomplished with great difficulty (see Luke 9:39; Acts 14:18; 27:7, 8, 16). The question is, if the just (i.e., the faithful Christians) achieve salvation only with great effort and difficulty (including perseverance in suffering—the major point of this section), where will this put the "godless, " i.e., those who are irreverent toward God *(ho asebēs)* and the "sinner" *(hamartōlos)*? The Christians by their very name stand in the sphere of Christ's triumphant power, but the nonbelievers stand alone before God.

19. *So then, those who suffer in accord with God's will should entrust their lives to a faithful creator in doing good:* With this final verse the author arrives at the ultimate point of his exhortation. The opening words "so then" *(hōste kai)* signal that the author is about to sum up his message and draw his conclusion. Suf-

fering "in accord with God's will" *(kata to thelēma tou theou)* refers to the unique character of Christian suffering that the author has spoken about throughout the letter and particularly in this last segment. It is not suffering that comes justly to the person who does something wrong and deserves punishment for it. No, suffering that is redemptive is in the pattern of Christ's own suffering, that is, suffering in doing what is good and just—namely, doing "God's will." The notion of doing God's will even at the cost of suffering is fundamental to the letter (see, for example, 2:15; 3:17; 4:2) and the author returns to this motif here. This leads to one of the most exquisite statements in the letter; the Christians are to "entrust their lives to a faithful creator." The verb "entrust" *(paratithemi,* literally to place one's life in the hands of another) connotes the total commitment and trust required of Christian faith and is reminiscent of the words of Ps 30:6 placed on the lips of Jesus at the moment of his death in Luke 23:46, "into thy hands I entrust *(paratithemai)* my spirit." The word *psychas* ("lives") implies the totality of one's life in all its dimensions, including that of action. God, the object of one's total trust, is beautifully described as "a faithful creator" *(pistō ktistē).* Although the term appears in Greco-Roman literature referring to the deity, this is the only time in the New Testament that God is explicitly called "creator." However, the notion of God as a "faithful creator" fits comfortably into the theology of the letter. That God is the origin and end of all things is a leitmotif of the letter's vision of human destiny (see 1:20; 4:7). The Christians themselves stand in the midst of creation as the beneficiaries of God's providence and were asked to properly "submit" to the authentic and legitimate demands of the "created structures" of the world for the sake of the Lord who had created them (2:13). The proper stance of the Christian even in the midst of suffering and in face of the approaching end of time is, therefore, not withdrawal from the world or living in fear, but confiding their lives to a faithful God while continuing "in doing good" *(en agathopoiią).* This last phrase is emphatic and gives the final punch to the author's exhortation. "Doing good" is not an additional bit of advice, but expresses what "entrusting one's life to God" means. Throughout the letter the author had repeatedly emphasized the importance of "doing good" as the authenticating expression of Christian faith (1:15; 2:12, 15, 20; 3:1-2, 6, 11, 13, 14, 16, 17). Trust in God and an active commitment to doing good constitute the stance the Christian must take as the day of judgment approaches.

Interpretation

The author begins the final section of the letter, summoning up many of the key ideas that appeared throughout, particularly those relating to suffering. Most of the author's previous reflections on suffering now pass in review. Christians should be the last to be surprised by the presence of suffering. The traditions of the biblical peoples, the pattern of Jesus' own life, and their own current experience demonstrate that suffering is an intrinsic part of the Christian vocation.

The letter offers a number of reasons why innocent suffering linked to the gospel can be of value. First of all, it is a "fiery ordeal" (4:12) that puts the Christians to the "test" and proves their commitment just as silver and gold are proven in the fire, a perspective found in the Old Testament and in other New Testament texts (see the Notes). The author had already discussed suffering as a "test" or "purification" in 1:6-7.

Paradoxically, suffering can also be a cause for "rejoicing" because in this way the Christian shares in the sufferings of Christ, who also was innocent but experienced rejection and persecution. Through his innocent sufferings life has come to the world, and the letter seems to imply that through suffering in the pattern of Jesus the Christians, too, will find new life (2:21, 24-25; 3:18-22; 4:1-2). They will be able to exult with joy on that day when the "glory" of Christ is fully revealed (4:13)—thus the sufferings of this age will ultimately issue in the glory that is to come.

The author never forgets the cost of discipleship, another dimension of suffering. Part of that "cost" is the inner struggle to free oneself from destructive cravings and to live a virtuous life (1:14; 2:11; 4:1-6). But the cost considered here is suffering that comes from the outside, from an uncomprehending and abusive world that does not share the values of the gospel and ridicules those who have thrown their lot with Christ (4:14). This, too, has been a strong current in the letter's message (2:12, 15, 18-25; 3:1-6, 9, 14, 16; 4:4). As in 3:14, the author seems to quote a beatitude similar to that found in the Gospel of Matthew—to be insulted in the name of Christ is, paradoxically, a "blessing" (4:14). Those who suffer in union with Christ are assured of the abiding presence of the Spirit, the Spirit of glory and of God, as the letter notes (4:14). "Glory" is one of the letter's key concepts (used ten times as a noun and four times as a verb). Traditionally the Bible associates "glory" with God's awesome and transcendent presence, a "glory" that is also inherent in Jesus Christ as God's Risen Son (1:7; 4:13). When that presence is manifest, "glory" streams out into the world. Conversely, when humanity properly acknowledges God's presence, this act of worship and praise is "glory" given to God. First Peter's use of the term fits into this perspective. It has linked the concept of glory to that final manifestation of God's saving presence that will be revealed at the end of the world (1:7; 4:13; 5:10). At that moment all the world must respond by glorifying God. This is what 1 Peter has just affirmed (4:16; see 2:12; 4:11). Now it extends this term to the Spirit of God. This powerful source of life and strength flows from the God of glory who will be fully revealed at the end-time. But even now this "Spirit of glory" "rests" with the Christians as they struggle and suffer courageously in the face of opposition and ridicule. That image of God's strengthening Spirit resting on the Christian seems to be drawn from the beautiful passage of Isa 11:2, where the Spirit of the Lord is described as "resting" on God's messiah, giving him a mission of justice. Now the Christians are portrayed as God's agents of salvation, armed with God's Spirit in the midst of the world.

Once again the author expresses the common-sense conviction that not all suffering is worthwhile (4:15; also 3:20). The just dues of a "murderer" or a "thief" or an "evildoer" or a "troublemaker" are not salvific. But to suffer "as a Christian" is another matter. The letter has made clear that the community was viewed with suspicion and hostility by the surrounding culture (see, for example, 3:16; 4:4); therefore the name "Christian" probably had a contemptuous ring to it as it came off the lips of outsiders. But true to the spirit of his entire message, the author calls on his people to make such abuse an opportunity for glory rather than shame. "Suffering as a Christian"—leading a life of integrity and beauty even when society derides it—unites one to the work of the suffering Christ (2:21-25). Thus a name used with hostility by the nonbeliever becomes a banner of glory for the believer.

A final dimension of suffering is brought forward, namely the link to final judgment (4:17-18). Twice before in the letter (2:8 and 4:5) the author had alluded to the nonbeliever's accountability before God for the suffering inflicted on Christians, and in 1:17 he had reminded the Christians themselves that they, too, were accountable to God as judge. The eschatological character of Christian life had risen to the surface in the latter part of the letter (4:7) and the author now makes the connection between the experience of suffering and the advent of the end-time (4:17-18). The time of God's final judgment of the living and the dead is near, and the process of judgment will begin with the "household of God" (4:17). As the author had already noted, the Christians must therefore be alert and responsive in this time of trial and suffering (4:7). The author tempers the threat of judgment for the Christians by contrasting their situation with that of those who cause the community to suffer. If the time of judgment is a crisis for those who believe in Christ and are strengthened by God's abiding spirit, what will it mean for those "who have not obeyed the gospel of God" (4:17)! As in 2:8 and 3:1, the author seems to refer not to unbelievers in general but to those who have deliberately rejected the Christian message. A quote from Prov 11:31 bolsters the author's argument: if salvation is a struggle for the "just" or faithful person, what will be the fate of the sinner and ungodly?

Verse 19 concludes this whole section on suffering in a spirit thoroughly typical of 1 Peter. The threat of suffering—whether as a purification, or a consequence of witness, or as part of the mysterious drama of judgment—must never immobilize the Christian with fear. Those who suffer "in accord with God's will" should entrust their lives to a "faithful creator." The taproot of Christian existence is complete trust in God; the entire lives of the Christians are in God's loving hands as they await the end of all things (1:5), and through Christ they can be confident of salvation (1:8-9). This message has been repeated in various ways throughout the letter and represents its underlying spirit of confident faith. This trust in God is the source of Christian hope (3:15) and the animating power of Christian witness to the world. The title "a faithful creator" is found nowhere else in the New Testament, but it beautifully expresses the theocentric vision of 1 Peter. The Christians were encouraged to participate in "created institutions" or structures (2:13) because of the author's conviction that God was truly at work in the world, bringing the divine creative task to a glorious conclusion. God is "faithful" to God's promises inherent in creation itself—promises sensed by the prophets (1:10) but now experienced by the Christians in the final age.

All of this should impel the Christian to "do good," one of the most insistent themes of the letter (e.g., 2:12, 15, 20; 3:1-2, 6, 11, 13, 16). In the Greek text of 4:19 these words conclude the sentence and stand in an emphatic position. All of the Christians' convictions about God, about creation, about human destiny, and about the meaning of suffering should lead them to persevere in their active witness of leading a good life.

FOR REFERENCE AND FURTHER STUDY

Borchert, Gerald L. "The Conduct of Christians in the Face of the 'Fiery Ordeal' (1 Pet 4:12–5:11)," *RevExp* 79 (1982) 451–62.

Elliott, John H. "Disgraced yet Graced: The Gospel according to 1 Peter in the Key of Honor and Shame," *BTB* 25 (1995) 166–78.

Holloway, Paul A. "*Nihil inopinati accidisse*—'Nothing unexpected has happened': A Cyrenaic Consolatory *topos* in 1 Pet 4.12ff.," *NTS* 48 (2002) 433–48.

Johnson, D. E. "Fire in God's House: Imagery from Malachi 3 in Peter's Theology of Suffering (1 Pet 4:12-19)," *JETS* 29 (1986) 285–94.

Rodgers, P. R. "The Longer Reading of 1 Peter 4:14," *CBQ* 43 (1981) 93–95.

Schutter, William L. "I Peter 4.17, Ezekiel 9.6, and Apocalyptic Hermeneutics," *SBL Seminar Papers 26.* Atlanta: Scholars, 1987, 276–84.

Villiers, J. L. de. "Joy in Suffering in 1 Peter," *Neot* 9 (1975) 64–86.

17. *Responsibility of the Elders* (5:1-5)

1. Therefore I exhort [the] elders among you, as a co-elder and witness of the sufferings of Christ, and also as one who shares in the glory expected to be revealed, 2. shepherd the little flock of God [entrusted] to you, providing oversight not under compulsion but willingly in God's own manner, not greedily but eagerly, 3. not as ones lording it over those

entrusted to you, but being examples to the flock. 4. And when the chief shepherd is revealed, you will receive the unfading crown of glory. 5. Likewise, younger men, be subject to the elders; all of you, put on humble-mindedness toward one another, because God resists the proud but gives grace to the humble.

NOTES

1. *Therefore I exhort [the] elders among you:* In a pattern used before, the author now moves from a consideration of the community's stance toward outside forces (4:12-19) to the quality of relationships within the community (5:1-5; see similarly the exhortations in 4:1-6 [dealing with outsiders] and 4:7-11 [life within the community]). The exhortations to the "elders among you" *(presbyterous . . . en hymin)* is linked to the previous material by the conjunction "therefore" *(oun)*. The inner logic of the connection is that given the crisis the community faces—with the need for discipline and fortitude in dealing with a hostile environment and the responsibility to maintain mutual love within the community—it is crucial that it have the support of authentic and understanding leaders.

   For the first time since the opening salutation (1:1) Peter, the purported author of the letter, refers to himself. His authority stands behind the exhortation to the elders (i.e., *parakalō*, "I exhort . . ."). The term "elders" is the literal translation of *presbyterous*. Because the author will subsequently address the "younger" ones (5:5), some interpreters take "elder" to be simply a reference to the older members of the community rather than to a group of leaders (J. Ramsey Michaels, for example, claims that the author is influenced by his allusion to Ezek 9:6 in 1 Pet 4:17, where Ezekiel describes the "elders" being slain in the destruction of the Temple [Michaels, *1 Peter* 277–79; as suggested in the Notes for 4:17, such an allusion seems dubious]; others suggest that both elders and "youth" [5:5] are addressed in function of 1 Peter's concern about the household: see F.-R. Prostmeier, *Handlungsmodelle* 453–57). However, given the author's reference to his own role as a "co-elder" and the instructions in vv. 2-3 about care for the community, it seems clear that the term "elder" in this context refers to a leadership role within the community (Achtemeier, *1 Peter* 322–23; Elliott, *1 Peter* 812–16). Evidence of "elder" as a generic designation for leadership is found in a number of New Testament texts (e.g., Acts 11:30; 14:23; 15:2-6, 22-23; 16:4; 20:17; 21:18; 1 Tim 5:17, 19; Titus 1:5; Jas 5:14). Christian usage of the term most probably derived from Judaism, although the term was also used to designate leaders in Greco-Roman literature. No hint is given of the particular role or responsibilities of these leaders, although the warning about greed may suggest that the elders had some responsibility for community funds (see a similar concern about the "overseer" being a good manager in 1 Tim 3:4-5). The letter's main concern is the spirit in which the elders exercise their authority on behalf of the community. The whole passage is similar in vocabulary and spirit to Paul's farewell speech to the elders of Ephesus at Miletus (Acts 20:18-35; note the references to "elders," "humility," "witness," "the flock," absence of greed) and is evidence of a rather mature tradition in the early community about the qualities needed for Christian leadership.

as a co-elder and witness of the sufferings of Christ, and also as one who shares in the glory expected to be revealed: The author cites three crucial realities that underwrite his authority to address the elders in the community. First of all, he himself shares in their role as leaders as a "co-elder" *(sympresbyteros)*. This term is found nowhere else in biblical or Greco-Roman literature up to this point (though it will be used widely in later Christian literature), and is probably a term coined by the author, who tends to favor compound words beginning with *syn* ("with" or "together"; see 3:7, "co-heir," 5:13, "co-elect," 3:7, "live with," 3:8, "sympathetic"—all of which are unique to 1 Peter in the New Testament; see Elliott, *1 Peter* 817). By identifying himself as a "co-elder" the purported author, "Peter," (see Introduction) links his apostolic authority (1:1, "an apostle of Jesus Christ") to that of the leaders in the local congregations addressed by the letter. The whole tone is one of gentle consideration for the local leaders, identifying with them as the author is about to offer advice to them.

Second, the author is also a "witness of the sufferings of Christ" *(martys tōn tou Christou pathēmatōn)*. The term "witness" *(martys)* can have several meanings, ranging from an eyewitness who gives testimony in a trial (e.g., the two witnesses required in Matt 18:16), to one who attests to something or someone, and finally to one who gives testimony by sacrificing his or her own life. The question here is: in what manner is "Peter" claiming to be a "witness" of the sufferings of Christ? Given the widespread gospel traditions about Peter's failure to remain with Jesus throughout his sufferings, it is unlikely that Peter is claiming to have observed Jesus' sufferings and death at first hand. More likely the word here has the sense of "attesting" to the sufferings of Christ, similar to the manner in which Peter claims to be a "witness" of the sufferings and resurrection of Christ in Acts (see Acts 2:32; 3:15; 5:32; 10:39, 41; cf. Luke 24:48; Acts 1:8). At the same time, because the one who attests is Peter, "the apostle of Jesus Christ" (1:1), it is also likely that the witness attributed to Peter implies a unique character. The letter may well assume that the readers are aware of Peter's historic role as the first witness to the resurrection (1 Cor 15:3; Mark 16:7; Luke 24:34) and that underscores his historic authority as a "witness." The recipients of the letter, by contrast, have never "seen" Jesus (see 1:8). That Peter claims his witness of the "sufferings of Christ" rather than of his resurrection fits into the overall context of the letter with its strong emphasis both on the exemplary sufferings of Christ (1:11, 19; 2:21-24; 3:18; 4:1) and the sufferings to be endured by the community (1:6; 2:19; 3:14, 17; 4:1, 13, 16, 19).

Finally, Peter is "one who shares in the glory expected to be revealed." The "glory expected to be revealed" *(tēs mellousēs apokalyptesthai doxēs)* is probably the glory associated with the end-time and the parousia of the triumphant Christ, a recurring motif in the letter and in harmony with the strong eschatological tone of the concluding section (see 4:7, 12-13; also 1:5, 7, 13, 20; 5:10).

Some have speculated that the author is referring to Peter's witnessing of the transfiguration as in 2 Pet 1:16-18 (see Mark 9:2-8; thus Edward G. Selwyn, *First Epistle* 228–29); but 1 Peter refers to a future, not a past event. On the score of his future destiny, therefore, Peter shares in common *(koinōnos)* the hope of all the Christians.

2. *shepherd the little flock of God [entrusted] to you:* The author now introduces a traditional biblical metaphor for leadership, that of the shepherd with the flock, an image found in both the Old and the New Testaments (see, for example, well-known passages such as Psalm 23, "The Lord is my shepherd . . ." and the prophetic critique of the leaders of Israel in Ezekiel 34; in the New Testament see Matt 9:36 [Mark 6:34]; Matt 26:31 [Mark 14:27]; John 10:1-18; 21:15-17—all passages strongly influenced by Old Testament use of the imagery). The connection of Peter with the image of "shepherd" is also made in the beautiful resurrection appearance story in John 21:15-17. Likewise here the aorist imperative *poimanate* ("shepherd" or "tend") implies attentive compassionate care (see the image of the sheep without a shepherd in Matt 9:36 and the famed parable of the lost sheep in Luke 15:3-7; the Gospel of Matthew applies the parable to leadership that is attentive to the vulnerable members of the community, Matt 18:12-14). The corresponding image for the community is the "little flock of God" *(to . . . poimnion tou theou);* the noun is in fact the diminutive, hence "the little flock" (see Luke 12:32; Acts 20:28, 29). The qualifying phrase, "of God," sets up a contrast with the phrase "[entrusted] to you" (literally "the to you flock," *to en hymin poimnion;* the word "entrusted" or "belonging to" has to be supplied). The community belongs to God, but is entrusted to the care of the elders.

providing oversight not under compulsion but willingly in God's own manner: Three contrasting statements illustrate the qualities of authentic pastoral leadership in the community. The participle "providing oversight" *(episkopountes)* is missing in many manuscripts but is probably authentic (some suggest that the notion of "elders" exercising oversight seemed problematic to some later scribes; see Achtemeier, *1 Peter* 320); it seems to have adverbial force here, explaining how "shepherding the flock of God" should be done. Those chosen or appointed (the method is not mentioned) as "elders" should accept their responsibility willingly and not under compulsion. The adverb *anangkastōs* ("under compulsion") is unique to 1 Peter; *hekosiōs* ("willingly," "freely") is also rare in the New Testament (see Heb 10:26). A willing spirit is *kata theon,* that is, "in God's own manner" or "in a godly way" as befits service to God's own little flock (see v. 2a); note that the phrase is missing in some manuscripts.

not greedily but eagerly: The adverb *aischrokerdōs* ("greedily") is also unique to 1 Peter. The adjectival form is found in lists of vices to be avoided in 1 Tim 3:8 (regarding qualities for deacons) and Titus 1:7 (qualities for bishop or "overseer"). The contrasting word *prothymōs* ("eagerly") implies that the elders should be ready for service to others rather than seeking their own gain (see the adjectival form in Rom 1:15 where Paul speaks of his eagerness to proclaim the gospel; also Mark 14:38, "the spirit is willing . . .").

3. *not as ones lording it over those entrusted to you, but being examples to the flock:* The third and final set of contrasts uses a vivid compound verb to describe abusive power, "lording it over" *(katakyrieuontes).* This word is found in a remarkably similar context in Mark 10:42 (see Matt 20:28), where Jesus warns his disciples not to act in the manner of "Gentile leaders" who "lord it over" their subjects and then goes on to invoke his own example as one who serves (10:45). The word *klērōn* (translated here as "those entrusted to you") is difficult. It derives from the word for a "lot" (as in casting lots; see Matt 27:35) but also extends to that which is assigned by lot or entrusted to someone as their share or portion. The latter is the meaning implied in 1 Peter, i.e., the flock of God has been assigned as portions or shares to the various elders for their care (see BDAG 548). Rather than "lording it over" these precious portions of God's flock, the elders should be "examples" *(typoi)* to the flock. While the kind of example the author has in mind is implicit in the contrasts he has mentioned in these verses ("willingly," "freely," "not lording it over"), the author has also previously cited the example of Jesus himself (see 2:21; there, however, the author used the word *hypogrammon*) as the "shepherd and guardian" (2:25) of the community and as the "chief shepherd" (5:4). Just as Peter himself as a "co-elder" was also a witness to the sufferings of Christ, so the "elders" too had to attest to and exemplify the spirit of Jesus the shepherd in their leadership.

4. *And when the chief shepherd is revealed, you will receive the unfading crown of glory:* Once again the author's eschatological view, so strong in this concluding part of the letter (especially beginning with 4:7), comes into view. Responsible exercise of leadership on the part of the elders will be rewarded at the parousia "when the chief shepherd is revealed" (literally, "the chief shepherd having been revealed" *kai phanerōthentos tou archipoimenos).* The word "chief shepherd" *(archipoimenos)* is found only here in the New Testament (but see a somewhat similar idea in Heb 13:20, "the great shepherd of the sheep," *ton poimena tōn probatōn ton megan).* The faithful elders will receive "the unfading crown of glory" *(ton amarantinon tēs doxēs stephanon).* Receiving a "crown" as an award for military, political, or athletic triumphs was commonplace in the ancient world (see 1 Cor 9:25, where Paul refers to the perishable crowns given to the athletes; in Mark 15:17 and parallels Jesus is mocked by being crowned with thorns). Metaphorical use of "crown" to refer to the reward expected at final judgment is found in other New Testament texts (see, for example, 1 Thess 2:19 [see a similar reference to the community as Paul's "crown" in Phil 4:1]; 2 Tim 4:8; Jas 1:12; Revelation frequently uses "crown" as a metaphor of final victory: see 2:10; 3:11; 4:4, 10; 6:2; 14:14). The adjective "unfading" *(amarantinon)* is used only in 1 Peter in the New Testament (see also 1:4); literally it derives from the "amaranth," a flower that was considered particularly durable. The term may suggest that 1 Peter had in mind the crowns used in athletic contests and other celebrations that were typically made from vegetation and therefore quickly wilted. From the outset the author has affirmed that the glorious reward conferred by God on the faithful Christians will never fade (see 1:3-9).

5. *Likewise, younger men, be subject to the elders:* The author's exhortation switches gears and now addresses the "younger men" (*neōteroi,* the comparative form). The adverb "likewise" (*homoiōs*) extends the exhortation about responsibility to this new category of people (see similarly 3:1, 7 where the same word extended exhortations to wives and husbands). Because of this shift some commentators suggest that the author resumes here the household code format broken off in 3:7, i.e., "younger men" would follow after exhortations to slaves, wives, and husbands (see Kelly, *Epistles* 204; Elliott, *1 Peter* 836–37, considers Kelly's view unlikely but concedes that this material may have originated as part of a "traditional instruction for households" and 1 Peter adapted it to the context). But such a "cut and paste" approach seems unlikely. The instructions in 2:18 to 3:7 do not follow the household code format, but single out those members of the community most vulnerable to social pressure (i.e., slaves and wives of non-Christian husbands); the exhortation to husbands is tacked on because of the preceding instructions to wives as a reminder to their spouses about the wives' inherent dignity. Hence the address to the "younger men" is not a residue from the preceding material, but stands on its own.

Yet the precise identification of the "younger men" and the purpose of addressing them here are not immediately clear. The term "elder" in the preceding verses did not refer simply to senior members of the community, but to those who exercised leadership. There is no evidence that "younger men" formed some kind of group or office in the community (as for example "widows" did; see 1 Tim 5:3-16). Thus the turn to "younger" members of the community is not a perfect balance with "elder" in this context. At the same time it is likely that the "elders" who were leaders were also, in fact, the older men in the community. Hence the term "younger men" may simply be a way of referring to those in the community who are not in leadership positions; thus it is equivalent to the "rest of the congregation" who must respect the elder's authority.

They are urged to "be subject to" (*hypotagēte*) the elders. This key word in 1 Peter was also used to describe the attitude of slaves to their masters (2:18) and wives to their husbands (3:1). More importantly, all the members of the community were urged to "be subject to all human authority for the sake of the Lord" (2:13). This latter text provides the best understanding of "being subject" as used in the letter. The notion is not one of servile obedience or submission but of proper respect for authority (as distinct from rebellion against authority). "Being subject to" the authority of the elders on the part of the younger men is in tandem with the instruction to the elders not to "lord it over" the community (4:3).

all of you, put on humble-mindedness toward one another, because God resists the proud but gives grace to the humble: Just as in 3:8, the author concludes his exhortations to individual clusters within the community by addressing everyone (*pantes,* i.e, "all of you"). As has been the case throughout this section of the letter, the author uses novel language to make his point. The community members are "to put on humble-mindedness toward one another"; the verb *engkombōsasthe* ("to put on") occurs only in 1 Peter and literally refers to a garment that is tied on like an apron or tunic. Some interpreters believe it may refer to the apron that laborers used to put over their regular clothes (Achtemeier, *1 Peter* 332; Elliott, *1 Peter* 846–47). If that is the case, its use with "humility" is enticing. The term "humble-mindedness" captures the literal sense of the word *tapeinophrosynēn* (literally "thinking humbly") and is especially appropriate in this segment of the letter, where the author speaks of the mutual attitudes of care and respect that should reign in the community. Acting out of a perspective of humility avoids the kind of arrogance or self-seeking that corrupts both leaders and followers (see also Phil 2:3; Col 3:12; Eph 4:2).

The author concludes with a quotation from the Septuagint version of Prov 3:34 (also quoted in Jas 4:6), prefacing it with the causative *hoti* ("because") to indicate that God's perspective is the ultimate guide for the community's life (see above, 5:2, "in God's own manner"), and changing the LXX "Lord" *(kyrios)* to "God" *(theos)*. God "resists" or "opposes" *(antitassetai)* the arrogant but gives grace *(charin)* to the humble, echoing the thought of 4:10 where God's "gifts" *(charisma)* were given precisely to serve one another within the community.

INTERPRETATION

As the letter moves to its conclusion the author links the community's fortitude in the midst of persecution and trial from without (4:12-19) with the proper exercise of leadership within its boundaries (5:1-5). For the first time since the opening greeting (1:1) the author brings himself into the picture as he urges the leaders of the community to be good pastors and calls on the rest of the community to be responsive to their leadership. As with a number of other New Testament references to leadership roles in the community (see, for example, 1 Tim 3:2-7, 8-13; Titus 1:5-9), the letter does not describe in detail the particular functions of the office, but is content to list the general qualities that should characterize the spirit in which leadership is exercised. In form and tone this passage in 1 Peter is reminiscent of Paul's farewell speech to the "elders" of Ephesus (Acts 20:17-36). As 1 Peter does here, Paul invokes his own apostolic leadership and then encourages the elders to care for the "flock" that God has placed in their charge.

The ones addressed are called "elders" *(presbyteroi)*, a term drawn primarily from Jewish tradition, referring not simply to age or status but to a more or less formalized role as leaders within the community. It is impossible to determine from the text of 1 Peter the extent to which such leadership roles were developed within the communities addressed by the letter. To bolster his own authority in advising this group the author describes himself as a "co-elder," as a "witness of the sufferings of Christ," and as "one who shares in the glory expected to be revealed" (5:1). As discussed in the Introduction and in the commentary on 1:1, it is not certain that the actual author of the letter is the apostle Peter. However, the letter does invoke the apostolic authority of Peter and now extends that authority to the leaders of communities in Asia Minor, presumably from the church in Rome (see below, 5:13).

The prerogatives cited by "Peter" are not unique to the apostle. He holds the office of "elder" in common with the leaders he addresses. He is a "witness" to Christ's sufferings, not in the sense of being an eyewitness to the Passion of Jesus, a boast unlikely in view of the gospel traditions about Peter's denial and desertion of Jesus during his Passion. Rather, Peter attests or witnesses to the suffering of Christ in the manner that all Christians were encouraged to do (see, for example, 2:21; 4:1), and he shares in the "glory expected to be revealed," just as every Christian has a stake in the day of salvation (1:4-5). Yet the readers of the letter were also aware that Peter was, in a sense, a first among equals; no other elder could claim to be "an apostle of Jesus Christ" in the way Peter could (1:1). Thus his "witness" bore a historic quality that legitimated his authority to address fellow elders with credibility.

The author uses traditional pastoral imagery in offering his advice to the elders, although in many instances the author finds novel language to do so. Earlier in the letter the author refers to Christ as the "shepherd and guardian" of the community (2:25). Now that same biblical image is applied to community leadership. The sacredness of the elder's responsibility rests on the fact that the community is "the little flock of God" and therefore leadership is to be exercised in a "godly manner" (5:2).

Three sets of contrasting attitudes define what pastoral leadership should be. It must be exercised "willingly" and not "under compulsion" (5:2). This may imply that the office of leadership was conferred by designation or election. The one so chosen must not perform this service as a grim duty. Likewise, elders should not be motivated by "greed," but be eager to be of service to the community (5:2b). The duties of the elders may have involved oversight of the community resources. The list of qualities for "overseers" *(episkopoi)* mentioned in 1 Timothy includes the ability to manage their own households and to be "no lovers of money" (1 Tim 3:3-4, 8 [for deacons]; also Titus 1:7).

Finally and most fundamentally, the elders should "not lord it over" those entrusted to them, but should be models or examples to the community (5:3). The word for "lording it over" is the identical and rare Greek word used in Mark 10:42 where Jesus decries the example of the Gentile leaders who oppress their subjects. To counter this example Jesus offers his own model of selfless service: "For the Son of Man came not to be served but to serve, to give his life in ransom for the many" (Mark 10:45).

Through the way the elders exercise leadership they can also witness to the redemptive sufferings of Christ (5:1).

The reward held out to the elders is the same vision that draws the entire community into the future: "the unfading crown of glory" (5:4). This share in glory will take place "when the chief shepherd is revealed" (5:4). This entire concluding section of the letter, beginning in 4:7, has a strong eschatological perspective. Just as the entire community eagerly awaits the day of glory and its imperishable inheritance (1:3-5), the leaders can expect the victor's crown, not made of perishable materials as was the Greco-Roman custom, but one that will endure forever and be emblazoned with God's own glory.

The author follows his directives to the leaders with an appeal for cooperation from the rest of the community. The "younger" ones should be properly respectful of the authority of the elders (5:5). The precise meaning of "younger" is not clear. The author may mean in effect everyone who is not a leader or "elder," playing off the term "elder" since in fact most religious leaders would be chosen from the older members. Or does he refer to the "younger" members as a specific group (see, for example, Titus 2:6-7), perhaps implying that the younger members might have a more difficult time submitting to the authority of the elders? In any case, the younger members were to "be subject to" the elders in the same way that all the members of the community were to be properly subject to legitimate human structures (2:13). The word "be subject to" does not connote blind obedience, but the deliberate commitment to involve oneself in a societal institution "for the Lord's sake." Here, in the case of "elders" chosen to lead the "flock of God," there was all the more reason to give them proper respect and obedience.

A final cast of the net draws in everyone, subjects and leaders: "all of you, put on humble-mindness toward one another" (5:5). The antidote for arrogance or resentment is "humble-mindedness." This was not considered a virtue generally in Greco-Roman society, but it was prized in Judaism and Christianity. To be humble meant that one understood one's standing before God. This is the attitude the community was urged "to put on." Similar clothing metaphors are found in other New Testament passages (see, for example, Rom 13:12; Eph 6:11, 14; 1 Thess 5:3; Col 3:12), but the word *engkombōma* used by 1 Peter is unique, suggesting the work apron or tunic used by laborers.

Following a typical pattern in the letter, the author concludes a series of exhortations with an Old Testament quotation (see also 1:24; 3:8; 4:18). The words of Prov 3:34 confirm the God-consciousness implied in the virtue of humble-mindedness. The proud who act as if God did not exist are opposed by God, but the humble who live in accord with God's truth receive "grace."

FOR REFERENCE AND FURTHER STUDY

Brown, Raymond E. *The Churches the Apostles Left Behind.* New York: Paulist, 1984, 75–83.

Brown, Raymond E., Karl P. Donfried, and John Reumann. *Peter in the New Testament.* Minneapolis: Augsburg; New York: Paulist, 1975.

Elliott, John H. "Ministry and Church Order in the New Testament: A Traditio-Historical Analysis (1 Pt 5,1-5 and parallels)," *CBQ* 32 (1970) 367–91.

Hiebert, D. Edmond. "Selected Studies from 1 Peter, Part 4: Counsel for Christ's Under-Shepherds—An Exposition of 1 Peter 5:1-4," *BS* 139 (1982) 330–41.

Perkins, Pheme. *Peter: Apostle for the Whole Church.* Columbia: University of South Carolina Press, 1994, 131–50.

Prostmeier, Ferdinand–Rupert. *Handlungsmodelle im ersten Petrusbrief.* FzB 62. Würzburg: Echter, 1990, 449–71.

Spicq, Ceslas. "La place ou le rôle des jeunes dans certaines communautés néotestamentaires," *RB* 76 (1969) 508–27.

Vancil, Jack W. "Sheep, Shepherd," *ABD* 5:1187–90.

18. *Confidence in the God of All Grace* (5:6-11)

6. Be humbled therefore under the mighty hand of God, in order that he might lift you up in due time, 7. throwing all your anxiety on him, because he cares about you. 8. Be sober, be watchful. Your opponent the devil goes about as a roaring lion, seeking [someone] to swallow up. 9. Oppose him, solid in faith, knowing that the same kinds of sufferings are being placed upon your brethren throughout the world. 10. For the God of all grace, who called you to his everlasting glory in Christ [Jesus], after [you] have suffered a little, will himself restore, confirm, strengthen, establish [you]. 11. To him [is] the power forever. Amen.

NOTES

6. *Be humbled therefore under the mighty hand of God:* While connected to the previous segment with the repetition of the word "humble" (see 5:5), these verses represent a distinct section, following upon the quotation of Prov 3:34. The author begins a "peroration" that summarizes major themes of the letter and leads to its final greetings and close in 5:12-14. The aorist passive imperative *tapeinōthēte* has the notion of "being humbled" or, as Achtemeier suggests, "accept being humbled" or "accept your humble status" (see Achtemeier, *1 Peter* 338). The conjunction "therefore" (*oun*) also draws a connection with the preceding quotation; since God "gives grace to the humble," it behooves

the Christians to accept their status before God. The metaphor "under the mighty hand of God" is found only here in the New Testament but is frequent in the Old Testament—another example of the ease with which the author absorbs biblical terms and metaphors. Here it is used to express God's protective power extended to those who are humble and in need (see, for example, Exod 3:19; 6:1; 13:9, 14, 16; Deut 3:24; 4:34; 9:26, 29; 26:8; Dan 9:15).

in order that he might lift you up in due time: First Peter's fundamental theology of suffering and exaltation is reasserted here. The Christians are humbled before God, but not in a servile spirit, because God will exalt the faithful Christians on the final day of judgment. Genuine humility is expressed in manifold ways—through a lack of arrogance on the part of leaders (5:3), through respect for the elders on the part of the "younger members" (5:5), and through mutual deference and respect on the part of the entire community (5:5). Such virtue will be rewarded by God; the humble will be "lifted up" (*hypsōsē*) by God "in due time." The "time" referred to here (*en kairō*) is without doubt the expected day of judgment; the term *kairos* is used repeatedly in this sense both in 1 Peter and in other New Testament texts (see 1:5, "in the last time" (*en kairō eschatō*); 4:17; also Mark 13:33; Matt 24:45; Luke 12:42). In a similar vein some variant readings add "of visitation" (*en kairō episkopēs*), but the shorter reading is preferred.

7. *throwing all your anxiety on him, because he cares about you:* The same dynamic of humility and exaltation is repeated, but now applied to the sufferings that threaten the Christians. The aorist participle *epiripsantes* ("throw" or "cast") could be construed as a participle imperative (i.e., "throw") or, as suggested here, as illustrative of what it means to be humble before God (i.e., "by throwing . . ."). The only other New Testament occurrence of the verb *epiriptein* is in Luke 19:35, where the disciples "throw" their cloaks on a colt as a saddle for Jesus to enter Jerusalem. That notion of casting or throwing one's anxieties on God to unburden oneself fits perfectly the author's meaning in 1 Peter. The term "anxiety" (*merimnan*) is generic, but in the context of the letter it must refer to the sufferings the community has had to endure, which have been a preoccupation of the letter.

Ultimate anxiety is dissolved in the knowledge that God "cares" (*melei*) for the community. This intimate sense of God's providence, too, is a deep current of the letter (see, for example, the sense of God's protective care in 1:5, 21; 2:9-10; 3:12; 4:14, 19). The sentiment echoes the sayings of Jesus found in Matt 6:25-34, with its encouragement "do not worry (*mē merimnate*) about your life . . ." (see also Luke 12:22-31; Phil 4:6-7; similarly, Ps 54:23 [LXX: *epirripson epi kyrion tēn merimnan sou*, "throw on the Lord your anxiety"). As in many instances in the letter, 1 Peter appears to tap into early Christian traditions rooted in the sayings of Jesus.

8. *Be sober, be watchful:* The author exhorts the Christians to adopt both of these stances in preparation for the end-time. Earlier (in 1:13) the author had encouraged the community to "be sober" (*nēpsate*), in the sense of self-controlled and focused, as it prepared for the final revelation of Jesus Christ, and again in 4:7 that the community be sober and prayerful in view of the approaching

end. Similarly, to be "watchful" or "awake" (*grēgorēsate*), although mentioned only here in 1 Peter, is an important virtue of readiness for the end-time in other New Testament traditions (see Matt 24:42; 25:13; Mark 13:35, 37; Luke 12:37; both verbs are paired in 1 Thess 5:6, "So then let us not fall asleep as others do, but let us keep awake and be sober [*grēgorōmen kai nēphōmen*] . . .")." These words give a strong eschatological dimension to a point the author has already made—namely, that the Christian was to live "conscious" of God (see 2:19; 3:7; 4:7). Now that consciousness also envelops an understanding that God's judgment is near and that the threats to the community are increasing.

Your opponent the devil goes about as a roaring lion, seeking [someone] to swallow up: With this verse the author adds another dimension to his analysis of the plight of the Christians in the world. Christians should be "sober" and "watchful" because their ultimate adversary is formidable; some manuscripts supply a causative *hoti*, "because," at the beginning of this phrase. The threat they face is not simply suffering caused by the abuse and alienation of the dominant non-Christian majority; lurking beneath and beyond all this is the power of the demonic. The demon is portrayed as an "opponent" *(ho antidikos)*; the term can mean an accuser or plaintiff in a lawsuit (see, for example, Matt 5:25; Luke 12:58; 18:3) but here has a more deadly meaning of adversary or enemy, a meaning the term also has in the Septuagint (see Isa 41:11; Sir 36:6) and in Josephus (*Ant.* 13:413). The demonic is also described as the "devil" *(ho diabolos)*, a term that has the basic meaning of one who "slanders" another but is used frequently in the New Testament to refer to Satan (see Matt 4:1, 5, 8, 11; 13:39; 25:41; Luke 4:2, 6, 13; 8:12; John 13:2; Acts 10:38; Eph 4:27; 6:11; Heb 2:14; Jas 4:7; 1 Tim 3:6; 2 Tim 2:26). The devil is an aggressive force who goes about as a "roaring lion," a vivid image of terror used only here in the New Testament but with similar echoes in 2 Tim 4:17 (". . . so I was rescued from the lion's mouth") and Heb 11:33 (referring to the faith of the Old Testament ancestors who "shut the mouth of lions"), as well the image of the lion as a powerful, threatening beast in Revelation (see Rev 4:7; 9:8, 17; 13:2). The notion of a "roaring lion" is found in the Old Testament (see particularly Ezek 22:25, "Its princes within it are like a roaring lion [*hōs leōntes hōryomenoi*]). The image of evil as a raging lion might have been prompted by the corresponding image of the community as God's "flock" who naturally would be vulnerable to such murderous attacks (see 5:2-4). The demon's intent is to totally consume its prey (the verb *katapiein* literally means to "drink down" or "swallow up"). The object of the devil's threat is not spelled out; a variant reading makes explicit the *tina* ("someone") that is to be understood here.

9. *Oppose him, solid in faith, knowing that the same kinds of sufferings are being placed upon your brethren throughout the world:* The Christians are to stand up against the power of evil; the imperative *antistēte* ("oppose" or "resist") is also found in Jas 4:7 ("Resist the devil, and he will flee from you"; see a similar motif in Eph 6:11-13). The Christians do so because they are "solid in faith"; the adjective *stereoi* denotes strength, solidity, something firmly established (see, for example, 2 Tim 2:19). The source of the Christian's strength against evil is found in their "faith" (*tē pistei;* see 1:5, 7, 9, 21). In other words, the source of

their strength is their trust in God, who protects them from all harm (1:5) and assures their salvation despite the threats of evil (1:9, 21; 4:21). The notion that trust in God is the ground of Christian existence is also implicit in the string of verbs in 5:10.

To reinforce the solidity of their faith the author reminds the Christians to keep in mind that their fellow believers throughout the world are also bearing such suffering. The grammar is somewhat complex here. The participle "knowing" (eidotes), followed by an accusative and an infinitive, is equivalent to indirect discourse, so that the sense is "knowing that . . ." (similar to 1:18; see J. Ramsey Michaels, 1 Peter 300–301). The phrase ta auta tōn pathēmatōn, with the word "sufferings" in the genitive plural, is somewhat obscure. It could mean "the same sufferings," but one might expect the author to use a simple noun and adjective formulation (i.e., ta auta pathēmata). The genitive "sufferings" is probably to be understood as a partitive genitive, i.e., "the same [kinds] of sufferings," as translated here (see Michaels, 1 Peter 301). The precise word used to describe the experience of suffering is significant; they are "being placed upon" (epiteleisthai) the Christians. The verb epitelein has the root meaning "complete" or "finish"; here in the passive infinitive form it has the sense of "causing something to happen as fulfillment of a purpose" or simply "fulfill" (BDAG 383). Thus the translation "placed upon" assumes intentionality and purpose; the passive voice suggests that the imposition of suffering, although it also has human and even demonic causalities, is ultimately something ordained by God. Throughout the letter the author has emphasized the redemptive force of suffering, principally the exemplary sufferings of Jesus (1:2, 11, 18-19; 2:21-24; 3:18-22; 4:1, 13) but also the innocent sufferings that Christians have to endure in remaining steadfast in faith (1:6-7; 2:19-21; 3:14, 17; 4:1, 13-16, 19; 5:1). Such redemptive suffering is placed upon en [tǭ] kosmǭ hymōn adelphotēti, literally "your brethren in the world." The word adelphotēs ("brethren") was used earlier in the letter when the author urged his addressees to love their fellow members of the community (3:17); now that bond of mutual love is extended to the whole network of Christian communities "in the world." The term "world" could mean the "world" as distinct from the realm of the divine, but that kind of stratification is not alluded to in the letter; more probably it is used geographically to mean "the whole world" (as, for example, in Matt 4:8; 26:13; 1 Cor 14:10). Given the probable origin of the letter from Rome (see the discussion at 5:13), this is an intriguing hint of the author's vantage point, addressing scattered communities in Asia Minor and linking their experience with that of other Christian communities in the wider Mediterranean world.

10. *For the God of all grace, who called you to his everlasting glory in Christ [Jesus]:* In a final burst of praise the author once again sounds his key conviction about God's fidelity in the midst of Christian suffering—the foundation of all his exhortations to the communities. God is named "the God of all grace" (ho . . . theos pasēs charitos). The term "grace" is used ten times in a variety of ways in 1 Peter, but fundamentally it refers to God's favor bestowed on the Christians through the redemptive work of Christ (see especially 1:2, 10, 13; 3:7; 4:10; 5:5,

12). Citing God in this conclusion to the letter as the source of all grace reaffirms the basic theocentric focus of 1 Peter. The author returns to the opening motif of the letter in reaffirming God as the "one who called" (*ho kalesas hymas;* see 1:15; 2:9, 21; 3:9) the Christians to "eternal glory in Christ [Jesus]." The intent of God's "call" has been variously described in the letter (to "holiness" 1:15; "into marvelous light" 2:9; "to follow in the footsteps of Christ" 2:21; "to inherit a blessing" 3:9), but in each instance the object of the call is to draw the Christian to final salvation, and that is also the sense of the term "eternal glory in Christ [Jesus]" used in 5:10 (on the meaning of "glory" *[doxa]* in this particular sense see especially 5:1, 4). Some manuscripts include the name "Jesus" with Christ, but the evidence is not compelling since it is less likely that a later scribe would eliminate it.

after [you] have suffered a little, will himself restore, confirm, strengthen, establish [you]: After a brief time *(oligon)* of suffering, God will bring the faithful Christians to their glorious end. The author has consistently emphasized the brevity of the time of suffering and here contrasts it with the "eternal glory" promised (see 1:6; 4:3, 5, 7, 17). The author assigns to God's personal action (the *autos,* "himself," is emphatic) a string of verbs similar in meaning: *katartisei* ("restore," "put in proper condition"), *stērixei* ("fix firmly in place," "confirm"); *sthenōsei* ("strengthen," "make strong"), *themeliōsei* ("provide a secure basis for something," "establish"). The object "you" is not expressed and can, as suggested in this translation, be supplied based on the "you" in 10a ("the one who called *you*") or omitted, leaving the focus solely on God's powerful affirming action (the notion of God's strengthening the Christian is found in Rom 16:25 *[stērixai]*; 2 Thess 2:17 *[stērixai]*). In any case the cumulative force of the author's rhetoric is to affirm without qualification the might and trustworthiness of the God who sustains the Christians in the midst of suffering and calls them to eternal glory (see also the exhortation of 4:19).

11. *To him [is] the power forever. Amen:* The peroration closes with a doxology, similar to the one that closed the main body of the letter (4:11) but with the single attribute of *kratos* ("power," "dominion," or "might"; see also 4:11)—the only time in the New Testament that it stands alone in a doxology. That singularity fits here, where the author stresses the power of God that ultimately overcomes all evil and brings life from death. The verb is not expressed, and although an imperative could be understood (i.e., "attribute to God the power") it is preferable to see this as an acclamation, acknowledging and implicitly giving praise for the divine power that belongs to God alone and is the taproot of all Christian hope (Achtemeier, *1 Peter* 346–47).

Interpretation

As the author brings his message to a conclusion, he returns to the starting point (see 1:3-5): trust in the God who calls the Christians to new life. That trust must not be shaken, even as the communities suffer on their way to glory. The whole passage, with its exhortation to resist evil and place one's trust radically in God, is reminiscent of Jas 4:6-10 and Eph 6:11-13, each author drawing on a common motif in early Christian tradition.

The reference to humility at the end of the previous segment (5:5) becomes the lead into this passage: the Christians are to "be humbled . . . under the mighty hand of God" (5:6). Being humble means recognizing the truth of one's standing before God; a truth that leads not to servile fear but to confidence in God's abiding strength. The Old Testament image of the "mighty hand of God" evokes God's protective power on behalf of Israel, especially during the Exodus (see, for example, Deut 26:8, "and the Lord brought us out of Egypt with a mighty hand and an outstretched arm . . .").

In a dynamic expressed throughout the letter and repeated here, the author affirms that humility before God is the prelude to exaltation. In the day of judgment that was fast approaching, God would exalt the Christians just as he had exalted the suffering Christ (3:18-22). This deep sense of hopefulness about the future, even in the midst of current suffering, is a hallmark of 1 Peter.

The next verse (5:7) is a corollary to the preceding. One expression of being humble before God is the willingness and trust that enable the Christians to "throw" their anxieties on God, knowing that the awesome and mighty God yet "cares" for the Christian. The author seems to borrow the language of this exquisite verse from the Septuagint version of Ps 54:23 ("Throw on the Lord your anxiety and he will sustain you"), yet the spirit of the passage also resonates with the sayings of Jesus in Matt 6:25-34 about God's unfailing providence and the uselessness of anxiety. Anxiety about life is useless when one considers the loving care of God for creation. While it is unlikely that 1 Peter draws directly on gospel material, the letter consistently echoes motifs that can be traced to the sayings of Jesus that had found their way into early Christian tradition (see also 3:9, 14; 4:14).

Confidence in God means more than casting one's anxieties into God's care; it also gives the strength to be alert and active in the Christian mission. For the first time in the letter the author identifies the demonic as the ultimate opponent of the community. Earlier the letter had described Jesus' own triumph over the evil spirits and his exaltation at the right hand of God over all cosmic "authorities and powers" (3:19-22). Now the Christians, too, must be "sober and watchful" because the demon as a roaring and ravenous lion also intends to "swallow them up" (5:8). Previously the author had placed the cause of the sufferings endured by the community on very human causes: the abuse and incomprehension of outsiders who resented the different ways of the Christians (2:12, 15; 3:16; 4:4, 16), a nonbelieving husband (3:1), an abusive slaveowner (2:18-21).

Now he suggests that behind this human agency there also lurked the aggressive evil of the devil. While 1 Peter does not share the viewpoint of Revelation that saw the Roman government itself as demonic, the author still views the world as a dangerous place in which evil prowls.

This reading of evil was no doubt fueled by the author's conviction that the end-time was approaching, a motif that comes strongly to the surface in the latter part of the letter (see 4:7, 12, 17). The end-time was expected to be a time of travail and of the final assault of evil. This, too, prompts the author's use of eschatological language about being "sober" and "watchful" (5:8), echoing similar calls for readiness at the beginning of the letter (see 1:13; see also 4:17). First Peter advises the Christians to draw on God's strength and to see evil as their "adversary" (5:8). Evil is not passive, but aggressive and active, prowling the world like a raging animal seeking to destroy human life. While the Christians were urged to respect proper authorities (2:13, 17) and to deal with their human opponents with "gentleness" (3:16; also 3:4), they are to actively "resist" the devil not by using their own strength but by the steadfastness of their faith and their conviction that God's own power would fully sustain them (5:9-10).

The author urges the communities to recall not only their own communion with God but also their fellowship in faith and suffering with their fellow Christians "in the whole world" (5:9). This consciousness of the "worldwide" church (probably the rim of the Mediterranean world known to Rome) is a unique glimpse into the dawning consciousness of the early community and its leadership. The sufferings endured by the communities addressed in the letter and by their fellow Christians are not isolated irritants but intrinsic to the experience of being a follower of Jesus. While human agency and the power of evil play their roles, ultimately the vocation to suffer as a Christian (4:16) finds its source in God, who leads the Christians from suffering to new life just as he had brought the suffering Christ to exaltation at his right hand. Suffering as a Christian is part of a cosmic transformation in which the power of evil and death will be overcome and the world will find its way to God.

That is the spirit of the final verses in this concluding section (5:10-11). Themes orchestrated throughout the letter crescendo in a triumphant and sustained chord. The author's convictions about the meaning of suffering as redemptive, about the strength and hope born of faith, and about the identity and destiny of the Christians called to salvation through Christ are fused into a firm promise: "after you have suffered a little" the "God of all grace" will utterly restore and strengthen his beloved Christians and give them a share in his "glory." God's people who have been living "in exile" and suffering alienation (1:1; 2:11) will be brought home and made whole. For those assured of this destiny the proper response is the acclamation of praise with which the body of the letter closes: "To him [is] the power forever. Amen" (5:11).

FOR REFERENCE AND FURTHER STUDY

Golebiewski, R. P. E. "Dieu nous console dans l'épreuve (1 P 5,6-11)," *AsSeign* 57 (1965) 17–23.
Richardson, R. L. Jr. "From 'Subjection to Authority' to 'Mutual Submission': The Ethic of Subordination in I Peter," *Faith and Mission* 4 (1987) 70–80.
Schwank, Benedikt. *"Diabolus tamquam leo rugiens* (I Petr. 5:8)," *Erbe und Auftrag* 38 (1962) 15–20.

19. *Final Word* (5:12-14)

12. Through Silvanus, the faithful brother as I regard him, I have written to you briefly, encouraging and testifying that this is the true grace of God; stand fast in it. 13. The co-elect in Babylon greets you, as also Mark my son. 14. Greet one another in a kiss of love. Peace be to all of you who are in Christ.

NOTES

12. *Through Silvanus, the faithful brother as I regard him, I have written to you briefly:* "Through Silvanus" *(dia Silouanou)* most likely refers to the bearer of the letter. While the preposition *dia* ("through" or "by means of") could indicate that Silvanus shared in the composition of the letter as co-author with "Peter," in almost every instance in early Christian literature the term "through" indicates the bearer of the letter and not its composer (see the discussion in Achtemeier, *1 Peter* 350; Elliott, *1 Peter* 872–74). The designation of Silvanus as "a faithful brother as I regard him" also makes it unlikely that Silvanus himself is writing this but rather that his trustworthiness is being endorsed by the author.

The identity of "Silvanus" has been the subject of much debate (see the Introduction). Since the name is not uncommon in the first-century Greco-Roman world it could refer to a "Silvanus" unknown to us from any other source. However, the majority of commentators agree that he is probably to be identified with the Silvanus who was a companion of Paul and Timothy (see 2 Cor 1:19, "for the Son of God, Jesus Christ, whom we proclaimed among you, Silvanus, Timothy, and I . . ."; 1 Thess 1:1 and 2 Thess 1:1, "Paul, Silvanus, and Timothy, to the church of the Thessalonians . . ."). The Latin form Silvanus is probably identical to "Silas," which may derive from the Aramaic *Šĕʾlîāʾ*, the name of the early missionary and companion of Paul, Barnabas, and John Mark in Acts. In a situation similar to his probable function in 1 Peter, the Jerusalem apostles appointed Silas and Barnabas to carry a letter to the church in Antioch and there to further elaborate the contents with the community (Acts 15:22-35). After a dispute broke out between Paul and Barnabas over John Mark, Silas joined Paul on his missionary journey through Syria and Cilicia (Acts 15:40-41) and continued to be a faithful companion of the apostle, along with Timothy (see Acts 16:19, 25; 17:4, 10, 14-15; 18:5). While there is no further mention of Silas or Silvanus in the New Testament apart from 1 Pet 5:12, the association with Peter and Mark in Rome is not improbable. Silvanus would have known both of these apostolic figures from his experience in the Jerusalem church (Acts 15) and would have had high standing in the Jerusalem and Pauline communities through his missionary association with Barnabas, Timothy, and Paul. The traditional evidence for Peter's eventual location in Rome and martyrdom there under Nero is strong. The reference in 1 Peter may suggest that Silvanus was part of an apostolic group in Rome (see the Introduction). Silvanus' long missionary experience, his knowledge of the apostolic church in Jerusalem, and his standing in Rome in association with Peter would all contribute to his credentials for bearing the letter to the churches of Asia Minor and even elaborating on its message upon delivery. The qualifying phrase, "the faithful brother as I regard him" *(tou pistou adelphou, hōs logizomai)* conveys this sense of endorsement on the part of "Peter" the presented author of the letter (1:1; 5:1). Silvanus is a "brother" not in the physical sense but as a trusted companion and a fellow member of the community; 1 Peter uses such familial terms in referring to the community itself (see the "brethren" *[adelphotēs]* in 2:17; 5:9). The comment "as I regard [him or it]" underscores Peter's own estimation of Silvanus (see a similar use of the verb *logizomai* in the sense of testimonial to one's own view in Rom 3:28; 8:18; 2 Cor 11:5).

Because of Silvanus' long association with Paul some interpreters have suggested that one of the purposes of citing his name in the letter is to demonstrate harmony between the Petrine and Pauline traditions. However, there is little indication in the content of the letter that such a problem is foreseen or that the author feels the need to do such reconciling (see the thorough discussion in Norbert Brox, "Tendenz und Pseudepigraphie," 116–19). At several points elements of style and theological perspectives in 1 Peter harmonize with Pauline tradition, while at the same time the theology of 1 Peter has its own distinctive and self-confident style with no sense of polemic or tension with other viewpoints (contrast, for example, 2 Pet 3:16-17).

Assuming that Silvanus is this known apostolic figure, the question remains whether or not he is cited in the letter as the actual historical bearer of the letter or whether this is part of the pseudonymous apparatus used by the actual author (see discussion in the Introduction).

The author notes that he has written "briefly" *(di ' oligōn)*. This comment is less a description of the actual length of the letter than it is part of a customary deferential remark whereby the author of a letter expresses consideration for the readers (see similar comments in Eph 3:3 *[en oligǭ]*; Heb 13:22 *[dia bracheōn]*, and numerous examples in Greco-Roman literature; see Achtemeier, *1 Peter* 352).

encouraging and testifying that this is the true grace of God; stand fast in it: The author's summation of the purpose of the letter is most apt; he has written, "encouraging" *(parakalōn)* and "testifying" *(epimartyrōn)*. The participle *parakalōn* means "urge" or "encourage"; the latter sense captures the spirit of the letter, whose fundamental purpose is to encourage Christians who suffer under duress from the dominant culture (see the same use of the word in 2:11 and 5:1). Likewise, the letter was written for "testifying"; *epimartyrōn* is an intensive form of the verb "witness" or "testify." This, too, captures the spirit of the letter. Peter had identified himself as a "witness *(martys)* of the sufferings of Christ" (5:1) and throughout the letter the author urges the Christians to remain steadfast in their commitment to the gospel even while having to suffer humiliation and abuse.

The precise referent of "this" is not immediately clear; it either refers to the letter itself, since *epistolē* is feminine, agreeing with the gender of the pronoun *tautēn* (e.g., J. Ramsey Michaels, *1 Peter* 309–10), or it may refer to the word "grace" *(charis,* also feminine gender) in 5:10, i.e., the "grace" given by the "God of all grace" that strengthens the Christians in the midst of suffering (so Elliott, *1 Peter* 878). That "grace" given by God is the "true grace" *(alēthē charin,* i.e., the "true" or "dependable" grace) and the ground of being on which the Christians are to stand. The final phrase, literally "stand in it" *(eis ēn stēte)* is a decisive imperative and probably the preferred reading, although a fairly well attested variant renders the verb as an indicative, *estēkate* ("in which you stand"). Note the similarity to Eph 6:14 *(stēte,* "stand therefore"), a passage whose affinity with the strong exhortations for resistance to evil in the latter part of 1 Peter was noted above (see 5:6-11).

13. *The co-elect in Babylon greets you:* The term "co-elect" *(syneklektē)* is unique to 1 Peter and reflects the author's preference for such compound words (e.g., see 5:1, "co-presbyter"). The notion of the Christian as "chosen" or "elected" by God was cited at the very beginning of the letter (1:2) and forms something of an inclusion here. Who precisely is the "co-elect"? The adjective is in the singular number and feminine gender. Some have speculated that Peter may be sending greetings from his wife or some other prominent woman known to the recipients (see J. K. Applegate, "The Coelect Woman of 1 Peter"), but there is no persuasive evidence for this. More likely this refers to the community from which Peter writes. The antecedent may be the term *ekklēsia* or "church," which is also feminine in Greek (a later variant in fact adds the word "church" to the text, i.e., the "co-elect church in Babylon"; see Achtemeier, *1 Peter* 353). However, since 1 Peter does not in fact use the term "church" in the letter, a better candidate may be the word "brethren" or "brotherhood" *(adelphotēs)* cited above in 5:9 (also 2:17). First Peter uses this feminine noun to stress the bonds that united the Christian community (either in a local sense as in 2:17 or to the entire worldwide community in 5:9), and that meaning would be appropriate here (Elliott, *1 Peter* 882).

The community is identified as that "which [is] in Babylon." While this term could refer to the actual city of Babylon in Mesopotamia (which was in ruins at the time) or to a military outpost by the same name in Egypt mentioned by Strabo and Josephus, it is almost certain that the author refers to Rome (a few manuscripts in fact read "Rome" here, but the variant is not well attested). Particularly after the destruction of Jerusalem in 70 C.E. and the intensification of the Jewish diaspora Rome was referred to by this name of Israel's ancient nemesis in both Jewish (for example, *2 Bar.* 11:1-2; 67:6; 4 Ezra 3:1-2, 28; *Sib.Or.* 5:143, 159-60) and later Christian literature, especially in the book of Revelation (Rev 14:8; 16:19; 17:5, 18; 18:2). While 1 Peter does not exhibit hostility to Roman authority and even encourages respect for the emperor (2:17), the experience of alienation from the surrounding culture and the resulting self-identification of the Christians as "exiles" (1:1; 2:11), members of the diaspora (1:1), and "aliens" (2:11) fit well with such a designation. Although the Christians were still honorably involved in the world and offered proper respect to authorities, they were to live with their minds and hearts fixed on God. They were, therefore—like Israel before them—exiles, living in "Babylon" but not at home there.

The bond of common faith, a common experience of suffering, and a common glorious destiny bound these small communities together. Now, from the political and symbolic center of the world, came "greetings" from their Christian brethren to the far-flung communities of Asia Minor.

as also Mark my son: Although it cannot be certain, this is probably the John Mark first mentioned in Acts in connection with the visit of Peter to his home (Acts 12:12), and then later with Paul, Barnabas, and Silas (see Acts 12:25; 15:37, 39). He is mentioned in Col 4:10 as a "cousin of Barnabas" and a co-worker with Paul (similarly in 2 Tim 4:11, where Paul instructs Timothy to bring Mark with him to aid Paul in his ministry and in Philemon 23 where he is listed, along with Luke and others, as Paul's coworker). Presumably he is one of the apostolic circle with Peter at Rome. The designation "my son" *(ho hyios mou)* is affectionate and corresponds to the relationship implied in Peter's visit to John Mark's family in Acts 12. Later Christian tradition also linked Peter to Mark as his mentor and apostolic father (see C. Clifton Black, *Mark. Images of an Apostolic Interpreter* 60–67).

14. *Greet one another in a kiss of love:* The encouragement to greet each other with a "holy kiss" is a typical element in the conclusion of several Pauline letters (see Rom 16:16; 1 Cor 16:20; 2 Cor 13:12; 1 Thess 5:26). First Peter's variant on that is to call it a "kiss of love" *(en philēmati agapēs).* Throughout the letter the author is unrestrained in urging the Christians to "love" each other (1:22; 2:17; 4:8) and addresses the community members with the term "beloved" *(agapētoi;* see 2:11; 4:12). While greeting a friend or family member with a "kiss" was part of Greco-Roman social conventions, the "holy kiss" or "kiss of love" may have also been included even at this stage in the community's assemblies and common worship. Perhaps the author foresees his letter being read at such an assembly; therefore the greeting with a "kiss of love" would be most appropriate.

Peace be to all of you who are in Christ: The letter ends with an eloquent farewell. Paul, too, concludes several of his letters in a similar fashion, but his more typical greeting is "The *grace* of our Lord Jesus be with you . . ." (as in Rom 16:20; 1 Cor 16:23; Gal 6:18; Phil 4:23; Col 4:18; 1 Thess 5:28; 2 Thess 3:18; but Paul can also include a greeting of "peace": see Rom 15:33; 2 Cor 13:11; Gal 6:16; Eph 6:23; 2 Thess 3:16). The greeting of "peace" is also traditional in the New Testament literature, including the risen Christ's greetings to his disciples (Luke 24:36; John 20:19, 21, 26; see also 14:27; 16:33) and was part of the mission instructions (Matt 10:13; Luke 10:5).

The author had opened the letter with a greeting of peace ("May grace and peace be yours in abundance" 1:2) and now concludes in the same fashion. "Peace" was the longing and the sure inheritance of all those who were "in Christ" *(en christō),* a phrase that signified the solidarity of the Christians with their Lord and the surety of their redemption through him (see 3:16; 5:10). The letter itself was meant to be an "encouragement" (5:11) that the final peace for which they longed in the midst of suffering was truly theirs because God was trustworthy.

INTERPRETATION

In these final verses the author closes the letter with some personal greetings and warm sentiments that capture the spirit of the letter as a whole. The style of this conclusion is not typical of Greco-Roman letters, which tend to end with a succinct final greeting (e.g., see Acts 15:29, "Farewell"), but is more in the manner of the Pauline letters, which may have had an influence on early Christian letter-writing as a whole. The greetings of coworkers, the summation of the intent of the letter, the greeting with a sacred kiss, and the final wish of peace are all characteristic of the conclusion of New Testament letters (see, for example, Rom 16:1-27; Gal 6:11-17; 1 Cor 16:1-24; see Achtemeier, *1 Peter* 348–49).

The author notes that the letter is "through Silvanus, the faithful brother as I regard him" (5:11). As mentioned in the Notes and discussed in the Introduction, "Silvanus" is most probably the apostolic figure, also known by the Aramaic form of his name, "Silas," who is mentioned in Acts and in Paul's letters as an important coworker with Peter, Paul, Barnabas, and John Mark. Early in the community's history "Silas" or "Silvanus" was delegated with Barnabas to bear a letter from the apostles at Jerusalem to the church of Antioch and there to elaborate on its contents. That is probably the kind of role implied in the term "through" Silvanus. Silvanus is the trusted bearer of the letter from Peter to the churches of Asia Minor and would be in a position to discuss its contents with the communities there.

Whether or not Silvanus was the actual historical bearer of the letter or whether the author uses this device to give his pseudonymous letter verisimilitude is another question (along with the question whether Peter is the actual historical author or not; see the Introduction). Just as Silvanus is most likely the figure mentioned in Acts and Paul's letters, so, too, Mark is probably the "John Mark" whose home Peter visits in Acts 12 and who is associated with the missionary work of Paul, Barnabas, and Silas (see above, Notes). The association of Mark with Peter at Rome is attested in Papias and in later Christian traditions. In any case, the authority of the letter is being bolstered not only by associating it with the apostolic authority of Peter as its author (1:1; 5:1) but also by adding the names of important figures in the apostolic church and the early Christian mission such as Silvanus and Mark (see 5:13). Peter's own authority stands behind both their roles in that he stresses Silvanus' status as "the faithful brother as I regard him" (5:11) and Mark as "my son" (5:13).

The author's stated purpose for the letter fits well with its actual style and message: "encouraging" and "testifying" (5:12). Through his eloquent letter the author has instructed the Christians on what is the "true grace of God" and urged them, even in the midst of suffering, to "stand fast in it." First Peter's brilliant and inspiring description of the basis for Christian hope and its thoughtful exhortations to refrain from violence and to remain faithful even while under duress in a hostile world give the letter extraordinary grace and power. The fact that it was included in the canon of the New Testament testifies to its effectiveness and the value with which it was held by the recipients.

The letter comes from "Babylon," a word used in first-century Jewish literature and in the book of Revelation as a code name for the imperial city of Rome. While the author does not demonize Rome and counsels respect for political authority (2:13, 17), he is well aware of the dangers to the community because of the vastly different values and practices that separate the non-Christian world from that of the community. If outright persecution is not the Christians' lot now, things could get worse and their sufferings would intensify (4:12). The choice of name for Rome shows the critical stance of the Christians toward the imperial city and its sphere of influence, which dominated their political and cultural life. They were, in fact, "exiles" (1:1; 2:11) and "aliens" (2:11) in their own land. Even in what might have been their ancestral home they were living as if in the diaspora (1:1), far from their true land where they would one day be at home with Christ and God the Father (1:4-5).

By adopting the code name "Babylon" the church at Rome signals to the communities of Asia Minor that it shares in their same call and destiny. No other New Testament book gives such explicit evidence of the strong bonds among the early communities of the church (see the Introduction). Invoking his own unique authority as "an apostle of Jesus Christ" (1:1) and a "witness of the sufferings of Christ" (5:1), as well as his common ground with the leaders of the communities (5:1) and as a sharer in the glory for which all the followers of Jesus longed (5:1), "Peter" brings the strength and wisdom of the church's newly emerging center to the scattered communities on the church's boundaries.

On the receipt of the letter these Christians are to "greet one another in a kiss of love" (5:14), a common gesture of friendship in the ancient world. But for the Christians bound together by a common call, a common faith, and a common glorious destiny the "kiss of love" was to be no perfunctory ritual but a joyous expression of their identity as God's people and members of the divine household.

The author leaves his Christians with the gift that belongs to those "in Christ" (see 3:16). People whose hope is based on Christ, who pattern their lives of witness on the crucified and risen Christ—to these "peace" belongs.

For Reference and Further Study

Applegate, J. K. "The Coelect Woman of 1 Peter," *NTS* 32 (1992) 587–604.

Brox, Norbert. "Tendenz und Pseudepigraphie im ersten Petrusbrief," *Kairos* 20 (1978) 110–20.

Elliott, John H. "Silvanus and Mark in 1 Peter and Acts," in Karl H. Rengstorf, ed., *Wort in der Zeit.* Leiden: Brill, 1980, 250–67.

Richards, E. Randolph. "Silvanus Was Not Peter's Secretary: Theological Bias in Interpreting *dia Silouanou . . . egrapsa* in I Peter 5:12," *JETS* 43 (2000) 417–32.

Soards, Marion L. "1 Peter, 2 Peter, and Jude as Evidence for a Petrine School," *ANRW* 2 (1988) 3827–49.

Jude and 2 Peter

Daniel J. Harrington, S.J.

JUDE AND 2 PETER

INTRODUCTION

1. *This Commentary*

In the expositions that follow, Jude and 2 Peter are treated as windows onto early Christian life in the late first or early second century. On the basis of close readings of these texts and modern scholarship, both letters are taken to be pseudepigraphical (that is, written under the names of Jude and Peter). Thus they are assumed to tell us more about the traditions associated with Jude and Peter in the late first century or the early second century than about them as historical figures in the early and mid-first century. I do, however, often refer to their implied authors as "Jude" and "Peter" as a way of avoiding awkwardness.

I regard the Epistle of Jude as a homily in the form of a letter and 2 Peter as a testament in the form of a letter. Both letters addressed real crises in church life, but the opponents—the "intruders" in Jude and the "false teachers" in 2 Peter—were probably not exactly the same. Both letters appeal frequently to the Old Testament as an authoritative source, while Jude uses other Jewish and Christian traditions and 2 Peter also includes some distinctively Greek terms and concepts. The Epistle of Jude seems to have been written in a more eastern (more "Semitic") setting in the Holy Land, Syria, or Asia Minor, while a plausible case can be made for 2 Peter as emanating from a Petrine "circle" in Rome. The two letters remind us that the late first to early second century was not entirely a "golden age" in Christian history. Although it remains hard to describe in detail the positions of the opponents in either letter, it is clear that for their authors what was at stake was the struggle for "the faith handed on to the saints once for all" (Jude 3), which was "a faith of equal standing" to that of the apostles (2 Pet 1:1).

The issues related to the text and language of Jude and 2 Peter (which are often "tricky") are treated in the (generally literal) translation and the

Notes. The Interpretations concern the literary form and structure of each passage, try to make clear the train of thought, and comment briefly on the wider theological significance.

2. *The Links between Jude and 2 Peter*

The NT writings known as Jude and 2 Peter are part of the collection (along with James, 1–3 John, and 1 Peter) traditionally called the General or Catholic Epistles. They appear under the names of one of Jesus' "brothers" (Jude) and one of Jesus' twelve apostles (Peter). The most obvious point of contact between them is that they share a large block of material that is so close in wording and in content as to suggest some kind of borrowing: Jude 4 = 2 Pet 2:1-3; 6 = 2:4; 7 = 2:6; 8 = 2:10a; 9 = 2:11; 10 = 2:12; 11 = 2:15; 12 = 2:13; 12-13 = 2:17; 16 = 2:18; 17 = 3:1-2; and 18 = 3:3. The occurrence of some very rare Greek expressions in parallel passages in these two works confirms the impression that one author was copying from the other. For example, "blemishes" (Jude 12; 2 Pet 2:13), "carouse together" (Jude 12; 2 Pet 2:13), "waterless" (Jude 12-13; 2 Pet 2:17), "loud boasts" or "bombast" (Jude 16; 2 Pet 2:18), and "scoffers" (Jude 18; 2 Pet 3:3).

While some earlier scholars (e.g., Charles Bigg) contended that Jude borrowed from 2 Peter and a few scholars (e.g., Anders Gerdmar) have argued that they may represent independent borrowings from a common source ("twins"), most interpreters today hold (correctly in my view) that the author of 2 Peter has borrowed (selectively) from the Epistle of Jude.

Several considerations regarding the use of OT material in particular make it more likely that Jude was the source for 2 Peter. The order of the OT examples in Jude 5-7 seems haphazard: the escape from Egypt and the destruction of the unfaithful Israelites (Exodus through Deuteronomy), the fall of the angels (Gen 6:1-4), and the punishment of Sodom and Gomorrah (Genesis 19). But in 2 Pet 2:4-10 the episodes flow according to their OT chronological order: the fall of the angels (Gen 6:1-4), the flood (Gen 6:5–8:22), and the destruction of Sodom and Gomorrah (Genesis 19). Moreover, 2 Pet 2:4-10 develops the theme of God's mercy toward the righteous alongside and as a supplement to Jude's theme of condemnation for the wicked by including the positive examples of Noah and Lot. To suppose that the author of 2 Peter has put the OT examples into their familiar biblical order and has inserted the positive theme of God's mercy toward the righteous seems more reasonable than to imagine that Jude has deliberately scrambled the order of events and omitted the theme of divine compassion.

Moreover, the use of "extracanonical" literature in Jude and its absence in 2 Peter suggest that "Peter" may have wished to impose on the text of Jude his own ideas about what is authoritative or "canonical" literature. The denunciation in Jude 8-16 mentions five figures from the Jewish tradition: the archangel Michael (v. 9), Cain (11), Balaam (11), Korah (11), and Enoch (14-15). But 2 Pet 2:15-16 focuses on and develops only the case of Balaam and omits the other four. The omission of the Michael and the Enoch material is especially significant. The dispute between Michael and the devil about Moses' corpse is not described in the OT and is probably taken from the Jewish writing known as the *Assumption (or Testament) of Moses*. The quotation ascribed to Enoch in Jude 14-15 corresponds to the Greek version of *1 Enoch* 1:9 (and 60:8). Perhaps the author of 2 Peter was satisfied with only one example. Yet his omission of the two extracanonical incidents may point to a more reserved attitude in 2 Peter toward what is an "authoritative" source for Christians and what is not. Thus the use of Jewish source material in the two letters also makes it more likely that Jude served as the literary source for 2 Peter.

Both letters confront crises within the early churches that were caused by other Christian teachers—described as the "intruders" in Jude, and as "false teachers" in 2 Peter. They both use examples taken from the OT and Jewish traditions to insist that God punishes evildoers and rewards the righteous. They both speak about Jesus in very exalted and formulaic terms: "our Lord Jesus Christ" in Jude, and "our God and Savior Jesus Christ" in 2 Peter.

In both letters it is difficult to get a clear idea about the exact nature of the opponents' teachings. The authors assume that their original readers had first-hand knowledge of the problems facing them on the local level and were concerned mainly to persuade them to resist the baleful influence of the "intruders" (in Jude) and the "false teachers" (in 2 Peter), respectively. The concerns of these late-first or early-second-century authors are not so much with enunciating Christian doctrines. Rather, they presuppose a familiarity with and acceptance of the apostolic preaching: "the faith handed on to the saints once for all" (Jude 3), and "a faith of equal standing to ours in the justice of our God and Savior Jesus Christ" (2 Pet 1:1).

The language in Jude and 2 Peter is both heated and vague. The letters contain some of the strongest polemics in the NT, which was written in a world in which philosophers and religious leaders often used very strong language against their opponents, and yet the texts offer few hints about the precise circumstances (time and place) in which they were composed. Those who accept direct authorship by Jude and Peter take the two letters as evidence for the earliest days in the history of the church. However, among the many interpreters who regard them as pseudepigraphical there are even those who place their origins well into the second century (as late as 160 C.E. for 2 Peter). Some take them as evidence for the phenomenon of "early catholicism" in the NT, a theological label that in some Protestant circles implies a falling away from the theological heights reached in Paul's letters to the Galatians and the Romans.

3. Are Jude and 2 Peter "Early Catholic" Documents?

The term "early catholicism" (*Frühkatholizismus* in German) had been a term used mainly by church historians to describe the form of Christianity that came to flourish in the late second and early third centuries C.E. under the influence of the Roman church. However, in a series of essays in the 1950s and 1960s the German Protestant NT scholar Ernst Käsemann contended that the roots of early catholicism can be found much earlier—in the late books contained in the NT canon: Luke's Gospel and Acts, Ephesians, 1 and 2 Timothy, Titus, Jude, and 2 Peter.

Käsemann interpreted these writings as attempts to control the enthusiasm rampant in the Pauline communities after Paul's interventions (as seen in 1 and 2 Corinthians) had met with practical failure. Käsemann's own theological sympathies lay with the theology in Paul's letters to the Galatians and the Romans. He regarded the so-called early catholic writings as a "falling away" (*Abfall*) from the heights of Paul's theology, and urged the churches today (Catholic and Protestant) to return to the authentic Paul and his teaching about justification by faith alone. (See Daniel J. Harrington, "Ernst Käsemann on the Church in the New Testament," *Heythrop Journal* 12 (1971) 246–57, 367–78; repr. in idem., *The Light of All Nations. Essays on the Church in New Testament Research* [Wilmington: Michael Glazier, 1982], 15–45.)

What is early catholicism? One quite comprehensive list of its characteristics was supplied by John H. Elliott in "A Catholic Gospel: Reflections on 'Early Catholicism' in the New Testament," *CBQ* 31 (1969) 214. Elliott's list included traces of, or tendencies toward, hierarchical rather than charismatic ministry, development of the monarchical episcopate, objectification of the kerygma and an emphasis on a strictly formulated rule of faith, stress on orthodoxy and sound doctrine, the moralization of faith and the conception of the gospel as the "new Law," faith as objective and static, the principle of apostolic succession and transmitted authority, the distinction between clergy and laity, an authoritative interpretation of Scripture, sacramentalism, the formulation of natural theology, concern for ecclesiastical unity and consolidation, and an interest in collecting apostolic documents. For a survey of these features in the pertinent NT writings (Luke–Acts, Ephesians, the Pastorals, Jude, and 2 Peter), see

Daniel J. Harrington, "The 'Early Catholic' Writings of the New Testament: The Church Adjusting to World-History," in *The Light of All Nations*, 61–78.

The letter of Jude has never played an especially prominent role in the debate about the presence of early catholicism in the New Testament. In fact, Jude became part of this controversy mainly through its association with 2 Peter, since almost its entire text has been integrated into 2 Peter. There is in Jude, of course, a great emphasis on proper moral behavior. What Jude criticizes most vehemently about the "intruders" is the immoral conduct they have displayed and the moral chaos they have created in the community being addressed.

The most important feature of "early catholicism" in Jude appears in its brief descriptions of Christian faith as something traditional and already fixed: "the faith handed on to the saints once for all" (3), and "your most holy faith" (20). There is also a reverence paid to the apostolic generation as a phenomenon of the past: "remember the words spoken beforehand by the apostles of our Lord Jesus Christ" (17). And the attribution of the letter's composition to Jude the Lord's brother (probably pseudonymous; see the discussion about authorship in the Introduction to Jude) attaches the document to the apostolic generation, if not to the circle of the Twelve Apostles. Finally, it is possible, as this commentary will suggest at various points, that the "intruders" combated through the letter of Jude may have represented an overly enthusiastic form of Paulinism promoted by Christians who considered themselves to be truly "spiritual" *(pneumatikoi)* but by their immoral conduct proved themselves to be only "natural" *(psychikoi)* and even "fleshly" *(sarkikoi)*.

If the letter of Jude has had a minor place in the "early catholicism" debate, the work known as 2 Peter has been very important, especially since Käsemann's famous essay on 2 Peter entitled "An Apologia for Primitive Christian Eschatology," in his *Essays on New Testament Themes*. SBT 41 (London: S.C.M., 1964) 169–95. In it Käsemann presented 2 Peter as the parade example of early catholicism in the NT canon and as the vehicle for everything he disliked about it.

As in the letter of Jude, there is in 2 Peter much emphasis on the moral shortcomings of the false teachers and the moral confusion they created. There is also (especially in 2 Pet 1:3-11 and 3:11-18) a positive vision of Christian life in which moral striving and the cultivation of the virtues are prominent.

The recipients of 2 Peter are assured at the outset that their faith is of equal standing with that of the apostles (1:1). Throughout the letter there are references to Peter as the apostle *par excellence* (1:12-16) and to the apostles as the medium for the communication of the gospel (3:2). Special care is given to showing that what Peter teaches in his letter agrees with what Paul wrote in his letters (3:15). That teaching is variously described as "the truth that is present within you" (1:12), "the way of truth" (2:2), "the holy commandment" (2:21), and "the commandment of the Lord and Savior" (3:2). These expressions all suggest that Christian "faith" is being viewed as something substantive and objective.

The author of 2 Peter seems also to hold firmer ideas about "Scripture" than Jude does, and so he excises legendary and extracanonical episodes from Jude (the angels' descent, the quarrel over Moses' corpse, and Enoch's prophecy) and rearranges the biblical events in their proper chronological order (see 2:4-8). He also criticizes the personal interpretation of Scripture and insists on Scripture's divine origin (1:20-21).

Second Peter is most noteworthy theologically for its treatment of the alleged delay of the parousia in 3:1-10. It first considers the complaint of certain scoffers ("Where is the promise of his coming?") and answers it by showing that the world has indeed changed throughout history and by reminding us that God's reckoning of time is not the same as ours: "One day with the Lord is like a thousand years" (3:8). In this way it is possible to leave time and space for the church to settle down in the world while encouraging the constant vigilance vis-à-vis the eschaton that is characteristic of most other NT writings.

While the "false teachers" in 2 Peter may not be the same as the "intruders" in Jude, they both may well represent an overly enthusiastic version of Paulinism, especially in the false teachers' focus on the present dimensions of salvation to the exclusion of future eschatology (3:3-4). The fact that in 3:15b-16 the author aligns himself with the authentic teaching of Paul while admitting the difficulties involved in interpreting Paul suggests that Paul's gospel was being used by the false teachers as a warrant for their own (distorted) version of the gospel.

Given the many "early catholic" features in Jude and 2 Peter, the question arises: Is it proper then to describe Jude and 2 Peter as proof of the presence of "early catholicism" in the NT? There are both historical and theological obstacles to doing so.

The so-called early catholic writings do not all come from the same time and the same place. Rather, Jude and 2 Peter (as well as the other pertinent documents) are better viewed as varied, though converging, responses to the crisis encountered in the late first century. Then the church was settling down in the Roman empire and was beginning to understand itself as an institution in world history rather than simply as an eschatological fellowship of believers. As Elliott states: "Early catholic documents in the NT are inevitable results of their own historical age" ("A Catholic Gospel," 215). Therefore the term "early catholicism" may be better left to the church historians as they describe what developed in the late second and third centuries.

It is probably preferable to speak about the "roots" or "elements" of early catholicism within the NT instead of full-blown early catholicism. In other words, the church of the second and third centuries found in these NT writings and in their own lived experience those features that later came to be regarded as formative and typical of early catholicism. And many of these features—emphasis on morality, the objective character of faith, an appeal to the apostolic generation, suspicions about an overly present-oriented Paulinism, explaining the "delay" of the parousia, and concern about the canon of Scripture and proper biblical interpretation—are prominent in Jude and/or 2 Peter.

While agreeing that "early catholic" elements or features may be present in Jude and 2 Peter, I do not accept the negative theological assessment of these phenomena represented by Käsemann (who regarded them as a deformation of the original Pauline kerygma) or even the approach of Richard Bauckham (who tends to explain them away). Rather, I regard these "early catholic" features as integral parts of the NT message that need to be taken seriously by all readers of the NT. And I contend that they also help us to understand better the lines of continuity between the NT and the later history of the church. There is no reason to neglect or despise the NT letters known as Jude and 2 Peter.

4. *Their Abiding Value*

Jude and 2 Peter are among the shortest documents in the New Testament, and no one can seriously claim that they rank in theological significance with the Gospels, Acts, Paul's letters, Hebrews, and Revelation. Nevertheless, they do possess some abiding significance not only for historians of early Christianity but also for serious Christians, especially in the areas of church life, inculturation, and Christian spirituality.

Church Life. The "intruders" in Jude and the "false teachers" in 2 Peter provide a vivid reminder that the early church did not exist in some untroubled golden age when everything ran smoothly. These two letters show that the first Christians not only faced persecutions from outsiders (as in 1 Peter) but also experienced divisions and factions within their own communities. And the highly emotional and polemical language that both authors used indicates how painful these conflicts must have been.

Inculturation. These two letters also provide contrasting snapshots of some early Christians living in the Greco-Roman world in the late first (or early second) century. With its many biblical and Jewish examples Jude represents a highly Jewish kind of Christianity—so much so that a plausible case can be made (as Bauckham does) for Jude the "brother" of Jesus as its real author. While in 2 Peter there is great respect for the Old Testament, there is also a concerted effort to translate the terms and concepts of Jewish Christianity into a (somewhat pretentious) Greek vocabulary. In both letters the writers push the Greek language beyond its ordinary vocabulary in their efforts at expressing what they believed so deeply.

Christian Spirituality. At the same time both letters bear witness to how quickly traditions and credal formulas developed in early Christian circles. They refer to Jesus in very reverent and exalted ways as Lord, Savior, and even God. They stand self-consciously in the tradition of "the faith handed on to the saints once for all" (Jude 3). However formulaic they may sound, their descriptions of Christian life (see Jude 20-21; 2 Pet 1:3-11; 3:11-18) are remarkably rich in their theology and sound in their spirituality.

5. *Issues in Scholarship*

In an article published in 1975, Douglas J. Rowston referred to the Epistle of Jude as "the most neglected book in the New Testament." A close runner-up in that contest would have been 2 Peter. In recent years, however, several full-scale commentaries and studies of the two letters have enriched our understanding of them.

Besides providing a guide to the larger bibliographies that follow, this survey of some major works (arranged according to their order of publication since 1975) can help to bring out the most important critical issues involved in the research on Jude and 2 Peter, and to illustrate the wide spectrum of scholarly opinions about their text, language, literary genre and structure, use of sources, authorship, historical setting, history-of-religions background, date and place of composition, and theological significance.

In *An Early Church in a Pluralistic Society. A Study of 2 Peter* (1977), Tord Fornberg argued that 2 Peter was addressed to Christians influenced by a Hellenistic urban culture, that the majority of its readers belonged to the poorer classes, that it mirrors the increasing dependence on pagan religious terminology, that it reflects a situation in which the Christians were not living under the aegis of the synagogue, that the conflict underlying the letter was cultural and religious rather than political, and that the Jewish influence was indirect and channeled through the Septuagint and early Christian traditions.

The most important commentary on the two letters is Richard J. Bauckham's *Jude, 2 Peter* (Word Bible Commentary, 1983), which takes account of previous studies and also serves as a vehicle for showing the author's wide knowledge of Jewish literature contemporary with the NT.

On the question of authorship Bauckham suggests that the Epistle of Jude reflects the direct activity of the Lord's brother whereas 2 Peter is a pseudepigraphical work composed around 90–100 C.E., probably at Rome.

In *Invention, Arrangement, and Style. Rhetorical Criticism of Jude and 2 Peter* (1988), Duane F. Watson argued that both letters incorporate the conventions of Greco-Roman rhetoric and follow similar classical rhetorical outlines: quasi-*exordium* (Jude 1-2; 2 Pet 1:1-2), *exordium* (Jude 3; 2 Pet 1:3-15), *narratio* (Jude 4), *probatio* (Jude 5-16; 2 Pet 1:16–3:13), and *peroratio* (Jude 17-25; 2 Pet 3:14-18).

Bauckham's case for the plausibility of Jude the Lord's brother as the real author of the letter that bears his name is developed and placed in a wider context in his essays collected in *Jude and the Relatives of Jesus in the Early Church* (1990). He situates Jude within the family of Jesus (the so-called *desposynoi*), who along with the Twelve were the most influential and respected leaders of Jewish Christianity in Jerusalem and in Galilee until the Bar Kokhba Revolt (132–135 C.E.).

J. Daryl Charles in *Literary Strategy in the Epistle of Jude* (1993) contends that Jude's chief concern was to strengthen and to exhort the faithful by painting in graphic terms the fate of the unfaithful. In developing his thesis that in Jude truth comes through literary form he examines the literary-rhetorical aspects of Jude's polemic, the letter's place in first-century Palestine (including Jewish Christianity), and its use of the OT (motifs and typological exegesis) and of extrabiblical (Jewish and pagan) source materials.

In *2 Peter, Jude* (Anchor Bible, 1993), Jerome H. Neyrey not only provides the standard features of a commentary (introductions, translations, expositions, notes, bibliographies) but also interprets the two letters with the help of five social-science models: honor and shame, patron and client relationships, purity and pollution, the physical body, and the group-oriented person.

Charles Landon in *A Text-Critical Study of the Epistle of Jude* (1996) contends that the Greek text of Jude should be reconstructed with much greater reliance on internal evidence than is apparent in modern editions such as the United Bible Societies' *The Greek New Testament* (4th ed. 1993). His discussion of the textual variants in the Greek manuscripts of Jude leads him to conclude that no single manuscript or group of manuscripts has a special claim to superiority and so there is a need for an eclectic approach that gives particular attention to style.

In *Rethinking the Judaism-Hellenism Dichotomy. A Historiographical Case Study of Second Peter and Jude* (2001), Anders Gerdmar seeks to turn "upside down" the traditional "consensus" of scholarly positions. He locates both Jude and 2 Peter in the context of early Jewish-Christian apocalypticism, suggests that 2 Peter could have been used as a source by Jude (though a common source is even more likely), and rejects the scholarly tradition of labeling 2 Peter as "Hellenistic" and Jude as "Jewish."

Thomas J. Kraus's *Sprache, Stil und historischer Ort des zweiten Petrusbriefes* (2001) is by far the most ambitious investigation of the Greek language and syntax of 2 Peter in the context of religious and secular documents from the classical and postclassical periods. He concludes that from the perspectives of language and style 2 Peter is a special text within the NT, and that it probably originated in the early second century C.E. against the background of the collection, circulation, reception, and misuse of the Pauline corpus (see 2 Pet 3:15-16).

6. General Bibliography

A. Commentaries on Jude and 2 Peter

Bauckham, Richard J. *Jude, 2 Peter.* Word Biblical Commentary 50. Waco: Word Books, 1983.

Bigg, Charles. *A Critical and Exegetical Commentary on the Epistles of St Peter and St Jude.* ICC. Edinburgh: T&T Clark, 1902.

Elliott, John H. *I–II Peter, Jude.* Augsburg Commentary on the NT. Minneapolis: Augsburg, 1982.

Fuchs, Eric, and Pierre Reymond. *La deuxième Épître de Saint Pierre. L'Épître de Saint Jude.* CNT XIIIb. Neuchâtel: Delachaux & Niestlé, 1980.

Green, Michael. *The Second Epistle of Peter and the General Epistle of Jude.* Tyndale NT. Grand Rapids: Eerdmans, 1968.

Grundmann, Walter. *Der Brief des Judas und der zweite Brief des Petrus.* THNT 15. Berlin: Evangelische Verlagsanstalt, 1974.

Kelly, J.N.D. *A Commentary on the Epistles of Peter and of Jude.* Harper's NT Commentaries. New York and Evanston: Harper, 1969.

Kraftchick, Steven J. *Jude/2 Peter.* Abingdon New Testament Commentaries. Nashville: Abingdon, 2002.

Mayor, Joseph B. *The Epistle of St Jude and the Second Epistle of Peter.* London: Macmillan, 1907.

Mazzeo, Michele. *Lettere di Pietro. Lettera di Guida.* Milan: Paoline, 2002.

Neyrey, Jerome H. *2 Peter, Jude.* AB 37C. New York: Doubleday, 1993.

Paulsen, Henning. *Der zweite Petrusbrief und der Judasbrief.* KEK 12.2. Göttingen: Vandenhoeck & Ruprecht, 1992.

Reicke, Bo. *The Epistles of James, Peter, and Jude.* AB 37. New York: Doubleday, 1964.

Schelkle, Karl H. *Die Petrusbriefe, der Judasbrief.* HTKNT 13.2. Freiburg: Herder, 1961.

Schrage, Wolfgang. *Die "Katholischen" Briefe.* NTD 10. Göttingen: Vandenhoeck & Ruprecht, 1980.

Senior, Donald. *1 & 2 Peter.* NTM 20. Wilmington: Michael Glazier, 1980.

Vögtle, Anton. *Der Judasbrief/Der 2. Petrusbrief.* EKKNT 22. Neukirchen-Vluyn: Neukirchener Verlag, 1994.

B. General Studies on Jude and 2 Peter

Cothenet, Edouard. "La tradition selon Jude et 2 Pierre," *NTS* 35 (1989) 407-420.

Desjardins, Michael. "The Portrayal of the Dissidents in 2 Peter and Jude: Does it tell us more about the 'Godly' than the 'Ungodly'?" *JSNT* 30 (1987) 89–102.

Gerdmar, Anders. *Rethinking the Judaism-Hellenism Dichotomy. A Historiographical Case Study of Second Peter and Jude.* CBNT 36. Stockholm: Almqvist & Wiksell, 2001.

Knight, Jonathan M. *2 Peter, Jude.* Sheffield NT Guides. Sheffield: Sheffield Academic Press, 1995.

Watson, Duane F. *Invention, Arrangement, and Style: Rhetorical Criticism of Jude and 2 Peter.* SBLDS 104. Atlanta: Scholars, 1988.

C. General Studies on Jude

Bandstra, Andrew. "Onward Christian Soldiers—Praying in Love, with Mercy: Preaching on the Epistle of Jude," *Calvin Theological Journal* 32 (1997) 136–39.

Bauckham, Richard J. *Jude and the Relatives of Jesus in the Early Church.* Edinburgh: T&T Clark, 1990.

_____. "The Letter of Jude: an Account of Research," in Wolfgang Haase, ed., *ANRW* II.25.5. Berlin: de Gruyter, 1988, 3791–3826.

Birdsall, J. Neville. "The Text of Jude in 𝔓72," *JTS* 14 (1963) 394–99.

Busto Sáiz, José Ramon. "La carta de Judas a la luz de algunos escritos judíos," *Estudios Bíblicos* 39 (1981) 83–105.

Charles, J. Daryl. "Jude's Use of Pseudepigraphical Source-Material as Part of a Literary Strategy," *NTS* 37 (1991) 130–45.

_____. "Literary Artifice in the Epistle of Jude," *ZNW* 82 (1991) 106–24.

_____. *Literary Strategy in the Epistle of Jude.* Scranton, Pa.: University of Scranton Press, 1993.

_____. "'Those' and 'These': The Use of the Old Testament in the Epistle of Jude," *JSNT* 38 (1990) 109–24.

_____. "The Use of Tradition-Material in the Epistle of Jude," *Bulletin of Biblical Research* 4 (1994) 1–14.

Eybers, I. H. "Aspects of the Background of the Letter of Jude," *Neotestamentica* 9 (1975) 133–23.

Greenlee, J. Harold. *An Exegetical Summary of Jude.* Dallas: Summer Institute of Linguistics, 1999.

Gunther, John J. "The Alexandrian Epistle of Jude," *NTS* 30 (1984) 549–62.

Hahn, Ferdinand. "Randbemerkungen zum Judasbrief," *Theologische Zeitschrift* 37 (1981) 209–18.

Heiligenthal, Roman. "Der Judasbrief. Aspekte der Forschung in den letzten Jahrzehnten," *Theologische Rundschau* 51 (1986) 117–29.

Joubert, Stephan J. "Facing the Past. Transtextual Relationships and Historical Understanding in the Letter of Jude," *BZ* 42 (1998) 56–70.

_____. "Language, ideology and the social context of the letter of Jude," *Neotestamentica* 24 (1990) 335–49.

_____. "Persuasion in the Letter of Jude," *JSNT* 58 (1995) 75–87.

Landon, Charles. *A Text-Critical Study of the Epistle of Jude.* JSOTSup 135. Sheffield: Sheffield Academic Press, 1996.

Müller, Peter. "Der Judasbrief," *Theologische Rundschau* 63 (1998) 267–89.

Reed, Jeffrey T., and Ruth A. Reese. "Verbal Aspect, Discourse Prominence, and the Letter of Jude," *Filología Neotestamentaría* 9 (1996) 181–99.

Rowston, Douglas J. "The Most Neglected Book in the New Testament," *NTS* 21 (1975) 554–63.

Seethaler, Paula-Angelica. "Kleine Bemerkungen zum Judasbrief," *BZ* 31 (1987) 261–64.

Sellin, Gerhard. "Die Häretiker des Judasbrief," *ZNW* 77 (1986) 206–25.

Thurén, Lauri. "Hey Jude! Asking for the Original Situation and Message of a Catholic Epistle," *NTS* 43 (1997) 451–65.

Webb, Robert L. "The Eschatology of the Epistle of Jude and Its Rhetorical and Social Functions," *Bulletin of Biblical Research* 6 (1996) 139–51.

Wendland, Ernest R. "A comparative study of 'rhetorical criticism', ancient and modern—with special reference to the larger structure and function of the Epistle of Jude." *Neotestamentica* 28 (1994) 193–228.

Wisse, Frederick. "The Epistle of Jude in the History of Heresiology," in Martin Krause, ed., *Essays on the Nag Hammadi Texts.* Leiden: Brill, 1972, 133–43.

Wolthuis, Thomas. "Jude and Jewish Traditions," *Calvin Theological Journal* 22 (1987) 21–41.

_____. "Jude and the Rhetorician: A Dialogue on the Rhetorical Nature of the Epistle of Jude," *Calvin Theological Journal* 24 (1989) 126–34.

D. General Studies on 2 Peter

Bauckham, Richard J. "2 Peter: an Account of Research," in Wolfgang Haase, ed., *ANRW* II.25.5. Berlin: de Gruyter, 1988, 3713–3752.

Boring, M. Eugene. "Gospel and Church in 2 Peter," *Mid-Stream* 35 (1996) 399–406.

_____. "The Historical Pilgrimage of the Church According to 2 Peter," *Mid-Stream* 35 (1996) 407–14.

Callan, Terrance. "The Christology of the Second Letter of Peter," *Bib* 82 (2001) 253–63.

_____. "The Soteriology of the Second Letter of Peter," *Bib* 82 (2001) 549–59.

Cavallin, Hans C. C. "The False Teachers of 2 Pt as Pseudo-prophets," *NovT* 21 (1979) 263–70.

Charles, J. Daryl. "The Function of Moral Typology in 2 Peter," in William P. Brown, ed., *Character and Scripture.* Grand Rapids: Eerdmans, 2002, 331–43.

Dschulnigg, Peter. "Der theologische Ort des Zweiten Petrusbriefes," *BZ* 33 (1989) 161–77.

Farkasfalvy, Dennis. "The Ecclesial Setting of Pseudepigraphy in Second Peter and its Role in the Formation of the Canon," *Second Century* 5 (1985–86) 3–29.

Fornberg, Tord. *An Early Church in a Pluralistic Society. A Study of 2 Peter.* CBNT 9. Lund: Gleerup, 1977.

Gilmour, Michael J. "Reflections on the Authorship of 2 Peter," *Evangelical Quarterly* 73 (2001) 291–309.

_____. *The Significance of Parallels between 2 Peter and Other Early Christian Literature.* SBL Academia Biblica 10. Atlanta: Society of Biblical Literature, 2002.

Käsemann, Ernst. "An Apologia for Primitive Christian Eschatology," in idem, *Essays on New Testament Themes.* London: S.C.M., 1964 169–95.

Klinger, Jerzy. "The Second Epistle of Peter: An Essay in Understanding," *St. Vladimir's Theological Quarterly* 17 (1973) 152-69.

Kraus, Thomas. *Sprache, Stil und historischer Ort des zweiten Petrusbreifes.* WUNT 2/136. Tübingen: J.C.B. Mohr (Paul Siebeck), 2001.

Kruger, Michael J. "The Authenticity of 2 Peter," *Journal of the Evangelical Theological Society* 42 (1999) 645–71.

Miller, Troy A. "Dogs, Adulterers, and the Way of Balaam: The Forms and Socio-Rhetorical Function of the Polemical Rhetoric in 2 Peter," *Irish Biblical Studies* 22 (2000) 123–44, 182–91.

Müller, Peter. "Der 2. Petrusbrief," *Theologische Rundschau* 66 (2001) 310–37.

Neyrey, Jerome H. "The Form and Background of the Polemic in 2 Peter," *JBL* 99 (1980) 407–31.

Picirilli, Robert E. "Allusions to 2 Peter in the Apostolic Fathers," *JSNT* 33 (1988) 57–83.

Robertson, T. "Relationships Among the Non-Byzantine Manuscripts of 2 Peter," *Andrews University Seminary Studies* 39 (2001) 41–59.

Snyder, John. "A 2 Peter Bibliography," *Journal of the Evangelical Theological Society* 22 (1979) 265–67.

Thurén, Lauri. "Style Never Goes Out of Fashion: 2 Peter Reevaluated," in Stanley E. Porter and Thomas H. Olbricht, eds., *Rhetoric, Scripture and Theology. Essays from the 1994 Pretoria Conference.* Sheffield: Sheffield Academic Press, 1996.

Wall, Robert W. "The Canonical Function of 2 Peter," *Biblical Interpretation* 9 (2001) 64–81.

THE EPISTLE OF JUDE

INTRODUCTION

1. *Text and Language*

The text of the Epistle of Jude that is translated and interpreted in this commentary generally follows the Greek text printed in *Novum Testamentum Graece* (27th edition), edited by Kurt and Barbara Aland (Stuttgart: Deutsche Bibelgesellschaft, 1981). This edition is based on the fourth- and fifth-century uncial manuscripts (Sinaiticus, Alexandrinus, Vaticanus, etc.) and other ancient evidence in Greek manuscripts and in early translations. For a full-scale analysis that is critical of this edition of the Greek text of Jude see Charles H. Landon, *A Text-Critical Study of the Epistle of Jude.* JSNTSup 135 (Sheffield: Sheffield Academic Press, 1996).

The Greek text of Jude is preserved, along with the texts of 1 and 2 Peter, in Bodmer Papyrus $\mathfrak{P}^{72}$, from the late third or early fourth century C.E. However early and valuable a witness $\mathfrak{P}^{72}$ may be, it cannot be simply equated with the "original" text. For example, in Jude 5 it reads (incorrectly it seems) *theos christos* instead of *(ho) kyrios,* and its short reading in Jude 22-23 gives the impression of smoothing out a passage that had already become a textual tangle. Both readings are controverted; see their treatment in the Notes and in the Interpretations of Jude 5 and 22-23.

By the end of the second century the text of the Epistle of Jude was numbered among the books of the NT by Tertullian in North Africa, Clement and Origen in Alexandria in Egypt, and the Muratorian Canon in Italy. Only afterward were doubts expressed about its canonical character (by Origen, Didymus, and Jerome), due mainly (it seems) to its appeals to the noncanonical works *1 Enoch* and *Assumption of Moses* as authoritative sources. Nevertheless, through the patristic period and after, the Epistle of Jude was generally considered part of the Christian canon of Holy Scripture.

The language of Jude is usually judged to be "good" Greek, with some Semitic influence. Most noteworthy are the fourteen *hapax legomena* ("said only once"), Greek words that are found only in Jude and not in other NT

175

books: *apodiorizein* (v. 19), *aptaistos* (v. 24), *gongystes* (v. 16), *deigma* (v. 7), *epagōnizesthai* (v. 3), *epaphrizein* (v. 13), *ekporneuein* (v. 7), *mempsimoiros* (v. 16), *pareisdyein* (v. 4), *planētēs* (v. 13), *spilas* (v. 12), *phthinōporos* (v. 12), *physikos* (v. 10), and *hypechein* (v. 7). Moreover, there are three Greek words that appear only in Jude and 2 Peter: *empaiktēs* (v. 18; 2 Pet 3:3), *syneuōcheisthai* (v. 12; 2 Pet 2:13), and *hyperongkos* (v. 16; 2 Pet 2:18). It is generally assumed that the author of 2 Peter took these words over from the text of Jude.

Jude's rich and varied vocabulary finds expression in relatively simple and clear sentences. There are instances of Greek idioms ("I was very eager," v. 3; "irrational animals" *[aloga zǭa]* in v. 10) as well as some constructions that are regarded as Semitisms ("woe to them, for they went in the way of Cain," v. 11; "showing partiality" *[thaumazontes prosōpa]* in v. 16).

The author has a special fondness for "triplets," or expressions consisting of three members: "called . . . beloved . . . kept safe," v. 1; "mercy and peace and love," v. 2; and so on. For a full list see Neyrey, *2 Peter, Jude* 28. He also makes abundant use of "catchwords" or keywords that keep the train of thought moving and give the impression of coherence to the letter: *asebēs/asebein/asebeia* in vv. 4, 15, 18; *blasphemein/blasphemia* in vv. 8-10; *planē/planētēs* in vv. 11, 13; and so on. See the full list in Bauckham, *Jude, 2 Peter* 5. The rhetorical highpoints include the list of colorful epithets in vv. 12-13 ("stains on our love feasts . . . waterless clouds . . . late autumn trees . . . wild waves of the seas . . . wandering stars") and the doxology used to conclude the letter in vv. 24-25: "Now to him who is able to keep you . . . glory, majesty, might, and authority before all time and now and for all time. Amen."

2. *Genre and Structure*

The Sinai and Vatican manuscripts give the title of this work simply as "Jude," while others entitle it the "Epistle of Jude" (including 𝔓⁷²), the "Epistle of Jude the Apostle," the "Catholic Epistle of Jude," or the "Catholic Epistle of Jude the [Holy] Apostle." In the manuscripts and printed editions of the NT (and in the modern translations) Jude appears in the part of the canon that includes the non-Pauline or Catholic/General Epistles: James, 1–2 Peter, 1–3 John, and Jude. In its gross structure the text of Jude conforms to the outline found in other NT letters as well as letters from the Greco-Roman world in general.

The most obvious epistolary feature in Jude is the salutation (vv. 1-2), which indicates the sender (Jude) and those who are being addressed ("those who are called . . ."), and offers a greeting ("mercy and peace and love"). The material in the body of the letter (vv. 3-23) consists of an opening in which the purpose and occasion are stated (vv. 3-4), a series of examples and prophecies along with applications (vv. 5-19), and an exhortation (vv. 20-23). The doxology in vv. 24-25 provides a fitting epistolary conclusion.

In vv. 3-4 the author, who had already identified himself as Jude the brother of James in v. 1, states that he had planned to write about "our common salvation" (v. 3). But the appearance of some other Christians who "secretly stole in" and were causing moral and theological confusion in the Christian commuity addressed in the letter (v. 4) led him to write a vigorous denunciation of those "intruders." Jude addresses those to whom he sends the letter as "beloved" *(agapētoi)* not only in v. 3 but also in vv. 17 and 20. Addressing fellow Christians who presumably had respect for him, Jude urges them "to contend for the faith handed on to the saints once for all" (v. 3). Indeed, the Epistle of Jude is part of their common struggle on behalf of the "most holy faith" (v. 20).

The main part of the letter (vv. 5-19) consists of examples and applications (vv. 5-13) as well as prophecies and applications (vv. 14-19). The examples in vv. 5-7 concern groups who sinned—ancient Israel in the wilderness, the rebellious angels, and the men of Sodom and Gomorrah—whose disbelief and disobedience brought about their condemnation and punishment by God. The example in v. 9 focuses on the archangel Michael's refusal to condemn his fellow angel Satan. And the three examples in v. 11—Cain, Balaam, and Korah—concern individuals who led others into sin. Each of the series of examples is accompanied by applications to "these men" *(houtoi)* in vv. 8, 10, and 12-13. Then there are prophecies from Enoch (vv. 14-15) and from "the apostles of our Lord Jesus Christ" (vv. 17-18), along with further applications to "these men" *(houtoi)* in vv. 16 and 19. An exhortation (vv. 20-23) consisting of a sketch of Jude's positive ideal of Christian life (vv. 20-21) and his advice about the pastoral care of those who may be influenced by the intruders (vv. 22-23) concludes the body of the letter. The letter is brought to a close with the doxology in vv. 24-25.

In light of this literary analysis the Epistle of Jude can be outlined as follows:

1. Salutation (1-2)

2. Purpose and Occasion (3-4)

3. Examples and Applications (5-13)

4. Prophecies and Applications (14-19)

5. Closing (20-25)

While Jude features the conventions of an ancient letter and has always been understood as a letter, the body of the document reads much like a sermon or at least the outline of a sermon (as is often postulated for Mark 4:13-20). The body skillfully interweaves biblical and related materials (episodes and characters) with practical applications in criticism of "these men" (*houtoi*). The use of catchwords and other rhetorical devices further enhances the impression that much of the material has been developed in a preaching situation. Indeed, some scholars describe Jude as an epistolary sermon, that is, a sermon in letter form.

In his use of biblical and other materials Jude adopts an interpretive approach that is common in the New Testament and is analogous to the Qumran Pesharim and other Dead Sea scrolls. In this context the biblical text (or character or episode) is a mystery *(raz)* to be resolved *(pesher)* by recourse to the life and history of the community in its present circumstances. Thus from the perspective of Jude and his readers all those examples and prophecies were being fulfilled in their own lives and experiences. In later Jewish writings this mode of reading is sometimes called "midrash." While earlier Christian interpreters spoke of this approach as "promise and fulfillment," modern Christian exegetes speak of it as "actualization."

Jude's collection of authoritative OT and Jewish texts was wider than what became the canon of Hebrew Scriptures. In his account of the rebellious angels (v. 6) and in his prophecy about the coming judgment (vv. 14-15) Jude relied on *1 Enoch,* a work that was very well known in Second Temple Judaism and well represented among the Dead Sea scrolls, but never became part of the Jewish canon (though it is part of the biblical canon in the Ethiopian Orthodox church). Likewise, in vv. 8-9 Jude seems to rely on a lost part of a work (or part of a lost work) known as the *Assumption (or Testament) of Moses* for the narrative about the struggle between Michael and Satan over the body of Moses. Jude certainly regarded materials in *1 Enoch* and *Assumption of Moses* as important and at least authoritative enough to cite on a par with biblical materials. Whether Jude considered them "canonical" raises the prior question whether he had any concept of a fixed "canon" of Holy Scriptures in the sense of an authoritative and normative collection of Old Testament Scriptures. For whatever reasons, the author of 2 Peter dropped the material from *1 Enoch* and *Assumption of Moses* in his partial rewriting of Jude, and replaced it with more solidly "canonical" biblical examples.

Some modern interpreters (following the lead of Duane F. Watson in *Invention, Arrangement, and Style. Rhetorical Criticism of Jude and 2 Peter*) are so impressed by the rhetorical features of Jude that they expound it according to the classical outline often found in ancient Greek and Latin speeches. According to this approach, Jude consists of the epistolary prescript or quasi-*exordium* (vv. 1-2), the *exordium* (v. 3), the *narratio* (v. 4), the *probatio* (vv. 5-16) consisting of three proofs (vv. 5-10, 11-13, and 14-16), the *peroratio* (vv. 17-21) consisting of a *repetitio* (vv. 17-19) and an *adfectus* or emotional appeal (vv. 20-23), and the doxology as a quasi-*peroratio* (vv. 24-25). Since the author had an extensive Greek vocabulary and could use various Greco-Roman rhetorical devices (see the list in Watson, *Invention* 194), it is very likely that he was exposed to speeches with such a rhetorical outline as part of his education and was even given the task of imitating them. But whether he purposely set out to follow this classical rhetorical outline or instinctively produced his work according to this outline is difficult to determine. In either case the Epistle of Jude is a letter with features both of a Jewish sermon and of a Greek/Latin speech.

3. *Jewish and Christian Traditions*

The Epistle of Jude is a rich mixture of Jewish and Christian traditions. Much of the body of the letter is devoted to examples taken from the OT: ancient Israel's disbelief and disobedience in the wilderness (v. 5 = Num 14:29-37), the rebellious angels (v. 6 = Gen 6:1-4), the men of Sodom and Gomorrah (v. 7 = Genesis 19), the death of Moses (v. 9 = Deut 34:5-6), Cain (v. 11 = Genesis 4), Balaam (v. 11 = Numbers 22–25), and Korah (v. 11 = Numbers 16). In several cases Jude seems to assume that his readers know not only the biblical texts but also the traditions that grew up around them ("even though you know all these things," v. 5).

In describing the fall and punishment of the rebellious angels Jude presupposes the extrabiblical account that is best known from the Book of Watchers in *1 Enoch* 6–11. In citing the debate over the corpse of Moses (v. 9), Jude seems to have relied on *The Assumption (or Testament) of Moses*. The first "prophecy" that Jude quotes in vv. 14-15 is taken from *1 Enoch* 1:9. The author shows no hesitation about citing these works as somehow authoritative in the course of his argument.

The "prophecy" from *1 Enoch* 1:9 quoted in Jude 14-15 is a good example of Jewish apocalyptic thinking: "Behold, the Lord comes with his holy myriads to execute judgment against all and to convict every soul for all their ungodly deeds that they committed in an ungodly way and for all the harsh words that those ungodly sinners spoke against him." The text contains some basic elements of Jewish apocalypticism: the sharp division between the ungodly and the righteous, the decisive appearance of God, and the negative (and definitive) judgment rendered by God against the wicked. The underlying presuppositon of the entire letter is that at God's judgment the wicked intruders will be severely judged and that their present success is only the fulfillment of the apostles' prophecy that "in

the last time there shall be scoffers" (v. 18). Meanwhile, the faithful need
to "wait for the mercy of our Lord Jesus Christ unto eternal life" (v. 21)
and to act in such a way that they will be presented "without blemish before his glory in joy" (v. 24).

The many Jewish traditions in the Epistle of Jude are used in the service of a defense of Christian faith, as the christological dimension of its
eschatology in vv. 21 and 24 shows. The explicitly "Christian" traditions
are generally mentioned in passing as if the readers were thoroughly
familiar with them and needed no explanation of them.

The references to Jesus are both exalted and formulaic: "our only
Master and Lord Jesus Christ" (v. 4), "our Lord Jesus Christ" (vv. 17, 22),
and "Jesus Christ our Lord" (v. 25). As vv. 21 and 24 show, there is an emphasis on the *parousia* or second coming of Jesus and on his role in the Last
Judgment. The two primary references to "faith" *(pistis)* suggest that faith
had a definite and objective content that was well known to the readers:
"to contend for the faith handed on to the saints once for all" (v. 3), and
"your most holy faith" (v. 20). Likewise, the apostles are referred to in a
formulaic manner that both gives them an exalted status and indicates
that knowledge of them is part of the Christian tradition: "the apostles of
our Lord Jesus Christ" (v. 17). The reference to Christian gatherings as
"your love feasts" (v. 12) and the doxology in vv. 24-25 give some insight
into early Christian community life and worship.

4. *The Opponents*

The Epistle of Jude is a polemical attack against certain Christian
teachers who had infiltrated the community (or communities) addressed
in the letter: "For some men secretly stole in" (v. 4). They seem to have
made themselves part of the community to the point of sharing in "your
love feasts" (v. 12). Since from Jude's perspective the opponents were
divisive and dangerous outsiders, some commentators have referred to
them as the "intruders"—a tradition carried on in this commentary.

The chief problem in identifying the intruders is Jude's "perspective."
Alarmed by the destructive effects of the intruders' inroads into the community, Jude issues a very strong and highly emotional warning against
them. He assumes that his readers are familiar with what "these men"
(houtoi) stand for in their actions and teachings. His task is not to provide
an objective and even-handed description (like a professor) but rather to
warn his readers about the moral and spiritual dangers that the intruders
represent (like a preacher). And so in Jude's letter we are exposed to only
one side of the dispute, which is expressed in very polemical language.

There is a real threat being met in the Epistle of Jude, but it is hard to know exactly what the precise content of the threat was.

In describing the intruders at the outset Jude calls them "ungodly persons, who exchanged the grace of our God for licentiousness" and accuses them of denying "the only master and our Lord Jesus Christ" (v. 4). Jude objects to the intruders on both moral and theological grounds. Other clues to what the intruders did and taught are found in the applications made to "these men" *(houtoi)* in vv. 8, 10, 12, 16, and 19. Amidst Jude's heated rhetoric there are only hints about the intruders' lifestyle and teachings.

According to Jude 8 "these men" rely on dreams or visions, commit and promote sexual immorality *(aselgeia)*, reject authority, and criticize or "revile" *(blasphemein)* the angels *(doxai* = "glorious ones"). These charges are repeated in various ways in the other *houtoi* passages. The focus on their speech in v. 16 suggests that they presented themselves as teachers, and the charge that they are "natural *(psychikoi)* people, not having the Spirit *(pneuma)*" in v. 19 indicates that they may have put themselves forward as truly "spiritual" *(pneumatikoi)*.

The biblical examples in vv. 5-7, 9, and 11 and the prophecies in vv. 14-15 ("ungodly sinners") and in v. 18 ("in the last time there shall be scoffers") confirm the impression that the intruders represented a moral and spiritual menace and at the same time contribute to the interpreter's frustration by not explaining exactly what they were doing and saying so as to evoke such a strong response from Jude.

In the interpretation of Jude it has often been customary to link the intruders to some early form of Gnosticism. But this approach involves explaining one unknown by another unknown, since the origin and character of early Gnosticism are matters of great dispute and unclarity. Another approach is to give up on the problem of the intruders' identity by saying that their precise character is beyond understanding because Jude's language is too general and stereotyped to allow any real insight into the group he was attacking. Others go even further and contend that the letter was simply a literary fiction (an exercise on "How to Write a Polemic") aimed at no particular historical circumstances.

For those who persist in connecting the intruders who are attacked in the Epistle of Jude with a group known from other early Christian sources, the most promising resource for a candidate is found in Paul's (often ironic) attack in 1 Corinthians against certain Christians who prided themselves on being especially "spiritual" or *pneumatikoi* (see 1 Corinthians 1–4; 12–14) as if they had received the fullness of resurrected life already in the present (1 Corinthians 15). Their claim to having experienced a fully realized eschatology led to immoral and divisive behavior (1 Corinthians

5–7) and to their regarding themselves as "strong" in contrast to other "weak" Christians (1 Corinthians 8–10).

These "spiritual" Christians were probably Gentile Christians or highly "liberated" Jewish Christians who had little respect for the biblical (OT) tradition. They very likely considered themselves as having been freed from and above the precepts of the OT Law (see Gal 5:18) and as superior even to the angels (see 1 Cor 6:3: "we are to judge angels") who (according to some traditions) were only mediators of the Mosaic Law (see Gal 3:19; Acts 7:53). These people may have thought that they were following Paul's gospel of freedom or at least taking it to its logical consequences. Paul wrote much of 1 Corinthians to correct what he regarded as their misinterpretations of his gospel.

The author of the Epistle of Jude may well have confronted this same (or a similar) group of radical Paulinists who in his judgment were perverting the authentic gospel by their actions and teachings. But it remains difficult to prove this definitively.

5. *Author, Date, and Place*

The author identifies himself as "Jude, servant of Jesus Christ, brother of James." This Jude seems to be neither the apostle "Judas the son of James" (Luke 6:16; Acts 1:13; John 14:22) nor "Judas called Barsabbas" (Acts 15:22), but rather the "Jude/Judas" listed among the "brothers" of Jesus (Mark 6:3; Matt 13:55). Whether this Jude/Judas was a full brother of Jesus, a half- or stepbrother, or a relative has been debated for many centuries. There is evidence for taking the Greek term *adelphos* in all three ways. At the least the salutation makes Jude the Lord's brother into the "implied author" of the letter, and so this commentary often refers to the author as "Jude" while withholding judgment about the identity of the "real author."

Was Jude the Lord's brother the real or actual historical author? Or was the letter only written in his name? That Jude the "brother" of Jesus and of James was the real author is usually argued along the following lines: the author's obvious familiarity with the OT and with traditions and books *(1 Enoch, Assumption of Moses)* at home among Palestinian Jews, his authority as a member of the family of Jesus, his apocalyptic outlook, ethical concerns, and interest in angels. The rich vocabulary and good Greek style, however, suggest that this Jude at least made use of the services of a secretary or scribe to put his letter into a more polished Greek form than might be expected from a first-century Galilean Jew whose primary language was Aramaic.

The chief arguments against direct authorship by Jude the brother of Jesus and of James include the high quality of the Greek vocabulary and style, the formulaic expressions about Jesus ("our Lord Jesus Christ"), the formulaic references to "faith" as an objective entity (see vv. 3, 20) and to "the apostles of our Lord Jesus Christ" (v. 17), the general or stereotyped nature of the polemical language, the references to "remembering" (vv. 5, 17), and the use of a doxology to close the letter (vv. 24-25). All these features tend to push the work's composition back into the late first century and beyond the lifetime of Jude the Lord's brother.

Most interpreters today regard the Epistle of Jude as pseudepigraphical (that is, only written in Jude's name), and this position is taken in the present commentary. Nevertheless, pronouncing Jude to be a pseudonym for the real author does not resolve all the questions about the letter's authorship and origin. For example, could the letter's genesis be explained by assuming that the historical Jude allowed his scribe great latitude in expressing his thoughts in Greek? Does the letter emanate from a movement within Jewish Christianity associated with the family of Jesus, especially James and Jude? Does the letter attack an actual movement that took up some of Paul's ideas and developed them in directions that other Christians (including Paul) regarded as perversions of the gospel (see 1 Corinthians; Jas 2:14-26; 2 Pet 3:15-16)? Or is it simply a "school exercise" that someone writing in the name of Jude composed as a general attack against heretics?

The position taken in this commentary is that the letter of Jude, written in the name of Jude the Lord's brother, responded to a real crisis in early Christianity from a Jewish-Christian perspective, and that the letter may well have had historical connections to Jude, James, and the family of Jesus.

One's view of the letter's date and place are linked to one's position on its authorship. If the real author was Jude the Lord's brother (with the help of his personal scribe), then the letter was most likely composed in the land of Israel before 70 C.E. If the letter is taken to be pseudepigraphical, then it probably was written sometime between 80 and 120 (before 2 Peter). It is possible that radical Paulinists like those envisioned in much of the polemic penetrated into Palestinian Jewish Christianity, though it is more likely that they flourished in Asia Minor (see Revelation 2–3) or Syria. It is possible that the letter of Jude represents a Jewish-Christian response to them. The position taken in this commentary is that the Epistle of Jude was composed in the late first century C.E., perhaps in the Holy Land but maybe outside the land of Israel, obviously for readers who were familiar with biblical and Jewish traditions and impressed by their importance.

TRANSLATION, NOTES, INTERPRETATION

1. *Salutation* (1-2)

1. Jude, slave of Jesus Christ, brother of James. To those who are called, beloved in God the Father and kept safe for Jesus Christ. 2. May mercy and peace and love be yours in abundance!

NOTES

1. *Jude:* The writer's name is Judas in Greek *(Ioudas)* and Judah in Hebrew. In the English Bible tradition his name is usually rendered "Jude," mainly to distinguish him from Judas Iscariot, the disciple who "handed over" Jesus. For Jude's identity as a "brother" of Jesus, see the Interpretation below. For a full treatment of early Christian traditions about Jude and about the relatives of Jesus and their place in the early church see Richard J. Bauckham, *Jude and the Relatives of Jesus in the Early Church* (Edinburgh: T&T Clark, 1990) 3–133.

   slave of Jesus Christ: In the Greek text there is a chiastic pattern: A "of Jesus Christ"; B "slave"; B "brother"; A "of James." Instead of claiming to be the brother of Jesus, Jude identifies himself as his "slave" *(doulos)* or "servant." Whether this was done out of reverence for Jesus and personal modesty, or whether it serves as a hint that Jude was the stepbrother or cousin of Jesus is not clear. For other uses of *doulos* in the salutations of NT epistles see Rom 1:1; Phil 1:1; Titus 1:1; Jas 1:1; and 2 Pet 1:1. The term (which is also applied to great figures in the OT) serves here to emphasize the superiority of Jesus and the lower status of the writers (Paul, James, Peter, and Jude) as instruments or agents of Jesus. The word *doulos* ("slave") is stronger than *diakonos* ("servant, minister").

   brother of James: In the NT lists of the twelve apostles there are two persons with the name "James" (or "Jacob"): (1) James the son of Zebedee and brother of John (Mark 3:17; Matt 10:2; Luke 6:14; Acts 1:13), and (2) James the son of Alphaeus (Mark 3:18; Matt 10:3; Luke 6:15; Acts 1:13). But here it is more likely that still another James—James the "brother" of Jesus (Mark 6:3; Matt 13:55)—is meant. While apparently not a follower of Jesus during his earthly ministry, this James was said to have been the recipient of an appearance of the risen Jesus (1 Cor 15:7) and a witness to the events of Pentecost (Acts 1:14). This

James became a leader in the church at Jerusalem and exercised a major role in the Jerusalem Council, according to Acts 15. He is at least the implied author of the NT letter of James and represents theological positions different from (and in some tension with) Paul and the Pauline movement (see Gal 2:12; Jas 2:14-26). According to Josephus (*Ant.* 20:200), this James suffered a martyr's death at Jerusalem around 62 C.E. when the high priest Ananus "convened the judges of the Sanhedrin and brought before them a man named James, the brother of Jesus who was called the Christ, and certain others. He accused them of having transgressed the law and delivered them up to be stoned." The high priest's actions so outraged "the inhabitants of the city who were considered the most fair-minded and who were strict in observance of the law" (20:201) that they complained to King Agrippa and the Roman procurator Albinus and got Ananus deposed from his office. Apparently James (and Jude?) represented a kind of Jewish Christianity that was not objectionable to observant Jews in Jerusalem.

To those who are called: For Christians as "those who are called" *(klētoi),* see Rom 1:6, 7; 8:28; and 1 Cor 1:2, 24. It is understood that God has done the calling and that believers are called to be holy. The term appears at the end of the verse, with the rest of the clause directed to the addressees ("beloved . . . Christ") placed between the article *tois* and *klētois.* The letter of Jude is not explicitly addressed to a specific person or community or group. Some manuscripts add "Gentiles" after *tois.*

beloved in God the Father and kept safe for Jesus Christ: Both verbs—"beloved" *(ēgapēmenous)* and "kept safe" *(tetērēmenous)*—are perfect passive participles, a construction that refers to an event in the past whose effects continue in the present. For the first verb some manuscripts read *hēgiasmenous* ("sanctified"), as in 1 Cor 1:2. The translation of the phrases that modify the two participles is difficult. Does the preposition "in" *(en)* govern only "God the Father," or does it also govern "Jesus Christ?" And in either case what is the precise sense? The idea seems to be that Christians who have experienced God's love for them ("beloved in God the Father") are now being "kept safe" as they await the second coming or *parousia* of Jesus (see v. 21: "wait for the mercy of our Lord Jesus Christ unto eternal life"). In this interpretation *en* governs only "God the Father."

2. *May mercy and peace and love be yours in abundance:* For "mercy" *(eleos)* and "peace" *(eirēnē)* together as members in epistolary greetings see 1 Tim 1:2; 2 Tim 1:2; 2 John 3. In Jude the greeting anticipates the exhortation near the close of the letter: "keep yourselves in the love of God; wait for the mercy of our Lord Jesus Christ unto eternal life" (v. 21). In the early Christian vocabulary "mercy and peace and love" refer to what believers have received from God's action in their lives through Christ. The proper response on their part is to show mercy, peace, and love toward other people. The verb *plēthyntheiē* ("be . . . in abundance") is an aorist optative passive, denoting a wish on the writer's part for those being addressed. The same verb appears in the greetings in 1 Pet 1:2 and 2 Pet 1:2. Literally it means "be multiplied, increased." In all three greetings "to you" *(hymin)* appears immediately after the first noun.

INTERPRETATION

The salutation follows the usual pattern in NT letters. It consists of the name of the sender ("Jude"), an indication of those to whom it is addressed ("to . . ."), and the greeting ("may mercy . . .").

The Sender (Jude 1a). The sender is identified as "Jude, slave of Jesus Christ, brother of James." As stated in the Introduction, this Jude is surely not "Judas called Barsabbas" in Acts 15:22, who was sent as an emissary from the Jerusalem Council to Antioch. Nor is it likely that he is "Judas the son of James" (Luke 6:16; Acts 1:13; John 14:22), one of the twelve apostles who is also identified with Thaddaeus or Lebbaeus (Mark 3:18; Matt 10:3). The suggestions that he is Judas Thomas or a symbolic "brother" only are even less likely. Rather, the implied author of this letter seems to be the Judas/Jude who is listed among the "brothers" (and sisters) of Jesus: "James and Joses and Judas and Simon" (Mark 6:3; see Matt 13:55 where Judas comes last, after Simon). Whether these were full brothers of Jesus (other children born to Mary and Joseph), his half- or stepbrothers (Joseph's children from an earlier marriage), or relatives (applying "brothers" to the extended family of Jesus) has been debated from patristic times onwards. The family of Jesus, though not among his first followers (see Mark 3:20-21, 31-35), did become prominent in the early church centered in Jerusalem. According to Eusebius (*Hist. eccl.* 3.20.6), the grandsons of Jude the Lord's brother became great Christian leaders renowned "for their testimony and for their relation to the Lord." It is even possible that the pseudepigraphic composition known as the letter of Jude was written in connection with their rise to prominence in Palestinian Christian circles.

The Addressees (Jude 1b). The letter of Jude is not explicitly addressed to one community in one place. Compare Paul's letters: "To all God's beloved in Rome," Rom 1:7; "To the church of God that is in Corinth," 1 Cor 1:2 and 2 Cor 1:1; "To the churches of Galatia," Gal 1:2; and so on. The attempt in some mansucripts to specify the audience as "to the Gentiles" must be judged a failure, since what follows would be most readily understood and appreciated by Jewish Christians. However, the absence of a specific place and group in the salutation does not necessarily mean that the letter of Jude is a "general" epistle (more like an essay) directed to no one or no group in particular or to no real situation. In fact, this letter is best interpreted as speaking to a Jewish Christian community whose identity and way of life were being threatened by the arrival of some "intruders" among them.

Having identified himself as a "slave *(doulos)* of Jesus Christ," Jude describes his readers as "called . . . beloved . . . and kept safe." As Richard J. Bauckham (*Jude, 2 Peter* 25) points out, these three terms figure prominently also in Second Isaiah (Isaiah 40–55) and in the Servant Songs in particular: "called" (Isa 41:9; 42:6; 48:12, 15; 49:1; 54:6), "loved" (42:1; 43:4), and "kept" (42:6; 49:8). This carefully chosen terminology suggests that the spirituality that characterized Christ the Servant/Slave of God (see Phil 2:7) provides the model for those who follow him. This pattern applies whether they be his "brother" like Jude or those whose kinship with him is entirely spiritual: "Whoever does the will of God is my brother and sister and mother" (Mark 3:35).

The description of the addressees also highlights the role of God ("beloved in God the Father") and Jesus ("kept safe for Jesus Christ") in Christian life. This "binitarian" (reference to the Father and the Son, without mention of the Holy Spirit) emphasis appears in the salutations of most NT letters (see Rom 1:1-6; 1 Cor 1:1-2; 2 Cor 1:1-2; Gal 1:1-5; and so on). Jude stresses that God's love is the origin of Christian life and that eternal life with the risen Christ in the fullness of God's kingdom is its goal or end. In the meantime, God's loving care makes it possible to withstand the dangers posed by the "intruders."

The Greeting (Jude 2). "May mercy and peace and love be yours in abundance!" The most common greeting in NT letters is the two-member formula "grace and peace" (Rom 1:7; 1 Cor 1:3; 2 Cor 1:2; Gal 1:3; etc.), which is usually explained as the combination of the Greek greeting *(chairein)* and the Hebrew greeting *(shalom/eirēnē)*. A three-member greeting appears in some NT epistles: "Grace, mercy, and peace" (1 Tim 1:2; 2 Tim 1:2; 2 John 3). These conventional forms are usually expanded with reference to God and to Jesus, and so they are given a distinctively Christian theological context and content. On reflection, the formulaic language is full of theological meaning. The attributes or virtues of mercy, peace, and love provide the dynamism for Christian life in the present, and the greeting is a prayer that these virtues may be in even greater abundance in the lives of those addressed in the letter.

The closest parallel to this greeting comes from the "Letter of Baruch" in *2 Bar.* 78–87, a Jewish pseudepigraphical work supposedly addressed to the exiles in Babylon in the sixth century B.C.E. but in fact intended for Palestinian Jews in the late first or early second century C.E. who were trying to come to grips with the destruction of Jerusalem and its Temple in 70 C.E. Baruch's letter begins in the following way: "Thus speaks Baruch, the son of Neriah. To the brothers who were carried away in captivity: Mercy (Syriac *rḥmh*) and peace (Syriac *šlmh*) be with you. I remember, my brothers, the love of him who created me, who loved us from the beginning and who never hated us but, on the contrary, chastised us" (*2 Bar.* 78:2-3). Here the greeting combines the three themes of mercy, peace, and love found also in Jude 2.

The salutation in the letter of Jude, while fulfilling its epistolary function, also provides a compact summary of Christian existence. This is a life of service after the pattern set by Christ the Servant/Slave of God. It consists in being called and loved by God, and being kept safe for the fullness of life in God's kingdom with Jesus Christ. And it is a life marked by the experience of God's mercy, peace, and love, which are to be shown to others in return.

2. *Purpose and Occasion* (3-4)

3. Beloved, though I was very eager to write to you about our common salvation, I had a need to write and exhort you to contend for the faith handed on to the saints once for all. 4. For some men secretly stole in— those who long ago were sentenced to this condemnation, ungodly persons, who exchanged the grace of our God for licentiousness and deny the only Master and our Lord Jesus Christ.

NOTES

3. *Beloved:* For *agapētoi* ("beloved") as an address for fellow Christians elsewhere in Jude see vv. 17 and 20. It is also prominent in 2 Peter 3 (see vv. 1, 8, 14, 17). Those who have experienced God's love in Christ are therefore "beloved."

though I was very eager to write to you about our common salvation: The participial phrase suggests that Jude planned to write a positive theological treatise (something like Paul's letter to the Romans) but was prevented by the need to address the crisis described in the main clause. The vocabulary in *pasan spoudēn poioumenos* is also prominent in 2 Peter (see 1:5, 10, 15; 3:14). The expression "our common salvation" refers to the salvation that all Christians share in Christ. This salvation has already begun but will reach its fullness with the Day of the Lord. Some manuscripts read "your common salvation."

I had a need to write: The crisis caused by the intruders described in v. 4 was so urgent that Jude had to put aside his original plan. Whereas the preceding clause consisted of a present participle and a present infinitive, the main clause has an aorist third-person verb ("I had") and an aorist infinitive ("to write"), thus indicating that Jude was carrying out his new plan with this letter.

and exhort you to contend for the faith handed on to the saints once for all: The present participle *parakalōn*, translated here as "exhort," is an important indication of the genre of the body of the letter: It is an exhortation *(paraklēsis)*. The dative plural pronoun "you" *(hymin)* can be taken with either "write" or "exhort" or (more likely) both. The infinitive "to contend" *(epagōnizesthai)* is an intensive form *(ep-)* of the root *agon-* and appears only here in the NT. In this context "the faith" *(pistis)* seems to refer to a body of teachings about God, Christ, and the Christian lifestyle (as in the Pastoral epistles). For faith as something that has been "handed on," see Acts 16:4; 1 Cor 11:2; and 15:3, as well as 2 Pet 2:21. Here "saints" *(hagioi)* is another term for Christians, comparable to "those who are called" and "beloved." They have been made holy by their contact with God the holy one *(hagios)*. Thus Jude exhorts his readers to join the struggle on behalf of the traditional faith, which he regards as endangered through the presence within the Christian community of those who are described in the next verse.

4. *For some men secretly stole in:* The reason for Jude's writing is given here ("For . . ."), though the precise identity of the troublemakers is left uncertain ("some men"). The verb *pareisedysan* appears only here in the NT, with the prefix *par-* adding the note of stealth or secrecy to their entry (see Gal 2:4; 2 Pet 2:1). While they are "outsiders" to the community that is addressed by Jude, they seem to have been Christians who intruded themselves into the community. On the basis of this phrase it has become customary among commentators to refer to Jude's opponents as the "intruders."

those who long ago were sentenced to this condemnation: While some kind of judgment or condemnation hangs over the intruders, the precise referent of this participial clause remains obscure. The phrase *palai progegrammenoi* (literally "long ago written beforehand") might suggest that something in the OT is meant. But what? Those who regard the writing of Jude as occasioned by the reception of 2 Peter point to similar language in 2 Pet 2:3 *(hois to krima expalai ouk argei)* for the proper context. But it is more likely that 2 Peter used Jude as its source.

ungodly persons, who exchanged the grace of our God for licentiousness: The description of the intruders as *asebeis* ("ungodly") is echoed in Jude 15 *(asebeias . . . asebeis)* and 18; see also 2 Pet 2:5; 3:7. That they "exchanged the grace of our God" suggests that they once enjoyed God's favor or grace. In other words, they had once become (and still were in their own minds) Christians. The accusation of "licentiousness" *(aselgeia)* in the sense of inappropriate sexual conduct is made also in 2 Pet 2:18. While such biblical terminology was often used as a metaphor for idolatry (as in Hosea), in Jude and 2 Peter it is best taken in its root sexual sense. Both in antiquity and today it is common in religious (and anti-religious) polemics to accuse opponents of sexual immorality (sometimes justly, and sometimes unjustly).

deny the only Master and our Lord Jesus Christ: Here the intruders are accused of denying the sovereignty of "the only Master" and of the risen Christ (see v. 8). Perhaps there is an even more specific reference, such as to Christ's second coming or *parousia* (as in 2 Peter). The most problematic feature here is trying to decide whether "the only Master *(despotēs)*" refers to God the Father or to Christ. Some manuscripts include the noun *theos* ("God") here, thus conforming this text to other NT passages where God is called *despotēs* (Luke 2:29; Acts 4:24; Rev 6:10). However, in 2 Pet 2:1 "the Master who bought them" seems to be Christ. The textual reading without *theos* seems to be certain (though for a defense of *despotēn theon* as original see Charles H. Landon, "The Text of Jude 4," and *A Text-Critical Study of the Epistle of Jude* 63–67). Still, the ambiguity as to whether there are two figures (God and Christ) or only one (Christ) remains. For Christ as "Lord" *(kyrios)* in Jude see vv. 17 and 21; for God as "Lord" *(kyrios)* see vv. 5, 9, and 14. What is said of God is also said of Christ, and vice versa—a common feature in the NT writings.

INTERPRETATION

Jude 3-4 supplies information about the purpose of the letter (3) and its occasion (4). The readers are addressed as "beloved" *(agapētoi)*, a common epithet for fellow Christians in the NT epistles, and one that is repeated in Jude 17 and 20. Jude first explains that his reason for writing was to "exhort you to contend for the faith handed on to the saints once for all." Then he describes the threat to the community posed by the appearance of certain "intruders" who seem to be leading some other Christians astray, at least in Jude's view.

The epistolary conventions found in Jude 1-2 (sender, addressees, greeting) have established the overall or gross identity of this document as a letter or an epistle. But after the salutation there is no customary thanksgiving for the good health and progress of the community such as appears in most of the Pauline letters (Galatians being a notable exception, since Paul was furious at them for listening to "another gospel"). Nor is there an epistolary closing containing news about travel plans and greetings. Rather, Jude looks more like an exhortation or sermon that has been made into a letter by the inclusion of an epistolary salutation in vv. 1-2. In this respect Jude is something like Hebrews, which is a long sermon or essay that has been given the trappings of a (Pauline?) letter by the inclusion of travel plans and greetings only at its very end (Heb 13:23-25).

Purpose (v. 3). Calling Jude a sermon does not deny its character as primarily a written work. As an oral piece only it would have been a very short and highly compressed sermon, one that an audience might find hard to grasp in all its details if they heard it only once, and needing to be put into written form. Moreover, the implied author "Jude" explicitly presents his work as something that he wrote: "I had a need to write . . ." (3). Indeed, as this commentary will try to show, the work known as the letter of Jude manifests a level of literary sophistication in its structure and vocabulary that suggests careful written composition.

The key to understanding the genre of Jude comes in the masculine singular present participle *parakalōn* in Jude 3, translated here as "exhort." The author of Hebrews describes his sermon as a "word of exhortation" *(logos tēs paraklēseōs)* in 13:22, and Hebrews, like Jude, is a combination of biblical (OT) expositions and exhortations to the readers. Likewise, the main part of Jude (5-19) consists of biblical examples and applications. The exhortation proper (20-23) provides positive advice to the readers, and the doxology (24-25) serves as a stirring conclusion to the sermon.

Jude claims to be contending "for the faith handed on to the saints once for all." In the Bible the word "faith" has both subjective and objective components. For example, in Gen 12:1-4 Abraham trusts the promise that God will make of him and his descendants "a great nation"—enough to leave his homeland and go to the land of Canaan. The objective component resides in the promise and its content, whereas the subjective component is Abraham's trust in acting upon the promise as God's word. The same subjective-objective character of faith appears throughout the OT and the NT. (See, for example, Paul's long meditation on Abraham as the person of faith in Romans 4.)

One of the earliest theological activities among the first Christians was constructing summaries of their beliefs about God and Jesus. The Pauline epistles are the earliest extant documents (from the fifties of the first century C.E.) in the NT, and they provide many examples of credal formulations that had become authoritative soon after Jesus' death.

One of the best and earliest examples pertaining to the content of Christian faith is found in 1 Cor 15:3-5: "For I handed on to you as of first importance what I in turn had received: that Christ died for our sins in accordance with the scriptures, and that he was buried, and that he was raised on the third day in accordance with the scriptures, and that he appeared to Cephas, then to the twelve." In his introduction (15:3a) to this traditional credal summary Paul claims that in evangelizing the Corinthians he delivered to them the tradition of faith that he himself had received, presumably from the apostles before him (see Gal 1:18-19). The language of 1 Cor 15:3a *(paredōka . . . parelabon)* suggests that the concept of "tradition" *(paradosis)* was already well established in Christian circles (a feature taken over from Judaism; see tractate *ʾAboth* in the Mishnah). The content of the credal formula in 1 Cor 15:3b-5 establishes the death and resurrection of Jesus as the core of Christian faith (the gospel). It also highlights the importance of the OT ("in accordance with the scriptures") and the apostolic witnesses ("to Cephas, then to the twelve").

While common in Paul's undisputed letters, the summaries of faith or credal formulas are especially prominent in the Pastoral epistles (1 and 2 Timothy, Titus). In the Pastorals these credal statements are often introduced in such a way as to promote their authority: "The saying is sure and worthy of full acceptance: that Christ Jesus came into the world to save sinners" (1 Tim 1:15). For other traditional summaries of the Christian faith in the Pastorals see 1 Tim 2:5-6a; 3:16; 2 Tim 2:11-13; Titus 3:4-7.

These Pauline texts provide important background for understanding the form and content of Jude's reference to "the faith handed on to the saints once for all" (3). While not devoid of subjectivity in the sense of trust, the phrase seems to stress the objective character of the Christian faith. First of all, "faith" is enough of an objective reality that Jude can exhort his readers to contend or struggle *(epagōnizesthai)* on its behalf. Also, the qualifying phrase "handed on to the saints once for all" appears between the definite article *tę* and the noun *pistei* in the dative case. More-over, the three elements in the qualifying phrase—the adverb *hapax* ("once for all"), the aorist passive participial form of the Greek verb used regularly to refer to the process of tradition *(paradonai)*, and the term used frequently to describe members of the Christian community in the early documents ("the saints")—all serve to strengthen the impression that the author and his readers had a clear idea about the content of their Christian faith. Their faith is both traditional and objective. There was no need here to specify its content further. In the author's perspective the traditional Christian faith was in danger of being distorted by some Christian teach-ers who had intruded themselves into the community he was addressing.

Occasion (v. 4). The occasion for the writing of the letter of Jude was the arrival of outsiders (who were Christians) and their intruding themselves into the life of the community addressed in the work. According to Jude 4 these persons gained access by stealth and were causing great harm. They are described as "ungodly" *(asebeis)* and are accused of licentiousness *(aselgeia)* and of denying "our only Master and Lord Jesus Christ." But in Jude 4 it is not clear what the logical link is between the charge about licentiousness and the charge about denying Jesus as Master. Was their immoral behavior effectively a denial of Jesus' authority? Or are there two components—ethical and theological—to the intruders' pernicious teach-ings?

Throughout the rest of the letter there are comments about "these men" *(hoi houtoi)* that can help the reader to add to the introductory description of the intruders in Jude 4 (see vv. 8, 10, 12-13, 16, and 19). Nevertheless, it is very difficult to know exactly what these "intruders" were teaching and doing. We know them only from what Jude says about them. In this re-spect we are overhearing one side of a conversation and cannot be sure that our (or Jude's) perception is accurate. Moreover, the language that Jude uses is so general (while at the same time polemical and even bom-bastic) that it sheds little clear light on the actual views of the intruders.

From Jude 4 we can be sure that the intruders were outsiders to the community he addresses. But they are not like the "judaizing" outsiders who are met in Paul's letter to the Galatians and in 2 Corinthians, who wanted Gentile Christians to live a full Jewish life. If anything can be said on the matter of Jude's opponents, it appears that the "intruders" were promoting a Christianity that gave little positive attention to the Jewish elements in Christianity. However, the Christianity represented by Jude and his first readers seems to have been very Jewish in orientation. So Jude responds to the crisis with examples culled from the OT and Jewish traditions.

Whether 2 Peter 3 can be of much help in developing the profile of the intruders in Jude is dubious. From that text we learn that the opponents denied the *parousia* of Jesus and appealed to Paul as their authority. Nevertheless, it is indeed tempting to classify the opponents in 2 Peter 3 and the intruders in Jude as radical Paulinists. Thus they would be Christians who pushed Paul's emphasis on the present dimensions of the saving effects of Jesus' death and resurrection to the exclusion of their future dimensions (something Paul did not do), and promoted Paul's stress on Christ as the "end" of the Jewish Law (Rom 10:4) and on Christian freedom to the point of paying little attention to morality (another thing Paul did not do).

The description of the letter's occasion and purpose in Jude 3-4 is a vivid reminder that Christians can and do fall away from their "common salvation" and from "the faith handed on to the saints once for all." To protect his readers from this danger Jude warns them against other Christians who have already (from Jude's perspective) chosen sexual immorality over God's grace and so have effectively denied God and God's Messiah, Jesus.

For Reference and Further Study

Landon, Charles H. "The Text of Jude 4," *Hervormde Teologiese Studies* 49 (1993) 823–43.

3. Examples and Applications (5-13)

5. Now I want to remind you, even though you know all these things, that the Lord once saved a people from the land of Egypt and then destroyed those who did not believe; 6. the angels who did not keep their own domain but abandoned their proper dwelling place he has kept for the judgment of the great day in chains forever in the underworld below; 7. and likewise Sodom and Gomorrah and the cities around them committed fornication in the same way as these and went after "other flesh." They set before (us) an example, undergoing the punishment of eternal fire. 8. Likewise these men too in their dreamings defile the flesh, reject authority, and revile the glorious ones.

9. But Michael the archangel, when he was disputing with the devil and debating about the body of Moses, did not dare to bring a judgment of blasphemy but said: "May the Lord rebuke you!" 10. But these men revile what they do not know; whatever they know by instinct like animals without reason, in these they are destroyed.

11. Woe to them, for they went in the way of Cain and poured themselves into the deceit of Balaam for a price and perish in the rebellion of Korah. 12. These men are stains on your love feasts, carousing without scruple, looking after themselves; waterless clouds carried away by winds; late autumn trees, twice dead, uprooted; 13. wild waves of the sea, churning up the foam of their own shame; wandering stars for whom the black darkness has been reserved forever.

NOTES

5. *Now I want to remind you, even though you know all these things:* Jude introduces the following biblical examples as though they were familiar to his readers from their Jewish heritage and/or had been part of the Christian catechesis that his audience had received. For terms related to "remind" *(hypomimnēskein)* see 2 Pet 1:12, 13, 15; and 3:1. The perfect tense accusative participle *eidotas* (literally "having known") has a present sense here (but depending on where the adverb *hapax* goes; see below).

that the Lord once saved a people from the land of Egypt: The aorist participial clause *(sōsas)* summarizes the exodus experience of ancient Israel as told in the book of Exodus. Some manuscripts lack the definite article *ho* before *kyrios* ("Lord"). Many manuscripts read "Jesus" instead of "Lord," and still others read "God" or "God Christ." These variants reflect a debate about the identity of the subject (see the Note on v. 4). Is "the Lord" God or Jesus? If it is Jesus, then he plays a proleptic or anticipatory role in OT history, like that of personified Wisdom in Wisdom 10–19 and of Christ in 1 Cor 10:4 ("the rock was Christ"). For defenses of "Jesus" as the original reading see Jarl Fossum, "Kyrios Jesus as the Angel of the Lord in Jude 5," and Carroll D. Osburn, "The Text of Jude 5." But since Jude never uses the name "Jesus" alone, it is probably better to read *ho kyrios* ("the Lord") and to interpret it as a reference to God. In some manuscripts the adverb *hapax* ("once") appears as part of the preceding clause ("though you once knew all these things"); for a defense of that as its original position see Osburn, "The Text of Jude 5."

and then destroyed those who did not believe: The adverb *deuteron* ("then" but literally "a second time, the next time, on a second occasion") forms a pair with *hapax* ("once"). Ancient Israel's failure in faith in the wilderness is a major OT theme not only in the Pentateuch but also in texts such as Ps 95:7-11 (and its NT application in Heb 3:7–4:11). One especially pertinent OT text is Num 14:26-35, where, in response to the many complaints by the Israelites whom God had rescued from slavery in Egypt, God promises that "not one of you shall come into the land" (14:30) except Caleb and Joshua, and that "your dead bodies shall fall in this wilderness" (14:32). The homiletical point of this example is that it is possible for Christians too, who have been saved through Christ, to fall away through lack of faith and so be destroyed (see Heb 6:4-6; 10:26-27). This warning applies most obviously to the Christian intruders, but it has relevance for Jude's readers also.

6. *the angels . . . abandoned their proper dwelling place:* The OT basis for the second example is Gen 6:1-4, according to which the "sons of God" (generally interpreted by Jews as angels) had sexual relations with human women and produced the "fallen ones" *(Nephilim).* In *1 Enoch* 6–16 (part of what is known as the "Book of Watchers") there is a full-scale account in which some angels plot and rebel against God and his good angels, and descend to earth where they introduce all kinds of sinful behavior among humans. See Matthias Delcor, "Le mythe de la chute des anges et de l'origine des géants," and André Feuillet, "Le péché évoqué aux chapitres 3 et 6,1-4 de la Genèse. Le péché des Anges de l'Épître de Jude et de la Seconde Épître de Pierre." In some Jewish circles the "original sin" seems to be the fall of the angels rather than the disobedience of Adam and Eve (Gen 3:1-24). The "domain" or "proper dwelling place" of the angels was where they were assigned by God in the heavenly court. Their sin consisted in leaving their proper place and introducing sinful behavior to people on earth. The point of the second example in Jude seems to be that there is an analogy between (1) the wicked angels who left their assigned places in heaven and caused sin on the earth and (2) the intruders who have stolen into the community and caused all kinds of trouble.

he has kept for the judgment of the great day: As in the previous example the subject is God. According to *1 Enoch* 22:11 the rebellious angels were bound forever "until the great day of judgment" (see also 10:6). These passages suggest that what is meant in Jude 6 is the Last Judgment when all (including angels) will receive their just rewards and punishments. The idea is that the intruders too will then receive the punishments they deserve.

in chains forever in the underworld below: According to *1 Enoch* 10:4-6 God instructed the angel Raphael to "bind Azazel hand and foot and throw him into the darkness." Raphael then cast Azazel into a hole in the desert and "threw on top of him rugged and sharp rocks. And he covered his face in order that he may not see the light. . . ." For other NT references to "the underworld below" *(zophos)* see Jude 13 and 2 Pet 2:4, 17.

7. *likewise Sodom and Gomorrah and the cities around them:* The primary OT text about the sin and destruction of Sodom and Gomorrah is Genesis 19. The "cities around them" that were destroyed were Adamah and Zeboiim, according to Deut 29:23 and Hos 11:8.

committed fornication in the same way as these and went after "other flesh": The fornication *(ekporneusasai)* of these cities is said to be like that of "these" *(toutois,* masculine in form), which is probably a reference to the evil angels of v. 6 rather than to the "cities" (which would be feminine in form). But Michael A. Kruger *("toutois* in Jude 7") claims that *toutois* refers back to the intruders mentioned in v. 4 who are accused of sexual sins. According to Genesis 19 the visitors to Sodom were (good) angels, and the inhabitants sought to have sexual relations with them and demanded: "Bring them out to us, so that we may know them" (Gen 19:5). While the roles are reversed, the sin in both Genesis 19 and Jude 7 consists in desiring "other flesh." Whereas in Jude 6 the rebellious angels of Gen 6:1-4/*1 Enoch* 6–11 wanted to have sexual relations with human women, in Jude 7 the human men of Genesis 19 wanted (knowingly or not) to have sexual relations with angels. Thus it is unlikely that the sin ascribed to the men of Sodom in Jude 7 (or in Genesis 19 either) is primarily one of homosexual (male-male or female-female) activity (but see Philo, *De Abrahamo* 135-136, who emphasizes the Sodomites' homosexual activity). What was most "unnatural" about the desire in both cases was the attempt at mixing humans and angels.

They set before (us) an example: The word *deigma* means "sample" or "evidence," but here it conveys the idea of "(negative) example" or even "warning." The term applies to all three examples cited in Jude 5-7: the rebellious Israelites in the wilderness (v. 5), the rebellious and lustful bad angels (6), and the lustful men of Sodom (7). The last two examples with their sexual overtones are linked to the charge of "licentiousness" (*aselgeia*) made against the intruders in v. 4 (see 2 Pet 2:7, 18). In all three examples rebellious behavior against God and his laws is to be punished both in history and at the Last Judgment.

undergoing the punishment of eternal fire: For fire as a punishment for sins see Jude 23: "snatching them out of the fire." See also Matt 5:22; 13:40, 42; 18:8; Mark 9:43-47; etc. for "hellfire" as a punishment for wicked behavior. In Jewish writings contemporary with the NT there is tension between the notions of eternal suffering in fire and annihilation as the proper divine punishment for the wicked.

8. *Likewise these men in their dreaming:* For other structurally significant references to "these men" (*houtoi*) see Jude 10, 12, 16, 19. The application comes back to the intruders mentioned in v. 4 as having caused the crisis in the community. The expression "in their dreaming" (*enypniazomenoi*) may allude to the intruders' appeals to visions, revelations, or other kinds of "mystical" experiences as the basis of their teachings.

defile the flesh, reject authority, and revile the glorious ones: At this point three charges are made against both the intruders of v. 4 and the figures in the examples of vv. 5-7. The charge of defiling the flesh fits well with the *aselgeia* imputed to the intruders in v. 4 and to the angels and men in the second and third examples (vv. 6-7). The charge of rejecting authority (*kyriotētēs*) may allude to the intruders' rejection of "the only Master and our Lord (*kyrios*) Jesus Christ" and the rebelliousness against God as Lord displayed in the first two examples (vv. 5-6). "The glorious ones" (*doxai*) seems to refer to a group of angels and fits with the last two cases (vv. 6-7), which involve angels. The intruders may have promoted heterodox teachings about angels. For what those teachings may have been, see the Interpretation on Jude 8.

9. *Michael the archangel:* In Hebrew the name Michael means "Who is like God?" Michael is a major figure in Jewish apocalypticism. In the book of Daniel,

Michael appears as the patron or guardian of Israel (see Dan 10:13, 21; 12:1) and may well be "the one like a son of man" (7:13) who receives power from the "Ancient of Days." In the Dead Sea scrolls the Prince (or Angel) of Light is very likely to be Michael. In Rev 12:7 Michael wages a cosmic battle against the Dragon (Satan).

when he was disputing with the devil and debating about the body of Moses: This incident is not found explicitly in the OT. But see Deut 34:1-8 for the mystery surrounding Moses' death and burial: "no one knows his burial place to this day" (34:6). The episode is usually traced to the now lost Jewish apocryphal work known as the *Assumption of Moses,* which may not be the same as the *Testament of Moses* unless the *Assumption of Moses* was part of that work's lost ending. See the Interpretation on Jude 9. According to traditions preserved in patristic writings that pertain to the work known as the *Assumption of Moses,* Michael was commanded to bury Moses but Satan opposed the burial because the body belonged to Satan as the lord of "matter" and because Moses was a murderer who had killed an Egyptian man (see Exod 2:11-15). See Klaus Berger, "Der Streit des guten und des bösen Engels."

did not dare to bring a charge of blasphemy: Despite the provocation from Satan's outrageous charges concerning Moses, Michael refrained from charging Satan directly with blasphemy. Rather, he left that judgment to God. In its narrow OT sense blasphemy refers to misusing the divine name YHWH (see Lev 24:14-16). In the NT and elsewhere, however, the term is used in a looser sense to refer to very inappropriate speech such as abusive language and slander (see Matt 26:65; Mark 2:7; 14:64; John 10:33). The translations of *krisis blasphēmias* in Jude 9 vary widely: "a reviling judgment" (RSV, NAB Rev.), "a condemnation of slander" (NRSV), and "the language of abuse" (NJB). The verbal form of the root *(blasphēmousin)* appeared in the list of charges made against the intruders in Jude 8: "(they) revile the glorious ones." The point seems to be that whereas Michael, though he was an archangel and was provoked by Satan in the debate about Moses' body, refrained from issuing a charge of blasphemy against Satan, these intruders ("those men"), though they are mere humans, are so bold as to slander, revile, or blaspheme angelic beings ("the glorious ones").

"May the Lord rebuke you!": The verb *epitimēsai* is a third-person singular aorist optative. Michael's words to Satan take the form of a wish that God might "rebuke" Satan. They show Michael's respect for a fellow angel (even though a bad one). It is likely that this formula was present in the now lost *Assumption of Moses.* But it also echoes Zech 3:2: "The Lord rebuke you, O Satan."

10. *But these men revile what they do not know:* "These men" *(houtoi)* is a recurrent formula to describe the intruders; see vv. 8, 12, 16, and 19. For *blasphēmousin* ("revile") as a description of what they do, see v. 8. What they do not know is the world of the angels. The example in Jude 9 and the uses of *blasphēmousin* in vv. 8 and 10 suggest that the intruders' teachings included a critique of angels in general or some group of angels known as "the glorious ones" *(doxai).*

whatever they know by instinct like animals without reason: This charge echoes the accusations of "licentiousness" *(aselgeia)* in v. 4 and defiling "the flesh" in v. 8.

The intruders are said to act like "animals without reason" *(aloga zōa)* because they allow themselves to be led by instinct or nature *(physikos)* only.

in these they are destroyed: The idea is that if the intruders live by their instincts only, these same instincts (especially their licentiousness) will bring about their destruction.

11. *Woe to them:* The interjection *ouai* ("woe, alas") is common in the synoptic gospels (e.g., Matt 11:21; 18:7; Mark 14:21; Luke 6:24-26; 11:42) and in Revelation (8:13; 9:12; 11:14; etc.) but appears elsewhere in the NT only in 1 Cor 9:16. *Autois* ("to them") refers back to the group ("these men") mentioned in v. 10 (see also vv. 8, 12, 16, and 19).

    for they went in the way of Cain: Although Cain was the subject of much speculation in early Jewish texts as a skeptic, a libertine, or even an atheist, the most obvious referent here is the biblical account in which Cain murders his brother Abel (Gen 4:8). The biblical example suggests that the intruders are effectively committing spiritual murder against their Christian brothers and sisters.

    poured themselves into the deceit of Balaam for a price: The verb *exechythēsan* ("pour out, abandon oneself") is strong and even graphic, suggesting enthusiasm for their evil deeds on the intruders' part. In Numbers 22–24 Balaam is hired by King Balak of Moab to prophesy against Israel. But despite his orders Balaam can only say good things about Israel and its God. However, in Num 25:1-5 Israelite men have sexual relations with Moabite women and join in the worship of their gods. In Num 31:16 this episode is blamed on Balaam: "These women here, on Balaam's advice, made the Israelites act treacherously against the Lord in the affair of Peor, so that the plague came upon the congregation of the Lord." This is what probably lies behind the phrase "the deceit of Balaam." The expression "for a price" *(misthou,* a genitive of price) suggests that the intruders were acting as they did both to deceive their fellow Christians and to make some kind of financial profit for themselves while doing so.

    perish in the rebellion of Korah: According to Numbers 16, Korah along with Dathan and Abiram challenged the authority of Moses and Aaron by asking them: "So why then do you exalt yourselves against the assembly of the Lord?" (Num 16:3). The implication here may be that the intruders are rejecting legitimate authority within the church.

12. *These men are stains on your love feasts:* For other references to "these men" *(houtoi)* see vv. 8, 10, 16, and 19. The term *spilades* here is best taken as derived from *spilas* and meaning "stain, spot." Another line of interpretation takes *spilades* to mean "hidden rocks" or "reefs" that present unseen dangers to ships off shore (and, by application, to unsuspecting Christians). The "love feasts" *(agapai)* refer to early Christian assemblies in which community members participated in festive meals and probably also the Lord's Supper (see 1 Cor 11:17-34). Jude charges that by their presence and divisiveness these men are staining the most important communal expressions of Christian fellowship. Some manuscripts, perhaps under the influence of the textual tradition of 2 Pet 2:13, read *apatais* ("deceits") rather than *agapais* ("love feasts").

See the discussion in Charles H. Landon, *A Text-Critical Study of the Epistle of Jude* 103–106). William Whallon ("Should We Keep, Omit, or Alter the *hoi* in Jude 12?") proposes that *achatais* ("agates") be read with the participle that follows: "these are the spots in your agates when they share a banquet."

carousing without scruple, looking after themselves: The participial phrase *syneuōchoumenoi aphobōs* could be translated literally in a more neutral way: "feasting together without fear." But given the polemical context something more negative (such as "carousing without scruple") seems called for here. Accusing opponents of dissolute personal behavior is a common feature in religious polemics. The verb in the expression *heautous poimainontes* translated here as "looking after themselves" features the "shepherd" root *(poim-)*. Some interpreters take this as an allusion to the intruders' rejection of legitimate authority in the church. At least it is a reference to their selfish concern with taking care of themselves.

waterless clouds carried away by winds: Like clouds that produce no rain and serve only to block the sun, the opponents *(houtoi)* are good for nothing. Like clouds that the winds drive away, they are ephemeral or transitory. See Prov 25:14: "Like clouds and wind without rain is one who boasts of a gift never given." For another possible source of the images in Jude 12-13 see Carroll D. Osburn, "*1 Enoch* 80:2-8 (67:5-7) and Jude 12-13."

late autumn trees, twice dead, uprooted: The adjective *phthinopōrinos* ("late autumn") appears only here in the NT. A tree that has not borne fruit by late autumn (harvest time) is never going to bear fruit at all. It is dead both in the current season and forever, and is effectively uprooted (but see Luke 13:6-9). The idea here is that barren trees—like waterless clouds—fail to fulfill their purpose and their promise, since they fail to produce good fruits (see Matt 7:15-20).

13. *wild waves of the sea, churning up the foam of their own shame:* This is the only occurrence of the verb *epaphrizein* ("cause to foam") in the NT. The image conveys all the rubbish and scum that waves can dredge up from the sea. See Isa 57:20: "But the wicked are like the tossing sea that cannot keep still; its waters toss up mire and mud." Its use here fits well with the interpretation of *spilades* in v. 12 as "hidden rocks" or "reefs." John P. Oleson ("An Echo of Hesiod's *Theogony* vv. 190-2 in Jude 13") links the verbal root *aphr-* to the Greek goddess Aphrodite.

wandering stars for whom the black darkness has been reserved forever: The expression *asteres planētai* ("wandering stars") reflects the ancient belief that planets "wander" *(planan)* across the sky among the fixed stars. For the stars as disobedient and so deserving punishment see Isa 14:12-15: "How you are fallen from heaven, O Day Star, son of Dawn! . . . But you are brought down to Sheol, to the depths of the Pit." See also *1 Enoch* 18:15-16: "And the stars who roll over upon the fire, they are the ones which have transgressed the commandments of God from the beginning of their rising because they did not arrive punctually. And he was wroth with them and bound them until the time of the completion of their sin in the year of mystery." See also *1 Enoch*

80:6-8, where the stars change their courses and functions, and sinners take them to be gods; see Carroll D. Osburn, "*1 Enoch* 80:2-8 (67:5-7) and Jude 12-13." For still another possible origin see Reinhold Merkelbach, "Zwei Beiträge zum Neuen Testament," who claims that the dark stars refer to two imaginary planets that played a role in eclipses according to the Ptolemaic system. The image in the context of Jude suggests that the intruders are off course in their lives and will be punished by God, thus foreshadowing the theme of judgment prominent in the quotation of *1 Enoch* 1:9 that follows in vv. 14b-15.

INTERPRETATION

In the Jewish and Christian traditions good preaching generally consists of the exposition of biblical texts (biblical interpretation) and their application to those who are being addresssed in the present (exhortation). The first main part of Jude's "sermon," which now functions as the body of his letter, fits this pattern very well. Jude 5-13 alternates between mentions of biblical (and some extrabiblical) texts and their applications to the "intruders" (*houtoi* = "these men").

After a brief rhetorical introduction in v. 5a ("Now I want to remind you"), Jude presents the material in three sections: three examples—Israel in the wilderness, the rebellious angels, and Sodom and Gomorrah—and an application (vv. 5-7, 8); another example—Michael and the devil—and an application (vv. 9, 10); and three more brief examples—Cain, Balaam, and Korah—and an application (vv. 11, 12-13). The Greek term *houtoi* ("these men") appears at the beginning of each application (vv. 8, 10, 12; see also 16 and 19). It serves not only as a demarcation between the biblical examples and the applications but also as a rhetorical device to keep the sermon focused and moving.

The discussions of the three sections in Jude 5-13 that follow will consider the literary structure of each unit, the historical background of the examples in the Bible and the Jewish tradition, and what can be said about the opponents from both the examples and the applications.

A. Three Examples and an Application (Jude 5-8)

In the rhetorical introduction in v. 5a ("Now I want to remind you, even though you know all these things"), Jude seeks to render his readers benevolent by appealing to their existing knowledge of OT and Jewish traditions. What he offers to them in the body of the letter/sermon then is presented as only by way of "reminder." The first three biblical examples are attached to the introduction by "that" (*hoti*) in v. 5b, by "that" (*hoti*) understood in v. 6, and by "just as" or "likewise" (*hōs*) in v. 7. Thus the

first three examples are subordinated to the introduction in one long and
awkward sentence that probably would have been more effective in its
oral form than it is in its present written form. The application in v. 8 is
marked by *houtoi* ("these men") and makes three charges against the opponents. Both the examples and the application illustrate the rhetorical
"rule of three" that is frequently used by preachers, teachers, and story-
tellers.

Ancient Israel in the Wilderness (Jude 5). The "spy narrative" in Numbers
13–14 is regarded as a turning point in the story of ancient Israel, since it
explains why the exodus generation did not enter the promised land.
Having been liberated from slavery in Egypt, most of the people became
discouraged about the "unfavorable report" (Num 13:32) regarding the
land of Canaan from the spies, apart from Joshua and Caleb, and so they
rebelled against the leadership of Moses and Aaron. God in turn swears
that "none of those who despised me shall see it [the land]" (14:23). God
also promises that "in the wilderness they shall come to a full end, and
there they shall die" (14:35). Among those sent to spy out the land only
Joshua and Caleb survive to enter the land, while "the men who brought
an unfavorable report about the land died by a plague before the Lord"
(14:38). For Jude the significance of the spy narrative lies in the fact that
people whom God once saved (the exodus generation and the Christian
"intruders") were and can be destroyed (in the wilderness, or at the Last
Judgment) for their lack of faith and obedience.

Another important description of the disobedience and punishment of
the exodus generation in the wilderness appears in Ps 95:8-11: "Do not
harden your hearts, as at Meribah, as on the day at Massah in the wilderness, when your ancestors tested me. . . ." Here ancient Israel's disobedience is put forward as a negative example to be avoided by later
generations. The penalty for their disobedience is expressed in God's
oath: "They shall not enter my rest" (Ps 95:11). The author of Hebrews in
3:7–4:11 takes Ps 95:8-11 as his main biblical text in exhorting his audience
to hear God's voice "today" and traces the failure of the exodus generation to their lack of faith: "they were unable to enter because of unbelief"
(Heb 3:19), and "they were not united by faith" (4:3).

In early Jewish and rabbinic writings, too, the destruction of the exodus
generation on account of its sinfulness serves as a negative example and a
warning. Ben Sira in Sir 16:7-10 uses them as one of several examples
(along with the giants, Sodom and Gomorrah, and the Canaanites) to
illustrate the destructive power of God's wrath against sinners: "He
showed no pity . . . on the six hundred thousand foot soldiers who
assembled in their stubbornness" (Sir 16:9-10). Likewise, in the *Damascus
Document* 3:7-9 the homilist uses the bad example of the exodus genera-

tion to illustrate the consequences of disobedience toward God: "But they chose their own will and did not heed the voice of their Maker, the commands of their Teacher, but murmured in their tents; and the anger of God was kindled against their congregation." And according to Mishnah *Sanhedrin* 10:4 "the spies have no portion in the world to come." This proposition is argued on the basis of the report in Num 14:37 that the spies (apart from Joshua and Caleb) "died by the plague," and on the reasoning that this somewhat redundant phrase must refer first to their physical death in the wilderness ("died—in this world") and then to their fate at the Last Judgment ("by the plague—in the world to come").

When read against the background of the pertinent biblical and extrabiblical texts the example of ancient Israel in the wilderness as used in Jude 5 suggests that the "intruders" are Christians who once were "saved" but now are headed for destruction because of their failure to believe properly and because of their disobedience. Jude intends his readers to interpret the present threat posed by the intruders in light of the sin and punishment associated with the exodus generation. At the same time the case of the exodus generation offers a warning to his readers along the lines of Heb 3:12: "Take care, brothers and sisters, that none of you may have an evil, unbelieving heart that turns away from the living God."

The Rebellious Angels (Jude 6). The second example reflects Jude's familiarity with the book known as *1 Enoch* or *Ethiopic Enoch,* a familiarity that is confirmed by the direct quotation of *1 Enoch* 1:9 in Jude 14-15. *First Enoch* is a collection of five books written between the third century B.C.E. and the first century C.E.: the Book of Watchers (chs. 1–36), the Book of Similitudes or Parables (37–71), the Astronomical Book (72–82), the Book of Dreams (83–90), and the Epistle of Enoch (91–107).

The fascination with the figure of Enoch was due in large part to the description of him in Gen 5:18-24, where he is said to have been the son of Jared and the father of Methuselah and to have lived piously ("Enoch walked with God," 5:22, 24) until "he was no more because God took him" (5:24). The mysterious description of Enoch's disappearance made him into a vehicle for recounting visions and dreams about the heavenly realm and about the future. The work known as *1 Enoch* is thus an anthology of Jewish apocalyptic writings associated with the figure of Enoch.

The most complete text of *1 Enoch* is the Ethiopic version (which is part of the canon of Scripture in the Ethiopian Orthodox church). There are also extant fragments of the Greek version, as well as many fragmentary manuscripts of the original Aramaic text that were found at Qumran among the Dead Sea scrolls. While *1 Enoch* is not directly tied in its origin to the Jewish sectarian movement based at Qumran (Essenes), the presence of this work in multiple copies there and the echoes of it in the language and concepts of the sect's own writings indicate that *1 Enoch* was very influential in some Jewish circles in Palestine in the first century. The author assumes that his first readers know and respect this book.

According to Jude 6 the rebellious angels failed to keep to their own heavenly domain and because of their rebelliousness they were consigned to be chained in the underworld until the Day of Judgment. While no such account appears in the OT, the Book of Watchers in *1 Enoch* 6–16 describes these events in great detail. Taking Gen 6:1-4 as its starting point, the Book of Watchers recounts a rebellion on the part of some two hundred angels under the leadership of Semyaz. Their rebellion consists in leaving their places in the heavenly court in order to have sexual relations with "the daughters of the people on earth" (9:7). In the process they revealed esoteric knowledge about magic, warfare, seduction, drugs, and astrology, and so they introduced sin and its consequences to humans (compare the Adam and Eve narrative of "original sin" in Genesis 3).

A prominent motif in the story of the fall of the rebellious angels according to *1 Enoch* is their leaving the places assigned to them in the heavenly court. For example, Enoch is instructed to "go and make known to the Watchers of heaven who have abandoned the high heaven, the holy eternal place, and have defiled themselves with women" (12:4). And Enoch is told to ask them: "For what reason have you abandoned the high, holy, and eternal heaven . . . for the dwelling of the spiritual beings of heaven is heaven?" (15:4, 7).

According to *1 Enoch* the punishment visited upon the rebellious angels was their being bound and imprisoned until the Day of Judgment. The angel Raphael is told to "bind Azazel hand and foot and throw him into the darkness" (10:4). And Enoch is instructed to inform the Watchers: "From now on you will not be able to ascend into heaven unto all eternity, but you shall remain inside the earth, imprisoned all the days of eternity" (14:5).

The story of the rebellious angels also appears in the homiletic section of the *Damascus Document:* "Because they walked in the stubbornness of their heart the Heavenly Watchers fell; they were caught because they did not keep the commandments of God" (*CD* 2:18-19). And in *2 Bar.* 56:11-13 the rebellious angels are put forward as another negative example: "For they possessed freedom in that time in which they were created. And some of them came down and mingled themselves with women. At that time they who acted like this were tormented in chains."

With its emphasis on the rebellious angels leaving their place in the heavenly court and their punishment in being bound in the underworld, Jude 6 provides a neat summary of *1 Enoch* 6–16. Read against the background of the Book of Watchers and other pertinent Jewish sources, Jude 6 suggests that the "intruders" were engaged in a rebellion against the divinely established order and that their disobedience will meet appropriate punishment from God both now and at the Last Judgment. The example of the rebellious angels also introduces the idea that the intruders were promoting theological views about angels at variance with the "orthodoxy" held by Jude (see vv. 8-9).

Sodom and Gomorrah (Jude 7). In Jude 7 the biblical episode of Sodom and Gomorrah is summarized in terms of the crime ("[they] committed fornication . . . and went after 'other flesh'"), its function as a negative example ("they set before [us] an example"), and the punishment for their sin ("undergoing the punishment of fire"). In the OT account found in Genesis 19 (see the parallel story in Judges 19) two angels come to Sodom and meet Lot, who invites them to spend the night at his house. After their meal all the men of Sodom surround Lot's house and demand to have sexual relations with the two visitors: "Bring them out to us, so that we may know them" (Gen 19:5). When the men of Sodom refuse Lot's offer of his two virgin daughters and begin to storm the house, the angelic visitors rescue Lot and strike the men of Sodom with blindness (19:10-11). Then after the angels arrange for the safety of Lot and his family in Zoar, the real punishment takes place: "Then the Lord rained on Sodom and Gomorrah sulfur and fire . . . and he overthrew those cities, and all the Plain, and all the inhabitants of the cities, and what grew on the ground" (Gen 19:24-25).

Early Jewish writings used the Sodom and Gomorrah episode in Genesis 19 as an example of God's preparedness to punish sinners. According to 3 Macc 2:5 Simon the high priest in his prayer reminds God how God punished evildoers in the past: "When the inhabitants of Sodom acted insolently and became notorious for their crimes, you burned them up with fire and brimstone and made them an example to later generations." Likewise, in *Jubilees* 16:5-6 there are descriptions of God's punishment of Sodom and Gomorrah ("he burned them with fire and sulfur and he annihilated them"), of their crime ("they were cruel and great sinners and they were polluting themselves and they were fornicating in their flesh and they were causing pollution on the earth"), and of their role as a negative example ("the Lord will execute judgment like the judgment of Sodom on places where they act according to the pollution of Sodom"; see also *Jub.* 20:6). The pattern of crime, punishment, and example in 3 Maccabees and *Jubilees* parallels the content (if not the order) of Jude 7.

More attention is given to the nature of the "crime" committed by the men of Sodom in the *Testaments of the Twelve Patriarchs.* In his testament the patriarch Naphtali uses the bad example of the men of Sodom to warn against departing from the order of nature: "do not become like Sodom, which departed from the order of nature. Likewise the Watchers departed from nature's order" (*T.Naph.* 3:4-5). As in Jude 6-7, the sin of the Watchers and the sin of the men of Sodom are linked and the violation of "the order of nature" takes place more on the angel-human level than with regard to homosexual (male-male) activity. In his testament Benjamin foresees that his sons "will be sexually promiscuous like the promiscuity of the Sodomites and will perish, with few exceptions" (*T.Benj.* 9:1). Benjamin cites as his authority for this prophecy "the words of Enoch the Righteous." Although no such prophecy survives in the extant Enoch materials, it is striking again that there is another link between the figure of Enoch and the men of Sodom as in Jude 6-7.

On the surface the example of Sodom and Gomorrah in Jude 7 accuses the intruders of sexual promiscuity or licentiousness (*aselgeia*) and threatens them with the punishment of fire (in this case, eternal fire) as just recompense for their evil deeds. In the background, however, is also the suggestion that the intruders' sin has something to do with their teaching about angels. This impression is strengthened by the proximity of the example of the rebellious angels in Jude 6 and by what follows in Jude 8-9. Whereas in *1 Enoch* 6–16 the Watchers wanted to have sexual relations with women, in Genesis 19 the men of Sodom wanted to have sexual relations with angels (whether they knew it or not). Thus the third example in the series points beyond the charge of sexual licentiousness to another issue: the order of nature and the place of angels and of humans within it.

The Application (Jude 8). This verse presents the first in a series of four applications of the biblical examples to "these men" (*houtoi*; see vv. 10, 12, and 16. As signalled already in Jude 4, it appears that, from Jude's perspective, the intruders were behaving immorally and promoting false teachings about divine authority and the angels. It seems that the intruders were appealing to their visions or dreams ("in their dreamings") as a warrant for their aberrant teaching and behavior. There is not necessarily a one-to-one correspondence between the three examples in Jude 5-7 and the three charges in Jude 8. As Richard J. Bauckham notes, "both the Watchers and the Sodomites defiled the flesh, all three types flouted the authority of the Lord, only the Sodomites abused angels" (*Jude, 2 Peter* 55).

The charge of defiling the flesh refers to sexual immorality or "licentiousness" (*aselgeia* as in v. 4) and echoes the descriptions of the rebellious angels who "defiled" themselves by having sexual relations with women (see *1 Enoch* 9:8; 10:11; 12:4; and 15:3, 4).

The charge of rejecting authority (*kyriotēta*) refers to the intruders' refusal to accept the divine authority of the "Lord" (*kyrios*), thus echoing Jude 4 ("[they] deny the only Master and our Lord Jesus Christ"). That "authority" here is to be understood as human authority (political or ecclesiastical) or as a class of angels are less likely interpretations.

The meaning of the charge about reviling or blaspheming the "glorious" ones depends on how the term *doxai* is understood. The word *doxa* means "glory" and here probably describes those beings who participate in the glory of God; that is, a class of angels or the angels in general. With the name *doxai* they could hardly be demons or fallen angels.

But why would the intruders revile or blaspheme the glorious ones *(doxai)*? Perhaps because of the intruders' emphasis on their experience of salvation in the present, they may have regarded themselves as somehow superior to the angels. See 1 Cor 6:3: "Do you not know that we are to judge the angels?" Moreover, perhaps their stress on freedom from the Mosaic Law (which Jude interpreted as licentiousness) led them to look down upon the angels who mediated the giving of the Law to Moses on Sinai (see Gal 3:19; Acts 7:53) and/or were associated with "the elemental spirits of the world" (see Gal 4:3, 9; Col 2:8, 18). The fact that the best parallels come from the Pauline writings suggests that the intruders may have been promoting a radical form of Paul's teaching that in the final analysis was a distortion of Paul's gospel (see 2 Pet 3:15-16).

B. Another Example and an Application (Jude 9-10)

The second part in the main section of the sermon proper consists of one (extrabiblical) example—the dispute between the archangel Michael and the devil over the body of Moses—in Jude 9, and another polemical application to "these men" *(houtoi)* in Jude 10.

The Dispute between Two Angels (Jude 9). According to Deut 34:5-6 Moses died in the land of Moab and was buried in a valley in Moab "but no one knows his burial place to this day." In retelling this event in his *Jewish Antiquities,* Josephus takes up the suggestion that Moses did not die but rather like Enoch (Gen 5:24) and Elijah (2 Kgs 2:11) was taken up into heaven: "And while he bade farewell to Eleazar and Joshua and was yet continuing with them, a cloud of a sudden descended upon him and he disappeared in a ravine" *(Ant.* 4:326).

Pseudo-Philo in his *Biblical Antiquities* 19:16 says that at his death Moses "was filled with understanding and his appearance became glorious." But he also insists that Moses "died in glory" and that God buried him. The Mishnah agrees that God buried Moses: "We have none so great as Moses, for only the Holy One, blessed be He, took care of his [bones]" *(m. Sotah* 1:9).

According to Philo's *Life of Moses* 2:291, Moses "was buried with none present, surely by no mortal hands but by immortal powers." The "immortal powers" in this context are presumably angels. Jude 9 agrees with the tradition that Moses was buried by angels and presents it as the occasion for a dispute between Michael, the chief among the angels, and Satan in his role as the erstwhile accuser in the heavenly court (see Job 1–2).

It is generally supposed that Jude 9 relies on an extrabiblical Jewish writing known as the *Assumption of Moses*. A work sometimes given that title but (according to some modern scholars) more accurately called the *Testament of Moses* exists in one Latin manuscript from the fifth century C.E. It was rediscovered and published in the nineteenth century. (For the Latin text, translation, commentary, and treatment of critical issues see Johannes Tromp, *The Assumption of Moses*.) The Latin text seems to have been the translation of a Greek version, and the Greek version may have been a translation of the Hebrew original composed in the first century. The problem is that the only extant manuscript of this work breaks off abruptly before it can narrate the story of Moses' death and burial. Nevertheless, it is likely that Jude had access either to this work or to something much like it. (See Bauckham, "Jude and the Testament of Moses," in *Jude and the Relatives of Jesus in the Early Church* 235–80.)

The only extant manuscript of the *Testament of Moses* takes as its starting point the biblical account of Moses' last days as narrated in Deuteronomy 31–34. As Moses' farewell speech it qualifies as his testament. And since chapter 10 provides a vision of the coming of God's kingdom and the vindication of the righteous, it is also an apocalypse.

In a testament a departing hero gives advice to his followers or children on the basis of what he has learned about life, and looks into the future. In Deuteronomy 32 Moses first surveys the displays of God's goodness in creation (32:6), in choosing Israel as his own portion (32:9), and in caring for Israel in the wilderness (32:10-14). But Moses foresees that Israel's prosperity will lead to apostasy and to seeking after new and abominable practices (32:15-18). Because Israel will have forgotten its Rock (God), God will hide his face and bring punishment upon Israel (32:19-25). Nevertheless, God will eventually vindicate his people, lest Israel's dispersion and destruction should lead its enemies to suppose that Israel's punishment was their own triumph and not God's judgment (32:26-43; see especially 32:36).

The biblical dynamic of apostasy, punishment, and vindication provides the outline for most of what is extant in the *Testament of Moses*. In his parting advice to Joshua, Moses foresees apostasy under the kings of Israel and Judah (ch. 2), the punishment in the destruction of the First Temple and the exile (3), and the partial vindication represented by the return from exile (4). Then the cycle occurs again, with further apostasy before the Maccabean revolt and then (probably as an addition to the earliest text) from the Maccabees to Herod the Great and his sons (6–7), punishment in the time of Antiochus IV Epiphanes (8), and vindication first through the martyrs' deaths (9) and then through the full coming of God's kingdom (10). The one surviving manuscript ends with talk about the burial of Moses (see Deut 34:5-6) but breaks off before describing the event itself.

Unless another manuscript of the *Testament of Moses* is discovered, we cannot be certain whether that work contained the account of Moses' death and burial alluded to in Jude 9. In patristic literature there are many descriptions of the events surrounding Moses's death and burial, and many references to the *Assumption of Moses* (for the full dossier see Bauckham, *Jude, 2 Peter* 67–76). For purposes of understanding Jude 9 it is sufficient here to quote only one version: "When Moses died on the mountain, the archangel Michael was sent to remove the body. But the devil resisted, wishing to deceive, saying, 'The body is mine, for I am the Master of matter,' or slandering the holy man, because he smote the Egyptian, and proclaiming him a murderer. The angel, not tolerating the slander against the holy man, said to the devil, 'May God rebuke you!'" (Bauckham, *Jude, 2 Peter* 74).

Jude 9 cites this tradition as if the readers were already familiar with it; see v. 5: "even though you know all these things." But it does not supply the reasons why there should have been any debate between Michael and the devil. However, the traditions preserved in the patristic writings indicate that the devil claimed that Moses' body belonged to him on the grounds that it was material ("I am the Master of matter") and that Moses had murdered an Egyptian (see Exod 2:11-12). While it is conceivable that the reasons for the dispute over Moses' body were supplied by Christian interpreters of Jude 9, it seems more likely that Jude 9 offers a truncated version of a Jewish tradition about the dispute surrounding the corpse of Moses and that this tradition was known from the (now lost) ending of the *Testament of Moses* or a work very much like it.

The precise role of the tradition about the dispute over Moses' body in the argument of Jude 5-13 is not entirely clear. The best clues come from the assumption that the devil belonged to the group of rebellious angels introduced in v. 6, from the charge that the intruders were reviling or slandering angels (taking *doxai* in v. 8 as a class of angels), and from the repeated use of the Greek root *blasphēm-* (see vv. 8, 9, and 10).

The basic points in Jude seem to be that God alone is the ultimate judge and that God will punish the intruders at the Last Judgment. When Michael the archangel responds to the devil in terms of Zech 3:2 ("May the Lord rebuke you!") Michael effectively leaves the ultimate judgment of Satan the rebellious angel to God. The intruders seem to have been criticizing the angels ("[they] revile the glorious ones," v. 8). Now if the archangel Michael refused to "revile" (*blasphēmein*) a rebellious angel like Satan, how much more should mere humans like the intruders refrain from reviling *(blasphēmein)* the "glorious ones." It seems less likely that Jude here is counseling his readers to avoid judging the intruders ("do not judge so that you may not be judged," Matt 7:1), since Jude himself does not hesitate to issue harsh judgments against them. Rather, the scandal is that the intruders are doing what Michael the archangel refused to do, even in the extreme case of the devil. They are judging angels *(doxai)* negatively ("revile, slander, blaspheme").

The Application (Jude 10). The intruders were apparently presenting themselves as intellectually and spiritually superior Christians. In some way and for some reason they were despising the angels. For possible reasons see the Interpretation of Jude 8. In response Jude claims that they are despising *(blasphēmein)* what they do not understand (the angels, or the spiritual realm in general), and that rather than being intellectually and spiritually superior they were in fact more like irrational animals. Jude foresaw that their negative attitudes and actions would eventually lead to their own destruction in this life and (especially) at the Last Judgment. Their eagerness to despise the angels was symptomatic of their pride and foolishness.

C. Three More Examples and an Application (Jude 11-13)

The examples of Cain, Balaam, and Korah are mentioned very briefly in v. 11, while the application in vv. 12-13 piles up colorful phrases in criticism of the intruders.

Three More Examples (Jude 11). In the cases of Cain, Balaam, and Korah individuals led large groups astray and into destruction. When the biblical accounts are read alongside their later extrabiblical developments in Jewish writings roughly contemporary with the NT there appear even more links between these three biblical characters and the vices that Jude attributes to the intruders. These three examples add to Jude's case that the intruders were promoting sexual immorality, were greedy, and were imparting false doctrines (very likely with regard to the Law of Moses).

THE WAY OF CAIN. According to Gen 4:1-16 Cain murdered his brother Abel. By walking "in the way of Cain" the intruders are effectively committing spiritual murder against their fellow Christians. A look at some parallel texts can "flesh out" what that spiritual murder might involve. Josephus describes Cain as "thoroughly depraved" and "with an eye only to gain" (*Ant.* 1:53). He goes on to accuse Cain of all kinds of evildoing: "He indulged in every bodily pleasure, even if it entailed outraging his companions; he increased his substance with wealth amassed by rapine and violence; he incited to luxury and pillage all whom he met, and became their instructor in wicked practices" (*Ant.* 1:60-61). *Targum Neofiti 1* of Gen 4:8 (see also *Targum Pseudo-Jonathan*) makes Cain into a proponent of skeptical and heretical (Sadducean?) theological views: "Cain answered and said to Abel: 'There is no judgment, and there is no judge and there is no other world. There is no giving of good reward to the just nor is vengeance exacted of the wicked.'" The profile of Cain's licentiousness, greed, and false teaching fits Jude's portrait of the intruders whom he is combating in his sermon.

THE DECEIT OF BALAAM. The "deceit" of Balaam most likely refers to the combination of Num 25:1 ("the people began to have sexual relations with the women of Moab") and Num 31:16 ("these women here, on Balaam's advice, made the Israelites act treacherously against the Lord in the affair of Peor"). Probably by attraction to the Balaam material in Numbers 22–24 a connection was made between Balaam and sinful actions on Israel's part. The implication is that Balaam led Israel into sin—just as the intruders are leading the Christian community addressed by Jude into sin.

Pseudo-Philo attributes to Balaam a much more conscious role in leading Israel into sin. According to *LAB* 18:13 Balaam counselled Balak the king of Moab about how to destroy Israel: "Pick out the beautiful women who are among us and in Midian, and station them naked and adorned with gold and precious stones before them. And when they see them and lie with them, they will sin against their Lord and fall into your hands; for otherwise you cannot fight against them." Why Balaam was with the kings of Midian when he was killed (Num 31:8) is explained by Rabbi Jonathan as due to his desire to get paid for his treachery against Israel: "He went to receive his reward for the 24,000 Israelites whose destruction he had encompassed" (*b.Sanh.* 106a). In Rev 2:14 certain Christian teachers who are accused of leading other Christians astray are said to promote "the teaching of Balaam, who taught Balak to put a stumbling block before the people of Israel, so that they would eat food sacrificed to idols and practice fornication." Against the background of such texts the "deceit of Balaam" in Jude 11 involves leading God's people into sin—a sin that includes sexual immorality, greed, and false teaching. (See Geza Vermes, *Scripture and Tradition in Judaism* 127–77.)

THE REBELLION OF KORAH. According to Numbers 16 Korah fomented a rebellion against the leadership of Moses and Aaron on the rather vague grounds, "You have gone too far" (Num 16:3). In Pseudo-Philo's *Biblical Antiquities* Korah's rebellion is linked to a protest regarding the laws about fringes on garments in Num 15:37-45 that immediately precede the biblical account of Korah's rebellion: "In that time he [God] commanded that man [Moses] about the tassels. And then Korah and two hundred men with him rebelled and said, 'Why is an unbearable law imposed upon us?'" (*LAB* 16:1). By joining Num 15:37-41 and 16:1-3 Pseudo-Philo gave specificity to the rebellion of Korah and made it into a protest against the imposition of the Mosaic Law in what could seem to be a trifling matter (that is, wearing tassels). Again it is tempting to view the intruders who are criticized by Jude as radical Paulinists who denied the validity of the Mosaic Law and tried to convince other Christians to disregard it totally. Jude, however, seems to defend a more conservative Jewish Christianity that held onto the Mosaic Law or at least refused to abrogate it in any sweeping way.

Application (Jude 12-13). While each of the three brief examples in Jude 11 conveys an implicit criticism of the intruders, the explicit application to them ("these men" = *houtoi*) in Jude 12-13 makes further criticisms of them, first by noting the harmful effects of their behavior and teachings on the life of the Christian community, and then by using four metaphors taken from nature to illustrate their negativity and disruptiveness.

The first set of criticisms ("stains on your love feasts, carousing without scruple, looking after themselves") assumes that the intruders have been participating in the life of the Christian community ("your love feasts" = *agapai*). But in Jude's perspective their outrageous and self-centered actions, probably undertaken in the name of Christian "freedom," were in fact only dangerous manifestations of self-indulgence.

The four images taken from nature correspond to four different spheres of the world: the clouds in the air, the trees in the ground, the waves in the sea, and the stars in the heavens. What unites Jude's development of these images is their fruitless and chaotic character: clouds that produce no rain, trees that bear no fruit, wild waves churning up scum, and stars that wander off their course.

The rhetorical effect of piling up all these negative images is to darken further the reputation of the intruders and to warn those Christians being addressed to have nothing more to do with the intruders, who are not conforming to the laws and the order set down by God.

For Jude and his readers the Old Testament was an authoritative source and a font of moral instruction. In this combination Jude (like the author of Hebrews) provides a sound model for preachers in all ages. And the basic model of scriptural exposition and application is being made even more attractive by recourse to such sources as *1 Enoch* and *Assumption of Moses* as well as by the skillful use of various rhetorical devices.

For Reference and Further Study

Bauckham, Richard J. "A Note on a Problem in the Greek Version of 1 Enoch i.9," *JTS* 32 (1981) 136–38.

Berger, Klaus. "Der Streit des guten und des bösen Engels um die Seele. Beobach-tungen zu 4Q Amr b und Judas 9," *JSJ* 4 (1973) 1–18.

Boobyer, G. H. "The Verbs in Jude 11," *NTS* 5 (1958-59) 45–47.

Delcor, Matthias. "Le mythe de la chute des anges et de l'origine des géants comme explication du mal dans le monde dans l'apocalyptique juive. His-toire et tradition," *RHR* 190 (1976) 3–53.

Feuillet, André. "Le péché évoqué aux chapitres 3 et 6,1-4 de la Genèse. Le péché des anges de l'Épître de Jude et de la Seconde Épître de Pierre," *Divinitas* 35 (1991) 207–29.

Fossum, Jarl. "Kyrios Jesus as the Angel of the Lord in Jude 5-7," *NTS* 33 (1987) 226–43.

Haacker, Klaus, and Peter Schäfer. "Nachbiblische Traditionen vom Tod des Mose," in Otto Betz, Klaus Haacker, and Martin Hengel, eds., *Josephus-Studien: Untersuchungen zu Josephus, dem antiken Judentum und dem Neuen Testament: Otto Michel zum 70. Geburtstag gewidmet.* Göttingen: Vandenhoeck & Ruprecht, 1974, 147–74.

Kruger, Michael A. "*toutois* in Jude 7," *Neot* 27 (1993) 119–32.

Landon, Charles H. "The text of Jude 4," *Hervormde Teologiese Studies* 49 (1993) 823–43.

Loewenstamm, Samuel E. "The Death of Moses," in George W. E. Nickelsburg, ed., *Studies on the Testament of Abraham.* Missoula: Scholars, 1976, 185–217.

Merkelbach, Reinhold. "Zwei Beiträge zum Neuen Testament," *Rheinisches Museum für Philologie* 134 (1991) 346–51.

Oleson, John P. "An echo of Hesiod's *Theogony* vv. 190-92 in Jude 13," *NTS* 25 (1979) 492–503.

Osburn, Carroll D. "*1 Enoch* 80:2 (67:5-7) and Jude 12-13," *CBQ* 47 (1985) 296–303.

_____. "The Text of Jude 5," *Bib* 62 (1981) 107–15.

Tromp, Johannes. *The Assumption of Moses: A Critical Edition with Commentary.* Studia in Veteris Testamenti Pseudepigrapha 10. Leiden: Brill, 1993.

Vermes, Geza. *Scripture and Tradition in Judaism.* Leiden: Brill, 1961, 127–77.

Whallon, William. "Should We Keep, Omit, or Alter the *hoi* in Jude 12?" *NTS* 34 (1988) 156–59.

Wikgren, Allen. "Some Problems in Jude 5," in B. L. Daniels and M. Jack Suggs, eds., *Studies in the History and Text of the New Testament (FS K. W. Clark).* Salt Lake City: University of Utah Press, 1967.

4. *Prophecies and Applications* (14-19)

14. And it was about these men that Enoch in the seventh generation from Adam prophesied when he said: "Behold the Lord comes with his holy myriads 15. to execute judgment against all and to convict everyone

for all their ungodly deeds that they committed in an ungodly way and for all the harsh words that those ungodly sinners spoke against him." 16. These men are grumblers, malcontents, walking according to their own passions; and their mouth speaks bombast, showing partiality to gain advantage.

17. But you, beloved, remember the words spoken beforehand by the apostles of our Lord Jesus Christ. 18. For they said to you: "At the last time there shall be scoffers walking according to their own ungodly passions." 19. These men are the ones who cause divisions, natural people, not having the Spirit.

NOTES

14. *And it was about these men that Enoch in the seventh generation from Adam prophesied when he said:* Early in the sentence we are told that 1 Enoch 1:9 was a prophecy about the intruders who are elsewhere referred to as "these men" *(houtoi)*. For Enoch as belonging to the seventh generation from Adam, see *1 Enoch* 60:8 and 93:3. According to Gen 5:24 "Enoch walked with God; then he was no more, because God took him." Since it was assumed that Enoch was taken up into heaven he became the recipient of revelations about the heavenly realm and about the future. And so there were books (see also *2 Enoch* and *3 Enoch*) produced that purported to tell what Enoch saw and learned. While not composed at Qumran, *1 Enoch* was preserved in multiple copies there and was very influential among the Essenes. For them as for Jude, *1 Enoch* was an authoritative (if not canonical) work. (For this Greek text see Richard J. Bauckham, "A Note on a Problem in the Greek Version of 1 Enoch i.9," and James C. VanderKam, "The Theophany of Enoch I 3b-7, 9.")

    "Behold the Lord comes with his holy myriads": The Greek version (based on the Aramaic original) of *1 Enoch* 1:9a reads: "for he comes with his myriads and his holy ones." Jude specifies "the Lord" *(kyrios)* as the subject, but again there is uncertainty as to whether the Lord is God or Christ. (See Carroll D. Osburn, "The Christological Use of I Enoch 1. 9 in Jude 14, 15.") Whereas the Greek of *1 Enoch* has the verb in the present tense *(erchetai)*, in Jude the verb is in the aorist *(ēlthen)*, where one would expect a present or future tense. Also, the Greek text of *1 Enoch* has two groups ("with his myriads and his holy ones"— probably both referring to angels), but in Jude 14 these become one group ("with his holy myriads").

15. *"to execute judgment against all and to convict everyone for all their ungodly deeds that they committed in an ungodly way and for all the harsh words that those ungodly sinners spoke against him":* Jude 15 presents a slightly abbreviated version of what appears in the Greek version of *1 Enoch* 1:9b. The message is that the Lord will bring to judgment (and punishment) all those (including and especially the intruders) who have acted in an "ungodly" way and have spoken badly against the Lord. The root *aseb-* ("impious, irreverent, ungodly") occurs three times in this verse: "ungodly deeds . . . in an ungodly way . . . ungodly

sinners" (see also Jude 4, 18). The characterization of the opponents as "ungodly sinners" taken over from *1 Enoch* is developed in even more colorful ways in Jude 16, with particular attention to their speech (teaching).

16. *These men are grumblers, malcontents, walking according to their own passions:* As in vv. 8, 10, 12 (and 19), the application of the example to the intruders is introduced by *houtoi* ("these men"). The term *gongystai* ("grumblers") suggests that they are conducting a campaign of complaint and slander. There may also be an allusion to the OT tradition of ancient Israel's murmuring against God and Moses in the wilderness (see Exod 16:7; 17:3). The word *mempsimoiros* ("malcontent"), which derives from *memphomai* ("blame") and *moira* ("fate"), occurs only here in the NT. The comment in BDAG apparently links the term to the following phrase ("walking according to their own passions"), and the whole unit is said to describe those "who choose a deviant life style and then complain (with tongue in cheek?) that this is their 'unfortunate fate'" (BDAG 629). See the reference to "ungodly passions" in v. 18.

and their mouth speaks bombast: The word *hyperonka*, here translated as "bombast," appears only here in the NT. It derives from the preposition *hyper* ("above") and the verb *ongkoō* ("swell"). It means literally "of excessive size, puffed up, swollen." When used in the context of speech it refers to haughty, pompous, or bombastic words.

showing partiality to gain advantage: Whereas the Greek expression *lambanein prosōpon* is the usual way of rendering the Hebrew idiom for showing partiality or respect *(naśaʾ pānîm)*, Jude uses *thaumazontes prosōpa* ("admire persons"), after the pattern set in the Septuagint of Lev 19:15 and Deut 10:17. The charge is that the intruders are mere flatterers whose smooth words are intended for their own gain.

17. *But you, beloved, remember:* The use of the plural pronoun "you" and the particle "but" *(de)* at the beginning of the sentence marks a new unit in the letter. The direct address "beloved" *(agapētoi)* links this section back to vv. 3-4, which also began with *agapētoi*. Whereas vv. 17-19 constitute a warning beginning with *agapētoi*, vv. 20-23 form an exhortation also beginning with *agapētoi*. Moreover, the aorist imperative *mnēsthēte* ("remember") derives from the verb *mimnēskomai* and so is related by the root *(mnēs-)* to the verb at the beginning of the previous section: "Now I want to remind *(hypomnēsai)* you" (v. 5).

the words spoken beforehand by the apostles: This phrase is often taken as proof for the later composition of the letter (since the apostles seem to belong to an earlier generation) and for the assumption that Jude the implicit author was not an apostle. Of course "Jude" does not claim to be an apostle. He is merely "slave/servant of Jesus Christ, brother of James" (v. 1). The perfect passive participle *proeirēmenon* is ambiguous. It could refer to words "spoken long ago," thus pointing to a long span of time between the apostles and this letter, or it could simply refer to some indefinite occasion "beforehand."

of our Lord Jesus Christ: For other uses of this solemn formula in Jude see vv. 4 and 21 (also v. 25 for a slight variation). This usage may suggest that *(ho) kyrios* alone in vv. 5, 9, and 14 refers to God the Father and not directly to Jesus.

18. *For they said to you: "At the last time there shall be scoffers"*: Compare 2 Pet 3:3:
"scoffers will come in the last days with scoffing, following their own passions." The "last time" presumably refers to the period preceding the *parousia*,
the general resurrection, and the Last Judgment. In the NT (e.g., Mark 13,
Matthew 24–25, Luke 21, Revelation) as in the Jewish apocalypses (e.g.,
1 Enoch, 4 Ezra, 2 Baruch) this "last" time is a period of trials and testings for
the faithful (see Matt 6:9-13; Luke 11:2-4). The emergence of "scoffers" is presented here as part of what Mark 13:8 describes as "the beginning of the birth-
pangs" (of the Messiah). The noun *empaiktēs* ("scoffer, mocker") appears in the
NT only here and in 2 Pet 3:3, though the verb *empaizein* and related nouns are
fairly common.

walking according to their own ungodly passions: For previous uses of "walking"
(poreuesthai) as a biblical idiom for conduct in Jude see vv. 11 and 16. For previous occurrences of the root *aseb-* ("ungodly") see vv. 4 and 15 (three times).
For a previous reference to "passions" *(epithymiai)* see v. 16. Jude finds the
prophecy of the apostles to be fulfilled in the disgraceful behavior of the intruders.

19. *These men are the ones who cause divisions:* For previous uses of *houtoi* ("these
men") to mark the applications of the various examples to the intruders see
vv. 8, 10, 12, and 16. The verb *apodiorizein* occurs only here in the NT. It combines the prefixes *apo* and *dia* with the word for "boundary" *(oros)*. While
diorizein means "to draw a boundary through," the more intensive *apodiorizein*
means "to divide or separate." The charge is that the intruders have been
causing divisions in the community addressed by Jude.

natural people, not having the Spirit: The masculine plural *psychikoi* is variously
translated as "natural, unspiritual, worldly." Derived from *psychē* ("soul"), it
refers "to the life of the natural world and whatever belongs to it, in contrast
to the realm of experience whose central characteristic is *pneuma*" (BDAG
1100). The best NT parallel appears in 1 Cor 2:14: "Those who are unspiritual
[or "natural"] do not receive the gifts of God's Spirit." In light of this parallel
it seems best to take *pneuma* as a reference to the Holy Spirit. However, the
pneuma ("spirit") as the aspect of the person open to the action of the Holy
Spirit is probably also in view. Those who propose a Gnostic background for
the intruders in Jude emphasize the contrast between "natural" *(psychikoi)* and
"spiritual" *(pneumatikoi)* persons. It is possible that the intruders, whether
they were Gnostics or not, claimed to be truly spiritual persons. If that is so,
Jude denies their claim and dismisses them as merely *psychikoi*. For the other
NT uses of *psychikos* see 1 Cor 15:44 ("a physical body" as opposed to a spiritual one) and Jas 3:15 ("such wisdom . . . is . . . unspiritual").

INTERPRETATION

This section follows the general literary pattern established in Jude
5-13. But instead of biblical and extrabiblical examples it presents two
prophecies or predictions—one from the patriarch Enoch (vv. 14-15) and

the other from the apostles (vv. 17-18), along with two applications of the prophecies to *houtoi* or "these men" (vv. 16, 19).

A. A Prophecy and an Application (Jude 14-16)

After three series of examples and applications (vv. 5-8, 9-10, 11-13), Jude presents a "prophecy" attributed to Enoch (actually a quotation of *1 Enoch* 1:9) in vv. 14-15 and an application to "these men" *(houtoi)* in v. 16 that focuses on their "ungodliness" *(asebeia)* in speech.

The Prophecy of Enoch (Jude 14-15). The quotation of *1 Enoch* 1:9 is called a "prophecy" in that Enoch, who belonged to the seventh generation from Adam (see Gen 5:21-24), is understood as speaking about those who are considered as "intruders" into a Christian community in the first century C.E. The text is part of the prologue (chs. 1–5) to the Book of Watchers in *1 Enoch* 1–36. In it Enoch claims that "I look not for this generation but for the distant one that is coming" (1:2), thus providing the warrant for the application or actualization of the prophecy in a later generation.

In the Ethiopic text *1 Enoch* 1:9 reads as follows: "Behold, he will arrive with ten million of the holy ones in order to execute judgment upon all. He will destroy the wicked ones and censure all flesh on account of everything that they have done, that which the sinners and the wicked ones committed against him" (*OTP* 1.13). Only a few words of the Aramaic version of this verse have been preserved among the Qumran manuscripts. There are full versions of the text in Greek and in Latin (see the synoptic chart in Bauckham, *Jude, 2 Peter* 95). The text in Jude 14-15 specifies the subject as the "Lord" *(kyrios)* and is somewhat shorter than the other versions. According to Bauckham (96), Jude knew the Greek version but made his own translation from the Aramaic.

For Jude the most important elements in Enoch's prophecy are the "Lord" *(kyrios*, which is present in no other text and has probably been supplied by Jude), the Greek root for "ungodly" *(aseb-)* that appears in three different forms *(asebeias, esebēsan, and asebeis)*, and the phrase "all the harsh words . . . [they] spoke."

As is common in NT writings, what was said about God as the Lord *(kyrios)* is transferred to the risen Jesus as *kyrios* whose second coming or *parousia* is awaited as part of the end-time scenario. The role attributed to the risen Jesus at his *parousia* is that of judge (as in Matt 25:31-46). According to the "prophecy" contained in *1 Enoch* 1:9 the condemnation issued by the Lord at his coming will especially involve the "ungodly" *(asebeis)* on account of their "ungodly" actions and their harsh words. The "ungodly" have sinned in deed and in word, and their punishment at the Lord's hand will constitute a display of divine justice.

The Application (Jude 16). The application of Enoch's prophecy to "these men" *(houtoi)* focuses on their sins involving speech: "for all the harsh words that those ungodly sinners spoke against him." This focus indicates that Jude's problem with the intruders went beyond their disgraceful behavior and included their teachings. Several of the epithets applied to the intruders in v. 16 directly concern their harmful words: "grumblers, malcontents . . . their mouth speaks bombast." These terms pertaining to speech suggest that the intruders presented themselves as teachers and regarded themselves as purveyors of a superior wisdom. For Jude, however, their false doctrine was mere "bombast" that proceeded from their enslavement "to their own passions" and their reliance on flattery to gain advantages for themselves. Jude portrays the intruders as the "ungodly" *(asebeis)* and so as the fulfillment of Enoch's prophecy against the "ungodly" belonging to the distant generation of the first century C.E.

B. Another Prophecy and an Application (17-19)

The second prophecy is attributed to "the apostles of our Lord Jesus Christ" and concerns "scoffers" *(empaiktai)* who will emerge in the last days (vv. 17-18). It is accompanied by the charge in v. 19 that "these men" foment divisions and are "natural" *(psychikoi)* rather than spiritual *(pneumatikoi)* persons.

The Prophecy of the Apostles (Jude 17-18). The way in which the second prophecy is introduced in v. 17 suggests that for Jude and his readers "the apostles" were a well known and revered group from the past. First there is a command to the readers to call to mind or remember: "But you, beloved, recall the words. . . ." Then there is the description of their words as having been "spoken beforehand," as if they were authoritative prophecies or predictions that only now are being fulfilled by the intruders. Finally there is the description of "the apostles" as a separate group within the early Christian movement and the application to them of the formulaic sounding phrase "the apostles of our Lord Jesus Christ."

The content of the apostles' prophecy according to Jude 18 ("In the last time there shall be scoffers walking according to their own ungodly passions") has many NT parallels, though the use of the noun "scoffers" *(empaiktai)* is unusual. See 2 Pet 3:3 for the only other use of the noun in the NT; there the object of the scoffing is the delay of the *parousia.* For Jude the intruders are false teachers (see the references to their speech in v. 16). By their false teachings they fulfill the various NT apocalyptic warnings against false teachers. For example, Matthew's eschatological discourse foresees the appearance of false prophets: "And many false prophets will arise and lead many astray. . . . For false messiahs and false prophets will appear and produce great signs and omens, to lead astray, if possible, even the elect" (Matt 24:11, 24; see also Acts 20:29-30; 1 Tim 4:1-3; 2 Tim 4:3-4). The prophecy attributed to the apostles in Jude 18 is more a summary of the apostolic warnings against false teachers than the direct quotation of a particular apostle or the statement of an apostolic council.

Application (Jude 19). While the intruders may have regarded their teaching as authentic Christian wisdom, Jude saw it as divisive. While they may have considered themselves to be truly spiritual, Jude viewed them as lacking the Holy Spirit and so as not spiritual at all.

From the several warnings about the Last Judgment scattered through the letter of Jude it is likely that the intruders questioned the Last Judgment entirely or at least raised doubts about its prominent place in the apostolic preaching of the Christian faith. In Jude's view the intruders deserved to be called "scoffers" on account of their skepticism, and Jude was especially concerned about the factionalism that their entry into the community was causing.

It appears that in their teaching and actions the intruders wanted to appeal to their own superior wisdom and spirituality. It is likely that they were presenting themselves as "spiritual" *(pneumatikoi)* in the sense of possessing the Holy Spirit *(pneuma hagion)* and doing everything in accord with the Holy Spirit. They may well have taken as their motto something like what is found in 1 Cor 2:15: "The spiritual person *(pneumatikos)* judges all things but is judged by no one." And just as Paul in 1 Cor 2:14 criticized those Corinthian Christians with pretensions to higher wisdom and spirituality as really "natural" or "unspiritual" *(psychikoi)* in the sense of their living on the level of the *psychē* or natural soul rather than on the level of the *pneuma* or spirit/Spirit, so Jude here turns the intruders' pretensions back upon themselves and describes them as "natural people, not having the Spirit" *(psychikoi, pneuma mē echontes).*

Not everyone who claims to be "spiritual" really is. That is the basic point of Jude 14-19. While the intruders may use the "right" words, their true character as "natural people" *(psychikoi)* is manifested by their evil deeds and their divisiveness. In fact, the intruders emerge as purveyors of bloated and empty words ("bombast"). On the contrary, the biblical ideal of spirituality is the perfect coherence between one's words and one's deeds (see Matt 7:13-27).

FOR REFERENCE AND FURTHER STUDY

Bauckham, Richard J. "A Note on a Problem in the Greek Version of I Enoch i.9," *JTS* 32 (1981) 136–38.

Black, Matthew. "The Maranatha Invocation and Jude 14, 15 (1 Enoch 1:9)," in Barnabas Lindars and Stephen Smalley, eds., *Christ and the Spirit in the New Testament*. Cambridge: Cambridge University Press, 1973, 189–96.

Dehandschutter, Boudewijn. "Pseudo-Cyprian, Jude and Enoch. Some Notes on Enoch 1:9," in J. W. Van Henten et al., eds., *Tradition and Re-interpretation in Jewish and Early Christian Literature: Essays in Honor of Jürgen C. H. Lebram*. Leiden: Brill, 1986.

Osburn, Carroll D. "The Christological Use of I Enoch i. 9 in Jude 14, 15," *NTS* 23 (1977) 334–41.

VanderKam, James C. "The Theophany of Enoch I 3b-7, 9," *VT* 23 (1973) 129–50.

5. *An Exhortation and Doxology* (20-25)

20. But you, beloved, build yourselves upon your most holy faith; pray in the Holy Spirit; 21. keep yourselves in the love of God; wait for the mercy of our Lord Jesus Christ unto eternal life. 22. Have mercy on those who are doubting; 23. save them, seizing them from the fire; have mercy on them in fear, hating even the garment stained by the flesh.

24. Now to him who is able to keep you from stumbling and to present (you) without blemish before his glory in joy, 25. to the only God our Savior through Jesus Christ our Lord, (be) glory, majesty, might, and authority before all time and now and for all time. Amen.

NOTES

20. *But you, beloved, build yourselves upon your most holy faith:* Just as the warning began in v. 17 with the address "But you, beloved," so the exhortation (vv. 20-23) is introduced in the same way. The verb *epoikodomein* means to "build something on something already built" (BDAG 387), and in this context it has the sense of growth and development in the Christian community founded on faith in God and Christ. The hortatory material in vv. 20-21 features three participles *(epoikodomountes, proseuchomenoi,* and *prosdechomenoi)* and only one true imperative *(tērēsate).* But in hortatory contexts in the NT it is not unusual to use participles in the sense of imperatives. The pronoun *heautous* very likely carries a collective or corporate overtone ("one another"). The foundation on which the addressees are to build is their "most holy faith," with the objective sense given to *pistis* in v. 3: "the faith handed on to the saints once for all."

pray in the Holy Spirit: Whereas the "natural" persons *(psychikoi)* do not have the Spirit, the Christians addressed by Jude can and do pray through the power of the Holy Spirit. For the Holy Spirit as empowering the prayer of Christians see Rom 8:26: "for we do not know how to pray as we ought, but that very Spirit intercedes with sighs too deep for words."

21. *keep yourselves in the love of God:* As the second member in the faith-love-hope triad so prominent in early Christian literature, *agapē* ("love") is probably meant here in both senses as God's love for us and our love for God in return. God's love for us provides the context in which we can love God and one another.

    wait for the mercy of our Lord Jesus Christ unto eternal life: The hope is for a positive verdict at the Last Judgment and the reward of eternal life. For the formula "our Lord Jesus Christ," see the Notes on v. 17. The reference to "mercy" (*eleos*) may refer to the soteriological effects of Jesus' death and resurrection already experienced in the present and to be enjoyed fully at the Last Judgment (as in Paul's letter to the Romans), or it may allude to the role of the risen Christ as the one who presides at the Last Judgment (as in Matt 25:31-46).

22. *Have mercy on those who are doubting:* For a full treatment of the textual problems posed by Jude 22-23 see Bruce M. Metzger, *A Textual Commentary on the Greek New Testament* (London and New York: United Bible Societies, 1971; corrected ed. 1975) 727–29 and Charles H. Landon, *A Text-Critical Study of the Epistle of Jude* 131–34. The Bodmer papyrus designated 𝔓⁷² presents a short and relatively smooth reading: "Some from the fire seize; but on those who are doubting have mercy in fear." For a defense of its originality see Carroll D. Osburn, "The Text of Jude 22-23." Some other early manuscripts (e.g., Sinaiticus, Alexandrinus) seem to distinguish three groups as in our translation, while other manuscripts (e.g., Vaticanus) have only two groups ("those whom you pity when they doubt [or, dispute] save, snatching them from the fire; but some pity in fear"). Sara C. Winter ("Jude 22-23") argues for two groups, while J. M. Ross ("Church Discipline in Jude 22-23") sees three groups. However, Joel S. Allen ("A New Possibility for the Three-Clause Format of Jude 22-3") suggests that all three clauses may refer to one and the same group ("those who are doubting") and may propose various pastoral approaches to them. The imperative *eleate* ("have mercy") reappears as part of the third clause, though some manuscripts read *elegechete* ("convince, refute") instead of *eleate* or *eleete* here in v. 22. The participle *diakrinomenous,* which derives from *diakrinein* ("separate, differentiate, judge, decide, dispute"), here carries the meaning "doubt, waver" found elsewhere in the NT (e.g., Matt 21:21; Mark 11:23; Rom 14:23).

23. *save them, seizing them from the fire:* While showing compassion to doubters, the addressees are to recognize that the doubters' eternal salvation is at stake. For the image of seizing something from the fire in the OT see Amos 4:11 and Zech 3:2. For "fire" as an everlasting punishment in the NT see Matt 5:22; Mark 9:43, 48; etc.

    have mercy on them in fear: For *eleate* ("have mercy") see the Note on v. 22. If we assume that there is only one group at issue ("those who are doubting"), then "in fear" probably conveys the idea of fear of contamination, an interpretation that fits well with the next clause.

    hating even the garment stained by the flesh: The *chitōn* ("garment") was worn next to the skin. For the verb *spiloō* see the dispute about translating *spilades* in

Jude 12 ("stains," or "hidden rocks"?). Here the perfect passive participle *espilōmenon* means "stained." The fear is that those who are doubting because of the false teachings they have received from the intruders may already be contaminated and can infect those who try to minister to them. The use of "flesh" *(sarx)* may be a further criticism of the intruders: Those who wrongly claim to be *pneumatikoi* are in fact not only *psychikoi* but even *sarkikoi* (see 1 Cor 3:1, 3; etc.).

24. *Now to him who is able to keep you from stumbling:* The doxology begins with the same expression ("Now to him who is able") as does the doxology in Rom 16:25-27 (which is generally regarded not as written directly by Paul but rather as a later addition to Paul's letter to the Romans). The referent is God (see v. 25), and the doxology ascribes to God "glory, majesty, might, and authority." The adjective *aptaistos* derives from the negative prefix *a-* (alpha privative) and the verb "stumble" *(ptaiein)*. This is the only occurrence of this adjective in the NT. Bodmer Papyrus $\mathfrak{P}^{72}$ reads "(able) to establish (you as) spotless, without blemish, purified" *(stērixai aspilous amōmous agneumenous);* for a defense of its originality see Landon, *A Text-Critical Study of the Epistle of Jude* 134–35.

and to present (you) without blemish before his glory in joy: God is praised as the only one capable of bringing righteous persons before his own judgment seat. The adjective *amōmos* means "without blemish" in a literal sense and is used frequently in a moral sense in the NT to mean "blameless" (see Eph 1:4; 5:27; Col 1:22; Phil 2:15; etc.). God makes salvation possible for humans, and rejoices to bestow it upon them.

25. *to the only God our Savior through Jesus Christ our Lord:* A similar formula appears in the doxology in Rom 16:27: "to the only wise God through Jesus Christ." While it is possible to translate *monǭ theǭ* as "to God alone," the NT parallels (see John 5:44; Rom 16:27; 1 Tim 1:17) make "to the only God" more likely. This is the only use of *sōter* as a title for God in Jude; in 2 Pet 1:1, 11; 2:20; 3:2, 18 it is a title for Christ. In the phrase "through Jesus Christ our Lord" Jude agrees in part with Rom 16:27 and departs from his own customary formula "our Lord Jesus Christ" (as in vv. 4, 17, 21).

(be) glory, majesty, might, and authority: There is no verb in the Greek text, and it is customary to supply one in translation; see Rom 16:27, where there is no verb either. The attribute of "glory" *(doxa)* makes the formula into a doxology, which involves ascribing glory to God. The other three attributes stress the sovereignty of God over all creation, whereas the preceding verse emphasized God's mercy and loving care for humans.

before all time and now and for all time. Amen: The divine attributes apply to the time before creation, the present age, and the time after the fullness of God's kingdom is made manifest. Whether one can find here a clear reference to the preexistence of Christ is dubious. The affirmatory "Amen" appears in its role as a seal or liturgical conclusion (see Rom 1:25; 9:5; 11:36; 15:33; 16:27; Gal 1:5; 6:18; etc.).

Whereas most of the letter of Jude thus far has presented stinging criticisms of the intruders and offered positive and constructive advice to the readers only by way of indirection, here another direct address to them ("But you, beloved"; see v. 17) introduces an exhortation (vv. 20-23) that first mentions the essential elements of Christian life (vv. 20-21) and then offers counsel regarding pastoral outreach to the struggling members of the Christian community (vv. 22-23). A doxology (vv. 24-25) that praises God as the one who is able to present faithful Christians "without blemish" at the Last Judgment provides a stirring ending or "seal" to the letter.

A. The Exhortation (Jude 20-23)

The exhortation consists of a brief description of the essentials of Christian theology (Father, Son, Holy Spirit) and of Christian life (faith, prayer, love, hope) in vv. 20-21, along with a plea for the pastoral care of those Christians who seem to be wavering under the influence of the intruders (vv. 22-23).

The Positive Ideal (Jude 20-21). The positive ideal of Christian theology and life is sketched in Jude 20-21 with four clauses that feature one true imperative ("keep") and three participles functioning as imperatives ("build[ing] . . . pray[ing] . . . wait[ing]"). The essentials of Christian life include faith ("your most holy faith"), prayer, love of God, and hope ("wait for the mercy . . ."). As in v. 3, "your most holy faith" appears as something objective, a body of beliefs or the deposit of faith. As in Rom 8:26-27, the Holy Spirit is understood to be the real agent in prayer ("pray in the Holy Spirit"). While "love of God" refers primarily to love for God (with God as the object of love), it is based on God's love for us and shows itself in love for others. And the note of hope ("wait") is present in that Christian life has "eternal life" as its goal and "the mercy of our Lord Jesus Christ" as its basis. These four clauses also place Christian life in a "trinitarian" framework: "in the Holy Spirit . . . the love of God . . . our Lord Jesus Christ." In two short verses Jude (perhaps relying on an established formula) provides a sketch of the essentials of Christian theology and Christian life.

A Call for Pastoral Outreach (Jude 22-23). Having offered a summary of the positive Christian ideal in vv. 20-21, Jude in vv. 22-23 provides his readers with some directions for pastoral outreach. His advice, however, is obscure in its OT background, object, and content.

The OT background is Zech 3:1-5. Part of this OT passage already appeared previously in the debate between Michael and Satan over the body of Moses (see Jude 9). There Michael, rather than rebuking his fellow angel directly, quotes Zech 3:2: "May the Lord rebuke you." That same OT verse goes on to describe the high priest Joshua as "a brand plucked from the fire" and is echoed in Jude 23: "save them, seizing them from the fire." Moreover, the image of the "garment stained by the flesh" at the end of Jude 23 seems to depend on Zech 3:4-5 where the angel tells Joshua that the removal of his filthy garment symbolizes the removal of his guilt and makes it possible for him to be clothed again in his priestly vestments. But why exactly Jude regarded this OT text as so important, especially since his use of the image of "filthy garment" is thoroughly negative, is puzzling.

The object of this pastoral care is a group described by the accusative masculine plural participle *diakrinomenous*. The verb *diakrinein* has several different meanings. In the context of Jude 22-23, however, the two most likely interpretations are (1) "those who are disputing" (see v. 9) and (2) "those who are doubting/wavering." In the first interpretation Jude urges his readers to reach out to the intruders or (more likely) those who are being influenced by them. In the second interpretation the objects of the pastoral care are envisioned as members of the community who are "on the fence" or wavering with regard to the intruders. Since up to this point Jude has shown no pastoral sensitivity toward the intruders, the more likely objects of his solicitude are those who were being influenced by the intruders. In that case those Christians who "dispute" on behalf of the intruders and those who "doubt" or waver because of them are in the final analysis the same people.

The content of Jude's pastoral advice is further complicated by the different textual forms in which vv. 22-23 appears in the Greek manuscripts. (See the full dossier in Bauckham, *Jude, 2 Peter* 108–11.) The simplest form is found in 𝔓⁷²: "Seize some from the fire; but have mercy in fear on those who dispute/doubt." Another early version appears in the Vatican manuscript (B): "Have mercy on some who are disputing/doubting; save them, seizing them from the fire. But have mercy on others in fear." In these forms of the text there seem to be two groups who are envisioned as the objects of pastoral care. In the Sinai and Alexandrian manuscripts, however, there appear to be three groups in need of pastoral care: "And have mercy on some who are wavering; save others by snatching them out of the fire; and have mercy on still others with fear" (NRSV). And in the Notes we have mentioned an interpretation that accepts the longer three-member text but takes the advice as directed to one group only ("those who are doubting").

Jude 22-23 represents one of the most difficult text-critical puzzles in the Greek NT. Whatever textual solutions are adopted, at its most basic level it reminds Christians of their obligation to seek out those "little ones" who have gone astray and are in danger of being lost (see Matt 18:10-14).

B. *The Doxology (Jude 24-25)*

In a doxology ("a word of praise") there are four basic elements: a mention of the person to be praised, usually in the dative case; a word of praise usually including *doxa* ("glory"); an indication of time or eternity ("forever"); and a response ("Amen") by which the hearers can make the prayer of praise their own.

The form of the doxology is presented at its simplest level in the *Prayer of Manasseh* 15: "and yours [God's] is the glory forever. Amen." Likewise, there is another very short example of a doxology in 4 Macc 18:24: "to whom [God] be glory forever and ever. Amen." Perhaps the best-known doxology appears at the end of the Lord's Prayer in Matt 6:13 but only in some (later and inferior) manuscripts: "For yours [God's] are the kingdom and the power and the glory forever. Amen." Most likely a later liturgical ending added to the biblical form of the prayer, it serves as a dramatic way to round off or "seal" the Lord's Prayer. Its wording echoes that of David's benediction in 1 Chr 29:11: "Yours, O Lord, are the greatness, the power, the glory, the victory, and the majesty."

The doxology in Jude 24-25 is most similar in form and function to the doxologies in Rom 16:25-27 (generally regarded as an addition to Paul's letter) and Eph 3:20-21 (generally regarded as part of a letter written not by Paul but in Paul's name by an admirer). All three doxologies begin with a mention of the power of God ("Now to him who is able . . ."), feature the word *doxa* ("glory"), mention the eternal character of God's glory, and conclude with a responsorial "Amen." In each case the doxology serves to end ("sealing" or "rounding off") a writing or a section on a triumphal note of praise directed to God.

The expansive form of the doxology in Rom 16:25-27; Eph 3:20-21; and Jude 24-25 allows the writer to develop particular reasons why God should be praised. In Rom 16:25-27 it is for the revelation of the gospel and in Eph 3:20-21 it is for the success of the Pauline mission. In Jude 24-25 the emphasis is on God's ability to sustain Christians in preparation for the Last Judgment: "to him who is able to keep you from stumbling and to present (you) without blemish before his glory in joy." The eschatological focus fits well with the many allusions to the Last Judgment throughout the letter of Jude.

The closing of the letter of Jude provides a beautiful sketch of Christian existence. The foundations are faith, prayer, love of God, and hope (vv. 20-21). It involves compassion toward others and a sense of mission toward them, however dangerous that may be (vv. 22-23). And the origin and the goal of all Christian life is God—the one in whom all glory, majesty, might, and authority reside (vv. 24-25). From start to finish, Christian life is an act of praise and thanksgiving to God.

FOR REFERENCE AND FURTHER STUDY

Allen, Joel S. "A New Possibility for the Three-Clause Format of Jude 22-3," *NTS* 44 (1998) 133–43.
Bieder, Werner. "Judas 22f," *Theologische Zeitschrift* 6 (1950) 75–77.
Deichgräber, Reinhard. *Gotteshymnus und Christushymnus in der frühen Christenheit.* SUNT 5. Göttingen: Vandenhoeck & Ruprecht, 1967, 25–40, 99–101.
Osburn, Carroll D. "The Text of Jude 22-23," *ZNW* 63 (1972) 139–44.
Ross, J. M. "Church Discipline in Jude 22-23," *ExpTim* 100 (1989) 297–98.
Winter, Sara C. "Jude 22-23: A Note on the Text and Translation," *HTR* 87 (1994) 215–22.

2 PETER

INTRODUCTION

1. *Text and Language*

The English version of 2 Peter that is translated and interpreted in this commentary generally reflects the Greek text printed in *Novum Testamentum Graece* (27th edition), edited by Kurt and Barbara Aland (Stuttgart: Deutsche Bibelgesellschaft, 1981). That edition is based on the fourth- and fifth-century Greek uncial manuscripts and other ancient evidence in Greek manuscripts and in early translations.

The oldest Greek text of 2 Peter is preserved (along with those of 1 Peter and Jude) in Bodmer Papyrus 𝔓⁷² from the late third or early fourth century C.E. However, as in the case of Jude, so in 2 Peter 𝔓⁷² itself shows signs of prior critical scribal activity. For example, in 2 Pet 3:10 𝔓⁷² adds to the mysterious expression *heurethēsetai* ("will be found") the participle *lyomena*, to yield "they will be found dissolved." This addition looks very much like a scribe's attempt to make sense out of a problematic text and to smooth it over. Here the reading in 𝔓⁷² probably does not reflect the "original" text.

The patristic evidence for the use of 2 Peter in the second century is quite thin. For a full dossier of the patristic witnesses see Charles Bigg, *A Critical and Exegetical Commentary* 199–215. The most important patristic observations on 2 Peter come from Jerome (see ibid. 199–200) who accepted all seven Catholic epistles as belonging to the NT canon but noted that some ancient writers denied the Petrine authorship of 2 Peter because of its very different style from that of 1 Peter. Jerome explained this "dissonance" as due to Peter's use of two different interpreters or secretaries in composing the two letters. Throughout the centuries Jerome's explanation has been embraced by those who argue for the direct Petrine authorship of both 1 and 2 Peter. However, recognition of the very different literary and theological styles in the two Petrine epistles still remains the strongest argument against the Petrine authorship of 2 Peter.

The language of 2 Peter is more ambitious but less successful than the language of Jude. The most striking feature in 2 Peter is the very large number of *hapax legomena*, that is, words not found elsewhere in the NT. According to Richard J. Bauckham (*Jude, 2 Peter* 135–38) there are fifty-seven words in 2 Peter that are not found elsewhere in the NT (and thirty-five of them are not found in the Septuagint either). The author shows a special fondness for the *alpha*-privative construction; that is, forming a negative word by prefixing an *alpha* (Greek *α*) to a stem: *amathēs* (3:16), *amōmētos* (3:14), *astēriktos* (2:14; 3:16), and so on. In some cases (e.g., *akatapaustos*, 2:14) the *alpha* is prefixed to a word that already contains a prefix. The author also likes to present pairs of words: e.g., *amatheis kai astēriktoi* ("the ignorant and unstable") in 3:16.

At times the author's linguistic ambitions outstrip his abilty to write clear Greek prose. The use of so many rare words and the occasional lapses in syntax have suggested to some modern critics that Greek was not his native language and that perhaps 2 Peter was written by someone whose native tongue was Aramaic or even Latin. Others have attributed the unusual language in 2 Peter to a deliberate effort at writing in the so-called Asiatic style of Greek, while still others have explained it as due simply to the writer's personal pomposity and ineptitude. The most complete analysis appears in Thomas Kraus, *Sprache, Stil und historischer Ort des zweiten Petrusbriefes*. WUNT 2.136 (Tübingen: J.C.B. Mohr [Paul Siebeck], 2001), who illustrates how within the NT 2 Peter stands out as a stylistically peculiar text.

2. *Genre and Structure*

Some manuscripts (including $\mathfrak{P}^{72}$) give the title of 2 Peter as the "Epistle of Peter B'." In the manuscripts and editions of the NT 2 Peter appears in the part of the canon that includes the non-Pauline or General/Catholic letters: James, 1–2 Peter, 1–3 John, and Jude. In its gross structure 2 Peter conforms to the conventions found in other NT letters and in letters from the Greco-Roman world in general.

What immediately marks 2 Peter as a letter is its salutation in 1:1-2: the sender ("Simeon Peter"), the addressees ("to those who received a faith of equal standing . . ."), and the greeting ("May grace and peace be yours . . ."). The occasion for this letter is said to be the imminent departure of the apostle Peter by death (1:12-15) and his desire to warn the addressees about certain "false teachers" *(pseudodidaskaloi)* who were bringing "destructive heresies" into the community and were promoting an immoral lifestyle (2:1-3). Especially controversial were their skeptical attitudes toward the second coming or *parousia* of Jesus ("Where is the promise of his coming?") and the dangerous consequences of this skepticism for Christian life (3:1-4).

The author explicitly identifies his work as a letter in 3:1: "Beloved, now this is the second letter that I write to you." He addresses his readers directly ("beloved") and creates the impression that they know him and he knows them. As most NT letters do, 2 Peter concludes with an exhortation or parenesis in 3:11-18a that spells out the practical implications of the "theological" exposition. And like Jude and Romans, 2 Peter ends with a doxology (3:18b).

While 2 Peter is clearly a letter, it also uses the literary conventions of a testament, that is, a farewell discourse in which a departing hero tells about the future and gives advice on proper behavior in the present and future. In 1:12-15 Peter describes his work as a "reminder" (see 1:12, 13, 15) that will serve as a substitute for his physical presence after he dies. He recognizes that "the putting off of my tent is imminent" (1:14) and assumes that his letter will be available to those who need it even when he is dead. Some of Peter's advice is cast in the future tense ("there will be false teachers among you," 1:12), but at other times his use of the present tense indicates that he was addressing an already present danger. In keeping with the eschatological framework of the testament genre in Judaism and early Christianity (see the Interpretation of 1:12-15), Peter portrays the danger posed by the false teachers as a sign that "the last days" (3:3) have begun. The duty of Christians is to remain faithful to the apostolic preaching and to conduct their lives in an appropriate manner. The positive ideal of Christian life is set forth in the initial paragraph (1:3-11), and its implications for Christian conduct in "the last days" are set out in the concluding exhortation (3:11-18a). So prominent are the conventions of the testament that 2 Peter can be described as a testament set within an epistolary framework (much as Jude can be called a sermon in an epistolary framework).

Some interpreters such as Duane F. Watson *(Invention, Arrangement, and Style. Rhetorical Criticism of Jude and 2 Peter)* are so impressed by the oratorical features of 2 Peter that they find in it (as in Jude) the classical rhetorical outline used in ancient Greek and Latin speeches: the epistolary prescript as a quasi-*exordium* (1:1-2), the *exordium* with features of the testament genre (1:3-15), the *probatio* (1:16–3:13) consisting of four accusations and the responses to them (1:16-19; 1:20-21; 2:3b-10a; 3:3-13), along with a *digressio* (2:10b-22) and a *transitio* (3:1-2), and the *peroratio* (3:14-18), consisting of a *repetitio* (3:14-16) and the *adfectus* or emotional appeal (3:17-18).

Watson also discovers in 2 Peter elements of the three classical rhetorical styles: deliberative, judicial (1:16–2:10a), and epideictic (2:10b-22). It is plausible and even likely that someone so fascinated with odd Greek words as the author of 2 Peter would have been exposed to classical oratorical training (for the author's familiarity with classical figures of speech see the list in Watson, *Invention* 195–97), which might lead him to produce a composition according to the classical rhetorical patterns. But this commentary will give more attention to 2 Peter as a testament in the Jewish tradition than as a speech in the Greco-Roman rhetorical tradition.

Since 2 Peter has the features of a letter, a testament, and a speech, perhaps the best approach to discerning its structure and flow of thought is to follow a topical or thematic outline:

1. Salutation (1:1-2)

2. Christian Life (1:3-11)

3. Peter's Testament (1:12-15)

4. The Witness of Peter and Holy Scripture (1:16-21)

5. False Teachers (2:1-3)

6. Biblical Precedents (2:4-11)

7. Denunciations (2:12-16)

8. More Denunciations (2:17-22)

9. The Delay of the Parousia (3:1-4)

10. Biblical Responses (3:5-10)

11. Final Exhortation (3:11-18)

In 2 Pet 2:4–3:3 the author makes abundant but selective use of Jude 6-18 as a source for terms and themes with which to denounce the "false teachers" he is opposing. However, he is not satisfied merely with copying from Jude. Rather, by strategic omissions, editorial changes, and additions he tailors his source to meet the threat posed by the opponents being confronted in this particular situation.

The literary and thematic unity of 2 Peter is neatly captured in its final two verses: "Therefore, beloved, knowing this beforehand, be on guard lest you be carried away by the error of unprincipled men and you lose your firm hold. But grow in the grace and knowledge of our Lord and Savior Jesus Christ" (3:17-18a). By the phrase "knowing this beforehand" the closing verses identify 2 Peter as a testament. It expresses the writing's basic purpose as a warning against the false teachers and the dangers they pose to the Christian community, and it holds out as the positive ideal for Christian life growth "in the grace and knowledge of our Lord and Savior Jesus Christ," thus sending the reader back to the program for achieving such growth set forth in 1:3-11.

The theological presupposition of 2 Peter is that God (especially in God's words and promises) and the apostolic preaching about God and Jesus are reliable. As the OT precedents prove, God has been faithful to past promises (to reward and to punish), and God's word is powerful. The writer assumes a "high christology" in his casual uses of epithets such as "Lord," "Savior," and even "God" with respect to Jesus. And there is an interweaving of eschatology and ethics, so that the visions of the "last days" function as a motive for correct behavior in the present as faithful Christians await their vindication at the Last Judgment.

3. *Jewish, Greek, and Christian Traditions*

One specific problem confronted in 2 Peter seems to have been the passing (by death) of the apostolic generation (see 3:4). Indeed, 2 Peter is presented as sound advice from the great apostle about how to continue the tradition begun by Jesus and spread by his apostles, but now without the physical presence of those apostles. In responding to this crisis 2 Peter calls upon a mixture of Jewish, Greek, and Christian traditions.

Jewish Traditions. The polemic in ch. 2 makes use of several examples taken from the OT: the rebellious angels (2:4 = Gen 6:1-4 and *1 Enoch* 6–11), the flood and Noah (2:5 = Genesis 7–8), the men of Sodom and Lot (2:6-8 = Genesis 19), the way of Balaam (2:15-16 = Numbers 22–25), and the proverb about the dog returning to its own vomit (2:22 = Prov 26:11).

While some of this material is taken over from Jude, the author of 2 Peter places the examples in their biblical chronological order, skips the debate between Michael and Satan over Moses' body from the *Assumption of Moses* found in Jude 9, and omits the "prophecy" from *1 Enoch* 1:9 that is quoted in Jude 14-15. While these changes may be due simply to lack of familiarity with these texts on the author's part and/or on the part of his readers, they may also reflect the author's uncertainty about the OT Apocrypha and his firmer ideas about the canon of OT Scriptures.

The author respects the OT as the prophetic word of God and gives a beautiful description of its role in Christian life as "a lamp in a gloomy place until day dawns and the morning star rises in your hearts" (1:19). In refuting the claim of the false teachers that the world remains the same (3:4) he invokes the OT accounts about God's creating the earth (Genesis 1) and bringing the flood upon the earth in Noah's time (Genesis 7–8). And to explain why the *parousia* is not really delayed he bases his argument that God does not follow our human reckoning of time on Ps 90:4: "For a thousand years in your sight is like yesterday."

One of the author's purposes is to keep alive among his readers the concepts and traditions of Jewish apocalypticism that provide the context for Christian teachings about the *parousia* of Jesus and the Last Judgment. The emergence of the false teachers is interpreted as a sign that "the last days" (3:3) have arrived. The Day of Judgment will be marked by a cosmic conflagration and the destruction of the godless (3:7). Its coming will be sudden ("like a thief," 3:10), and then the old heavens and earth will pass away (3:10) and give way to "new heavens and a new earth in which justice dwells" (3:13). And this advice about the future is presented to a large extent in the form of Peter's testament—a literary genre that was popular among apocalyptically oriented Jews in the first century.

Greek Traditions. Greek terms and concepts are also very prominent in 2 Peter. The most striking examples include the call to "become partakers of the divine nature" *(genēsthe theias koinōnoi physeōs)* in 1:4, the use of the aorist participle *tartarōsas* ("cast into hell," or more literally "hold captive in Tartarus") in 2:4, and the prophecies of a world conflagration (see 3:7, 10, 12) also present in Plato *(Timaeus* 22BC) and in Stoic philosophy. Moreover, the author makes abundant use of words and ideas taken over from the Greek mystery religions and popular philosophy: *theia dynamis* (1:3), *epoptēs* (1:16), *eusebeia* (1:3, 6, 7; 3:11), *aretē* (1:3, 5), *engkrateia* (1:6), *philadelphia* (1:7), and *gnōsis* and *epignōsis* (1:2, 3, 6, 8; 2:20; 3:18). These quasi-technical terms and the many Greek *hapax legomena* suggest that the author of 2 Peter was trying to speak in a way that would communicate effectively with Greek-speaking Gentile Christians living in a pagan milieu while defending the apostolic teachings about Jesus' *parousia* and the Last Judgment (whose original context was Jewish apocalypticism).

Christian Traditions. The author's familiarity with early Christian traditions is shown by his use of Christian sources and his references to Christian doctrines. In 3:1 he notes that this letter is "the second letter that I write to you." Most interpreters identify the previous letter as 1 Peter, though there is little or no discernible influence from 1 Peter on the language and ideas in 2 Peter. Likewise, in 3:15-16 he mentions "our beloved brother Paul" and "all his letters," but again it is difficult to point to any distinctively Pauline influences in 2 Peter. The author seems more concerned simply to deny that he and Paul are in conflict.

At several points 2 Peter contains material found also in the synoptic tradition. The most obvious example is the account of the transfiguration of Jesus in 2 Pet 1:16-18 (see Matt 17:1-8; Mark 9:2-8; Luke 9:28-36). Whether the author read the full text of any gospel (Matthew would be the most likely candidate) is not clear. Also, the saying in 2 Pet 2:20 ("then the last state becomes worse for them than the first") is close to what appears in Matt 12:45 and Luke 11:26 (presumably from the Sayings Source Q). Other links with the gospel tradition include Jesus' prophecy about Peter's death (1:14; see John 21:18-19), the theme of rescue from *peirasmos* or trial (2:9; see Matt 6:13), and the warning that "the Day of the Lord will come like a thief" (3:10; see Matt 24:43-44; Luke 12:39-40; 1 Thess 5:2; Rev 3:3; 16:15).

There are, of course, numerous parallels between Jude 6-18 and 2 Pet 2:1–3:3. So close is the wording in many cases that some borrowing must be assumed. These parallels have been explained in four different ways: (1) 2 Peter used Jude; (2) Jude used 2 Peter; (3) both used a common source; or (4) the same author wrote both letters. The first explanation is generally regarded as the best and most likely, and is adopted in the following commentary. See the discussion at the beginning of the General Introduction to Jude and 2 Peter.

Analysis of how the author of 2 Peter used Jude 6-18 (see the Notes on the individual texts) shows that while he took over much of the polemical language from Jude, he tailored it to bolster his criticisms of those he called "false teachers" *(pseudodidaskaloi)*. However, in the process of redaction he sometimes did harm to the intricate patterns and careful constructions in the Epistle of Jude (e.g., compare Jude 9-10 and 2 Pet 2:10b-11).

Second Peter is partly exhortation (1:3-11; 3:11-18) and partly polemical warning. It was written in response to a crisis fomented by the appearance of *pseudodidaskaloi* ("false teachers"). Rather than producing a doctrinal treatise (see Jude 3), the author has integrated Christian beliefs and formulas into his arguments against the opponents. For example, in the first two verses (the epistolary salutation in 1:1-2) he refers to the Christian faith of the readers as of "equal standing" with that of the apostles and to Jesus as "our God and Savior" and "our Lord." While insisting that all Christians share the same (apostolic) faith, the author presents Peter as the apostle *par excellence* and exhorts the readers to hold on to the faith they were taught.

Throughout the letter the author prescribes a balance between eschatological hope and ethical action in the present. The second coming of Jesus and the Last Judgment are certain to happen. But their precise timing remains unknown. Therefore the Christian should live in constant vigilance (but in confidence of vindication rather than in fear of punishment) as if the judgment was to occur in the next moment. In this ethical-eschatological stance 2 Peter stands close to what is taught in the synoptic eschatological discourses (Matthew 24–25, Mark 13, Luke 21).

Second Peter also reminds us that in the early church there were controversies about the interpretation of the OT Scriptures ("no prophecy of Scripture is a matter of personal interpretation," 1:20) and of Paul's writings ("In them there are some things that are hard to understand, which the ignorant and unstable twist, as they do the other writings, to their own destruction," 3:16).

4. *The Opponents*

At the heart of 2 Peter (2:1–3:10) is a vigorous denunciation of a group the author calls *pseudodidaskaloi* ("false teachers") in 2:1. They are accused

of introducing "destructive heresies" into the community (2:1) and of promoting a licentious or immoral lifestyle (2:2). They are further accused of
exploiting people with their false or fabricated words out of a desire for
their own financial gain (2:3).

The attack becomes more specific in 3:3-4 when the "false teachers" are
reported to be questioning the second coming of Jesus and (by implication) the Last Judgment to which Jesus' *parousia* is a prelude. They are reported to be saying (skeptically): "Where is the promise of his coming?"
There seems to be a link made between the false teachers' eschatological
skepticism and their moral laxity. If the *parousia* and Last Judgment are
merely "cleverly devised tales" (1:16, which seems to reflect the false
teachers' dismissal of these articles of faith rather than Peter's judgment
on their teachings) made up by the apostles, then there is no ultimate
sanction for immoral behavior, and most everything is allowed.

The "false teachers" are clearly Christians. According to 2:20-22, by becoming Christians they thought that they had escaped "the defilements of
the world," but they now find themselves "entangled in them again." By
promoting theological skepticism about Jesus' *parousia* and the Last Judgment and by displaying what the author regards as a pagan lifestyle the
false teachers are like a dog returning to its own vomit or like a pig, once
having been washed clean, going back to rolling in the mud.

The false teachers seem to be having their greatest influence and success among recent converts to Christianity: "those who are barely escaping those who live in error" (2:18). They take as their slogan the word
"freedom": "they promise them freedom" (2:19). The false teachers seem
to have been Gentile Christians who appealed primarily to other Gentile
Christians and promoted a kind of Christianity more at home in a pagan
milieu than in a Jewish society or a Jewish-Christian community, especially with regard to eschatology and ethics.

As with the "intruders" in the Epistle of Jude, it is difficult to be more
precise about the identity of the "false teachers." Again we have only the
author's side of the conflict, and he could apparently presume firsthand
knowledge of the opponents and their teachings among the first readers.
Moreover, the author was mainly concerned to warn the readers against
the dangers that the false teachers posed and to refute their teachings, not
to provide a fair and objective description of the movement fit for inclusion in a modern encyclopedia.

The task of identifying the opponents in 2 Peter is rendered even more
difficult by the author's extensive use of Jude 6-18 as a source for his
polemics. While attention to the author's redaction of the parallel material
in Jude is enlightening, it is hard to know how seriously or literally we can
take what he does retain from Jude as reliable evidence about the false
teachers. Does the material drawn from Jude 6-18 also really describe the

attitudes and behaviors of the false teachers? Or is it now only stereo-typed or "boilerplate" polemical language that was close at hand to the author and used at his covenience?

The old hypothesis that the false teachers were Gnostics runs into the same methodological problems (insufficient data in 2 Peter, questions of definition regarding Gnosticism) as it does with respect to Jude. More-over, as in Jude, there is no evidence of cosmological dualism (spirit versus matter), which is often taken as a defining feature of Gnosticism.

It is tempting to identify the "false teachers" of 2 Peter with the "intruders" of Jude. But as Bauckham notes (*Jude, 2 Peter* 155–56), the only certain point in common is their ethical libertinism—a charge that is made against almost every set of opponents in antiquity and today. The oppo-nents in Jude claim to enjoy prophetic revelations (Jude 8) and to possess the Holy Spirit (Jude 19), whereas these claims are deleted in 2 Peter. And the ethical libertinism of the false teachers has more to do with their eschatological skepticism (2 Pet 3:3-4) than with the antinomian perver-sion of the grace of God as seems to have been the case with the intruders (Jude 4). According to Bauckham, "redaction-critical study reveals the false teachers in 2 Peter to be very different from the opponents in Jude" (*Jude, 2 Peter* 155).

The mention of "our beloved brother Paul" (2 Pet 3:15) could suggest that the false teachers were radical Paulinists who had pushed Paul's em-phasis on the saving effects of the Christ-event in the present to the exclu-sion of all futurist eschatology. However, the author of 2 Peter portrays Paul as his own ally in protecting the apostolic teaching and condemns the false teachers' appeal to Paul as a distortion. How central Paul's authority was to the false teachers' program is something we cannot know from our only source—the text of 2 Peter. Did they really think that they were simply drawing out the implications of Pauline theology? Or did they merely enlist Paul's writings as a cover for their own heterodox teachings? Despite all these caveats, however, there does appear to be some connection between the false teachers in 2 Peter and some kind of Pauline Christianity.

5. *Author, Place, and Date*

Few interpreters today accept the text's claim that 2 Peter was com-posed directly by the apostle Peter. Some scholars dismiss it as a pious fiction entirely. Others follow Jerome's lead and propose that a secretary or an interpreter was responsible for the actual writing. Still others sug-gest that 2 Peter emanated from a Petrine "circle" at Rome and was writ-ten in his name. For a survey of the methodological problems involved in

identifying the author see Michael J. Gilmour, "Reflections on the Authorship of 2 Peter," *Evangelical Quarterly* 73 (2001) 291–309.

The strongest argument against direct Petrine authorship is the author's frequent use of rare Greek words and traditional Greek ideas—to
an extent that one would not expect from a Galilean fisherman. Moreover,
the author's extensive use of the Epistle of Jude as a source, his apparent
references to the first generation of Christians and the apostles as "forefathers" (3:2, 4), and his positive picture of Paul and his writings as authoritative (if sometimes misunderstood) sources (3:15-16; cf. Gal 2:11-14)
all fit better with the period after the passing of the pioneer apostles than
they do during Peter's lifetime. And as Jerome noted, if one accepts both
1 and 2 Peter as directly composed by the apostle Peter it is difficult to
explain the striking differences in their vocabulary, style, and tone. And if
Peter did employ a secretary in both or in either letter, he must have given
him very great freedom—to the extent that even under this hypothesis the
claim of direct "Petrine" authorship becomes dubious.

The actual writer of 2 Peter appears to have been a Hellenized Jewish
Christian. The Christian element in his identity is obvious from his use of
early Christian formulas (e.g., "our Lord and Savior Jesus Christ") and his
championing the cause of Christian faith. His Jewish identity can be de-
duced from the many appeals to biblical characters and incidents as well
as the use of the testament form. And the Hellenized dimension in his
identity emerges not only from his inclusion of unusual Greek terms and
allusions to Greek ideas but also from his efforts at inculturating the
gospel while retaining its original Jewish character.

The composition of 2 Peter has been assigned to many different places:
Egypt, Asia Minor, Syria, Palestine, and Rome. Any of these proposals is
at best an educated guess, since the text provides no hard clues. But a
good case for Rome as the place of 2 Peter's origin has been made by
Richard Bauckham (*Jude, 2 Peter* 159–62). The cosmopolitan culture of
Rome would fit well with the profile of a Hellenized Jewish Christian
writer. The apostle Peter was associated with the city of Rome and died
there in 64 or 65 C.E. The work known as 1 Peter was apparently written at
Rome under the code-name "Babylon" (1 Pet 5:13) to churches in northern
Asia Minor, and provides evidence for a Petrine "circle" (not "school,"
which may suggest too much organization) in Rome. Moreover, 1 Peter
and *1 Clement* both illustrate the tendency of the church at Rome to show
pastoral concern for churches elsewhere (Corinth in the case of *1 Clement*).
So it is at least plausible that a Hellenized Jewish Christian writer in a
Petrine circle at Rome composed 2 Peter as the testament of Peter, the
apostle *par excellence,* to provide advice for meeting a pastoral threat in
some other Christian community.

The location of the Christians being addressed in 2 Peter is even more problematic. They seem to have been Gentile converts to Christianity, obviously Greek speakers, and living in a highly Hellenized society. The "false teachers" were raising questions about Jesus' *parousia* and the Last Judgment ("Where is the promise of his coming?" 3:3) and promoting a morally "loose" lifestyle. Their approach could be viewed as a reaction against the eschatological consciousness and ethical rigorism of early Jewish Christianity. To the author of 2 Peter, however, the false teachers were encouraging a reversion to paganism (2:20-22) and posed a great danger among recent converts.

The author of 2 Peter seems to have been trying to develop a "middle way" by showing off his familiarity with Greek language and ideas on the one hand and by insisting on Jewish-Christian eschatological consciousness and ethical seriousness on the other hand. While giving the impression of meeting the needs of Gentile Christians and inculturating the gospel, the author of 2 Peter clearly favors a somewhat traditional Jewish Christianity marked by respect for the OT, lively expectation about the second coming of Jesus, and a lifestyle that is appropriate to Jesus' followers who expect to face their Lord and Savior at the Last Judgment.

The date of the composition of 2 Peter has been placed almost everywhere between 60 and 160 C.E. If the letter was composed directly by the apostle Peter or under his personal supervision, then a date in the early 60's (before his death in 64 or 65) is necessary. Those who regard 2 Peter as an extreme example of "early catholicism" (as Ernst Käsemann did) generally tend to place it very late, around the middle of the second century. However, if the phrase "from the time when the forefathers fell asleep" refers to the passing of the apostles and their generation of Christians, then a date in the very late first or early second century C.E. seems most likely.

When placed in this context 2 Peter can be read as pseudepigraphical advice from Peter about how a new generation of Christians can carry on the movement founded by Jesus and nurtured by the apostles. Being assured that they possess "a faith of equal standing" to the apostles (1:1), the first readers are provided in 2 Peter with a positive ideal for living a Christian life (1:3-11; 3:11-18) and a warning against "false teachers" who would play down eschatological consciousness and its ethical consequences in favor of what appeared to the author (and/or to the Petrine circle at Rome) to be a return to pagan ways.

TRANSLATION, NOTES, INTERPRETATION

1. *Salutation* (1:1-2)

1. Simeon Peter, slave and apostle of Jesus Christ. To those who received a faith of equal standing to ours in the justice of our God and Savior Jesus Christ. 2. May grace and peace be yours in abundance in the knowledge of God and Jesus our Lord.

NOTES

1. *Simeon Peter, slave and apostle of Jesus Christ:* The manuscript evidence is divided between the names "Simeon" and "Simon." Since the form "Simon" came to predominate in the Christian tradition and "Simeon" is more Semitic (see Acts 15:14 for the only other NT occurrence of Simeon), it is likely that "Simeon" is the better reading here. According to various gospel passages (see Mark 3:16; Matt 16:18; Luke 6:14; John 1:42), Jesus gave to Simon (Simeon) bar Jona the name *Kephâ*, meaning "rock" in Aramaic. For the title *doulos* ("slave, servant") used for the writers of NT letters see Rom 1:1; Titus 1:1; Jas 1:1; Jude 1 (see the discussion there). For "apostle" as a title for NT letter writers see Rom 1:1; 1 Cor 1:1; 2 Cor 1:1; Gal 1:1; Eph 1:1; 1 Tim 1:1; Titus 1:1; 1 Pet 1:1. According to the gospels Peter was one of the first persons called to follow Jesus (see Mark 1:16-20; Matt 4:18-22; Luke 5:1-11; John 1:41-42), is always named first in the lists of the twelve apostles (Mark 3:16; Matt 10:2; Acts 1:13), and often serves as the spokesman for the group. In Matt 16:17-19 Peter is said to be the "rock" on which Jesus will build his church, and in 1 Cor 15:5 Cephas/ Peter is listed first among the recipients of appearances of the risen Christ. While he was infamous for his threefold denial of Jesus during the Passion (Mark 14:66-72; Matt 26:69-75; Luke 22:56-62; John 18:17, 25-27), his experience of the risen Christ transformed Peter into a fearless preacher of the gospel (see Acts 1–5). In many ways Simeon Peter is the "slave/servant and apostle of Jesus Christ" *par excellence.*

To those who received a faith of equal standing to ours: The idea is that in their faith the addressees (who are not apostles, and in fact most likely belong to the postapostolic generation) are on the same level as the apostles like Peter. A similar point is made in John 20:29: "Blessed are those who have not seen and yet have come to believe." The dative plural aorist participle *lachousin* ("received") derives from the verb *langchanein,* which often carries the notion of casting lots. The use of this verb here conveys the "gift" character of Christian faith as something received from God. The word *pistis* ("faith") here has an objective sense; it is something that has been given by God and received by humans. The adjective *isotimos,* which derives from *isos* ("equal") and *timē* ("value, honor") appears only here in the NT. Thus the apostle *par excellence* confirms that the faith of those who came to know and believe in Jesus only later (after Jesus' death and resurrection) is of equal value and honor to the faith of Jesus' twelve apostles.

in the justice of our God and Savior Jesus Christ: It is tempting to render *dikaiosynē* as "righteousness" in the light of Paul's letter to the Romans and its thesis statement (1:16-17) about the revelation of God's "righteousness" in Jesus' life, death, and resurrection. But it is probably sounder exegesis to link the use of *dikaiosynē* here to the preceding phrase about "a faith of equal standing to ours" and to translate it as "justice." Here *dikaiosynē* refers to the "justice" of God (reconciling or restorative justice as opposed to narrow human justice) as the reason why the addressees can possess such faith. The formulaic expression "of our God and Savior Jesus Christ" presents some interpretive problems. There is only one article (the genitive singular *tou*) governing the two members *theou* ("of God") and *Iēsou* ("of Jesus") in the phrase. The grammatical construction suggests that the reference is to one and the same person, and that here Jesus is called "God" (as perhaps also in John 1:1; 20:28; Titus 2:13; Heb 1:8-9). However, such usage is very rare in the NT. For "Savior" *(sōtēr)* as a title for Jesus in 2 Peter see 1:11; 2:20; and 3:2, 18. For Jesus as Savior and its implications for the eschatology and ethics of 2 Peter see Terrance Callan, "The Soteriology of the Second Letter of Peter."

2. *May grace and peace be yours in abundance:* The same basic formula appears in 1 Pet 1:2 and Jude 2. The pair "grace" *(charis)* and "peace" *(eirēnē)* occurs in the salutations of most Pauline epistles (see Rom 1:7; 1 Cor 1:3; 2 Cor 1:2; Gal 1:3; Eph 1:2; Phil 1:2; Col 1:2; 1 Thess 1:1; 2 Thess 1:2; Phlm 3). It combines the usual Greek epistolary greeting *(chairein)* and the usual Hebrew epistolary greeting *(shalom* = "peace"). In the Christian context these terms refer to what God has made possible through Jesus' death and resurrection: divine favor ("grace"), and "peace" with God and with other persons. The aorist optative passive verb *plēthyntheiē* (see 1 Pet 1:2; Jude 2) expresses the wish that these divine gifts might be experienced ever more abundantly by the letter's recipients.

in the knowledge of God and Jesus our Lord: The noun *epignōsis* ("knowledge") is prominent in 1 Peter; see also 1:3, 8; 2:20. The object of *epignōsis* is in every case God and/or Christ: "of God and Jesus our Lord" (1:2); "of him who called us . . ." (1:3); "of our Lord Jesus Christ" (1:8); and "of our Lord and Savior Jesus Christ" (2:20). As in 1:1, the question arises here: Is there one object of this knowledge (God = Christ) or two objects (God and Christ)? See the Interpretation below. Early Christians were apparently less bothered by these ambiguities than some modern interpreters are. For a good treatment of the compatibility between Jewish monotheism and early Christian claims about Jesus' divinity see Richard J. Bauckham, *God Crucified. Monotheism and Christology in the New Testament* (Grand Rapids: Eerdmans, 1999).

INTERPRETATION

The letter known as 2 Peter follows the usual epistolary outline with its salutation in 1:1-2: sender (Simeon Peter), addressees ("To those who . . ."), and greeting ("grace and peace").

The Salutation (2 Pet 1:1-2). For the salutation pattern in general see the treatment of Jude 1-2; for points of detail see the Notes above. The use of the "Semitic" form "Simeon" in identifying the sender is a subtle reminder that Peter was one of the first disciples called by Jesus at the shore of the Sea of Galilee in the Holy Land, while the phrase "slave and apostle of Jesus Christ" underlines both his subordination to Jesus and his pivotal role in spreading early Christianity in the Greco-Roman world.

The identification of the recipients in 1:1b emphasizes the gift-character of Christian faith and serves as a reminder of the fundamental equality of all Christians according to the justice/righteousness of God. It indicates that there is no essential difference in the quality of faith between distinguished members of the apostolic generation like Simeon Peter and Christians of the second and third generations (and beyond).

The greeting is similar to those in 1 Pet 1:2 ("May grace and peace be yours in abundance") and Jude 2 ("May mercy and peace and love be yours in abundance"). What is distinctive here is the reference to the "knowledge" *(epignōsis)* of God and Jesus our Lord"—a theme developed in the body of the letter. As the Pauline epistles illustrate (see Rom 1:1-6; 1 Cor 1:2; Gal 1:3-5; etc.), it was customary to use the salutation as a vehicle for introducing some of the major ideas or motifs in the letter taken as a whole. And "knowledge" is surely one of them in 2 Peter.

The salutation in 2 Pet 1:1-2 contains two phrases that appear to apply the title *theos* ("God") to Jesus. While not unique in the NT (see John 1:1; 20:28; Titus 2:13; Heb 1:8-9), the application of the epithet *theos* to Jesus is unusual since Jesus is more commonly called the "Son of God" by the evangelists and Paul.

In both 2 Pet 1:1 and 1:2 there are some grammatical problems associated with the use of these titles. In each case the divine epithet appears in the genitive case as part of clauses governed by phrases in the dative case: "in the justice of . . ." (1:1) and "in the knowledge of . . ." (1:2). It is possible to read the following genitive phrases as referring to two distinct figures: "our God and [our] Savior Jesus Christ" (1:1), and "God and Jesus our Lord" (1:2). But in 1:1 the more likely reading takes the two epithets ("our God and Savior") as both referring to Jesus Christ. And given its proximity to 1:1, the more likely reading of 1:2 is that it too refers to Jesus as both *theos* and *kyrios*. Thus it seems that the salutation in 2 Pet 1:1-2 refers to Jesus twice as "God" *(theos)* and also as "Savior" *(sōtēr)* and "Lord" *(kyrios)*.

One must ask, of course, what people in the Mediterranean world of the late first and early second century understood by these terms. While *kyrios* could simply refer to any powerful person or great teacher, for Greek-speaking Jews *kyrios* had become a way of referring to the God of Israel (who is the God of all). The term "Savior" *(sōtēr)* was often applied to civic benefactors, persons of wealth and influence who provided funding for important buildings or monuments or extricated the people of a city or region from great danger. It was also applied to Roman emperors beginning with Augustus, and became part of the vocabulary that was attached to the emperor in imperial propaganda and in the imperial cult. The emperor Domitian is said to have been greeted as "my Lord and my God." It is in this context that we need to place the application of the epithet *theos* to Jesus Christ. The use of this language in the NT (especially in Revelation and in John 20:28) had definite political implications. If the risen Jesus really is "Lord and God," then the Roman emperor is not.

In other words, granted that in 2 Pet 1:1-2 Jesus is called *theos* ("God"), we probably should interpret this title more in its first-century Greco-Roman context where *theos* and *theios* had fairly broad meanings rather than from the perspective of the great fourth-century epitomes (or creeds) of Christian beliefs ("true God from true God"). That means that attempts either at explaining away the references to Jesus as *theos* in 2 Pet 1:1-2 as historically impossible or at holding them up as the definitive proofs for the divinity of Jesus as understood in the later conciliar sense are probably both misguided. The NT does call Jesus "God." But it may not mean everything that people in the fourth (or twenty-first) century attached to that term. See Terrance Callan, "The Christology of the Second Letter of Peter."

The salutation in 2 Peter emphasizes both the greatness of Jesus (who is called God, Savior, Christ/Messiah, and Lord) and the relative lowliness of Peter ("slave and apostle of Jesus Christ"). At the same time Peter invites his readers to enjoy "a faith of equal standing" to his faith as one of Jesus' first apostles, and traces the gifts of God's grace and peace back to knowledge of God and Jesus.

For Reference and Further Study

Callan, Terrance. "The Christology of the Second Letter of Peter," *Bib* 82 (2001) 253–63.

_____. "The Soteriology of the Second Letter of Peter," *Bib* 82 (2001) 549–59.

Fitzmyer, Joseph A. "The Name Simon," *HTR* 54 (1961) 91–97.
Picirelli, Robert E. "The meaning of 'Epignosis,'" *Evangelical Quarterly* 47 (1975) 85–93.

2. *Christian Life* (1:3-11)

3. [As] his divine power has bestowed on us all that pertains to life and godliness through the knowledge of him who called us to his own glory and excellence 4. through which the precious and sublime promises to you have been bestowed, that through these you might become partakers of the divine nature, escaping from the corruption in the world because of inordinate desire.

5. And for this very reason bring to bear every effort and supplement your faith with virtue, virtue with knowledge, 6. knowledge with self-control, self-control with patience, patience with godliness, 7. godliness with affection for others, affection for others with love.

8. For if these are increasingly yours, they make you neither useless nor fruitless with regard to the knowledge of our Lord Jesus Christ. 9. For whoever lacks these is so nearsighted as to be blind, forgetting the purification of his sins committed in the past. 10. Therefore, brothers and sisters, be even more eager to make firm your calling and election. For in practicing these you will never stumble. 11. For so there will be richly provided for you an entrance into the eternal kingdom of our Lord and Savior Jesus Christ.

NOTES

3. *[As] his divine power has bestowed on us:* The clause beginning with *hōs* ("as, whereas, since") looks back to the end of 1:2 and forward to the list of virtues in 1:5-7. The referent of the "divine power" *(theia dynamis)* is generally understood to be God rather than Christ, though in view of the ambiguity noted already in 1:1-2 it could be either or both. The genitive absolute in the form of the perfect passive participle *dedōrēmenēs* ("having been bestowed") emphasizes the gift character (as in 1:1: "those who received") of Christian faith. The dative plural pronoun *hēmin* ("on us") presumably includes not only the apostles but also the addressees, who possess "a faith of equal standing to ours."

all that pertains to life and godliness: Throughout 2 Peter but especially in 1:5-7 there is an insistence that faith must express itself in appropriate actions. The two nouns "life" *(zōē)* and "godliness" *(eusebeia)*, while pointing toward the fullness of eternal life with God, also refer to human existence in the present.

through the knowledge of him who called us: For God/Christ as the object of *epignōsis* ("knowledge") see the Note on 1:2. While the gospels frequently portray Jesus as calling persons to follow him, in the NT epistles God is generally the subject of the verb "call" *(kalein)* when used in a religious sense.

to his own glory and excellence: The phrase *idią doxę kai aretę* refers to the glory and excellence (rather than "virtue") of God (and/or of Christ). Many manuscripts have the reading *dia doxēs kai aretēs* ("through glory and excellence"). In favor of the reading with *idią* plus the two nouns in the dative case (see Bruce M. Metzger, *A Textual Commentary on the Greek New Testament* [London and New York: United Bible Societies, 1971; corrected ed. 1975] 699) are its wide attestation in the manuscripts, the presence of several other instances of *dia* in the context, and the frequency of *idios* in 2 Peter (see 1:20; 2:16, 22; 3:3, 16, 17).

4. *through which the precious and sublime promises to you have been bestowed:* The referent of "through which" is "his own glory and excellence" in 1:3. The noun *epangelma* ("promise") is said to be "a declaration to do something, with implication of obligation to carry out what is stated" (BDAG 356). According to 2 Pet 3:13 the content of God's promises is "new heavens and a new earth where righteousness dwells." There are several different word orders in the manuscripts, but the variations make little impact on the translation or sense.

that through these you might become partakers of the divine nature: The purpose of God's gifts and promises is that believers may become sharers or partakers *(koinōnoi)* in the deity. The phrase "divine nature" *(theia physis)* is generally regarded as a Hellenistic expression and the root of the patristic theology of human divinization in and through Christ; see James M. Starr, *Sharers in the Divine Nature.* Interpreters who are not persuaded by the alleged Hellenistic background of this phrase (see Al Wolters, "'Partners of the Deity'") take it to refer to participation by humans in the heavenly court and its worship (as in Revelation 4–5).

escaping from the corruption in the world because of inordinate desire: Here the word *phthora* ("corruption") is used in the sense of moral depravity (see "slaves of corruption" in 2 Pet 2:19), while *epithymia* ("passion") carries the sense of inordinate desire (see BDAG 1055). Those who participate in the divine nature through God's gift in Christ are no longer enslaved to moral depravity and inordinate desire. This is, of course, a major theme in Paul's letter to the Romans.

5. *And for this very reason bring to bear every effort:* The "reason" has been given at length in 1:3-4: It is what God has made possible for humans in and through Christ. This gift demands an appropriate response in character formation and actions from those to whom it has been given. The masculine plural participle *pareisenengkantes* (with two prefixes, *par-* and *eis-*) functions as an imperative here: "bring to bear every effort." Readers are challenged to summon all their zeal and earnestness *(spoudē)* in developing their character as Christians.

and supplement your faith with virtue, virtue with knowledge: The verb *epichorēgein* means "give, grant" (see 2 Pet 1:11), but here it has the sense of "supply, furnish, supplement." The list of virtues in 1:5b-7 provides a program for those seeking to make progress in Christian life. The program begins with "faith" *(pistis)* and ends in "love" *(agapē)*. The six virtues in between faith and love might be regarded as "natural" human virtues. But in the context of an early Christian list ranging from faith to love and built upon God's gift in Christ the natural virtues are infused with a distinctively Christian content. While *pistis* (faith) here may have its basic biblical sense of "trust in, remain faithful," it probably also conveys the idea of accepting an objective body of truth (see the Note on 1:1). Whereas *aretē* in 1:3 was rendered "excellence" because it pertained to God and/or Christ, here in an obviously human context it means "excellence of character" or "virtue." Apart from Phil 4:8 and 1 Pet 2:9 the important Greek moral philosophical word *aretē* appears in the NT only in 2 Pet 1:3 and 1:5 (twice). Since *epignōsis* in 2 Peter (see 1:2, 3, 8; 2:20) refers to knowledge of God and/or Christ, *gnōsis* in this list of virtues most likely refers to human wisdom and moral knowledge.

6. *knowledge with self-control, self-control with patience, patience with godliness:* The virtue of *enkrateia* ("self-control") involves the restraint of one's emotions, impulses, and desires. It is part of Paul's list of the fruits of the Holy Spirit in Gal 5:22-23. The virtue of *hypomonē* ("patience") refers to the ability to hold out or bear up in difficult circumstances. It is prominent in both the gospels and the NT epistles, and frequently appears in an eschatological context where patience is sure to be vindicated and rewarded (see Luke 21:19; Rom 5:3-5). The virtue of *eusebeia* ("godliness, piety") describes the respect and devotion that humans owe to God (see 2 Pet 1:3; 3:11).

7. *godliness with affection for others, affection for others with love:* The virtue of *philadelphia* ("brotherly/sisterly love") is used in the NT in a metaphorical or extended sense of affection for fellow Christians (see Rom 12:10; 1 Thess 4:9; Heb 13:1). The virtue of *agapē* ("love") refers most obviously here to love for God, since *philadelphia* has already covered love for one's fellow Christians. Love for God on the part of Christians has its root in God's love for them experienced in and through Christ. For love as the climax and pinnacle of Christian virtues see 1 Cor 13:13: "And now faith, hope, and love abide, these three; and the greatest of these is love."

8. *For if these are increasingly yours:* The word "these" *(tauta)* refers to the virtues listed in 1:5-7. In the Greek text there is no "if" and the two neuter plural participles *hyparchonta* and *pleonazonta* form the subject of the main verb *kathistēsin* ("make"). It is possible to translate the second participle as the equivalent of an adverb, and so the translation here as "if these are increasingly yours." The specification "increasingly" continues the emphasis on human effort and cooperation with God in Christian life.

they make you neither useless nor fruitless: The two accusative plural adjectives *argous* and *akarpous* are examples of the *alpha*-privative construction that is very common in 2 Peter: *a* plus *ergon* ("without work") and *a* plus *karpos* ("without fruit"). The use of negative expressions to make a positive statement is called litotes, a figure of speech that makes its positive point by denying the opposite.

with regard to the knowledge of our Lord Jesus Christ: For similar phrases featuring *epignōsis* see 2 Pet 1:2 and 3 (and 2:20). This knowledge is the origin and dynamism of Christian life.

9. *For whoever lacks these is so nearsighted as to be blind:* In Greek the construction is literally: "for to whom these are not present." As in 1:8, *tauta* refers to the virtues listed in 1:5-7. Such persons are "blind" *(typhlos)* because they lose sight of the knowledge *(epignōsis)* of Christ, and they are "nearsighted" with respect to that knowledge. The verb *muōpazein* refers to "closing or contracting the eyes = squinting as nearsighted (myopic) people do." The two terms for lack of sight can be put in a sequential order: "so nearsighted as to be blind" (BDAG 663).

forgetting the purification of his sins committed in the past: The reference is to baptism and the washing away of past sins (see 1 Pet 3:21). The adverb *palai* ("long ago") can refer to a relatively short time seen from the perspective of the present ("in the past").

10. *Therefore, brothers and sisters, be even more eager to make firm your calling and election:* This is the only use of *adelphoi* ("brothers") in direct address in 2 Peter. The term is generally regarded as including men and women in the new family of Jesus (see Mark 3:31-35). The verb *spoudazein* ("be eager, zealous") appears also in 2 Pet 1:15 and 3:14; in both 1:10 and 3:14 the aorist imperative is used where one expects the present imperative. Some manuscripts add after this imperative the phrase "in order that through (your) good works you may make. . . ." The idea of Christians as called by God and/or Christ was raised in 1:3: "the one who called us to his own glory and excellence." For the theme of the divine "election" of Christians see 1 Pet 1:2 ("who have been chosen") and 2:9 ("a chosen race").

For in practicing these you will never stumble: As in 1:8 and 9, the referent of *tauta* ("these") seems to be the virtues listed in 1:5-7. The clause with the verb *ptaiein* ("stumble") does not guarantee a life totally without sin, but it does promise that those who practice the virtues will not lose their footing on the way to the kingdom of Christ mentioned in 1:11.

11. *For so there will be richly provided for you:* The Christian way not only is a sure and steady path through life in the present but also issues in the fullness of life with God and Christ. The verb *epichorēgēthēsetai* ("be provided") here is in the passive, thus suggesting divine initiative and activity; that is, God/Christ provides the entrance. Compare the active form of the same verb in 1:5 ("supplement") where the stress is on the human effort demanded from those who seek to practice the Christian virtues.

an entrance into the eternal kingdom of our Lord and Savior Jesus Christ: For the image of "entering" the kingdom of God see Mark 9:47; 10:15, 23-25; etc. There are references to the kingdom of Christ in Eph 5:5; Col 1:13; and 2 Tim 4:1. In 1 Cor 15:24 the kingdom of Christ seems to be a temporary or interim stage: "Then comes the end, when he [Christ] hands over the kingdom to God the Father." But in 2 Pet 1:11 it functions as a synonym for the kingdom of God. In the NT the combination "Lord and Savior" applied to Jesus Christ occurs only in 2 Peter (see also 2:20; 3:2, 18).

INTERPRETATION

What follows the salutation in 1:3-4 is best taken as both the elaboration of themes in the salutation and a bridge to the body of the letter in 1:5ff. The list of Christian virtues in 1:5-7 gives a sample of attitudes and actions that are necessary for progress in Christian life, and the consequences—positive and negative—of the practice of these virtues are spelled out in 1:8-11. The passage taken as a whole provides a firm theological and practical foundation for understanding Christian life.

Inculturating Christian Faith (2 Pet 1:3-4). The application of the titles *theos* ("God") and *sōtēr* ("Savior") to Jesus in 2 Pet 1:1-2 is an example of translating the beliefs of a messianic Jewish movement rooted in Palestine into the terminology and conceptuality of the Greco-Roman world in which Greek was the most common language. The elaboration of the salutation in 1:3-4 provides further evidence for what might be called the early Christian program of inculturation.

While the ideas conveyed in 1:3-4 are not entirely foreign to the OT and to early Jewish writings, many expressions in the passage cannot be translated readily back into Hebrew or Aramaic. Rather, it seems that the author of 2 Peter was deliberately using distinctively Greek expressions as a way of expressing the gospel in an idiom that native Greek speakers could more easily grasp. Some examples in 1:3-4 include *theia dynamis* ("divine power"), *eusebeia* ("godliness"), *epignōsis* ("knowledge"), *aretē* ("excellence"), *timia kai megista . . . epangelmata* ("precious and sublime promises"), *theias koinōnoi physeōs* ("sharers of the divine nature"), and *en epithymią phthoras* ("corruption . . . because of passion").

The results of the effort at inculturating the gospel in 2 Peter are not always linguistically successful or aesthetically pleasing. The author's attempts at using an extensive and impressive Greek vocabulary often end up sounding pretentious and pompous. And sometimes the syntax gets away from him, as in 1:3-4 where the unit introduced by "since" (*hōs*) is left dangling between 1:1-2 and 1:5ff. While in some cases the author chooses terms that had become part of the Christian vocabulary (e.g., *eusebeia* = "godliness"), in many instances he is obviously trying (sometimes too hard) to speak to readers whose religious vocabulary was shaped more by Hellenism than by Judaism.

What is the author saying in 1:3-4? He is basically describing what God has done for us in Christ, much as Paul does at great length in his letter to the Romans. Through God's gift in Christ it is possible for all people to escape the corruption of this world and to share in the divine life and power, and through knowledge of God and of Christ to live a virtuous and godly life.

The Virtuous Life (2 Pet 1:5-7). The emphasis on God's gift to humankind in the process of salvation described in 1:3-4 ("his divine power has bestowed on us . . . promises to you have been bestowed") is balanced in 1:5-7 by an exhortation to personal effort in the life of Christian virtue. The closest NT parallel appears in Rom 5:3-5: "knowing that suffering produces endurance, and endurance produces character, and character produces hope, and hope does not disappoint us." This kind of "chain" of virtues is called a sorites. The OT Book of Wisdom contains a list that moves from instruction in wisdom to "a kingdom" (Wis 6:17-20). And the Mishnah presents a chain of virtues from zeal to the resurrection of the dead: "Zeal leads to cleanliness, and cleanliness leads to purity, and purity leads to self-restraint . . ." (*m. Sotah* 9:15).

The list of virtues in 2 Pet 1:5-7 begins with faith and ends with love. What is not so clear in this list is whether it assumes that there is straight-line progress or movement as in the three examples listed in the preceding paragraph: from suffering to hope (Rom 5:3-5), from instruction to a kingdom (Wis 6:17-20), and from zeal to resurrection (*m. Sotah* 9:15). While love may be regarded as the greatest or crowning Christian virtue (see 1 Cor 13:13), it is hard to imagine a NT writer teaching that all the other virtues could be practiced without the presence of love from the beginning or that living out all the other virtues could produce love as the highest virtue. From beginning to end faith and love (and hope) must suffuse all Christian efforts at living the virtuous life.

The (by no means exhaustive) list of virtues in 2 Pet 1:5-7 contains items that fit well in Hellenistic popular philosophy and Stoicism, and so continues the program of theological inculturation begun in 1:3-4. The virtues included in this list are *pistis* ("faith" here understood in its Christian theological sense), *aretē* ("virtue" or "moral excellence"; cf. 1:3 where *aretē* refers to the excellence of God), *gnōsis* ("knowledge" in the sense of practical wisdom), *enkrateia* ("self-control" in the sense of self-mastery especially in the matter of sexuality), *hypomonē* ("patience" in the sense of retaining perspective and hope in the midst of danger or suffering), *eusebeia* ("godliness" in the sense of piety or respect for and devotion to God), *philadelphia* ("affection for others" or "brotherly love" in the sense of reaching out to help others), and *agapē* ("love" that embraces God, self, and others). The terms most at home in the Greco-Roman moral philosophical vocabulary are *aretē, enkrateia, eusebeia,* and *philadelphia.* The terms most characteristic of early Christian ethical discourse are *pistis, hypomonē* (with its note of hope), and *agapē.*

The Christian quest for virtue proceeds from faith and is guided by love and hope. It respects the divine initiative in calling persons to holiness and recognizes that human efforts are required to grow in holiness. In the life of Christian virtue it is love that "binds everything together in perfect harmony" (Col 3:14). The development of Christian character involves the theological virtues (faith, hope, and love) and the "natural" virtues as linked together and informing one another. See J. Daryl Charles, "The Language and Logic of Virtue in 2 Peter 1:5-7."

The Consequences of the Virtuous Life (2 Pet 1:8-11). That the cultivation of the virtues is necessary for progress in Christian life is emphasized by the contrast drawn in 1:8 and 1:9. According to 1:8 the practice of the virtues makes useful and fruitful the knowledge *(epignōsis)* one has of "our Lord Jesus Christ." On the other hand, according to 1:9, those who lack the virtues listed in 1:5-7 (or more accurately, fail to work at their practice) grow spiritually blind and run the risk of forgetting entirely what God has done for them through Christ (the forgiveness of their sins). It is not enough to make an act of faith or to proclaim the forgiveness of sins. Rather, one must put into practice the theological and natural virtues that characterize ongoing progress in Christian life, and one must act in a manner that is consistent with one's faith and identity as a forgiven sinner.

Commitment to the practice of the Christian virtues has consequences both in the present (1:10) and in the future (1:11). In the present (1:10) the practice of these virtues is an affirmation of one's seriousness about Christian faith. It is a sign that one's call to be a Christian is not a one-time action (receiving the Spirit and baptism) but rather a long-term commitment for the whole of one's life. The familiar image of life as a way or journey appears in both 1:10 and 1:11. Those who continue their journey through the practice of Christian virtue will not stumble or be tripped up on their way (1:10). And the goal of that journey is entrance into "the eternal kingdom of our Lord and Savior Jesus Christ" (1:11). The claim is that the cultivation of the Christian virtues mentioned in 1:5-7 will guide believers on their way through life in the present and will lead them to the goal of eternal life with Christ.

Thus 2 Pet 1:3-11 describes a "pilgrim's progress" that balances faith and works. It is not a matter of faith alone or of works alone. Indeed, faith comes first and is ultimately a gift from God, as 1:3-4 makes clear. But faith is not simply an intellectual or emotional assent. Faith manifests itself in attitudes and actions that are made concrete in the practice of the theological and natural virtues (1:5-7). The practice of these virtues equips believers for living out their faith in everyday life and leads them toward the fullness of life with God and "our Lord and Savior Jesus Christ" (1:8-11).

The theological-ethical stance promoted in 2 Pet 1:3-11 is close to that defended in the letter of James, especially in those passages that seek to correct a misinterpretation of Paul's teachings: "So faith by itself, if it has no works, is dead . . . faith without works is also dead" (Jas 2:17, 26).

In fact, the position defended in 2 Peter and James is consistent with Paul's own teaching. While emphasizing the centrality of faith and its gift-character (grace), Paul also stresses in every letter the need for attitudes and actions that are consistent with the profession of Christian faith. Paul's historical problem with "works" came from Jewish Christian teachers who tried to convince Gentile Christians that they had to become Jews and to practice "the works of the Law" (circumcision, Sabbath observance, food and purity rules). Paul's theological problem with "works" came from those who believed that by doing the "right" actions one could earn justification and salvation on the basis of one's own merits. In this context Paul insisted on the primacy of God's grace and on faith as the proper response, and he resisted attempts to force Gentiles who clearly had received the Holy Spirit to become Jews and observe all 613 commandments in the Torah. But for Christians who had received the Holy Spirit and made their profession of faith, Paul joined with James and Peter (and Jesus) in emphasizing the importance of both faith and works. Whereas the earliest NT writer (Paul) was intensely interested in faith and initial conversion, the latest NT writer (the author of 2 Peter) focused on the challenge of Christian life over "the long haul" and so insisted on the importance of cultivating the Christian virtues as a guide toward fullness of life with God and acting in an appropriate manner.

Modern scholars sometimes dismiss 2 Peter as lacking in positive theological significance. However, 2 Pet 1:3-11 provides an excellent short description of the dignity and the challenge of Christian existence. The initiative is with God, and the divine calling makes it possible to become "partakers of the divine nature" (1:4). Yet this great dignity demands by way of response religious and moral seriousness (the practice of and growth in the virtues) on the part of those who have been called and gifted by God. What results is a useful and fruitful life in the present as well as entrance into "the eternal kingdom of our Lord and Savior Jesus Christ" (1:11).

FOR REFERENCE AND FURTHER STUDY

Charles, J. Daryl. "The Language and Logic of Virtue in 2 Peter 1:5-7," *Bulletin of Biblical Research* 8 (1998) 55–73.

Danker, Frederick W. "2 Peter 1: A Solemn Decree," *CBQ* 40 (1978) 64–82.

Fischel, Henry A. "The Use of Sorites *(Climax, Gradatio)* in the Tannaitic Period," *HUCA* 44 (1973) 119–51.

Starr, James M. *Sharers in Divine Nature. 2 Peter 1:4 in Its Hellenistic Context.* Stockholm: Almqvist & Wiksell, 2000.

Wolters, Al. "'Partners of the Deity': A Covenantal Reading of 2 Peter 1:4," *Calvin Theological Journal* 25 (1990) 28–44.

_____. "Postscript to 'Partners of the Deity.'" *Calvin Theological Journal* 26 (1991) 418–20.

3. *Peter's Testament* (1:12-15)

12. Therefore I intend to remind you always about these matters, though you know them and are established in the truth that is present with you. 13. But I think it right, as long as I am in this tent, to stir you up by a reminder, 14. knowing that the putting off of my tent is imminent as our Lord Jesus Christ showed me. 15. And I will see to it that after my departure you may be able at any time to recall these matters.

NOTES

12. *Therefore I intend to remind you always about these matters:* In this section first-person singular language ("I") predominates. Peter explains his situation and his reason for writing the letter. The future form of *mellein (mellēsō)* has the sense of "intend, propose." Some manuscripts read *ouk amelēsō* ("I will not be negligent"), a reading that is attractive for its use of the *alpha*-privative so common in 2 Peter and the rhetorical figure of litotes (see the Note on 1:8). By writing a letter Peter creates a document that can be read in his physical absence or after his death, and so it can serve as a perpetual ("always") reminder regarding God's action in Christ and the challenge of Christian life, as well as a warning against "false teachers."

    though you know them and are established in the truth that is present with you: This assurance to the readers prepares for the attack on the charge about "cleverly devised myths" that begins in 1:16. Given the emotional tone and the intensity of the polemic in the rest of the letter, it seems that in the writer's mind this assurance about the readers was probably more wishful thinking than reality.

13. *But I think it right, as long as I am in this tent:* The initial verb is in the present tense. The new element here (compared with 1:12) is the reference to Peter's personal situation: "as long as I am in this tent." The word *skēnōma* ("tent") functions as a metaphor for the body understood as a temporary dwelling as opposed to a permanent structure. Compare Paul's statement in 2 Cor 5:1: "For we know that if the earthly tent we live in is destroyed, we have a building from God, a house not made with hands, eternal in the heavens."

    to stir you up by a reminder: The present infinitive *diegeirein* ("to stir up") suggests that the process can be repeated frequently. For another use of "by a

reminder" *(en hypomnēsei)* see 2 Pet 3:1. Insofar as the author was making present the apostolic tradition, he could legitimately claim apostolic authority (see
Joseph Zmijewski, "Apostolische Paradosis und Pseudepigraphie"). For the
possible nature of this reminder see the Note on 1:15.

14. *knowing that the putting off of my tent is imminent:* Since Peter expects to die
soon, this letter serves as his farewell discourse or "testament." In the testament genre the dying person looks into the future and imparts good advice
about life in the present and the future. While the term "tent" *(skēnōma)* is retained (though some manuscripts read *sōma*, meaning "body"), the imagery
seems to shift to clothing, as in 2 Cor 5:2-4: "longing to be clothed with our
heavenly dwelling . . . we wish not to be unclothed but to be further clothed."
The adjective *tachinē* can mean "quick, in haste" (as in 2 Pet 2:1), but here it
seems to have the sense of "coming soon, imminent."

as our Lord Jesus Christ showed me: For the title "our Lord Jesus Christ" see 2 Pet
1:8 and 1:16. For Jesus' revelation about Peter's death the most obvious referent is the tradition preserved in John 21:18-19 in which the risen Jesus says to
Peter: "'But when you grow old, you will stretch out your hands, and someone else will fasten a belt around you and take you where you do not wish to
go.' (He said this to indicate the kind of death by which he would glorify
God)." But whether this specific text or even the tradition behind it directly
influenced 2 Peter is not certain.

15. *And I will see to it that after my departure:* The discourse returns to the first person singular future tense as in 1:12: *mellēsō . . . spoudasō.* For other uses of
spoudazein see 2 Pet 1:10 and 3:14. For "departure" *(exodos)* as a metaphor of
Jesus' death see Luke 9:31: "They [Moses and Elijah] appeared in glory and
were speaking of his departure, which he was about to accomplish at Jerusalem."

you may be able at any time to recall these matters: The most obvious candidate for
fulfilling the role of a perpetual reminder is the letter we know as 2 Peter. In
other words, this letter will serve as the "reminder" that Peter promised
would be circulated after his death. Another possibility is the Gospel of Mark,
which is traditionally associated with Peter. This kind of language also generated a Gospel, an Acts, and an Apocalypse associated with Peter. These works
constitute the theological trajectory of Peter in early Christianity.

Interpretation

Having set forth in 1:3-11 the basic elements of the apostolic teaching
about Christian life, in 1:12-15 "Peter" presents himself as the implied
author and uses the conventions of the testament genre to give added
authority to his advice about dealing with the "false teachers" and the
apparent delay of Jesus' *parousia.*

As the salutation (1:1-2) and the final doxology (3:18) indicate, 2 Peter
is formally a letter. But within that epistolary framework it uses the con-

ventions of the testament genre to promote its message. Just as Jude can be regarded as a sermon within a letter (an epistolary sermon), so 2 Peter can be viewed as a testament within a letter (an epistolary testament).

As a biblical literary form the testament is a discourse attributed to a great figure whose death is imminent. It offers predictions about the future and exhortations about behavior in the present. The biblical prototypes are Jacob's last words to his twelve sons (Genesis 49) and Moses' farewells to Joshua and the people (Deuteronomy 31–32). The genre is based on the assumption that at the end of a lifetime a great figure wants to share wisdom with the coming generation(s) and can be trusted to tell the truth.

The most extensive example of the genre is the *Testaments of the Twelve Patriarchs,* a work in which each of Jacob's twelve sons takes a turn in looking into Israel's future and imparting warnings about life in the present. There are also testaments attributed to Abraham, Isaac, and Jacob, as well as Moses, Solomon, Job, and Adam. (For their texts see James H. Charlesworth, *OTP* 1:771–995.) Of course, in every case the protagonist or implied author is long dead, and the real author uses the figure as a vehicle for imparting advice about confronting some present danger. Much of what the implied author presents as future has already taken place, a phenomenon (prophecy after the fact) that is supposed to bolster the work's credibility.

In Luke's gospel the celebration of the Last Supper becomes the occasion for Jesus' short farewell speech or testament about the service of others as true greatness in his community (Luke 22:24-38), and in John's gospel Jesus delivers a series of much longer discourses about how the movement begun by him can continue after his departure (John 13–17). Among the Pastoral epistles it is possible to describe 2 Timothy as Paul's testament in that he imparts wise pastoral advice and warns about godlessness in the last days (see 3:1-9). So both in early Jewish writings and in the NT the testament was an established literary form.

The Testament of Peter (2 Pet 1:12-15). As the implied author, the apostle Peter recognizes that his own death is close: "knowing that the putting off of my tent is imminent as our Lord Jesus Christ showed me" (1:14). He presents his letter as a lasting reminder of his prescient wisdom when he is no longer physically present: "always to remind you" (1:12), "to stir you up by a reminder" (1:13), and "you may be able at any time to recall these matters" (1:15). Second Peter is thus a substitute for the apostle's earthly presence and serves as his testament. As the apostle *par excellence* Peter functions as the guarantor of the apostolic tradition as he offers advice about meeting the threat posed by the "false teachers." In doing so he preserves the apostolic message (1:3-11) and adapts it to meet the present crisis.

As Peter looks into the future he foresees that "false teachers" will arise and introduce "destructive heresies" (2:1). He also warns about "scoffers" who will come in the "last days" and raise questions about the apparent delay of Jesus' *parousia* or second coming (3:3-4). Much of the letter is given over to describing the destructive power of the false teachers and to correcting misunderstandings about the *parousia*. And so 2 Peter, with its warning about the "future" crises facing the community, is rightly understood as a testament.

However, from the perspective of the first readers the future envisioned by "Peter" was already present in large part. In fact, the real author was not entirely successful in keeping up the literary pretense that he is the apostle Peter gazing at a distance into the future. It soon becomes obvious that when 2 Peter was composed there were already "false teachers" active in the community being addressed and already people who were asking hard questions about the *parousia*.

The testament is an appropriate vehicle for the apostle Peter, whom various NT authors portray as a wise teacher and a pastor. Having been declared "blessed" by Jesus, in Matt 16:16-19 Peter is designated as the rock on which the church is to be built, and is given the keys to God's kingdom and the power of binding and loosing. In John 21 the risen Jesus commissions Peter to "feed my lambs" and "tend my sheep" (21:15-16). According to Acts 2, Peter is the first apostle to proclaim the gospel on Pentecost, to provide the correct interpretation of Jesus' death and resurrection, and to invite others to repent and be baptized. In 1 Peter the apostle instructs Christians who were suffering social ostracism and even persecution from outsiders to follow the example of Jesus as God's suffering servant. In the apostle's testament presented in 2 Peter the NT trajectory of Peter as teacher and pastor reaches its fullness.

For Reference and Further Study

Brown, Raymond E., et al. *Peter in the New Testament.* New York: Paulist, 1973.

Gnilka, Joachim. *Petrus und Rom. Das Petrusbild in den ersten zwei Jahrhunderten.* Freiburg: Herder, 2000.

Kolenkow, Anitra B. "The Genre Testament and Forecasts of the Future in Hellenistic Jewish Milieu," *JSJ* 6 (1975) 57–71.

Perkins, Pheme. *Peter. Apostle for the Whole Church.* Minneapolis: Fortress, 2000.

Zmijewski, Joseph. "Apostolische Paradosis und Pseudepigraphie im Neuen Testament. 'Durch Erinnerung wachhalten' (2 Petr 1,13; 3,1)," *BZ* 23 (1979) 161–71.

4. *The Witness of Peter and Holy Scripture* (1:16-21)

16. For we did not follow cleverly devised tales when we made known to you the power and coming of our Lord Jesus Christ. But we were eyewitnesses of his majesty. 17. For he received from God the Father honor and glory, when a voice came to him from the Majestic Glory: "This is my Son, my beloved one, with whom I am well pleased." 18. And we heard this voice coming from heaven when we were with him on the holy mountain.

19. And we have the prophetic word as something that is all the more reliable. To it you do well to pay attention as to a lamp in a gloomy place until day dawns and the morning star rises in your hearts. 20. First of all, you must understand this: that no prophecy of Scripture is a matter of personal interpretation. 21. For not by an act of human will was prophecy ever brought, but persons moved by the Holy Spirit spoke from God.

NOTES

16. *For we did not follow cleverly devised tales:* The Greek noun *mythos* has a variety of meanings: "tale, story, legend, myth." Here, as in the Pastorals (see 1 Tim 1:4; 4:7; 2 Tim 4:4; Titus 1:14), it carries a negative or pejorative sense. This impression is strengthened by the perfect passive participle *sesophismenois* ("cleverly devised, concocted") that modifies it. The phrase probably represents a charge made against the teachings associated with Peter and the apostles about Jesus' *parousia* and the Last Judgment rather than Peter's charge against the opponents.

when we made known to you the power and coming of our Lord Jesus Christ: In this section first person plural ("we") language is prominent. The main verb in the verse is *egnōrisamen* ("we made known"), which is accompanied by two participles, *exakolouthēsantes* and *genēthentes*. The "coming" of Jesus refers to his glorious return or second coming, designated in NT Greek as the *parousia* (see Matt 24:3; 1 Cor 15:23; 1 Thess 2:14; 2 Thess 2:8; Jas 5:7-8; 1 John 2:28). The dispute about Jesus' *parousia* is the main topic in 2 Pet 3:1-13 and probably provided the specific occasion for the letter's composition. The opponents seem to have been calling the teachings about the *parousia*, the general resurrection, and the Last Judgment "cleverly devised tales." For the title "our Lord Jesus Christ," see 2 Pet 1:8, 14.

But we were eyewitnesses of his majesty: "Peter" does not specify the group of three disciples—Peter, James, and John—mentioned in the gospel accounts of the transfiguration (see Mark 9:2-8; Matt 17:1-8; Luke 9:28-36). Nor does he mention his own awkward response: "He did not know what to say, for they were terrified" (Mark 9:6). The noun *epoptēs* ("careful observer, eyewitness") appears only here in the NT (but see the verb *epopteuein* in 1 Pet 2:12 and 3:2). Besides affirming the reliability of the witness, it can also designate those who have been initiated into the highest grade of the mystery religions (BDAG

388). While used here in very different religious context, *epoptēs* is an appropriate Greek word for describing Peter's experience of the transfiguration of Jesus. The term *megaleiotēs* ("majesty") is used generally with reference to divine beings. Here Peter interprets the transfiguration as the expression of Jesus' divine glory and the anticipation of his glorious return at the *parousia.*

17. *For he received from God the Father honor and glory:* The word translated "he received" is actually the aorist participle *labōn;* there is no finite verb in the sentence. Jesus' honor and glory came not only with his transformation but also with the words uttered by the heavenly voice. The "glory" *(doxa)* of Jesus reflects the glory of God, who is aptly called "the Majestic Glory" in the next clause.

when a voice came to him from the Majestic Glory: Second Peter specifies God as the origin of the voice, whereas in the gospels it simply comes "out of the cloud" (Mark 9:7; Matt 17:5; Luke 9:35). The use of the "divine passive" (literally "a voice was conveyed") and the unusual title for God ("the Majestic Glory") draws further attention to the content of the saying that follows. See Daniel P. Kuske, "Conveyed from Heaven—2 Peter 1:17, 18, 21," who argues that the meaning "convey" fits best since in all four cases a divine message is "conveyed" to humans.

This is my Son, my beloved one, with whom I am well pleased: The wording is closest to Matt 17:5: "This is my Son, the beloved, with whom I am well pleased." Compare Mark 9:7 ("This is my Son, the beloved") and Luke 9:35 ("This is my Son, the chosen one"). A heavenly voice says similar words at the baptism of Jesus (see Mark 1:11; Matt 4:17; Luke 3:22). The saying is a pastiche of OT phrases: Ps 2:7 ("You are my Son"—about the king/messiah); Gen 22:2 ("your only son"—about Isaac); and Isa 42:1 ("my chosen, in whom my soul delights"—about the Servant of God).

18. *And we heard this voice coming from heaven:* Not only were Peter and his companions "eyewitnesses" *(epoptai)* to the transfiguration of Jesus; they also heard the authoritative interpretation of the identity of the one who was transformed before them. As in 1:17a, a (divine) passive participle of the verb *pherein* ("was borne, brought, carried, conveyed") is used to describe how the voice came.

when we were with him on the holy mountain: While the point of the passage is to establish Peter as the authoritative witness, the language is cast in the first person plural ("we"), as in 1:16. The mountain (whose exact location is unknown) is holy because of what happened there: The glory of God was made manifest in Jesus. Mountains were naturally regarded as places of divine revelation since they put humans closer to heaven and to the gods. In the Jewish tradition Sinai/Horeb and Zion (Jerusalem) were the holy mountains *par excellence.*

19. *And we have the prophetic word as something that is all the more reliable:* The expression "prophetic word" in 1:19 and the references to "prophecy" in 1:20 and 1:21 prepare for the attack on the false prophets/false teachers in 2:1, but the precise referent of the term and its relation to 1:16-18 are less obvious.

Some possibilities include the OT taken as a whole, some OT passages (e.g., Dan 7:13-14 about the coming of "one like a son of man," which in the NT was applied to the second coming of Jesus), the various passages that made up the message of the heavenly voice at the transfiguration (Ps 2:7; Gen 22:2; Isa 42:1), or the transfiguration itself taken as a prophetic action pointing to the *parousia* of Jesus. The uncertainty about the referent of the prophetic word raises the further question about the meaning of the comparative adjective *bebaioteron* ("more reliable") in this context. It can hardly mean that the prophetic word is more reliable than the transfiguration and Peter's witness to it. Rather, the idea seems to be that the transfiguration and all that pertains to Jesus fulfills and thus confirms what the prophets said and so makes them even "all the more reliable."

To it you do well to pay attention as to a lamp in a gloomy place: In the Greek text this is a relative clause introduced by the dative *hō* ("to which"). The adjective *auchmēros* usually means "dry," but in this context it must mean "gloomy, dreary, dark." Until the Day of the Lord the prophetic word provides guidance and direction—like a light shining in the darkness.

until day dawns and the morning star rises in your hearts: Here "day" (*hēmera*) must allude to the Day of the Lord, which involves the *parousia*, the general resurrection, and the Last Judgment. The "morning star" (*phōsphoros*, literally "the light bearer" = *Lucifer* in Latin) is generally taken to be the planet Venus, which is the first "star" visible in the morning. See Rev 22:16 where the risen Jesus is given the title "the bright morning star."

20. *First of all, you must understand this:* As an adverb *prōton* means "in the first place, above all, especially." The participle *ginōskontes* functions here as an imperative ("you must understand"), a common usage in 2 Peter and other NT and Jewish texts.

    that no prophecy of Scripture is a matter of personal interpretation: One papyrus ($\mathfrak{P}^{72}$) reads "every prophecy and scripture," while some other manuscripts have "every scripture of prophecy" (as in 2 Tim 3:6). The "prophecy of Scripture" must refer to the OT, since it is highly unlikely that a NT writer (however late 2 Peter may be dated) referred to NT books as Scripture. The Bible of the early church was the OT, usually in its Greek version. The word *epilysis* ("explanation, interpretation") means literally a "loosing or setting free" and alludes to an understanding of the OT as a book of mysteries or puzzles to be solved. In the Pesharim the Qumran community "solved" the mysteries of the OT Prophets and Psalms in the light of their history, theology, and life together. Likewise, early Christians interpreted the OT in light of the Christ event. Here 2 Peter emphasizes the need for interpreting the OT in the context of the Christ-event and the life of the community rather than on one's own.

21. *For not by an act of the human will was prophecy ever brought:* The two parts of the sentence concern the origin of prophecy. In the first part Peter denies that any genuine prophecy ever came from human beings on their own without divine aid. As in 1:17 and 1:18 with regard to the heavenly voice, so here the verb *ēnechthē* is an aorist passive form of *pherein* ("bring, bear, convey").

but persons moved by the Holy Spirit spoke from God: The genuine prophets served
as instruments of the Holy Spirit, and so their prophecies had a divine origin
("spoke from God") rather than only a human origin. The verb that describes
the prophets as "moved" *(pheromenoi)* by the Holy Spirit also derives from
pherein and literally means "borne about." Some manuscripts read "holy
persons *(hagioi)* of God" rather than "persons . . . from God."

INTERPRETATION

Reacting to the opponents' charge that Peter's version of the gospel and
his teaching about Jesus' *parousia* in particular are only "cleverly devised
tales" (2:16a), "Peter" appeals to his experience as an eyewitness to the transfiguration of Jesus (2:16b-18) and to the witness of Holy Scripture (2:19-21)
to establish that his teaching represents sound Christian doctrine.

The Transfiguration of Jesus (2 Pet 1:16-18). There is a longstanding debate
among exegetes about the genre or nature of the transfiguration accounts
in the synoptic gospels (Matt 17:1-8; Mark 9:2-8; Luke 9:28-36). Do they
narrate an event from the life of the earthly Jesus (much as the gospels
present it)? Or has a story about an appearance of the risen Jesus after
Easter been retrojected into the earthly career of Jesus? Or is the transfiguration an apocalyptic vision that serves as a preview or anticipation of what
the glorified Jesus is to be with the full coming of the kingdom of God?

The contours of this debate can help in explaining why, in defense of
his apostolic teaching about Jesus' *parousia,* "Peter" appeals to his status
as a witness to Jesus' transfiguration. In the gospels the transfiguration
accounts are attached to a mysterious saying about the coming kingdom
of God: "Truly I tell you, there are some standing here who will not taste
death before they see the Son of Man coming in his kingdom" (Matt 16:28;
see Mark 9:1; Luke 9:27). In the gospel context, whatever else it may be,
the transfiguration narrative is presented as a preview or anticipation of
"the Son of Man coming in his kingdom." And, of course, the glorious Son
of Man is Jesus after his death and resurrection—the risen Christ. As
Jerome H. Neyrey ("The Apologetic Use of the Transfiguration," 519)
states, the transfiguration functions as a prophecy of Jesus' *parousia,* and
the apology in 2 Pet 1:16-21 defends that prophecy "as divine in source,
authoritatively revealed, and inspiredly interpreted."

In anticipation of his argument about Jesus' *parousia* in 3:1-13, "Peter"
presents himself as a witness to the transfiguration of Jesus. Whether the
author of 2 Peter had access to a gospel account (Matt 17:1-8 is the most
likely candidate; see Robert J. Miller, "Is There Independent Attestation")
or relied on an independent tradition, his goal is to establish Peter as a
witness to Jesus' transfiguration in its role as a pledge or anticipation of

Jesus' *parousia*. The author shows no interest in the many fascinating details in the gospel accounts: the time ("six days later"), the presence of the sons of Zebedee, the offer to construct booths, the appearance of Moses and Elijah, and so on. What counted for this author were the majesty of Jesus, the voice from heaven, and Peter's role as an eyewitness. As in the gospels, the transfiguration is interpreted in 2 Peter as the anticipation or prolepsis of "the Son of Man coming in his kingdom."

Of pivotal importance in Peter's account of the transfiguration is what the voice from heaven says: "This is my Son, my beloved one, with whom I am well pleased" (1:17). For its OT roots (Ps 2:7; Gen 22:2; Isa 42:1) see the Note on 1:17. The lead text here is Ps 2:7: "You are my son." Psalm 2 was a royal psalm composed for and used at the coronation of kings in ancient Jerusalem. These kings were crowned on Mount Zion ("my holy hill," 2:6). In early Christian circles when Jesus was identified as the Messiah and the Son of God it was natural to take Psalm 2 as a prophecy fulfilled in the person of Jesus. Jesus then became the key to interpreting Psalm 2, since Psalm 2 was viewed as really speaking about Jesus by way of prophecy. Thus there was a thematic continuity (Jesus the Messiah and Son of God) stretching from Psalm 2 (the psalm of the Davidic kings) through the transfiguration of Jesus (on the holy mountain) to the coming of the Son of Man in his glory at the *parousia*.

The Prophetic Word (1:19-21). As mentioned in the Note on 1:19, the relationship between Peter's appeal to his status as a witness to Jesus' transfiguration (1:16-18) and Peter's appeal to the prophetic word (1:19-21) is not immediately clear. The options include the OT taken as a whole, some specific OT text(s), and the transfiguration itself. Maximum coherence is obtained if we take the "prophetic word" as a reference to the content of the statement from the heavenly voice as a combination of OT texts: "This is my Son (Ps 2:7), my beloved one (Gen 22:2), with whom I am well pleased (Isa 42:1)." In this interpretation Peter moves relatively smoothly from his description of Jesus' transfiguration to his reflection on the OT as Holy Scripture, its divine origin, and its proper interpretation.

According to 2 Pet 1:19, Holy Scripture (the OT) functions as a "lamp in a gloomy place" until God's kingdom appears in its fullness and Jesus returns as the glorious Son of Man. Like other early Christians, the author of 2 Peter understood the OT as the revelation of the divine plan and divine will that reached a certain fullness in the earthly Jesus and will reach its absolute fullness with the coming of God's kingdom and Jesus' *parousia*.

In 2 Pet 1:20-21 there seems to be a defense of what came to be known in Christian circles as the "fuller sense" *(sensus plenior)* of Scripture on the basis of its divine origin. In this perspective the interpretation of Psalm 2 (and Gen 22:2 and Isa 42:1) does not depend entirely on the intention of the historical prophet or author. Nor does it depend on an individual interpreter at a later time: "No prophecy of Scripture is a matter of personal interpretation" (1:20). For the author of 2 Peter (and for other early Christians) the OT Scriptures were really speaking about Jesus Christ (a christological hermeneutic). They held this view because they were convinced that God speaking to human authors through the Holy Spirit was the ultimate author of Holy Scripture. With the first coming of Christ the "fuller sense" of the OT as a book of prophecies about Jesus became manifest. In this framework the true significance of the (OT) words from the heavenly voice was revealed at the transfiguration of Jesus: "This is my Son, my beloved one, with whom I am well pleased."

Before beginning his critique of the "false teachers," "Peter" establishes his credentials as a wise teacher who has been enlightened by his personal experience of Jesus' glory at the transfiguration and by the (OT) Scriptures. He correctly interprets the glory of the transfigured Jesus as reflecting the honor and glory of God the Father and as ratified by the voice of God, whom he calls "the Majestic Glory." He also insists that the prophetic word of Scripture interpreted properly in the light of Jesus' death and resurrection serves as "a lamp in a gloomy place." Peter's personal experience and his reading of Scripture are set in the context of the Christ-event.

FOR REFERENCE AND FURTHER STUDY

Curran, J. T. "The Teaching of 2 Peter i. 20," *Theological Studies* 4 (1943) 347–68.

Kuske, Daniel P. "Conveyed from Heaven—2 Peter 1:17, 18, 21," *Wisconsin Lutheran Quarterly* 99 (2002) 55–57.

Miller, Robert J. "Is There Independent Attestation for the Transfiguration in 2 Peter?" *NTS* 42 (1996) 620–25.

Neyrey, Jerome H. "The Apologetic Use of the Transfiguration in 2 Peter 1:16-21," *CBQ* 42 (1980) 504–19.

5. *False Teachers* (2:1-3)

2:1. But there were false prophets among the people, as there will be false teachers among you, who will introduce destructive heresies, denying the Master who bought them, bringing upon themselves swift destruction. 2. And many will follow their licentiousness; because of them the way of truth will be reviled. 3. And in greed they will exploit you with false words; for a long time their condemnation has not been idle and their destruction is not dozing.

NOTES

1. *But there were false prophets among the people:* For the problem of false prophets in ancient Israel see the contest between Jeremiah and Hananiah in Jer 28:1-17 and the rules for discerning true and false prophets in Deut 18:20-22. The terms *pseudoprophētēs* is fairly common in the NT; see Matt 7:15; 24:11, 24; Mark 13:22; Luke 6:26; Acts 13:6; 1 John 4:1; Rev 16:13; 19:20; and 20:10.

   as there will be false teachers among you: Much of the language in 2 Pet 2:1-10a is in the future tense as befits the genre of testament, when the departing hero looks into the future and warns the listeners about what will happen and how they are to act then. But the switch into the present tense from 2:10b on indicates that these problems are already going on. This is the only use of *pseudo-didaskaloi* ("false teachers") in the NT.

   who will introduce destructive heresies: The verb translated as "introduce" *(pareisaxousin)* contains two prefixes *(par-* and *eis-)*, which is a common linguistic feature in 2 Peter. The word *hairesis* has as its basic sense a political preference or group loyalty, and so it can be used to describe a sect, party, school, or faction (as Josephus does when he talks about the Pharisees, Sadducees, and Essenes; see Josephus' *Jewish War* 2:119-20, 122, 137-42, 152-53, 162-66). In Gal 5:20 and 1 Cor 11:19 Paul uses the term in the negative sense of factions or divisions within a community. In later Christian literature it came to refer to a "heretical" sect in the sense of a group holding unorthodox or false positions. In 2 Pet 2:1 *hairesis* is on its way from referring simply to factionalism and toward meaning false teaching, as the use of "false teachers" indicates. The Greek text reads *haireseis apōleias* ("heresies of destruction"), that is, heresies that bring destruction to the community and to the false teachers themselves (see 2:1, 3).

   denying the Master who bought them: For *despotēs* ("Master") as a divine and/or christological title see the Note on Jude 4. The imagery presupposes the institution of slavery and the theological concept of redemption: "for you were bought with a price" (1 Cor 6:20; 7:23). According to Paul, God's action in Christ involved a change of masters from Sin and Death (with the Law) to Christ. Peter claims that in effect the false teachers are denying the reality of the redemption accomplished by Christ, even though they had been redeemed by Christ (see Andrew D. Chang, "Second Peter 2:1 and the Extent of the Atonement").

   bringing upon themselves swift destruction: Those who promote "destructive heresies" *(haireseis apōleias)* end up by bringing "destruction" *(apōleia)* upon themselves. Whereas in 2 Pet 1:14 *tachinē* meant "imminent," here it seems to mean "swift" (though the two meanings are not entirely separable).

2. *And many will follow their licentiousness:* Again Peter looks into the future and foresees the destructive excesses brought into the community by the false

teachers. The noun *aselgeia* refers to "lack of self-constraint which involves one in conduct that violates all bounds of what is socially acceptable" (BDAG 141). In the NT (see Eph 4:19; 1 Pet 4:3; Jude 4; etc.) it often refers to sexual excesses. It is possible that the false teachers promoted a libertine lifestyle in the name of Christian freedom. But it is also possible that the charge of sexual misconduct is being used here without much thought or evidence, simply to vilify the opponents and their teachings.

because of them the way of truth will be reviled: In the Greek text this is a relative clause that is connected to the preceding by *di' hous* ("through whom"). For Christianity as "the way" see Acts 9:2; 18:25-26; 19:9, 23; 22:4; and 24:24. By referring to "the way of truth" Peter distinguishes his true Christian teaching from the false teaching of the dissidents. He further charges that through their teachings and conduct the Christian faith is becoming an object of ridicule for outsiders and is being corrupted for insiders. As is common in the NT (especially in Jude), *blasphēmein* is used not in the technical sense of blasphemy, meaning the misuse of the divine name (see Lev 24:10-23), but rather in the more general sense of "defame, revile, slander."

3. *And in greed they will exploit you with false words:* The charge of greed or avarice is repeated in 2 Pet 2:14: "having hearts trained in greed." As with sexual excess *(aselgeia),* so greed *(pleonexia)* is also a standard charge made against religious or philosophical rivals. In his earliest extant letter Paul denied the charge that he was motivated by greed: "As you know and as God is our witness, we never came with words of flattery or with a pretext for greed" (1 Thess 2:5). Paul's mention of "words of flattery" is echoed in Peter's remark about "false words." The adjective *plastos* ("false") derives from the verb *plassein* ("form, mold") and carries the sense of "fabricated" (and so without a basis in fact or reality).

for a long time their condemnation has not been idle and their destruction is not dozing: According to BDAG (307), the adverb *ekpalai* here pertains "to a relatively long interval of time since a point of time in the past"; compare 2 Pet 3:5 where *ekpalai* ("for a long time") pertains to "a point of time long before a current moment." But when this condemnation was first issued is hard to say. Was it in Genesis 3? Or was it in Deut 18:20: "But any prophet . . . who presumes to speak in my name a word that I have not commanded the prophet to speak—that prophet shall die"? The two verbs *argein* ("slack off, become idle") and *nystazein* ("be almost asleep, nod, become drowsy, doze") used with negative markers constitute another case of litotes, where negative expressions are used to make a positive point. They may also reflect the language used by the false teachers in raising their cynical questions about the apparent delay of Jesus' *parousia.*

INTERPRETATION

One of the elements of the testament form is the hero's predictions or prophecies about the future or the last days. In 2:1-3 "Peter" foresees the emergence of "false teachers" who will gain many followers and bring about destruction *(apōleia)* for themselves and for others. In his denunciation of them Peter makes selective use of elements from Jude 4: the charge that the false teachers "deny the Master," the accusation about their "licentiousness" *(aselgeia)*, and the warning that they were long ago slated for condemnation *(krima)*.

The Opponents (2 Pet 2:1-3). The author's use of the Epistle of Jude as a source here and throughout ch. 2 raises some methodological questions about the possibility of identifying precisely the opponents being confronted in 2 Peter. The basic issue is: Does 2 Pet 2:1-3 supply reliable historical information about those persons who are called "false teachers" *(pseudodidaskaloi)* by the author? Or is it possible that the author took over without much reflection the polemical material found in Jude and applied it to some group that was annoying him and some other early Christians? It is even conceivable to some scholars that 2 Peter was merely a literary exercise, an example for other early Christian writers on how to compose a polemic.

However, the author of 2 Peter did not simply copy the Epistle of Jude. Rather, he made selective and often clever use of certain parts of it. The best approach to 2 Peter is to take a middle road between excessive credulity (the view that 2 Peter offers a totally accurate portrait of the opponents) and excessive skepticism (the view that 2 Peter is only a copy of Jude or a literary exercise). While 2 Peter is full of stereotypes, it most likely uses this kind of material in confronting some real group that was causing trouble within a Christian community.

The best clue to identifying the opponents in 2 Peter comes from 2 Pet 3:3-4: "scoffers will come in scoffing, walking according to their own passions, and saying: 'Where is the promise of his coming?'" According to 3:3-4 the opponents expressed doubts about the *parousia* of Jesus and exhibited licentious behavior in keeping with their theological skepticism about the Last Judgment. Thus their teaching had a doctrinal component (no judgment) and a practical component (moral laxity because there will be no judgment). When 2 Peter 2 is read in the light of 3:3-4 some of the stereotypes come into sharper focus as aimed (or re-aimed) at Christian teachers who constituted a real threat to the life and wellbeing of a Christian community addressed in 2 Peter.

The opponents are labeled "false teachers" *(pseudodidaskaloi)*. They stand in line with the OT "false prophets" *(pseudoprophētai)* who led ancient Israel astray and brought destruction upon the people. These false teachers are said to import into the community "destructive heresies" *(haireseis apōleias)*, that is, positions or choices that lead to destruction. They are accused of (sexual) licentiousness and of exploiting people out of greed. The result is that they will bring shame upon "the way of truth" (the Christian religion) and condemnation upon themselves and others.

The theme of condemnation or judgment *(krima)* in 2:3 and the motif of "destruction" *(apōleia)* in 2:1, 3 provide further clues toward a more precise identification of the opponents. The threat from Peter that the false teachers will bring upon themselves "swift destruction" (2:1) contrasts sharply with their own skepticism about the Last Judgment expressed in 3:3-4. In their skepticism regarding Jesus' *parousia* as part of the scenario of end-time events they effectively deny "the Master who bought them" (2:1) and so cut away an essential element of Christian faith—the glorious return of the risen Jesus at the Last Judgment.

There are also hints in 2 Pet 2:1-3 that the author may be "turning the tables" on the "false teachers." Whereas they seem to have accused "Peter" of promulgating "cleverly devised tales" (1:16), presumably about the *parousia* of Jesus and the Last Judgment, in 2:3 Peter accuses them of greedily exploiting people by their "false (or fabricated) words" *(plastois logois)*. Whereas the false teachers denied Jesus' *parousia* and the Last Judgment in 3:3-4, in 2:1 and 2:3 Peter warns them that they will soon find themselves condemned before the judgment seat of God with the risen Jesus as their Master *(despotēs)*.

There is little reason to doubt that 2 Peter confronted some real threat in early church life. What was most characteristic of that threat was the appearance of Christian teachers who raised questions about beliefs in the *parousia* of Jesus and the Last Judgment and drew some dangerous implications regarding moral behavior. Their views are expressed most clearly in 2 Pet 3:3-4. In warning against them the author used the figure of the apostle Peter, the genre of testament (with its look into the future), and polemical material taken over from the Epistle of Jude. While the conventions of the testament genre required that "Peter" speak as if the threat posed by the false teachers was in the distant future ("there will be false teachers among you," 2:1), it is clear from 2:10b-16 that they were already present in the community when 2 Peter was composed.

Peter begins his critique of the false teachers by stressing the inevitability of the appearance of such persons. He accuses them of bringing "destructive heresies" into the community, as well as sexual immorality ("licentiousness") and greed ("they will exploit you"). While the false teachers will harm other Christians and the Christian movement as a whole ("the way of truth"), they will just as certainly bring destruction upon themselves both in their own time and before the judgment seat of God. It is always tempting to regard the days of the early church as the "golden age." But a careful reading of the NT and other pertinent sources shows that the first Christians not only suffered persecution from outsiders but also experienced severe problems within their own communities.

FOR REFERENCE AND FURTHER STUDY

Chang, Andrew. D. "Second Peter 2:1 and the Extent of the Atonement," *BS* 142 (1985) 52–63.
Charles, J. Daryl. "On Angels and Asses: The Moral Paradigm of 2 Peter 2," in *Proceedings: Eastern Great Lakes and Midwest Biblical Societies* 21 (2001) 1–12.

6. *Biblical Precedents* (2:4-11)

4. For if God did not spare the angels when they sinned but cast them into hell and consigned them to the pits of darkness to be kept for judgment, 5. and if he did not spare the ancient world but preserved Noah, a herald of righteousness, as the eighth, when he brought the flood upon the world of the ungodly, 6. and if he reduced to ashes the cities of Sodom and Gomorrah and condemned them to extinction and made them an example for what will happen to the ungodly, 7. and if he rescued righteous Lot who was worn down by the licentious behavior of unprincipled persons 8. (for by what he saw and heard while dwelling among them, that righteous man day by day tormented his righteous soul with their lawless deeds), 9. then the Lord knows how to rescue the godly from trial and to keep the unrighteous punished until the day of judgment, 10. especially those who go after flesh in depraved desire and despise authority. Bold and arrogant, they do not fear to revile the "glorious ones," 11. whereas angels who are greater in strength and power do not pronounce a demeaning judgment against them from God.

NOTES

4. *For if God did not spare the angels when they sinned:* The sentence begins here in 2:4 with the "if" clause (the *protasis*) and only ends with the "then" clause (the *apodosis*) in 2:9-11. For the sin of the "sons of God" with the daughters of humans see Gen 6:1-4. The episode is told at much greater length in *1 Enoch* 1–36 (the Book of Watchers). For the details, see the Notes on Jude 6. See also André Feuillet, "Le péché des Anges de l'Épître de Jude et de la Seconde Épître de Pierre." In 2 Pet 2:4-11 this is the first in a series of what turns into a set of alternating bad and good examples designed to illustrate God's justice toward sinners and God's mercy toward righteous persons like Noah and Lot.

but cast them into hell: For the binding of the fallen angels see *1 Enoch* 10:4-6, and for their being kept until the Last Judgment see *1 Enoch* 22:11 (again see the Notes on Jude 6). The aorist participle *tartarōsas* ("cast into hell") derives from the noun "Tartarus," which was regarded by the Greeks as "a subterranean place lower than Hades where divine punishment was handed out" (BDAG 991). The root made its way into the Greek version of *1 Enoch* 20:2. The only NT occurrence of either the verb or the noun is in 2 Pet 2:4.

and consigned them to the pits of darkness to be kept for judgment: The translation "pits of darkness" reflects the reading *sirois zophou*, in which *siros* means "deep hole, pit, cave." Other manuscripts contain the reading *seirois zophou*, in which *seira* means "cord, rope, chain." The reading *seirois*, "cords, etc.," does fit better with Jude 6 *(desmois)* and is found in the oldest manuscript ($\mathfrak{P}^{72}$). But it is also possible to take *seirois* as an alternative spelling for *sirois* and still meaning "pits." For the idea of the fallen angels being kept for judgment on the Day of the Lord see *1 Enoch* 10:6 and 22:11 (see the Notes on Jude 6). While 2 Pet 2:4 shares many features with Jude 6, it passes over the motif of the rebellious angels leaving their proper positions and their assigned dwelling places and emphasizes more clearly God's initiative in punishing these wicked angels.

5. *and if he did not spare the ancient world:* Instead of the negative example of ancient Israel's rebellion in the wilderness, which is featured in Jude 5 (before the fall of the angels), 2 Peter calls upon the account of the great flood in Genesis 7–8 as a second example of God's justice in punishing sinners. Flood stories were common in pagan literature, and the reference to the flood in the "ancient world" anticipates the discussion about the end of the present world in 2 Pet 3:5-7 (see also the references to Noah and the flood in 1 Pet 3:20). The use of the flood example also correlates the sequence of examples (fallen angels, flood generation, Sodom and Gomorrah) with the biblical order (Genesis 6, 7–8, and 19). The latter two negative examples are also balanced off with the positive examples of Noah and Lot (which are not in Jude).

but preserved Noah, a herald of righteousness, as the eighth: For the preservation of Noah and his family see Genesis 7–8. For a very positive evaluation of Noah as a righteous person (based on Gen 7:1) see Wis 10:4: "When the earth was flooded, because of him [Noah] wisdom again saved it, steering the righteous man by a paltry piece of wood." Likewise, according to Josephus, "God loved Noah for his righteousness" (*Ant.* 1:75). The reference to Noah as "the eighth" *(ogdoos)* means Noah plus seven other persons, that is, Noah and his wife along with his three sons Shem, Ham, and Japheth, and their wives (see Gen 6:12, 18). This usage is different from Jude 14, where *hebdomos* ("the seventh") refers to Enoch as being in the seventh generation from Adam.

when he brought the flood upon the world of the ungodly: For God's motive in destroying the world by the flood see Gen 6:11: "Now the earth was corrupt in God's sight, and the earth was filled with violence." For the "ungodly" *(asebeis)* as those who will be condemned on the Day of the Lord see 2 Pet 3:7. The term *asebeis* is used several times for the "intruders" in Jude (vv. 4 and 15 [twice]).

6. *and if he reduced to ashes the cities of Sodom and Gomorrah:* The biblical basis for this example is Gen 19:1-29. In 2 Pet 2:6 there is no mention of "the cities around them" as there is in Jude 7, nor is there any reference to the sexual

improprieties committed by the people of those cities. The aorist participle *tephrōsas* constitutes the only use of *tephroein* ("cover with or reduce to ashes") in the NT.

and condemned them to extinction: For the biblical description of the fate of these cities see Gen 19:24-29. The manuscripts of 2 Peter are divided with regard to including *katastrophē* ("to extinction") before *katekrinen* ("condemned"). Its omission can be explained by the presence of the same prefix *(kat-)* at the beginning of both words (which may have caused a scribe to skip over the first word). The strongest argument against its inclusion is that it is unnecessary. But the language of 2 Peter tends to be repetitious and full of "unnecessary" items.

and made them an example for what will happen to the ungodly: In Greek a *hypodeigma* ($\mathfrak{P}^{72}$ reads *eis to deigma*) is an example of behavior used for purposes of moral instruction. The translation "for the ungodly" follows the reading *asebesin* (dative plural) after the genitive plural participle *mellontōn*. Some manuscripts have the present infinitive *asebein*: "for those who act in an ungodly way."

7. *and if he rescued righteous Lot:* As with Noah in 2:5, Lot serves as a positive example to be imitated. For Lot as "righteous" *(dikaios)* see Wis 10:6: "Wisdom rescued a righteous man when the ungodly were perishing; he escaped the fire that descended on the Five Cities." See T. Desmond Alexander, "Lot's Hospitality: A Clue to His Righteousness," who traces Lot's righteousness to the parallels between Abraham and Lot in Genesis 18 and 19.

who was worn down by the licentious behavior of unprincipled persons: The only other use of *kataponein* ("wear or weigh down") in the NT is in Acts 7:24 ("the oppressed man"). The basic meaning of the verb is to cause distress through oppressive means, and so it can be rendered "subdue, torment, wear out, oppress." The rest of the clause piles up charges against the opponents. For the charge of sexual misconduct *(aselgeia)* see 2 Pet 2:2 and Jude 4. For the claim that the opponents are unprincipled or lawless *(athesmoi)* see 2 Pet 3:17. See John Makujina, "The 'Trouble' with Lot in 2 Peter: Locating Peter's Source for Lot's Torment," who traces the source to the Septuagint of Gen 19:16 and its verb *etarachthēsan* ("be disturbed, thrown into confusion").

8. *for by what he saw and heard while dwelling among them:* The clause translated "by what he saw and heard" is made up of two nouns, *blemmati . . . kai akouē* ("by sight and hearing"). It describes the corrupt moral climate to which Lot was exposed while living among the people of Sodom.

the righteous man day by day tormented his righteous soul with their lawless deeds: The repetition of the adjective *dikaios* ("righteous man . . . righteous soul") and the omission of Lot's name are reminiscent of Wis 10:6 (see the Note on 2:7). The use of the verb *basanizein* ("torture, harass, torment") is somewhat awkward here. See the suggestion in BDAG (168): "(Lot) felt his upright soul tormented by the lawless deeds (of the Sodomites)." The idea is that Lot's moral sensitivity made his life among the Sodomites unbearable, just as the life of faithful Christians among the false teachers and those influenced by them will become unbearable. In the translation it seems necesssary to specify that the lawless deeds are committed by the opponents ("their lawless deeds").

9. *then the Lord knows how to rescue the godly from trial:* Whereas the *protasis* ("if . . .") began in 2:4, the *apodosis* ("then . . .") begins here in 2:9. Noah and Lot serve as outstanding examples of God's ability to save the righteous among corrupt fellow humans from the flood and from the destruction of Sodom and Gomorrah, respectively. For the theme of divine rescue from the (eschatological) trial *(peirasmos)* in the Lord's Prayer see Matt 6:13: "And do not bring us to the time of trial, but rescue us from the evil one."

and to keep the unrighteous punished until the day of judgment: The reference is to the paradigmatic evildoers set forth in the three examples given so far: the rebellious angels (Gen 6:1-4), the generation destroyed by the flood (Gen 8–9), and the sinners of Sodom and Gomorrah (Gen 19:1-29). For a vivid description of the punishments visited upon the wicked after death and before the day of judgment see *4 Ezra* 7:78-87. See Nick Lunn, "Punishment in 2 Peter 2:9," who finds an iterative aspect ("God knows how to keep the unrighteous whom he punishes for the day of judgment") rather than a continuous aspect.

10. *especially those who go after the flesh in depraved desire:* The three "specific" charges in 2 Pet 2:10-11 echo the charges made in Jude 8. Here the charge about "defiling the flesh" is made more graphic by the phrases "who go after the flesh" (see Jude 7) and "in depraved desire" (literally "in the desire of pollution").

and despise authority: Whether *kyriotēs* refers to the lordship of God and/or Christ or that of church leaders/apostles like Peter is not entirely clear. The former interpretation, however, is more likely in the context of 2 Peter (and Jude).

Bold and arrogant, they do not fear to revile the "glorious ones": The third charge is also based on Jude 8, where it is suggested that the intruders were promoting heterodox teachings about angels. While *tolmētai* ("bold") appears only here in the NT, *authadeis* ("arrogant") occurs also in Titus 1:7. The main verb *tremousin* means "tremble," and so it brings out the notion of fear in a graphic way. It is in the present tense, suggesting that what Peter describes is not in the future only (see 2:1-3). As in 2 Pet 2:2, 12 and in Jude 8, 10, *blasphēmein* has a general sense of "revile" rather than the narrow sense of taking the divine name in vain (as in Lev 24:10-23). "The glorious ones" *(doxai)* seems to refer to "majestic beings" in the sense of transcendent beings deserving of honor (BDAG 258); that is, angels of some sort (as in Jude).

11. *whereas angels who are greater in strength and power:* This clause in 2 Peter summarizes Jude 9–10 but omits any allusion to the contest between Michael the archangel and the devil over the corpse of Moses (which was apparently based on the noncanonical *Assumption of Moses*). The effect is to generalize the topic and make it into a paradigm for understanding the situation addressed in 2 Peter.

do not pronounce a demeaning judgment against them from the Lord: Following the lead of Jude 9-10, it appears that the good angels refused to condemn the rebellious angels of Gen 6:1-4 (and *1 Enoch*) on the grounds that this task should be left to God, who is superior over all the angels and is thus the judge of all creatures. The phrase "demeaning judgment" *(blasphēmon krisin)* might also be rendered "judgment of blasphemy" in the sense of referring to what the wicked angels did in their rebellion against God. Some manuscripts read *para kyriou,* while others have *para kyriǭ,* and still others omit the phrase altogether. See Thomas J. Kraus, *"Para kyriou, para kyriǭ* oder *omit* in 2Petr 2,11," who prefers the reading *para kyriǭ.*

INTERPRETATION

The bulk of 2 Peter 2 is a vigorous attack on the false teachers that relies heavily on phrases and motifs taken over from the Epistle of Jude. The starting point seems to be the skepticism of the false teachers about Jesus' *parousia* and the Last Judgment (see 2 Pet 3:3-4). In fact, the second part of 2 Pet 2:3 may echo their own cynical charge that God (and/or Jesus) is "idle" and "dozing." In response, Peter insists that for the false teachers "condemnation has not been idle and their destruction is not dozing."

The first part of Peter's direct attack on the false teachers (2:4-11) takes the form of a long conditional sentence ("if . . . then"). The *protasis* ("if") in 2:4-8 consists of three negative examples (about the rebellious angels, the generation destroyed by the flood, and the men of Sodom and Gomorrah) and two positive examples (Noah and Lot). The point of these examples is made clear in the beginning of the *apodosis* ("then") in 2:9: "then the Lord knows how to rescue the godly from trial and to keep the unrighteous punished until the day of judgment." By mentioning punishment for the wicked in second place Peter leaves an opening for the further denunciations of the false teachers in 2:10-11 and in the remainder of ch. 2.

The Protasis (2 Pet 2:4-8). In rewriting Jude 5-8 the author of 2 Peter has omitted the example of the exodus generation (Jude 5) and added the case of the flood generation (2 Pet 2:5). Also he has put all the examples in their biblical chronological order: rebellious angels, flood, and Sodom and Gomorrah. Moreover, he has added two positive examples (Noah, Lot) to balance the second and third items in the series.

In the case of the rebellious angels 2 Pet 2:4 may be dependent (as in Jude) to some extent on the extrabiblical narrative preserved in *1 Enoch* 6–11 as well as Gen 6:1-4. Whether the author or his audience knew *1 Enoch* directly is not certain. But the idea that the author of 2 Peter objected to "noncanonical" works (and so already had a firm concept of the canon of biblical books) is not explicit here and can be at most inferred. He does simplify Jude 6 by omitting the motif of the rebellious angels leaving their assigned positions in the heavenly court. Instead, his emphasis is on

God's past punishment of sinners that will be in effect until the Last Judgment. The point is that God has punished sinners in the past and will certainly punish them on the Day of Judgment.

In 2:5 the negative example of the flood generation is passed over quickly: "(he) did not spare the ancient world . . . when he brought the flood upon the world of the ungodly." It is balanced by the positive example of Noah, who is described as "a herald of righteousness"; that is, Noah proclaimed righteousness or justice by his life and words. The point is that just as God has punished the wicked and rewarded or saved the righteous in the past, so God will do at the Last Judgment.

In 2:6-8 (see Jude 8) some attention is given to the evils done in Sodom and Gomorrah and their just punishment (2:6), but even more to the righteousness of Lot and his personal horror at the wicked deeds that were being committed around him (2:7-8). By inserting the two positive examples of Noah and Lot the author encourages the readers to recognize that their fidelity and resistance to the false teachers will be rewarded by God. At the same time the three negative examples assure the readers that the false teachers will eventually be sanctioned by God. The very judgment that the false teachers question will be the occasion for their own condemnation as well as for the vindication of those who have resisted their pernicious teachings about it.

The Apodosis (2 Pet 2:9-11). The *apodosis* first, in 2:9, draws the appropriate general conclusion from the negative and positive examples in the *protasis* and then in 2:10-11 begins to "specify" the charges against the false teachers.

The general conclusion (2:9) is that just as in the distant biblical past God has rescued righteous persons like Noah and Lot and punished evildoers (the rebellious angels, the flood generation, and the men of Sodom and Gomorrah), so at the future judgment (which the false teachers are denying) God will rescue the righteous and punish the wicked.

The "specific" charges (2:10-11) are taken from Jude 8, and are in fact not very specific at all: sexual immorality ("[they] go after flesh in depraved desire"), rejecting authority (probably divine authority; that is, the authority of God and/or Christ as *kyrios*), and reviling the "glorious ones" (*doxai*: here, as in Jude, most likely angels). The general character of these charges and the dependence of 2 Peter on Jude make it impossible to be more precise about the exact nature of these charges or their accuracy.

The charge about reviling "the glorious ones" (2:11) is even more enigmatic than it appears in Jude 8-9, since the author has omitted the reference to the debate between Michael and Satan over the corpse of Moses and generalized the matter into the charge that what good angels refuse to do, the false teachers are presuming to do. But there is no indication elsewhere in 2 Peter that the false teachers were setting themselves above the angels (even the fallen ones). Nevertheless, the dramatic introduction ("bold and arrogant") suggests that some importance is being given to this charge.

In 1:19 Peter compared the prophetic Scriptures of the OT to a lamp shining in a gloomy place. The present passage illustrates what Peter meant by that comparison, for in it he uses OT examples not only negatively to help his readers discern the fate that awaits the false teachers (wicked angels, flood generation, Sodom and Gomorrah) but also positively to encourage them to preserve their integrity as Christians during these painful community conflicts (Noah, Lot). Despite his very critical attitude toward the false teachers, Peter nevertheless leaves their final judgment and punishment to God and so urges a certain tolerance upon his readers (as in the parable of the wheat and the weeds in Matt 13:24-30, 36-43).

FOR REFERENCE AND FURTHER STUDY

Alexander, T. Desmond. "Lot's Hospitality: A Clue to His Righteousness," *JBL* 104 (1985) 289–91.

Dalton, William J. "The Interpretation of 1 Peter 3,19 and 4,6: Light from 2 Peter," *Bib* 60 (1979) 547–55.

Feuillet, André. "Le péché évoqué aux chapitres 3 et 6,4 de la Genèse. Le péché des Anges de l'Épître de Jude et de la Seconde Épître de Pierre," *Divinitas* 35 (1991) 207–29.

Kraus, Thomas J. "*Para kyriou, para kyriō* oder *omit* in 2Petr 2,11. Textkritik und Interpretation vor dem Hintergrund juristischer Diktion und der Verwendung von *para*," *ZNW* 91 (2000) 265–73.

Lunn, Nick. "Punishment in 2 Peter 2:9," *Notes on Translation* 12 (1998) 15–18.

Makujina, John. "The 'Trouble' with Lot in 2 Peter: Locating Peter's Source for Lot's Torment," *WTJ* 60 (1998) 255–69.

Pearson, Birger A. "A Reminiscence of Classical Myth at II Peter 2.4," *Greek, Roman and Byzantine Studies* 10 (1969) 71–80.

7. *Denunciations* (2:12-16)

12. But these men, like irrational animals, creatures of instinct, born to be caught and destroyed, reviling in matters that they do not understand, in their destruction they too will be destroyed, 13. suffering the penalty for wrongdoing, regarding dissipation in the daytime as pleasure, blots and

blemishes, reveling in their lusts, carousing with you, 14. having eyes full
of desire for an adulteress and unceasingly looking for sin, enticing unstable souls, having a heart trained in greed, accursed children. 15. Leaving behind the straight way they went astray, following the way of
Balaam the son of Bosor who loved gain from wrongdoing. 16. But he
received a reproach for his own transgression. A donkey incapable of
speech, speaking with a human voice, restrained the prophet's madness.

Notes

12. *But these men, like irrational animals, creatures of instinct, born to be caught and
destroyed:* Most of the ideas and words in 2 Pet 2:12 are based on Jude 10. In
Jude the term *houtoi* ("these men") as a way of referring to the intruders is
prominent in the structure of the homily in letter form (see Jude 8, 10, 12, 16,
19). As in Jude 10 the opponents are vilified as lacking reason (*aloga*, the *alpha*-
privative plus the root *log*-) and as operating only by instinct or nature
(*physika*). They are no better than wild animals. The phrase translated as "to be
caught and destroyed" consists of two nouns (*halōsis* and *phthora*); the latter
noun, *phthora* ("destruction"), is echoed twice at the end of the verse.

    reviling in matters that they do not understand: This charge follows Jude 10
in content but not in wording. The false teachers claim knowledge about
spiritual matters: God, Jesus, the angels, humankind, and Christian life. But as
irrational animals living only on instinct they could hardly have real understanding about them. What they really "know" has nothing to do with true
knowledge (*epignōsis*) regarding God and Jesus (see 2 Pet 1:2, 3, 8, 12, 16).

    in their destruction they too will be destroyed: Picking up on the reference to
phthora ("destruction") early in the verse, this clause contains two more uses
of the same roots: *phthora* and *phtharēsontai*. The warning here has two levels:
the present or near future in which the false teachers will destroy themselves
by bringing false teaching into the community, and the Last Judgment in
which they will surely be destroyed on account of their destructive deeds.

13. *suffering the penalty for wrongdoing:* The Greek text features a play on words:
adikoumenoi misthon adikias, though some manuscripts read *komioumenoi*. The
basic point seems to be the same as that of the preceding clause: The false
teachers will be punished for their evil deeds, both now and at the Last Judgment. The New Jerusalem Bible presents the following paraphrase: "being
injured in return for the injuries they have inflicted."

    regarding dissipation in the daytime as pleasure: While the term *tryphē* can be used
positively ("joy, delight") or neutrally ("luxury"), in this context it is clearly
negative ("dissipation, revelry, debauchery"). The fact that such activity takes
place in the daytime instead of under the cover of darkness adds to the portrayal of the lifestyle of the false teachers as both shameful and shameless.

    blots and blemishes, reveling in their lusts, carousing with you: These phrases echo
material in Jude 12. Here, however, there is no textual dispute about *spiloi* (not

spilades), which clearly means "blots," and not "hidden rocks" or "reefs." The reading *en tais apatais autōn* ("in their lusts") seems certain, though some manuscripts, following Jude 12, read *agapais* ("in their love-feasts"). Whether *apatai* should be rendered "lusts" or "deceits" is debated, though the context favors "lusts." The phrase *syneuōchoumenoi hymin* is literally "feasting together with you," but here (as in Jude) it seems to carry a pejorative sense ("carousing with you"), especially when *apatais* is read rather than *agapais*. The phrase "with you" suggests that the false teachers have infiltrated themselves into the community, and that the community is in great danger of being corrupted by them. What looks like the community meal (*agapē*) has become an occasion for the false teachers to "carouse" in shameful ways (in *apatē*).

14. *having eyes full of desire for an adulteress and unceasingly looking for sin:* The first phrase is literally "having eyes full of an adulteress." The false teachers are said to be always on the lookout for an adulterous woman and so always seeking an opportunity to commit sexual sin. The adjective *akatapaustos* ("unceasing") appears only here in the NT; it consists of the *alpha*-privative, the prefix *kata*, and the root *pauein* ("rest, cease").

    enticing unstable souls, having a heart trained in greed, accursed children: The verb *deleazein* ("entice, lure") also occurs in 2 Pet 2:18 (see also Jas 1:14). The adjective *astēriktos* ("unstable") has an *alpha*-privative and appears only here in the NT. For the charge of "greed" (*pleonexia*) made against the false teachers see 2 Pet 2:3. Here it is said that they have even been "trained" (*gymnazein*) to be greedy. They are "accursed children" or (more literally) "children of the curse" in the sense that whatever they do ends in destruction and death; see Sir 41:5-10 for a reflection on the "curse" under which the wicked live and act.

15. *Leaving behind the straight way they went astray:* For the image of Christian life as "the way" see the Note on "the way of truth" in 2 Pet 2:2. In 2:21 there is reference to "the way of righteousness." The word "way" (*hodos*) leads into the treatment of the way (*hodos*) of Balaam in 2:15b-16. Here the adjective "straight" (*eutheia*) probably comprises both doctrinal and moral matters, if we are to follow the double thrust of the polemic against the false teachers thus far.

    following the way of Balaam the son of Bosor who loved gain from wrongdoing: Jude 11 cites the examples of Cain, Balaam, and Korah. Second Peter omits mention of Cain and Korah, and focuses on the case of Balaam, who was hired by Balak the king of Moab to prophesy against Israel. The description of Balaam here echoes the charges made against the false teachers in the preceding verses: *adikia* ("wrongdoing") in 2:13, and *pleonexia* ("greed") in 2:14. All the ancient witnesses except 2 Pet 2:15 give the name of Balaam's father as "Beor." The form "Bosor" is peculiar to 2 Peter and is either the author's error or an early scribal error. Attempts at explaining it with a punning reference to the Hebrew word for "flesh" (*basar*) are not convincing.

16. *But he received a reproach for his own transgression:* Balaam's transgression, according to 2 Peter, was his attempt to profit from his prophesying. The

reproach came from the donkey according to 2:16b. These are the only occurrences of *elengxis* ("reproach, reproof, rebuke") and *paranomia* ("trangression, lawlessness") in the NT.

a donkey incapable of speech, speaking with a human voice: The animal called in Greek *hypozygion* ("beneath the yoke") is a beast of burden or pack animal, and in the Bible (see also Matt 21:5, following Zech 9:9) it is identified as a donkey or an ass. The usual translation is "dumb ass." The adjective *aphōnon* (with an *alpha*-privative) has the sense of being unable to speak by nature and so incapable of communicating with humans. For Balaam's ass speaking with a human voice see Num 22:28-30: "Then the Lord opened the mouth of the donkey. . . ."

restrained the prophet's madness: According to Num 22:21-35 the donkey acted as an instrument of the angel of the Lord in preventing Balaam from continuing his journey: "The donkey saw the angel of the Lord standing in the road with a drawn sword in his hand" (Num 22:23). In the OT the donkey speaks only to complain about the harsh treatment it received from Balaam. This is the only occurrence of the noun *paraphronia* ("madness, insanity") in the NT, though a participial form appears in 2 Cor 11:23.

INTERPRETATION

The expression "these men" *(houtoi)* serves to introduce the next two sections of denunciations leveled against the false teachers (2:12-16; 2:17-22). While *houtoi* does not have the same structural significance it carries in the Epistle of Jude (vv. 8, 10, 12, 16, 19), in 2 Peter 2 it does function at least as a paragraph marker and signals the start of a new section.

Much of the polemical language in 2 Pet 2:12-16 is taken from Jude 10-12, and so the problem of knowing how seriously to take this language and how applicable it may actually have been to the false teachers in 2 Peter arises once more. In rewriting Jude 10-12 the author omits the examples of Cain and Korah to concentrate on the case of Balaam and passes over some of Jude's most colorful language about the intruders as waterless clouds, late autumn trees, wild waves, and wandering stars. Instead he reshapes the material in Jude 10-12 to focus on the false teachers' stupidity (2:12-13a), sensuality (2:13b-14a), and greed (2:14b-16).

Their Stupidity (2 Pet 2:12-13a). The false teachers' stupidity is highlighted by calling them "irrational animals" *(aloga zōa)* and claiming that they rant on about matters that they do not understand. And just as the fate of irrational animals is to be destroyed, so the false teachers are hurtling toward their own destruction. The evaluation of them as irrational animals is underscored by the final remarks in 2:16b about Balaam's ass restraining the madness of the prophet. Just as the dumb animal knew more than the ancient prophet did, so "irrational animals" are even wiser than the false teachers. See also the proverbs about the dog and the pig in 2:22.

Their Sensuality (2 Pet 2:13b-14a). The false teachers' sensuality is brought out by a series of highly charged phrases: "regarding as pleasure dissipation in the daytime . . . enticing unstable souls." Not only do they display immoral behavior on their own for all to see, but they also seduce others into similar actions. Whereas Jude 12 accuses the intruders of being "stains on your love feasts *(agapais)*," 2 Pet 2:13 goes further by judging the false teachers to be "blots and blemishes, reveling in their lusts *(apatais)*." Rather than making any connection with the Christian love feasts *(agapai)*, 2 Pet 2:13 characterizes gatherings marked by the presence of the false teachers as *apatai* ("lusts") and occasions for mere carousing. The criticism of the false teachers' sensuality is intensified when they are said to be always on the lookout for an adulterous woman with whom they might have a sexual affair.

Their Greed (2 Pet 2:14b-16). The false teachers' greed is developed by accusing them of "following the way of Balaam . . . who loved gain from wrongdoing" (2:15). Passing over the figures of Cain and Korah mentioned in Jude 11, the author develops at some length the strange story of Balaam in Numbers 22–25 and contrasts the wisdom shown by an irrational animal (Balaam's ass) with the madness displayed by the greedy prophet. The concentration on Balaam's ass and endowing her with a human voice and a wisdom superior to that of the prophet Balaam serve to link the greed of the false teachers (the third charge) back to the accusation about their stupidity (the first charge). The thrust of 2 Pet 2:12-16 is that the false teachers are leading other Christians astray into destruction, seducing them into an immoral lifestyle, and using them to satisfy their desire for their own financial profit.

According to the law of retribution people get what they deserve. The wise and righteous are rewarded, and the foolish and wicked are punished—whether in this life or in the next. We know, of course, from the book of Job and other biblical texts that life does not always work according to the law of retribution. But sometimes it does! At the heart of Peter's further denunciations in 2:12-16 is the conviction about the false teachers that "in their destruction they too will be destroyed" (2:12).

For Reference and Further Study

Skehan, Patrick W. "A note on 2 Pet 2,13," *Bib* 41 (1960) 69–71.

8. *More Denunciations* (2:17-22)

17. These men are waterless springs and mists driven by a storm; for them the black darkness has been reserved. 18. For by uttering bombastic and empty words they entice in the licentious passions of the flesh those who are barely escaping those who live in error. 19. They promise them freedom, but they themselves are slaves of depravity. For by whatever one has been overcome, to this one has been enslaved.

20. For if after escaping the defilements of the world through the knowledge of [our] Lord and Savior Jesus Christ but by becoming entangled in them again they are overcome, then the last state becomes worse for them than the first. 21. For it would have been better for them if they had not known the way of justice than after knowing it to turn back from the holy commandment handed on to them. 22. For what the proverb says has turned out to be true for them: "A dog returns to its own vomit," and "a pig when washed (returns) to rolling in the mud."

Notes

17. *These men are waterless springs and mists driven by a storm:* For the false teachers as "these men" *(houtoi)* see the Note on 2:12. In Jude 12 the intruders are called "waterless clouds carried away by winds." In 2 Pet 2:17 these images are divided and modified, perhaps on the basis of the empirical observation that all clouds have some water. The adjective *anydroi* (with an *alpha*-privative) fits better with "springs" *(pēgai)* as a way of criticizing the false teachers as incapable of giving life and satisfying spiritual thirsts. The description of them as "mists driven by a storm" suggests a lack of substance and a transitory character. This is the only NT occurrence of *homichlē* ("mist," or more generally according to BDAG 705 "an atmospheric condition that darkens the sky").

    for them the black darkness has been reserved: The expression is borrowed directly from Jude 13. Second Peter omits the other comparisons in Jude 12-13 ("late autumn trees . . . wild waves . . . wandering stars") and moves directly to the fate prophesied for these "waterless springs" and "mists." For other references to *zophos* as the dark place where sinners are kept see Jude 6, 13 and 2 Pet 2:4. The omission of "forever" *(eis aiōna)* as found in Jude 13 may reflect the author's theological correction that after the Last Judgment the wicked will undergo a different kind of punishment or even annihilation.

18. *For by uttering bombastic and empty words:* The verb *phthengomai* ("utter") occurred in 2:16 with reference to Balaam's ass; see Acts 4:18 for the only other NT occurrence. The term *hyperongka* ("bombast") appears only here and in Jude 16 in the NT. The phrase is literally "bombast of emptiness" *(hyperongka mataiotētos).*

    they entice in the licentious passions of the flesh: For *deleazein* ("entice") see 2 Pet 2:14 and Jas 1:14. Building on Jude 16 ("walking according to their own passions"), 2 Peter strengthens the expression with the aid of "licentiousness" (*aselgeia;* see Jude 18; 2 Pet 2:7) and "flesh" *(sarx).*

those who are barely escaping those who live in error: The charge here is that the false teachers prey especially on recent converts. The reading *oligōs* ("barely") is preferable to *ontōs* ("really") on the grounds of its manuscript attestation, linguistic probability (the adverbial form *oligōs* is very rare; only here in the NT), and sense. Those who live in error are pagans still living a pagan lifestyle.

19. *They promise them freedom, but they themselves are slaves of depravity:* Given the prominence of *eleutheria* ("freedom") in the Pauline letters (Rom 8:21; 1 Cor 10:29; 2 Cor 3:17; Gal 2:4; 5:1, 13), there may be some connection between Paul's theology and the slogan of the "false teachers" of 2 Peter. This impression is strengthened by the explicit reference to whose who twist Paul's words to their own destruction in 2 Pet 3:15b-16. See also the polemical uses of *eleutheria* in Jas 1:25 and 2:12. The term *phthora* here (as in 2 Pet 1:4) has the sense of depravity or moral corruption rather than destruction (as in 2:12). The charge is that, while the false teachers promote their gospel of "freedom," in fact they are enslaved in and to their own depravity.

For by whatever one has been overcome, to this one has been enslaved: This sounds like a proverb, and the dramatic position in which it appears confirms this impression. In ancient warfare those who were overcome in battle were frequently taken into slavery. In the moral sphere the idea is that one's evil deeds and desires can turn into habits that cannot be broken. The use of the perfect tenses in both verbs underlines the perduring effects of sin.

20. *For if after escaping the defilements of the world:* The reference in 2:20-22 seems to be primarily to the false teachers rather than to the recent converts on whom they prey. This is the only NT occurrence of *miasma* ("defilement"); see 2 Pet 2:10 for the related term *miasmos.*

through the knowledge of our Lord and Savior Jesus Christ: For the importance of knowledge *(epignōsis)* about God and Jesus in 2 Peter see the Note on 1:2. For the formula "our Lord and Savior Jesus Christ" see 2 Pet 1:11 and 3:18. There is some variation about the place of "our" *(hēmōn)* in the manuscripts of 2 Pet 2:20. For Jesus as "the Lord and Savior" see 2 Pet 3:2.

but by becoming entangled in them again they are overcome: The basic meaning of the verb *emplekein* is "to be involuntarily interlaced to the point of immobility," as with an animal being caught up in a thornbush (BDAG 324). In a metaphorical sense it describes becoming involved in an activity to the point of interference with one's other activities and objectives. It may refer to involvement in civilian or secular pursuits (as in 2 Tim 2:4) or (more negatively) in "the defilements of the world" (as is the case here). The verb *hēttōntai* ("they are overcome") links this charge to the "proverb" at the end of 2:19: "by whatever one has been overcome *(hēttētai).* . . ." For another NT treatment of the problem posed by Christians who have sinned after their baptism see Heb 6:4-6: "For it is impossible to restore again to repentance those who have once been enlightened . . . and then have fallen away."

then the last state becomes worse for them than the first: See Matt 12:45 (and Luke 11:26): "the last state of that person is worse than the first." Whether 2 Peter quotes a common proverb, the Sayings Source Q, or one of the gospels is not clear. At any rate, there is no effort to ascribe the saying directly to Jesus. The point here is that the false teachers, having once embraced Christian faith, have (at least from the author's perspective) perverted the gospel and effectively returned to pagan ways. In that sense they are in an even worse state than when they began their spiritual journey. This theme is elaborated in 2:21-22.

21. *For it would have been better for them if they had not known the way of justice:* The construction "it would have been better" *(kreitton . . . ēn)* describes an unfulfilled or unreal condition (see Matt 26:9, 24; Heb 9:26). The perfect infinitive *epegnōkenai* ("had known") indicates that the false teachers had once come to a solid knowledge *(epignōsis;* see 2 Pet 1:2, 3, 8; 2:20) of the Christian faith. The "way of justice" here seems to function as a synonym for the Christian faith or the object of *epignōsis* ("our Lord and Savior Jesus Christ," 2:20). For rendering *dikaiosynē* as "justice" rather than "righteousness" in 2 Peter see the Note on 1:1. For "the way of truth" see the Note on 2:2.

than after knowing it to turn back from: The dative plural participle in the aorist tense *(epignousin)* continues the play on *epignōsis* as genuine knowledge of God and Christ. The aorist infinitive *hypostrepsai* means "to turn away and go back" (BDAG 1041). Other manuscripts read *epistrepsai* (see 2:22) and *eis ta opisō anakampsai* ("to turn back again to the former things," which is probably a gloss on *hypostrepsai).*

the holy commandment handed on to them: The "holy commandment" is very likely another way of talking about the Christian faith, like "the way of truth" (2:2), "the knowledge of our Lord and Savior Jesus Christ" (2:20), and "the way of justice" (2:21). However, it may especially evoke the ethical dimensions of that faith. For the Christian faith as something "handed on," see Jude 3 ("the faith handed on to the saints") and 1 Cor 15:3a ("For I handed on to you as of first importance what I in turn had received").

For what the proverb says has turned out to be true for them: A *paroimia* is a "proverb, saw, or maxim" here and in most Greek writings, though in John's gospel (see 10:6; 16:25, 29) it refers to veiled speech in which lofty ideas are concealed. The Greek construction is somewhat awkward: "the [point or thrust] of the true proverb has happened to them." In fact there are two proverbs cited in 2:22. But their message is the same, and both serve as commentaries on the spiritual condition of the false teachers.

"A dog returns to its own vomit": See Prov 26:11: "Like a dog that returns to its vomit is a fool who reverts to his folly." The proverb is based on the empirical observation that dogs sometimes go back to their vomit and eat again the chunks of food. In biblical times dogs were mostly regarded as scavengers (rather than pets) and had a negative image, and so enemies set to devour (Ps 22:16; Isa 56:10-11), the unclean (Matt 15:26-27; Rev 22:15), and male prostitutes (Deut 23:18) are called "dogs." This is the only occurrence of *exerama* ("vomit") in the NT.

and "*a pig when washed (returns) to rolling in mud*": The *Story of Ahikar* contains a saying close to this proverb in its Arabic version: "you have been to me like the pig who went into the hot bath with people of quality, and when it came out of the hot bath, it saw a filthy hole and it went down and wallowed in it" (8:15). In the OT it is forbidden to eat meat from pigs (Lev 11:17; Deut 14:8), and in NT times the pig had become a symbol for uncleanness (1 Macc 1:47; 2 Macc 6:18; Mark 5:1-20). Again the proverb is based on empirical observation of pigs wallowing in mire. It is possible that the passive participle *lousamenē* ("when washed") was taken by 2 Peter's readers as an allusion to the baptism the false teachers had undergone in the past. For another combination of proverbial sayings about dogs and pigs see Matt 7:6: "Do not give what is holy to dogs; and do not throw your pearls before swine." The two proverbs in 2:22 illustrate what, according to the author, the false teachers have done in departing from the way of truth and justice.

INTERPRETATION

Having assailed the false teachers for their stupidity, sensuality, and greed in 2:12-16, the author of 2 Peter reflects on the harmful effects they bring on other Christians (2:17-19) and on themselves (2:20-22). "Peter" is no longer looking into the "future," but is speaking clearly about the present. In 2:17-18 he relies on Jude 12-13, 16, while in 2:19-22 he makes use of some traditional sayings and proverbs.

When depicting the low state into which the false teachers have fallen in 2:18-20 the author alludes back to his picture of the Christian ideal as sketched in 1:3-4 by way of contrast. The two passages have many words in common: "knowledge" (1:3 and 2:20), "passion" (1:4 and 2:18), "corruption" (1:4 and 2:19), "escape" (1:4 and 2:18, 20), "world" (1:4 and 2:19), and "promise" (1:3 and 2:19). Whereas 2 Pet 1:3-4 presents Christian life at its best, 2:17-22 portrays it at its worst, with both passages using the same vocabulary.

The Harmful Effects on Others (2 Pet 2:17-19). The false teachers are especially dangerous to recent converts to Christianity: "those who are barely escaping those who live in error" (2:18). Their teaching has no real substance, a point the author makes by breaking up a phrase in Jude 12 ("waterless clouds, carried away by winds") and creating out of it two striking images: "waterless springs and mists driven by a storm" (2:17). The irony is that the teachers who cast doubt on the Last Judgment will be confined (like the fallen angels of *1 Enoch* and Jude) to the "black darkness" as they await their judgment and punishment at the Last Judgment (see Jude 13).

By denying the Last Judgment and the related doctrine of rewards and punishments the false teachers seduce new converts into sexual immorality ("in the licentious passions of the flesh," 2:18) and so entice them to go back to the ways of paganism. The idea seems to be that where there is no ultimate sanction at the Last Judgment people will act as if every kind of action is allowed. Liberty becomes license.

The false teachers' promise of "freedom" (2:19) is probably associated with their skepticism about the Last Judgment. Freed from the constraints involved in having to face such a scrutiny, those who embrace their false teaching feel free to construct their own moral codes and to act with impunity. Or so they think! But in fact not only will all have to face the divine judgment in the future, but also in the present they will find themselves enslaved to sin (see Rom 1:18–3:20). The point is emphasized by what sounds like a proverb and is at least an apt summary of human existence before and apart from Christ: "For by whatever one has been overcome, to this one has been enslaved" (2:19).

The Harmful Effects on Themselves (2 Pet 2:20-22). The focus shifts from the harm the false teachers are causing to recent converts to the harm they are doing to themselves by their teaching and lifestyle. The false teachers are Christians. When they became Christians they escaped "the defilements of the world through the knowledge of [our] Lord and Savior Jesus Christ" (2:20). But now (whether they know it or not) they find themselves entangled again in these same defilements and so are in an even worse position. While regarding themselves as enlightened Christians, they are effectively in a state of apostasy.

In 2:21 Peter goes so far as to speculate that the false teachers would have been better off if they had remained in their paganism. At least then they would not have to add apostasy to their list of sins. By effectively turning away from authentic Christian teaching ("the holy commandment handed on to them") and enticing others to do so they have made themselves even worse sinners than they ever were. According to the two proverbs quoted in 2:22 they are indeed acting like "irrational animals"— like the dog that returns to its own vomit and like the pig that, having once been washed (a possible reference to their baptism?), goes back to wallowing in the mud.

After repeating his now-familiar criticisms of the false teachers, Peter presents a subtle analysis of moral freedom and slavery. While the false teachers were promising "freedom" to recent converts, in fact they were enslaved to their own vices. What made their condition even more tragic was the fact that the false teachers were Christians. They had once attained true freedom in Christ, but now they had entangled themselves once more in the defilements of the world. The images of the dog going back to its own vomit and the pig rolling about again in the mud after having been washed clean are effective ways of making the point that "the last state becomes worse for them than the first" (2:20).

For Reference and Further Study

Dunham, Duane A. "An Exegetical Study of 2 Peter 2:18-22," *BS* 140 (1983) 40–54.

9. *The Delay of the Parousia* (3:1-4)

3:1. Beloved, now this is the second letter that I write to you. In them I stir up your pure mind by a reminder, 2. that you may recall the words spoken beforehand by the holy prophets and the commandment of the Lord and Savior through your apostles.

3. First of all you must understand this—that in the last days scoffers will come in scoffing, walking according to their own passions, 4. and saying: "Where is the promise of his coming? For from the time when the forefathers fell asleep, all things remain the same since the beginning of creation."

Notes

1. *Beloved, now this is the second letter that I write to you:* For "beloved" (*agapētoi*) as a mode of address see 2 Pet 3:8, 14, 17, as well as Jude 3, 17, 20. The statement in 3:1a places the authority of the apostle Peter behind the content of this letter. The first letter has been identified variously as Jude, 2 Peter 1, some lost letter, or 1 Peter. Most interpreters take it to be 1 Peter, though the style and content of 1 and 2 Peter are very different and it is hard to find any direct influence from 1 Peter in 2 Peter.

   In them I stir up your pure mind by a reminder: In the Greek text this is a relative clause (*en hais*) dependent on the preceding statement in 3:1a. For an earlier use of the expression "stir up by a reminder" to characterize the nature of this document see 2 Pet 1:13. The expression "pure mind" (*eilikrinēs dianoia*) appears in Plato's *Phaedo* 66A. But in 2 Peter the emphasis is more likely on the moral aspect ("sincere, free of dissimulation") rather than on the intellectual aspect, and so "pure heart" would have been even more appropriate.

2. *that you may recall the words spoken beforehand by the holy prophets:* 2 Pet 3:2-3 follows Jude 17-18 for the most part. The infinitive *mnēsthenai* ("recall") serves as the equivalent of a purpose clause and picks up on "by a reminder" in 3:1. By attributing "the words spoken beforehand" (see Jude 17) to "the holy prophets" the author broadens the range of the Christian tradition to include the OT prophets and indeed the whole OT. That the reference here is to Christian prophets only is very doubtful.

   and the commandment of the Lord and Savior through your apostles: For an earlier use of *entolē* ("commandment") see 2 Pet 2:21. In both cases it refers not so much to one commandment (e.g., the love command) but rather to the substance of the Christian faith proclaimed by the apostles (though probably again with a moral emphasis). For Jesus as "Lord and Savior" see 2 Pet 1:11; 2:20; 3:18. The author's rewriting of Jude 17 is awkward, especially with regard to the genitival phrase "your . . . apostles." Some interpreters point to "your apostles" as evidence for the post-apostolic composition of 2 Peter, though the author (necessarily in view of the conventions of pseudepigraphy) seems to play down that impression. Given the literary framework in which 2 Peter is presented (as a letter from the apostle Peter, who was an "eyewitness" to Jesus' transfiguration), the term "apostles" here most likely refers narrowly to the twelve apostles (for whom Peter serves as the spokesman) rather than to the wider group including figures such as Paul and Barnabas. According to Richard J. Bauckham, however, they are the apostles from whom the readers themselves had received the gospel ("your apostles").

3. *First of all you must understand this:* The same construction—the adverb *prōton* ("first of all") and the present participle *ginōskontes* as the equivalent of an imperative ("you must understand this")—was used also in 2 Pet 1:20.

   that in the last days: For this and similar expressions in the NT see John 6:39, 40, 44, 54; 11:24; 12:48; Acts 2:17; 2 Tim 3:1; Heb 1:2; and Jas 5:3. It reflects the early Christian consciousness that "the last day" (as in John) is near and that the whole period from the present to that day constitutes "the last days." By his testament (2 Peter), the apostle warns about the trials that are associated with this period (see Mark 13; Matt 24–25; Luke 21) and affirms that they will issue in the *parousia* of Jesus, the general resurrection, the Last Judgment, and definitive rewards and punishments.

   scoffers will come in scoffing: Peter looks into the future (in good testament form) and foresees the emergence of false teachers who will challenge the "orthodox" Christian teaching about the last days. The repetitious construction *en empaigmonę empaiktai* ("in scoffing scoffers") is generally regarded as a Hebraism and gives the sentence a "biblical" flavor. The term *empaiktēs* ("scoffer, mocker") appears only here and in Jude 18 in the NT. However, the verb *empaizein* is quite common in the NT, and the noun *empaigmōs* is found also in Heb 11:36. The basic meaning of the root is "ridicule, make fun of, mock." It can also mean to trick someone or make a fool out of someone. Whereas in Jude the "scoffing" takes the form of immorality and divisiveness in a general sense, in 2 Peter it pertains explicitly to skepticism about the second coming or *parousia* of Jesus.

   walking according to their own passions: The same phrase is found in Jude 18, which includes the adjective *asebios* (see 2 Pet 3:7) in describing the *epithymiai* ("passions") of the intruders. For "walking" as a way of describing moral conduct see Jude 11, 16, and 18, as well as 2 Pet 2:10. In 2 Peter the context in which *epithymia* appears is always very negative: "the corruption of the world because of passion" (1:4); "in the desire of pollution" (2:10); and "in the licentious passions of the flesh" (2:18).

4. *and saying: "Where is the promise of his coming?:* Only here in 2 Peter (and in Jude) do we get a clear idea about what the opponents were teaching. Their

"scoffing" takes the form of skeptical questions posed in the OT: "Where is your God?" (Pss 42:3, 10; 79:10; etc.); and "Where is the word of the Lord?" (Jer 17:15). For similar questions in the NT see Luke 8:25 and 1 Cor 1:20; 15:55. The noun *epangelia* ("promise") refers to a "declaration to do something with implication of obligation to carry out what is stated" (BDAG 355). In the NT it often refers to God's promises, and here it refers specifically to the "promise" of the *parousia* of Jesus. In 2 Pet 1:4 there is reference to "the precious and sublime promises *(epangelmata),*" and 2:19 criticizes the false teachers in terms of their false promises: "They promise them freedom but they themselves are slaves of depravity." The noun *parousia* derives from the verb *pareinai* ("be present") and refers to a "presence, coming, advent." Outside the NT it is used sometimes to describe the visit of a high official (a king or a governor) to a province or a city. In the NT it becomes a technical term for the second coming of Christ (see Matt 24:3, 27; 1 Cor 15:23; 1 Thess 2:19; 3:13; 4:15; 2 Thess 2:1, 8; Jas 5:7, 8; 2 Pet 1;16; 3:12; 1 John 2:28).

For from the time when the forefathers fell asleep: This sentence purports to give the reason ("For . . .") behind the opponents' skepticism about the *parousia* of Jesus, and prepares for the response beginning with 3:5. The "forefathers" *(hoi pateres)* could include the great figures of the OT (Abraham, Moses, David, etc.). Some interpreters, however, confine the *pateres* to the first generation of Christians who were dying off (see 1 Thess 4:13–5:11) and in particular to the apostles like Peter. They take this as another indication of the letter's postapostolic and pseudepigraphical composition. (See the Interpretation of 3:3-4 below.) In 1 Thessalonians a major pastoral problem Paul faced was concern about the fate of those Christians who had passed away before the second coming of Jesus.

all things remain the same since the beginning of creation: The opponents' reasoning, while stated explicitly, is obscure. Their denial of Jesus' *parousia,* according to 2 Peter, is based on their observation that "all things remain the same." From that premise they apparently dismissed the teachings about the *parousia* of Jesus and the Last Judgment as "cleverly devised tales" (2 Pet 1:16) or mythology. As Christians they may have believed that God's promise had already been fulfilled in the resurrection of Jesus and in their baptism as their participation in Jesus' death and resurrection (see Rom 6:3-4). Several early Christian hymns (John 1:1-18; Col 1:15-20; Heb 1:1-4) depict Christ the Wisdom of God as present at the beginning of the creation of the world and sustaining the world in the present. See Sam Meier, "2 Peter 3:3-7—An Early Jewish and Christian Response to Eschatological Skepticism," who notes that the skeptics were overlooking the fact that if all things (the paradigmatic nature of God's action) remain the same, then judgment is certain.

INTERPRETATION

Chapter 3 makes repeated use of "beloved" *(agapētoi)* in direct address (see vv. 1, 8, 14, 17). After the first such use in 3:1 there is first a solemn introduction that calls upon various sources of authority (3:1-2) and then Peter's statement about the false teachers' skeptical question regarding the apparent delay of Jesus' *parousia* and the reasons for their skepticism (3:3-4).

Sources of Authority (2 Pet 3:1-2). The solemn introduction in 2 Pet 3:1-2 takes up again the idea of the letter as the testament of Peter. It also marshals the following authorities as support for the summary and critique of the false teachers' views that begins in 3:3: Peter the apostle *par excellence,* his previous letter (1 Peter?), the OT prophets, and the apostolic message.

In the solemn introduction Peter refers to the present letter as his "second letter," a statement that appears to presume the existence and circulation of 1 Peter or something like it among his readers. He also notes the function of these letters as reminders and so as substitutes for the apostle's physical presence. In what follows Peter will look into the future ("scoffers will come," 3:3) and provide advice about living as good Christians during "the last days." Thus he echoes the characterization of 2 Peter as his farewell discourse or testament that was first developed in 1:12-15.

In addition to his personal authority as the apostle *par excellence* and the enduring value of his written reminders, Peter also invokes the authority of the prophets (perhaps the OT as a whole, taken as a book of prophecy about Jesus) and "the commandment of the Lord and Savior through your apostles" (the apostolic preaching handed on to the readers). In what follows Peter appears as the chief spokesman for the apostles. Compare Jude 17-18, where the quotation is attributed to the apostles as a group: "they said to you."

The Alleged Delay of Jesus' Parousia (2 Pet 3:3-4). In accord with the conventions of the testament genre Peter proceeds to describe what will take place in "the last days" (the period leading up to the *parousia*). But for the author and his first readers, of course, these matters clearly belonged in the present rather than in the distant future. The irony is that the appearance of "scoffers" who cast doubt upon the *parousia* of Jesus and the Last Judgment is a sign that those very events are near. As has been the case throughout the letter thus far, the false teachers are accused of leading immoral lives ("walking according to their own passions").

According to 2 Pet 3:4 the scoffers were raising their question about Jesus' *parousia* in a form that manifested their skepticism: "Where is the promise of his coming?" According to Peter their rationale included the passing of the "forefathers" and the idea that "all things remain the same since the beginning of creation." This statement, of course, is the position of the false teachers as it was understood and expressed by the author of 2 Peter. The most important elements are the non-occurrence of Jesus' *parousia*, the death of the "forefathers," and the notion that everything in the world remains the same.

Near the end of the eschatological discourse in Mark 13, Jesus says: "Truly I tell you, this generation will not pass away until all these things have taken place" (13:30; see Matt 24:34). The most obvious referent of "all these things" is the whole scenario of signs and events described thus far in Mark 13, especially the second coming or *parousia* of Jesus as the Son of Man according to Mark 13:24-27. The expression "this generation" is most obviously understood as referring to those who belonged to the same age group as Jesus and his first followers. So the gospel saying gives the impression that the *parousia* of Jesus will take place during the lifetime of the apostles.

The impression that Jesus' second coming would occur during the apostles' lifetime is strengthened by other gospel texts. In a saying that now introduces the synoptic transfiguration narratives Jesus asserts that "there are some standing here who will not taste death until they see that the kingdom of God has come with power" (Mark 9:1; Matt 16:28; Luke 9:27). In the Matthean missionary discourse Jesus urges the twelve apostles to proclaim the good news of God's reign to "the lost sheep of the house of Israel" (Matt 10:5) and promises that "you will not have gone through all the towns of Israel before the Son of Man comes" (10:23). And John 21:22-23 suggests that Jesus' second coming might take place before the death of the beloved disciple: "If it is my will that he remain until I come, what is that to you?"

The crisis that gave rise to the scoffers' skepticism about Jesus' second coming seems to have been the passing of the apostolic generation ("this generation") without the *parousia* of Jesus having occurred. The purpose of 2 Peter as the farewell discourse or testament of Peter the apostle *par excellence* is to provide both an answer to the skeptics within the Christian community ("Where is the promise of his coming?") and advice to those Christians who regarded Jesus' *parousia* as an integral part of the apostolic message. In what follows, Peter rebuts the skeptics' contention that "all things remain the same" (3:5-10) and exhorts other Christians to be faithful to the apostolic message and to act accordingly (3:11-18).

After almost two thousand years the *parousia* of Jesus has still not come, and so it may be easy to sympathize with the view of the scoffers/false teachers that "all things remain the same since the beginning of creation" and the implication that there will be no last judgment. Yet from earliest times Christians have insisted on the second coming of Jesus and the final judgment (whenever they may take place) as articles of faith.

For Reference and Further Study

Allmen, Daniel von. "L'apocalyptique juive et le retard de la parousie en II Pierre 3:1-13," *Revue de Théologie et de Philosophie* 16 (1966) 255–74.

Bauckham, Richard J. "Delay of the Parousia," *TynBull* 31 (1980) 3–36.

Green, G. L. "'As for Prophecies, They Will Come to an End': 2 Peter, Paul and Plutarch on 'The Obsolescence of Oracles,'" *JSNT* 82 (2001) 107–22.

Meier, Sam. "2 Peter 3:3-7—An Early Jewish and Christian Response to Eschatological Skepticism," *BZ* 32 (1988) 255–57.

Talbert, Charles H. "II Peter and the Delay of the Parousia," *Vigiliae Christianae* 20 (1966) 137–45.

Zmijewski, Joseph. "Apostolische Paradosis und Pseudepigraphie im Neuen Testament. 'Durch Erinnerung wachhalten' (2 Petr 1,13; 3,1)," *BZ* 23 (1979) 161–71.

10. *Biblical Responses* (3:5-10)

5. For they deliberately ignore this fact—that the heavens and the earth came together long ago from water and through water by the word of God, 6. through which the world then was deluged by water and was destroyed. 7. But the heavens and the earth now by that same word have been stored up for fire, being kept until the day of the judgment and the destruction of the godless.

8. Beloved, do not ignore this one fact—that one day with the Lord is like a thousand years, and a thousand years like one day. 9. For the Lord is not slow about the promise as some reckon slowness; but he is patient toward us, wishing not that any should perish but that all should come to repentance. 10. But the day of the Lord will come like a thief. On it the heavens will pass away with a roar; and the elements will be dissolved by burning; and the earth and the works on it—will they be found?

Notes

5. *For they deliberately ignore this fact:* What follows is a refutation of the opponents' contention that "all things remain the same since the beginning of creation" (3:4). In the Greek text the construction is impersonal: "It escapes their notice . . ." (see 3:8). The first response to the opponents' objection to the *parousia* is based on the creation account of Genesis 1:1–2:3 and the flood narrative of Genesis 7–8.

that the heavens and the earth came together long ago: "The heavens" and "the earth" form the subject of the verb *ēsan . . . synestōsa:* "In the beginning when God created the heavens and the earth" (Gen 1:1). The verbal construction is an example of the "divine" or "theological" passive frequent in the NT. The perfect participle *synestōsa* is a compound of the prefix *syn* ("with") and the verb *histēmi* ("stand"), and carries the ideas of cohering, consisting, existing, or being held together. The adverb *ekpalai* here (in contrast to 2 Pet 2:3) refers to a point in time long before the current moment ("long ago").

from water and through water by the word of God: According to Gen 1:2, before the first creative word from God "the earth was a formless void and darkness covered the face of the deep." On the second day, according to Gen 1:6, God said: "Let there be a dome in the midst of the waters, and let it separate the waters from the waters." And on the third day, according to Gen 1:9, God said: "Let the waters under the sky be gathered together into one place, and let the dry land appear." See Roselyne Dupont-Roc, "Le motif de la création selon 2 Pierre 3."

6. *through which the world then was deluged by water and was destroyed:* The referent of the relative clause beginning with *di ' hōn* is most likely both "water" and "the word." Here "the world" is the equivalent of "the ancient world" (that is, the world before the flood) in 2 Pet 2:5. The point of calling on the biblical flood story (Genesis 7–8) again is to disprove the opponents' contention that all things have remained the same since the creation of the world. For the flood as a worldwide phenomemon see Gen 7:21-23: "And all flesh died. . . . He blotted out every living thing that was on the face of the ground. . . . Only Noah was left." Whether one can say that the whole world was destroyed by the flood is debatable (since Noah and his family survived). Compare the use of the flood story in 2 Pet 2:5, where the emphasis is moral—on God's punishing the ungodly and preserving Noah, "the herald of righteousness." For a vision of the ancient world being destroyed see *1 Enoch* 83:3-5: "I saw in the vision the sky being hurled down and snatched and falling upon the earth. When it fell upon the earth, I saw the earth being swallowed up in the great abyss. . . . And I began crying aloud, saying: 'The earth is being swallowed up.'"

7. *But the heavens and the earth now by that same word:* A distinction is drawn between the world "then" *(tote)* and the world "now" *(nyn)*. But the language ("the heavens and the earth" and "by the same word") echoes the language of 3:5.

have been stored up for fire: The use of the verb *tethēsaurismenoi* may be associated with the image of souls in storehouses or treasuries until the day of the Last Judgment (see *4 Ezra* 7:77, 83-84). The roots of the idea of a coming world destruction by fire are to be found in late OT and Jewish apocalyptic texts, perhaps under Persian influence. See, for example, Isa 66:15-16: "For the Lord will come in fire . . . by fire will the Lord execute judgment," and Mal 4:1: "See, the day is coming, burning like an oven, when all the arrogant and all evildoers will be stubble; the day that comes shall burn them up, says the Lord of hosts." While this theme is not found elsewhere in the NT, it became common in later Christian writings and has found a firm place in Christian consciousness ("the fire next time"). Since the world was once created by God's word and was once destroyed by God's word, we can expect it to be destroyed again as a prelude to the Last Judgment. See Carsten P. Thiede, "A Pagan Reader of 2 Peter: Cosmic Conflagration in 2 Peter 3 and the *Octavius* of Minucius Felix."

being kept until the day of judgment and the destruction of the godless: For similar (eschatological) uses of *tērein* ("keep, hold") see 2 Pet 2:4 ("to be kept for the judgment"), 2:9 ("to keep the unrighteous punished until the day of judgment"), and 2:17 ("for them the black darkness has been reserved"). The nouns "judgment" *(krisis)* and "destruction" *(apōleia)* both modify "day" *(hēmera)*. For the "godless" *(asebeis)* see 2 Pet 2:5 ("when he brought the flood upon the world of the ungodly") and Jude 4, 15 (twice). The expression suggests that the eternal punishment of the wicked will be annihilation (rather than eternal punishment by fire).

8. *Beloved, do not ignore this one fact:* For *agapētoi* ("beloved") as a form of direct address see 2 Pet 3:1, 14, 17, as well as Jude 3, 17, and 20. The impersonal verbal construction ("this one thing should not escape your notice") is similar to that in 3:5.

   that one day with the Lord is like a thousand years, and a thousand years like one day: The saying is based on Ps 90:4: "For a thousand years in your sight is like yesterday." The point is that God's reckoning of time is not bound to follow human calculations. Its use in 2 Peter serves to counter the scoffers' talk about the delay or nonappearance of the *parousia.* It reminds readers that God works *sub specie aeternitatis* and so takes a larger view than is possible for humans to take. In 2 Peter there is no direct interest in equating the six days of creation in Genesis 1 with six thousand years or in the concept of "chiliasm" that divides history into thousand-year periods (based to some extent on Rev 20:3, 7).

9. *For the Lord is not slow about the promise as some reckon slowness:* The verb *bradynein* ("be slow, hesitate, delay") appears only in 1 Tim 3:15 elsewhere in the NT. Its occurrence with the genitive *tēs epangelias* is somewhat awkward— so much so that some propose taking it with *ho kyrios:* "The Lord of the promise is not slow." The problem with the scoffers is that they try to make God conform to their human timetable when they ask (skeptically): "Where is the promise of his coming?" (3:4). Jerome H. Neyrey ("The Form and Background of the Polemic in 2 Peter") contends that the charge about the Lord's slowness to act in 2 Pet 3:9 resembles in form and function the Epicurean arguments against divine providence. Implied in the opponents' position is a corresponding denial of divine judgment, afterlife, and post-mortem retribution.

   but he is patient toward us: While "patience" *(makrothymia)* is often a human virtue in the NT, it is also a divine attribute (see Rom 2:4; 9:22; 1 Pet 3:20) and an attribute of Christ (1 Tim 1:16; 2 Pet 3:15). The claim here is that the alleged delay of the *parousia* is in fact a demonstration of divine forbearance on behalf of humankind. See Roselyne Dupont-Roc, "Le motif de la création selon 2 Pierre 3," who links the theme of God's patience and the openness of creation. See also Thomas H. Duke, "An Exegetical Analysis of 2 Peter 3:9."

   wishing not that any should perish but that all should come to repentance: The idea here is similar to that in Rom 2:4: "Or do you despise the riches of his kindness and forbearance and patience? Do you not realize that God's kindness is meant to lead you to repentance?" For God's will that all persons should have the opportunity to come to salvation in the NT see John 3:16 ("so that everyone who believes . . . may have eternal life"); Rom 11:32 ("so that he may be merciful to all"); 1 Tim 2:4 ("who desires everyone to be saved and to come to the knowledge of the truth"). However, the NT writers understood "universal salvation" always in relation to Christ and to the gospel. In 2 Peter 3 this theme helps to explain why it appears that the *parousia* of Jesus has been delayed. The delay is due to God's willingness to give all humans the opportunity to find their way to Christ and the gospel.

10. *But the day of the Lord will come like a thief:* For the comparison of the day of the Lord coming like a thief *(kleptēs)* see 1 Thess 5:2 ("the day of the Lord will come like a thief in the night") as well as Matt 24:43-44; Luke 12:39-40; Rev 3:3; 16:15. The image supports the common NT perspective that since the precise time of the day of the Lord remains uncertain one should always be on guard in one's behavior (e.g., Matt 24:36–25:46). See Gert Malan, "Die metafoor: 'Dag van die Here' in 2 Petrus en die dood as marginale ervaring."

On it the heavens will pass away with a roar: In the Greek text this (and what follows) is a relative clause introduced by *en hē.* The adverb *roizēdon* ("with a roar") describes a "noise made by something passing with great force and rapidity" (BDAG 907); it occurs only here in the NT. For another description of heaven and earth passing away see Matt 24:29, 35. See also Isa 34:4a: "All the host of heaven shall rot away, and the skies roll up like a scroll."

and the elements will be dissolved by burning: For *stoicheia* as referring to the "elements" see Gal 4:3, 9; Col 2:8, 20; Heb 5:12; and 2 Pet 3:12. But the precise meaning of *stoicheia* here is disputed. They could be (1) the four elements—earth, air, fire, and water; (2) the heavenly bodies—sun, moon, stars, etc.; (3) a combination of them—air, earth, sea, sun, moon; or (4) hostile angelic powers presiding over nature. Given the clear references to the heavens and the earth in 3:10, it seems most likely that *stoicheia* refers to the "heavenly bodies" (sun, moon, stars, etc.). The passive participle *kausoumena* ("by burning") also appears in 3:12; otherwise the verb does not occur in the NT. See Mal 4:1: "See, the day is coming, burning like an oven . . . the day that comes shall burn them up." For the motif of cosmic conflagration see Carsten P. Thiede, "A Pagan Reader of 2 Peter."

and the earth and the works on it—will they be found?: In this context *erga* ("works") refers to whatever happens on the earth—activities, occupations, tasks, products, and so on. The final verb *heurethēsetai* ("will be found") presents many textual problems. Some manuscripts and many modern scholars dismiss it as an error, and read instead some form of a verb that can be rendered "will be burned up." The form *heurethēsetai* can be retained only if one inserts the negative participle *ouk* ("will not be found") or takes it as a question ("will they be found?") that implies that the earth and its works will be totally destroyed. For discussions of this text see Hellmut Lenhard, "Noch einmal zu 2 Petr 3:10d"; R. Larry Overstreet, "A Study of 2 Peter 3:10-13"; G. A. van der Heever, "In purifying fire: World view and 2 Peter 3:10"; David Wenham, "Being 'Found' on the Last Day: New Light on 2 Peter 3.10 and 2 Corinthians 5.3"; and Al Wolters, "Worldview and Textual Criticism in 2 Peter 3:10."

INTERPRETATION

According to Peter's summary in 3:4 the false teachers were casting doubt about the occurrence of Jesus' *parousia* (3:4a) and claiming that everything remains the same since the creation (3:4b). In 3:5-10 Peter deals with their positions by appealing to various biblical texts. He does so in reverse or chiastic (ABB'A') order by showing that everything does not remain the same (3:5-7) and that the apparent "delay" of Jesus' *parousia* can be explained in terms of God's forbearance and mercy (3:8-10).

Rather than continuing the use of future-tense language (as in 3:3: "scoffers will come") in keeping with the testament genre, 2 Peter reverts to the present tense in 3:5 ("they deliberately ignore"), thus showing that the false teachers were posing an immediate threat and that these are "the last days." The testament setting in which Peter the apostle *par excellence* delivers his teachings helps to rebut the suggestion that the non-occurrence of Jesus' *parousia* before the death of the apostles means that it will never take place. The point of 2 Peter is that the apparent delay had already been explained by Peter the apostle before his passing.

Everything Does Not Remain the Same (2 Pet 3:5-7). Peter's rebuttal of the false teachers' claim that the world remains the same since the creation is more concerned with the theological theme of divine judgment than with cosmology. To refute their claim he appeals first to the OT account of the creation of the earth out of the waters. The initial emergence of the dry land out of the waters took place by the word of God: "And God said: 'Let the waters under the sky be gathered together into one place, and let the dry land appear'" (Gen 1:10). Then Peter appeals to the story of the flood in the days of Noah according to Genesis 7, through which the earth became submerged again in the waters. God's word announced the flood beforehand to Noah: "every living thing that I have made I will blot out from the face of the ground" (Gen 7:4).

Taken together, the OT creation account and the flood narrative prove that the world has not remained the same since creation. The flood story also proves that God enters into human history, that God's word is powerful enough to create and to destroy, and that God can and does punish human wickedness. The vision of history conveyed in the Bible and in Jewish apocalyptic is linear and goal-oriented rather than cyclical or static. The end or goal toward which human history is moving, according to 2 Peter and other NT writings, is the full manifestation of God's kingdom, and integral to this manifestation are the second coming of Jesus and the Last Judgment.

That the present heavens and earth will be destroyed once more is part of Jewish and early Christian eschatology (see Mark 13:24-25; Matt 24:29). This cosmic catastrophe will make way for the emergence of the new heaven and new earth: "Then I saw a new heaven and a new earth; for the first heaven and the first earth had passed away, and the sea was no more" (Rev 21:1).

The idea that fire will be God's instrument of destruction the next time is based on the "word of God" found in various passages such as Isa 66:15-16 and Mal 4:1 (see the Note on 3:7). For fire as a vehicle of divine judgment in the OT see Deut 32:22: "For a fire is kindled by my anger, and burns to the depths of Sheol; it devours the earth and its increase, and sets on fire the foundations of the mountains." Even though God promised not to destroy humankind and other creatures again by a flood ("as I have done," Gen 8:21), God can and will use fire to destroy the godless on the Day of Judgment.

The "Delay" Explained (2 Pet 3:8-10). The second part of the response deals directly with the skeptical question posed by the false teachers as stated in 3:4a: "Where is the promise of his coming?" It meets their skepticism first by arguing with an obvious allusion to Ps 90:4 that God's reckoning of time is not necessarily the same as the human reckoning of time: "one day with the Lord is like a thousand years, and a thousand years like one day" (2 Pet 3:8). What can seem like a long delay to humans may well be but a moment in the divine consciousness and divine plan. The alleged delay or non-occurrence of Jesus' *parousia* is a matter of perspective, and the false teachers are accused here of imposing their all-too-human mode of calculating time on God's plan regarding Jesus' *parousia* and the Last Judgment.

The second argument (3:9) attributes God's apparent slowness in bringing about the *parousia* and Last Judgment to God's mercy and compassion, based upon the biblical definition of God: "a God merciful and gracious, slow to anger, and abounding in steadfast love and faithfulness" (Exod 34:6). By allowing more time before the Last Judgment than was expected, God has made it possible for more people to come to know Jesus Christ as their Lord and Savior and to transform their lives. According to this line of argument God has deferred the *parousia* and the Last Judgment according to God's own saving purposes: to make it easier for all persons to come to true knowledge of God and so to enjoy the benefits of eternal life in God's kingdom. This kind of theological reasoning stands in some tension with the notion expressed in Mark's apocalyptic discourse: "And if the Lord had not cut short those days, no one would be saved; but for the sake of the elect, whom he chose, he cut short those days" (Mark 13:20). It would be perverse logic to argue from 2 Pet 3:9 that human sinfulness alone can retard the *parousia* or from Mark 13:20 that human merits alone can accelerate the *parousia*. In both cases the point is that the precise time of the Last Judgment is ultimately God's decision and according to God's plan.

In any case the apparent delay of Jesus' *parousia* does not mean the non-fulfillment of God's promise. The OT background for 2 Pet 3:10 is Hab 2:3: "For there is still a vision for the appointed time; it speaks of the end, and does not lie. If it seems to tarry, wait for it; it will surely come, it will not delay." According to 2 Peter and the rest of the NT the second coming of Jesus is certain, but exactly when he will come is up to God and is not known by humans: "But about that day or hour no one knows, neither the angels in heaven, nor the Son, but only the Father" (Mark 13:32).

The image of the Day of the Lord coming like a "thief" expresses well the human uncertainty about its precise timing. But the images of the heavens passing away with a roar, the cosmic conflagration, and the disappearance of the (old) earth indicate that its actual arrival will be clear to all. The description of the Day of the Lord in Luke 17:20-37 preserves the tension between the stealth of its coming (see Luke 17:20: "The kingdom of God is not coming with things that can be observed") and the obviously public character of its arrival ("For as lightning flashes and lights up the sky from one side to another, so will the Son of Man be in his day," Luke 17:24). Luke also uses the OT examples of life in "the days of Noah" and the men of Sodom (Luke 17:26-30; see 2 Pet 2:5-8) to describe what things will be like "on the day that the Son of Man is revealed" (17:31).

The dissolution of the elements and the disappearance of the (old) earth signal the coming of the Lord as judge. Since that coming is certain but its time remains unknown, the moral lesson is that Christians should be perpetually vigilant and always on guard in their actions so that the Last Judgment will be for them a vindication and not a condemnation. And so 2 Peter draws to a close with an exhortation (3:11-18) about how Christians should live in preparation for Jesus' *parousia* and the Last Judgment.

The Bible promotes a linear and purposeful (rather than a cyclical or purposeless or static) view of history. Second Peter's defense of the position that the world has already indeed undergone change (in creation and at the flood) seeks to open up the possibility that it will undergo further dramatic change with the coming of God's kingdom in its fullness and the *parousia* of Jesus. Second Peter agrees with other NT writers in insisting on the certainty of these eschatological events while leaving their precise timing to God.

For Reference and Further Study

Duke, Thomas H. "An Exegetical Analysis of 2 Peter 3:9," *Faith & Mission* 16/3 (1999) 6–13.

Dupont-Roc, Roselyne. "Le motif de la création selon 2 Pierre 3," *RB* 101 (1994) 95–114.

Heever, G. A. van den. "In purifying fire: World view and 2 Peter 3:10," *Neot* 27 (1993) 107–18.

Lenhard, Hellmut. "Noch einmal zu 2 Petr 3:10d," *ZNW* 69 (1978) 136.

Malan, Gert. "Die metafoor 'Dag van die Here' in 2 Petrus en die dood as marginale ervaring," *Hervormde Teologiese Studies* 55 (1999) 656–70.

Neyrey, Jerome H. "The Form and Background of the Polemic in 2 Peter," *JBL* 99 (1980) 407–31.

Overstreet, R. Larry. "A Study of 2 Peter 3:10-13," *BS* 137 (1980) 354–71.

Thiede, Carsten P. "A Pagan Reader of 2 Peter: Cosmic Conflagration in 2 Peter 3 and the *Octavius* of Minucius Felix," *JSNT* 26 (1986) 79–96.

Wenham, David. "'Being Found' on the Last Day: New Light on 2 Peter 3.10 and 2 Corinthians 5.3," *NTS* 33 (1987) 477–79.

Wolters, Al. "Worldview and Textual Criticism in 2 Peter 3:10," *Westminster Theological Journal* 49 (1987) 405–13.

11. *Final Exhortation* (3:11-18)

11. Since all these are to be dissolved in this way, what kind of persons ought you to be in holy conduct and piety, 12. awaiting and hastening the coming of the day of God, because of which the heavens will be set on fire and dissolved, and the elements will be burned and melt away! 13. But according to his promise we await new heavens and a new earth in which justice dwells.

14. Therefore, beloved, since you await these, be eager to be found without fault and without blemish, at peace, 15. and regard the forbearance of our Lord as salvation. So also our beloved brother Paul, according to the wisdom given to him, wrote to us, 16. speaking about these matters as he does in all the letters. In them there are some things that are hard to understand, which the ignorant and unstable twist, as they do the other writings, to their own destruction.

17. Therefore, beloved, knowing this beforehand, be on guard lest you be carried away by the error of unprincipled men and you lose your firm hold. 18. But grow in the grace and knowledge of our Lord and Savior Jesus Christ. To him be the glory both now and unto the day of eternity. [Amen.]

NOTES

11. *Since all these are to be dissolved in this way:* The expression "all these" refers to the heavens, the elements, and the earth (as in 3:10). Their "dissolution" was described in 3:10 with the Greek verb *lyein,* and that verb reappears here.

what kind of persons ought you to be in holy conduct and piety: While the word *potapos* is sometimes interrogative, here it carries an exclamatory sense; see the exclamation point placed in the translation at the end of 3:12. Some manuscripts read "we" *(hēmas)* rather than "you" *(hymas)*, and others have neither word. In 2 Peter the expectation of the dissolution of the old creation is used as a stimulus to acts of moral goodness and piety in the present; compare 2 Thess 3:6-13, which addresses the problem of some Christians taking their imminent expectation of the Day of the Lord as an excuse for laziness. Whereas the false teachers apparently regarded the non-occurrence of the *parousia* as grounds for moral laxity, 2 Peter uses its certain occurrence in the future (but with unknown timing) as a challenge toward proper moral and religious behavior in the present in the typical NT spirit of constant vigilance.

12. *awaiting and hastening the coming of the day of God:* The Greek verb *prosdokaō* ("await, look for, expect") appears in various forms in 3:12, 13, and 14. The verb *speudein* ("hurry, hasten") is related to *spoudasate* in 3:14. That humans can "hasten" the coming of the kingdom of God is not a common theme in Jewish apocalyptic writings, and 2 Pet 3:12 is the only NT text that makes such an assertion. The term *speudein* can also mean "be zealous, exert oneself, be industrious." But if that were the sense here one would expect it to be followed by a noun in the dative case ("be zealous for . . .") rather than the accusative *hēmeran* as its object. The "coming of the day of God" is also a unique expression in the NT, though its elements are familiar from 2 Peter and from the NT in general. For earlier uses of *parousia* ("coming"), see 2 Pet 1:16 and 3:4. For *hēmera* ("day") in its eschatological sense see 2 Pet 1:19; 2:9; 3:3, 7, 10, 18. There is no obvious difference between "the day of the Lord" (3:10) and "the day of God" (3:12).

    because of which the heavens will be set on fire and dissolved, and the elements will be burned and melt away: What was said about the "elements" *(stoicheia)* in 3:10 is now said also about the "heavens" *(ouranoi)*. Compare the description in 3:10, where the expectation is that the heavens will pass away with a roar. Both clauses here contain a passive participle and a main verb also in the passive (one in the future and the other in the present): "being set on fire will be dissolved" and "being burned melt away." These passive verbs imply that divine agency is at work.

13. *But according to his promise we await new heavens and a new earth:* For previous references to God's promises see 2 Pet 1:4; 3:4, 9; for the (false) promise of freedom made by the false teachers see 2:19. For the content of the promise see Isa 65:17 ("For I am about to create new heavens and a new earth"); Isa 66:22 ("For as the new heavens and the new earth, which I will make, shall remain before me, says the Lord"); and *1 Enoch* 91:16 ("The first heaven shall depart and pass away; a new heaven shall appear; and all the powers of heaven shall shine forever sevenfold"). The OT motif is taken up in Rev 21:1: "Then I saw a new heaven and a new earth; for the first heaven and the first earth had passed away."

    in which justice dwells: For earlier uses of *dikaiosynē* see 2 Pet 1:1; 2:5, 21. The idea is similar to the petition in the Matthean version of the Lord's Prayer:

"Your will be done, on earth as it is in heaven" (Matt 6:10). In the fullness of God's kingdom the rule of God's justice will prevail completely: "Then justice will dwell in the wilderness, and righteousness abide in the fruitful field" (Isa 32:16).

14. *Therefore, beloved, since you await these:* For other uses of *agapētoi* ("beloved") as a form of direct address see 2 Pet 3:1, 8, and 17. For previous uses of *prosdokaō* ("await") see 2 Pet 3:12 and 13. The word "these" *(tauta)* here refers to the new heavens and the new earth described in 2:13.

be eager to be found without fault and without blemish, in peace: For an earlier use of *spoudasate* ("be eager, zealous") as an imperative see 2 Pet 1:10. The primary referent of the aorist passive infinitive *heurethēnai* ("to be found") is the Last Judgment. The pair of adjectives *aspiloi* and *amōmētoi* ("without fault and without blemish") illustrates again the author's predilections for pairs and for words with the *alpha*-privative. See *spiloi kai mōmoi* ("blots and blemishes"), used in 2 Pet 2:13 to describe the false teachers, and *aptaistous kai . . . amōmous* in Jude 24 to describe the Christian ideal. Their "peace" will come from having a clear conscience.

15. *and regard the forbearance of our Lord as salvation:* The instruction looks backward to the reflection on the "delay" of the *parousia* as due to God's patience or forbearance *(makrothymia)* in 2 Pet 3:9 and as providing an opportunity for repentance and salvation: "he is patient toward us, wishing not that any should perish but that all should come to repentance." In this context it appears that "Lord" *(kyrios)* refers to God rather than to Christ.

So also our beloved brother Paul: For the relationship between Peter and Paul see Gal 2:1-14 and Acts 15. The description of Paul as "our beloved brother" implies that Paul is held in high esteem by the writer and his "beloved" (see 2 Pet 3:1, 8, 14, 17) readers, and that "Peter" feels obliged to present Paul as being on the same side over against the false teachers, who were apparently invoking Paul as support for their views.

according to the wisdom given to him, wrote to us: Paul himself usually refers to his own charism as "the grace given to me" (see Rom 12:3, 6; 15:15; Gal 2:9). The formula insists on the divine origin and agency of Paul's apostleship. The reference to Paul's writings presupposes that the writer and his readers are familiar with a collection of Paul's letters. John P. Meier, "2 Peter 3:8-18: Forming the Canon on the Edge of the Canon," observes that the history of the NT canon that started with Paul correcting Peter at Antioch (see Gal 2:11-21) concludes with "Peter" here correcting erroneous interpretations of the Pauline gospel.

16. *speaking about these matters as he does in all the letters:* What "these matters" are may well be what Paul says in his letters about the topics raised in 2 Pet 3:14-15a: the mercy of God, salvation, appropriate behavior, and the Last Judgment. The reference to "all the letters" suggests a fairly substantial collection, certainly more than one or two.

In them there are some things that are hard to understand: For another case of controversy about interpreting Paul's views see Jas 2:14-26 ("so faith apart from works is dead," 2:26). In the context of 2 Peter the problems seem to involve Paul's emphasis on the present dimension of participation in Jesus' resurrection and his teaching about freedom from the Law. Paul himself balanced these views with a lively sense of future eschatology and an understanding of freedom as serving God as Master in ways appropriate to that service. This is the only occurrence of *dysnoēta* ("hard to understand") in the NT.

which the ignorant and unstable twist: Again there is a pair of adjectives, *amatheis* and *astēriktoi* ("ignorant and unstable"), with the *alpha*-privative construction. The writer seeks to make a sharp division between the authentic Paul (a revered figure whose letters are well known) and the false teachers (who may be appealing to Paul's authority). This is the only occurrence of *strebloō* ("twist, distort") in the NT; it labels the opponents' teachings as distortions of Paul's teachings.

as they do the other writings, to their own destruction: The word *graphai* ("writings") can be (and usually is) translated as "scriptures." These "writings/scriptures" would certainly include the OT as the Bible of the early church. Whether Paul's writings are included in or excluded from "the other writings" as part of a kind of canon is a matter of debate, as is the inclusion or exclusion of other Christian writings such as the gospels and Acts. By distorting the writings of Paul and the OT (and perhaps the evangelists), the false teachers are bringing "destruction" (*apōleia;* see 2 Pet 2:1-3, 7) upon others and upon themselves.

17. *Therefore, beloved, knowing this beforehand:* This is the fourth and last use of *agapētoi* ("beloved") in 2 Peter 3 (see vv. 1, 8, 14) as a form of direct address. By using the participle *proginōskontes* ("knowing this beforehand") 2 Peter resumes the conventions of the testament in which the dying person gives a look into the future (see 1:12-15).

    be on guard lest you be carried away by the error of unprincipled men: Whereas Jude 24 appeals to God as the one "who is able to keep you *(phylaxai)* from stumbling," with the imperative middle form *phylassesthe* 2 Peter here puts the initiative on and the challenge to the readers. The rest of the warning picks up terms used in 2 Peter 2 to describe the false teachers: "error" (*planē,* 2:18) and "unprincipled men" (*athesmoi,* 2:7).

    and you lose your firm hold: The verb *ekpesēte* here means "to change for the worse from a favorable condition" (BDAG 308). The noun *stērigmos* (only here in the NT) can refer to a "safe position" or to a "firm commitment to conviction or belief, steadfastness" (BDAG 945).

18. *But grow in the grace and knowledge of our Lord and Savior Jesus Christ:* Contrary to the translation here, one could argue that the two nouns *charis* ("grace") and *gnōsis* ("knowledge") should be taken separately ("grow in grace and in the knowledge of our Lord . . ."). While 2 Peter uses *gnōsis* in a positive context in 1:5-6 (with regard to the virtues), it prefers *epignōsis* when referring to knowing God and Christ (see 1:2, 3, 8; 2:20). For "Lord and Savior" as a compound title for Jesus see 2 Pet 1:11; 2:20; 3:2. Its appearance here in the genitive case raises the question whether "the grace and knowledge" have Jesus as

their object (objective genitive) or as their origin and source (subjective genitive)—or both.

To him be the glory both now and unto the day of eternity. [Amen]: Like Jude, 2 Peter ends not with epistolary conventions (travel plans, greetings, etc.) but rather with a doxology. The doxologies in 2 Pet 3:18 and 2 Tim 4:18 are the only ones in the NT that are directed solely to Jesus. The "day of eternity" *(eis hēmeran aiōnos)* is best explained in the light of Sir 18:10 *(en hēmerą aiōnos)* as a synonym for "eternity" or "forever." Many doxologies in the NT end with "Amen" (see Rom 1:25; 9:5; 11:36; 15:33; 16:27; Gal 1:5; 6:18; Eph 3:21; etc.), and it became customary for scribes to conclude NT books by inserting "Amen" at the end of the text. However, not all manuscripts of 2 Pet 3:18 contain the closing "Amen," and its absence is the more difficult reading (and so more likely original).

INTERPRETATION

Many NT letters end with advice about conduct or ethics, and frequently this ethical advice is put in the context of the Last Judgment or eschatology. Also, the testament genre is constructed so as to provide a forecast of future events and to offer instruction about appropriate behavior in the present and in the future. As a testament in letter form 2 Peter comes to a close with a series of exhortations that offer ethical advice in an eschatological setting. For Christians who live according to the apostolic message set forth in 2 Pet 1:3-11, the Day of the Lord will be the occasion for their vindication and reward, not for their condemnation. The mood of the closing exhortation in 2 Peter is more triumphant than fearful—something like what is found in Luke 21:28: "Now when these things begin to take place, stand up and raise your heads, because your redemption is drawing near."

The closing exhortation can be divided into three sections (3:11-13, 14-16, 17-18), and in the exhortation taken as a unit there is a rich mixture of ethics and eschatology. Throughout the letter Peter has criticized the false teachers for their licentiousness and has suggested that their immoral behavior is a corollary to their skepticism about Jesus' *parousia* and the Last Judgment. The exhortation here illustrates how eschatology (or the prospect of the Last Judgment) can serve as an effective motive for righteous behavior in the present. The thrust of the exhortation is to encourage righteous behavior in the present. Along the way, however, there are references to the Day of the Lord and other matters that have attracted considerable attention among exegetes.

In Holy Conduct and Piety (2 Pet 3:11-13). The initial segment in Peter's exhortation has at its heart the call for good Christians to live "in holy conduct and piety" (3:11). This call is set in the context of apocalyptic

descriptions about the dissolution of the elements, the great cosmic conflagration, and the appearance of the "new heavens and a new earth in
which justice dwells." For those who have cultivated justice or righteousness throughout their lives as Christians the images of the end-time are
not a threat, but rather a promise that their vindication (or salvation)
is near.

The reference to "hastening the coming of the day of the Lord" (3:12)
might lead readers today to imagine that they can and should bring about
or build the kingdom of God. But Peter and all other NT writers insist that
it is God's kingdom, and that God will bring about its full manifestation
when and how God sees fit. The idea that humans bring in or produce the
kingdom of God is foreign to the NT and to Jewish apocalypticism (and is
bad theology). However, one can say that human actions may influence
God in deciding when is the right time to bring about the Day of the Lord
(and so we pray "thy kingdom come," Matt 6:10), and whether to defer
(as in 2 Pet 3:9) or to hasten its arrival (as in 2 Pet 3:12 and Mark 13:20). As
Richard J. Bauckham says, "their repentance and holy living may therefore, from the human standpoint, hasten its coming. This does not detract
from God's sovereignty in determining the time of the End . . . but means
only that his sovereign determination graciously takes human affairs into
account" (*Jude, 2 Peter* 325).

To Be Found Without Fault (2 Pet 3:14-16). In the second segment of the
concluding exhortation, ethics and eschatology are linked subtly in the
admonition: "be eager to be found without fault and without blemish"
(3:14). The aorist passive infinitive *heurethēnai* ("to be found") refers to the
Last Judgment. The ideal of Christian life is to be found without fault or
blemish on the Day of the Lord. The consequence of this hope is constant
vigilance in the present and confident expectation regarding the Last
Judgment. Those who embrace the Christian lifestyle outlined in 1:3-11
will have nothing to fear at the Last Judgment. In keeping with the explanation for the apparent delay of the *parousia* given in 3:9, Christians
should regard their present lives as an opportunity given by God the
all-merciful one to prepare for the judgment that leads to their ultimate
salvation.

The reference to "our beloved brother Paul" in 3:15b-16 introduces a
positive picture of Paul. It suggests that Peter and Paul, far from being
rivals, teach the same doctrines and are on the same side over against the
"false teachers." It also implies that the false teachers were appealing to
Paul's writings as support for their positions. While it may be possible to
develop Paul's emphasis on present or realized eschatology so as to play
down or even exclude Jesus' *parousia* and the Last Judgment, such an approach would be a distortion of Paul's thinking as expressed, for example,
in 1 Corinthians 15. Peter agrees with Paul (and vice versa) in stressing

both the present and the future dimensions of salvation. By their skepticism about the Last Judgment and their licentiousness in the present the false teachers have gone so far beyond Paul's theology that they pervert his clear teaching and make it unrecognizable.

Be On Guard (2 Pet 3:17-18). For the last time (see 3:1, 8, 14), Peter addresses his readers as "beloved" *(agapētoi).* Peter's closing words in 3:17-18a are an apt summary of the whole letter. First, 3:17a again identifies the work as a testament (see 1:12-15; 2:1-3; 3:14) designed to let the readers know "beforehand" the threat that they face from the false teachers: "knowing this beforehand." Second, according to 3:17b the letter is intended negatively as a warning to prevent the readers from "being carried away by the error of lawless men." In other words, its purpose is to point out and refute what the author regarded as "destructive heresies" (2:1) in order that the Christians addressed in it might not fall away from the apostolic teaching and Christian ethical conduct. Third, 3:18a balances the negative message directed against the false teachers with a restatement of and encouragement toward the positive ideal of progress in Christian life outlined in 1:3-11: "But grow in the grace and knowledge of our Lord and Savior Jesus Christ."

It is fitting that 2 Peter should end in 3:18 by calling Jesus "our Lord and Savior" (see 1:11; 2:20; 3:2) and by making Jesus the object of a doxology ("to him be the glory"). The chief contribution of 2 Peter to NT christology is its frequent use of formulaic expressions that take for granted a very exalted view of Jesus. The final verse of 2 Peter shows what Christians had come to believe and confess about Jesus of Nazareth at a relatively early stage in their theological history. In both form and content it is a fitting summary of the letter's christology.

Just as 2 Peter began with a positive description of Christian life (1:3-11), so it concludes with a reflection on the implications of belief in the Last Judgment for Christian behavior in the present (3:11-18). Since the occurrence of eschatological events is certain and there will be a final judgment (whenever that may be), Christian life in the present involves awaiting these decisive events and being "eager to be found without fault and without blemish, at peace" (3:14).

FOR REFERENCE AND FURTHER STUDY

Conti, Martino. "La Sophia di 2 Petr 3,15," *RivBib* 17 (1969) 121–38.
Meier, John P. "2 Peter 3:8-18: Forming the Canon on the Edge of the Canon," *Mid-Stream* 38 (1999) 65–70.

INDEXES

SCRIPTURAL INDEX

301

INDEX OF ANCIENT WRITINGS

SUBJECT INDEX

AUTHOR INDEX